Economy and Society in the Modern South

edited by Douglas Flamming and Bryant Simon

During the past half century, the American South has undergone dramatic economic and social transformations. Gone is the South of cotton fields and cotton mills, of monocrop agriculture and rudimentary industries, of desperate poverty and stultifying racial segregation. Gone is the South that Franklin Roosevelt saw as "the Nation's Number One economic problem." But if that South is gone, how can we explain the rise of the "Sunbelt," and what has economic change meant to southerners—their daily lives, their attitudes, their culture? This series aims to answer these critical questions through a multidisciplinary analysis of the region's economic and social development since World War II. It seeks to present the best new research by historians, economists, sociologists, and geographers—fresh scholarship that investigates unexplored topics and boldly reinterprets familiar trends.

THE POLITICS OF WHITENESS

THE POLITICS OF WHITENESS

RACE, WORKERS, AND CULTURE IN THE MODERN SOUTH

Michelle Brattain

THE UNIVERSITY OF GEORGIA PRESS *Athens & London*

Paperback edition published in 2004 by
the University of Georgia Press
Athens, Georgia 30602

Chapter 6 appeared in a somewhat different form as "Making Friends and Enemies: Textile Workers and Political Action in Post–World War II Georgia," *Journal of Southern History* 63 (February 1997): 91–138.
It appears here by permission of the publisher.

Set in Sabon
Printed and bound by Thomson-Shore
The paper in this book meets the guidelines for permanence and durability of the Committee on Production Guidelines for Book Longevity of the Council on Library Resources.

Printed in the United States of America
08 07 06 05 04 P 5 4 3 2 1

Library of Congress Cataloging-in-Publication Data

Brattain, Michelle, 1968–
The politics of whiteness : race, workers, and culture in the modern South / Michelle Brattain.— Pbk. ed.
p. cm. — (Economy and society in the modern South)
Includes bibliographical references (p.) and index.
ISBN 0-8203-2604-6 (pbk. : alk. paper)
1. Labor—Southern States—History. 2. African Americans—Employment—Southern States—History. 3. Labor movement—Southern States—History. 4. Southern States—Race relations—History. I. Title. II. Series.
HD8072.5.B727 2004
331'.0975—dc22 2003022977

British Library Cataloging-in-Publication Data available

This book was originally published in hardcover by Princeton University Press.

For Andrew

Contents

Acknowledgments

So many people have helped me with this project that I scarcely know how to begin acknowledging the support I received along the way. I owe my first and most outstanding debt to my adviser and friend Dee Garrison, who taught me so much about writing, research, history, and life. She has provided invaluable encouragement and advice through every step of this project. There are no words to express how much I value her wisdom and friendship.

I was also extraordinarily lucky to have begun this research at Rutgers University in the company of warm, generous, and brilliant people. Each member of my dissertation committee—Sue Cobble, Alice Kessler-Harris, David Oshinsky, and Robert Zieger—made a unique contribution to this project, and I am grateful to have had a chance to learn from each of them. Norma Basch, Gerald Grob, Jan Lewis, and Clement Price were wonderful mentors and friends. I am also grateful to fellow graduate students at Rutgers, Erika Bsumek, Kari Frederickson, Grace Hale, Lisa Kannenberg, Lisa Phillips, Linda Reeder, and Martin Summers. Much of what I have learned has come from conversations with them. Other friends—Amy and Andy Forbes, David Tager, John Sarnecki, Tiph Crenn, Gina Cox, and Skip Davis—made contributions that may not appear directly in these pages but mean very much to me. My parents, Jane and Dan Brattain, and my sister, Kim, also deserve a special mention for helping out with money, cars, and havens in the middle of research trips, long after it was appropriate for me to ask them for help. My mother's pride in this book will always be a precious and special memory to me, as is she. I am also grateful to my grandmother Edna Gathings Whitley, who taught me a lot about the working class before I even knew what to call it. I wish that my mother and grandmother could have seen the completed book.

Since I left Rutgers, many colleagues and friends have shared their time and knowledge. During a brief visit to Caltech, Jennifer Tucker was a model of what a colleague should be. Members of the history department at the University of Auckland provided a critical but supportive audience for an early presentation on this project. I am especially indebted to Deborah Montgomerie, who was extraordinarily generous with her time and insight. I am also grateful to my colleagues at Georgia State University for encouragement in the final, most trying, points in this project. Along the way many people have commented on ideas, chapters, or presentations from this book, and their questions, criticism, and advice have been invaluable. Anne Brophy, Elizabeth Faue, Gary Fink, Kari Frederickson, Doug Flamming, Cliff Kuhn, Jonathan Prude, Mal Murray, Bryant Simon, Christopher Tomlins, David Roediger, the members of the Emory–Georgia Tech–Georgia State Seminar in the Comparative History of Labor, Industry, Technology, and Society (SCHLITS), the graduate students in the SCHLITS seminar, and the readers at the *Journal of Southern History* and Princeton University Press have all made this a better work.

I am grateful to Rutgers University, the Rieve Pollock Foundation of the Amalgamated Clothing and Textile Workers Union (now UNITE), the Georgia State History Department, and the National Endowment for the Humanities for providing the support that helped make the project possible.

Support from the many archivists and library staff members has also been essential. Staff at the State Historical Society of Wisconsin, Madison, accommodated a tight schedule and requests for a truly unreasonable number of boxes with exceptional mercy. Research aid from Marty Hackett at the University of Pennsylvania archives in the late stages of revision made an enormous contribution to the final product. I also owe a special thanks to Bob Dinwiddie, Chris Paton, Annie Tilden, Peter Roberts, Julia Young, and the staff at the Southern Labor Archives, who continue to make work at Georgia State a great pleasure. I am especially grateful to Peter Roberts, Vincent Rehder, Robbyn Morrison, and James Heitzman, who helped me with illustrations. Final thanks are also due to Brigitta van Rheinberg, Jonathan Lawrence, and Princeton University Press for all their help in the final stages of editing the manuscript.

Finally, my greatest debt by far is to Andrew Milne, who has been an exacting critic and unfailing source of moral support through every step of my research and writing. To a degree that he probably will never know, Andrew has made me a better thinker and a better historian. Without my most treasured friend and collaborator in things academic and otherwise, I never could have completed this project.

Abbreviations

ADA	Americans for Democratic Action
AFL-CIO	American Federation of Labor–Congress of Industrial Organizations
CIO	Congress of Industrial Organizations
COPE	Committee on Public Education
CTNIRB	Cotton Textile National Industrial Relations Board
EEOC	Equal Employment Opportunity Commission
FEPC	Fair Employment Practices Commission
HEW	U.S. Department of Health, Education, and Welfare
NAACP	National Association for the Advancement of Colored People
NIRA	National Industrial Recovery Act
NLRB	National Labor Relations Board
NRA	National Recovery Administration
TWOC	Textile Workers Organizing Committee
TWUA	Textile Workers Union of America
USES	U.S. Employment Service
UTW	United Textile Workers
WLB	War Labor Board
WMC	War Manpower Commission

THE POLITICS OF WHITENESS

Introduction

THERE HAS EXISTED throughout the twentieth century, to borrow the words of W. J. Cash, a "profound conviction that the South is another land." In his influential book *Mind of the South* (1941), Cash argued that the region's history was a continuous and internally logical progression straight from slavery to modern industrial capitalism. Old South and New, Cash contended, stood apart from the rest of the nation, warped by mistaken notions of progress and white supremacy and by the demagogues who represented them. The failings of workers in textiles, the low-wage industry that dominated the whole region, played a central role in Cash's "southern mind." Scarcely concealing his disgust, Cash portrayed millhands as foolish pawns who were duped by boosters, racism, and a naive trust in the mill barons who transferred plantation social relations to the company town. If they participated in politics at all, southern workers were easily distracted from their "real" class interests. By fanning the fears and insecurities of the South's poor whites, the perennial Ben Tillmans, Huey Longs, and Eugene Talmadges of the South had co-opted working-class unrest and funneled racial antagonism into support for a white Democratic coalition that sustained one of the most rigid and oppressive social systems in American history. Though Cash's analysis sometimes betrayed a mean-spirited "want of feeling for the seriousness of human strivings," in the words of C. Vann Woodward, his book anticipated much of the current scholarly interest in whiteness and articulated much of what became the conventional wisdom on class, race, and politics in southern life.[1]

This persistent image of southern workers as cheap, contented, and anti-union, recycled by social scientists, journalists, historians, and sociologists throughout the twentieth century, also indirectly shaped much of the "new" labor history, and scholars who hoped to investigate southern workers from a more sympathetic point of view first had to contend with that traditional stereotype. In the 1980s and early 1990s, the publication of several innovative and creative studies of the southern textile working class nearly banished the sacred cow of southern exceptionalism. In those works, southern textile workers emerged as the creators of an authentic, vibrant culture, the shapers of the modern industrial system, the defenders of a more humane moral economy, and realistic political actors inspired

[1] W. J. Cash, *The Mind of the South* (New York: Vintage Books, 1941), quote from vii.

by the events and opportunities around them.[2] In other words, southern workers emerged as nearly the polar opposite of all that Cash had claimed for them. But with a few notable exceptions, the revisionist project has not addressed the contention by Cash and others that race determined the social order that emerged in the South's largest industry. Nor have many scholars addressed the role played by the working class in twentieth-century southern Democratic politics.[3]

This book is a study of textile workers, race, and politics in the twentieth century. Though it is not intended to revive faith in southern exceptionalism, particularly not in the caricature of the South offered by Cash, it does seek to restore his approach to southern political, social, racial, and economic history as an organic whole. Cash frequently condemned southern workers' actions as self-defeating, irrational displays of racism. This book, in contrast, seeks to understand not simply racism, but the construction, reconstruction, and manipulation of race itself. In particular, it examines how whiteness—a racial identity and a cultural phenomenon grounded in the unique historical context of the Jim Crow South—shaped working-class history and southern politics in the twentieth century. Workers' advocacy of whiteness was, as Cash implied, tragic and selfish, but unfortunately it was not irrational or unfounded. Whiteness was, and continues to be, a very real determinant of social relationships and material benefits.

My research builds on a growing body of literature in history and cultural studies on the phenomenon of whiteness, or the ways that white racial identity serves as a token of privilege and entitlement, though sometimes unacknowledged, in American society.[4] This line of inquiry has par-

[2] The most influential revisionist work on textile workers is Jacquelyn Dowd Hall et al., *Like a Family: The Making of a Southern Cotton Mill World* (Chapel Hill: University of North Carolina Press, 1987); for recent reevaluations of southern workers and exceptionalism, see, for example, Robert Zieger, "Introduction: Is Southern Labor History Exceptional?" in *Southern Labor in Transition, 1940–1995*, ed. Zieger (Knoxville: University of Tennessee Press, 1997), 1–13; idem, "Textile Workers and Historians," in *Organized Labor in the Twentieth-Century South*, ed. Zieger (Knoxville: University of Tennessee Press, 1991), 35–59; and Bryant Simon, "Rethinking Why There Are So Few Unions in the South," *Georgia Historical Quarterly* 81 (Summer 1997): 465–84.

[3] David Carlton's *Mill and Town in South Carolina, 1880–1920* (Baton Rouge: Louisiana State University Press, 1982) and, more recently, Bryant Simon's *A Fabric of Defeat: The Politics of South Carolina Millhands, 1910–1948* (Chapel Hill: University of North Carolina Press, 1998) are important exceptions.

[4] On the construction of southern whiteness, see Grace Elizabeth Hale, *Making Whiteness: The Culture of Segregation in the South, 1890–1940* (New York: Pantheon, 1998). See also the essays in Mike Hill, ed., *Whiteness: A Critical Reader* (New York: New York University Press, 1997); Richard Dyer, *White* (New York: Routledge, 1997); and George Lipsitz, *The Possessive Investment in Whiteness: How White People Profit from Identity Politics* (Philadelphia: Temple University Press, 1998). On the impact of this new scholar-

ticular resonance for the southern textile industry, which began, and remained for much of its history, wholly captive to race. Ensconced in the unique, paternalistic milieu of mill village welfare, whites maintained exclusive access to jobs in the industry from the 1880s to the late 1960s. At the very time that white southerners were seemingly obsessed with codifying Jim Crow practices and were themselves sorely divided, the cotton mill campaigns created a healing mythology of common racial interests and provided a new institutional form to express racial difference.[5] Surrounded by seas of rural poverty, textile mills also made a significant material contribution to segregation by creating and sustaining disparities in black and white wealth. Moreover, race was not simply encoded into the structures of employment, nor were the effects of whiteness simply economic. For much of the twentieth century, textile workers lived and labored in a society where every facet of social life was meticulously segregated. Recipients of what W.E.B. DuBois described in 1935 as a "sort of psychological wage," all white workers received respect, courtesy, and access to public spaces merely for being white citizens of the segregated South. Whiteness also granted whites a special status in the region's politics. Candidates flattered and deferred to poor whites, validating their participation and indicating their inclusion, if not always their electoral significance, in southern political culture.

DuBois also speculated that the psychological effects of whiteness had served as a smoke screen, hiding from white workers their common interests with black workers. Much of the story that follows here, however, is about why white workers did not in fact share identical interests with black workers. If whiteness initially served, as David Roediger has argued, as a way for antebellum northern workers to come to terms with wage work and working-class status, I argue that whiteness in the South became something that largely determined the ability to become part of the industrial working class.[6] In the context of southern rural poverty and the general acceptance of wage work by the turn of the century, this did not represent a decline in status. The creation of wage work actually intro-

ship on labor history, see Bruce Nelson, "Class, Race, and Democracy in the CIO: The 'New' Labor History Meets the 'Wages of Whiteness,' " and responses by Elizabeth Faue and Thomas Sugrue in *International Review of Social History* 41 (1996): 351–420; and Michelle Brattain, "The Pursuits of Post-exceptionalism: Race, Gender, Class, and Politics in the New Southern Labor History," in *Labor in the Modern South*, ed. Glenn T. Eskew (Athens: University of Georgia Press, 2001).

[5] For a insightful analysis of the similar role race played in structuring the iron and steel industry, see Henry M. McKiven, Jr., *Iron and Steel: Class, Race, and Community in Birmingham, Alabama, 1875–1920* (Chapel Hill: University of North Carolina Press, 1995).

[6] W.E.B. DuBois, *Black Reconstruction in America, 1860–1880*, 3rd ed. (New York: Macmillan, 1992), 700; David Roediger, *The Wages of Whiteness: Race and the Making of the American Working Class* (New York: Verso, 1991), 12–13.

duced a much higher standard of living to the rural South in the late nineteenth and early twentieth century, and whites had nearly exclusive access to it.

At the same time, it is clear that whiteness often served to disguise differences in power, status, and control. I am not arguing that white workers were ever as powerful as the southern elites who actually set the limits on political discourse. Nor am I suggesting that they were as contented as southern apologists claimed.[7] Rather, I am arguing that it would be a mistake to allow an awareness of differences among whites to obscure, or divert scholarly attention from, the advantages that whites of all classes gained from race in the Jim Crow South. Working-class southern whites relied on race to serve as their entrée to politics, jobs, and, later, union jobs. In George Lipsitz's words, segregation gave whites a "possessive investment" in whiteness. Because they profited from the "spoils of discrimination"—in this case, the franchise, jobs, welfare, and status—they had, unfortunately, much to gain in the short term by defining and defending their interests in racial terms. Thus although the history of class formation in the South did not significantly alter existing inequalities between classes of whites, it did leave open the possibility for creating mutually advantageous *intra*racial cross-class alliances among whites. And more significantly, it provided disincentives for *inter*racial working-class relationships that would undermine the value of whiteness.[8]

Based on a community study of Rome, a midsize industrial town in northwest Georgia, this book examines how whiteness shaped the class identity and politics of textile workers from the introduction of industrial wage work at the turn of the century to the official elimination of discriminatory employment policy in the 1960s. A primary concern of this book is to examine how workers' culture and politics incorporated, expressed, and contributed to emerging definitions of whiteness. Here my work owes a major debt to historian David Roediger's example, especially his keen analysis of language and folklore and his insight into how seemingly race-blind terms, such as "boss," incorporated and expressed contemporary ideas about race.[9] Even in the Jim Crow South, I discovered, concepts of whiteness were implicit rather than explicit in much of the discourse on

[7] Some scholars have emphasized the extent to which whiteness has disguised inequalities among whites. See, for example, Neil Foley, *The White Scourge: Mexicans, Blacks, and Poor Whites in Texas Cotton Culture* (Berkeley: University of California Press, 1997); and Annalee Newitz and Matthew Wray, *White Trash: Race and Class in America* (New York: Routledge, 1997).

[8] Lipsitz, *Possessive Investment in Whiteness*, vii; I thank David Roediger for this insight. On the material value of whiteness and its treatment as "property" under the law, see Cheryl I. Harris, "Whiteness as Property," *Harvard Law Review* 106 (June 1993): 1709–91.

[9] Roediger, *Wages of Whiteness*, 65–92.

workers, politics, and policy. The pervasiveness of race often allowed speakers, writers, workers, and candidates to take their audience's understanding of whiteness for granted. Southern workers, the greatest majority of whom never joined unions, left few documents in the archives and even fewer that provide explicit declarations of their racial ideology. At the same time, whiteness, as a historical phenomenon, was an idea that changed over time. Although I have interviewed dozens of people, I am not naive enough to believe that oral histories can overcome the revolutionary changes that have altered the boundaries of acceptable discourse since the 1950s.

On the other hand, armed with the recognition of how whiteness was so often invisible, unspoken, and understood, I discovered that ideas about race were, more often than not, an implicit facet of all aspects of southern culture. Even though southerners in the early twentieth century did not use the term, whiteness was deeply embedded in social relations, politics, and class formation. For example, when white southerners spoke of "the South," they almost always meant, and were invariably understood as meaning, the *white* South. Through a close reading of working-class culture that pays attention to the symbols, assumptions, and ideas that guide it, this book examines these racial dimensions of working-class identity and the contributions workers made to southern racial ideology. From expressions of loyalty to their paternalistic benefactors, to racial designations institutionalized in union contracts, to humor in plant newspapers, I argue, textile workers inscribed and gave meaning to working-class whiteness.

Politics, in particular, provides an important point of entry into the world of whiteness. Although southern politics is ordinarily assumed to be an elite affair, I discovered that working-class notions of racial privilege and labor itself occupied a critical position in the rhetoric of state politics, especially as labor practices increasingly came under the purview of federal policy. And contrary to another aspect of the conventional wisdom about southern politics, ordinary white working-class Georgians also assumed an important role in the practice of popular politics, from the stump speeches they attended, to the issues they elicited, to the ballots they did cast. In spite of their reputation as anti-union supporters of a conservative business elite, Georgia's Eugene and Herman Talmadge often incorporated specifically working-class issues into their platforms and made direct appeals to working-class voters as whites, as workers, even as union members.

White workers did respond to political appeals to maintain segregation, but to dismiss their politics as simply a privileging of race over class is to miss an opportunity to better understand workers and the way southern Democratic politics worked. As Bryant Simon has demonstrated, southern workers' political identities were "a subtle overlapping of multiple identities and ideas about the state, public power, class, gender, and race."[10] As I hope this book demonstrates, the South's single party was an equally complex phenomenon. While southern Democrats clearly never embraced unions over the "right to work," this does not mean they were wholly unresponsive to working-class or union issues. In fact, what is most striking about Georgia Democrats, and the Talmadges in particular, is their remarkable flexibility in accommodating so many white agendas. The southern party's success owed as much to its ability to accommodate an extraordinarily diverse group of white interests as it did to the limited franchise. Despite the general anti-union climate in postwar Georgia, for example, Rome millhands were able to carve out an effective and influential role for themselves in Georgia politics that expressed a distinctly white working-class union perspective.

As a community study, this book has strengths and limitations. I would not make any claim for Rome or its workers as representative of the South.[11] For the study of politics, racial ideology, and textile workers, however, it does offer advantages. The format of community study, which provides a way to examine how various elements of a community interact with each other, offers an ideal place to investigate intraracial interactions and the context-dependent meanings of race and class. As a majority-white community whose economy was dominated by several textile mills, Rome also presented an opportunity to compare the experiences of different groups of workers—organized and unorganized, urban and rural, cotton and rayon. Rome's political divisions also provided a unique insight into politics. For much of the twentieth century, the electoral precincts within Rome and Floyd County corresponded to significant social and class divisions among whites, such as union and non-union, and this permits a comparison of various constituencies' responsiveness to candidates and issues. Finally, Rome's history upsets some of the tidiest narratives about southern workers, from the impact of the 1934 General Textile Strike, to the effects of World War II's Fair Employment Practices Commission (FEPC), to the postwar economic fortunes of southern industry. And even within Rome, I found a surprising level of diversity among white textile workers.

Organized chronologically, this book places this history within the context of major events of the twentieth century from the New Deal to the

[10] Simon, *Fabric of Defeat*, 7.

[11] In fact, recent studies of race and employment in northern locales suggest that the South's workers had no monopoly on whiteness or preferential hiring. See Thomas Sugrue, *The Origins of the Urban Crisis: Race and Inequality in Postwar Detroit* (Princeton: Princeton University Press, 1996).

civil rights movement. Several overlapping narratives emerge. First, whiteness played an important role in facilitating the acceptance of industrial development among all classes of whites from the cotton mill campaigns of the 1880s through the 1950s reign of "moderates" such as Herman Talmadge. Although the ideology of boosterism was rarely expressed in terms of race after the New South era, southerners understood development as a project carried out for the benefit of whites that would maintain established racial hierarchies. Race also facilitated southern apologists' version of paternalism and encouraged many millhands to internalize its morals. This did not, however, necessarily prevent independent working-class actions. How well paternalistic benefactors lived up to this intraracial ideal played a significant role in determining workers' reactions to such events as the 1934 strike and later organizing campaigns by the CIO. Whiteness and boosterism disguised some of the exploitative elements of southern industry, but because they also made an implicit promise to workers, millhands could appeal to them in ways that served their interests.

This book also examines how racial discrimination in employment, and the occupational segregation that resulted, actually contributed to the very definitions of whiteness and blackness by constantly reconstructing and confirming racial difference. Thus not only did race determine occupation, but in time occupation played a determining role in defining race. Jobs themselves became important tokens of racial identity. The significance of this connection was repeatedly demonstrated in the visual symbols and iconography whites chose to represent race. A third narrative, that of white southerners' fierce resistance to the encroachment of federal fair employment initiatives under the New Deal, the FEPC, and later the Civil Rights Act, also indicates the centrality of work to the South's racial order. The story of this resistance and the political support it elicited also provides a unique insight into southern ideas about whiteness and the deep roots of massive-resistance politics.

The central narrative concerns the use that workers made of whiteness. Because textile factories employed whites almost exclusively, the unions that formed in Rome did not initially challenge workers' commitment to segregation. The failure of race-baiting to prevent union organization, in fact, paradoxically revealed workers' understanding of their unions as white. Workers re-created racial difference in a labor movement that, until the 1960s, permitted a fair amount of space for segregation. However, the labor movement's increasing emphasis on both political action and civil rights as elements of the working-class agenda foisted a complex set of negotiations on Rome's union members. By the time AFL-CIO leaders adopted a more aggressive support of civil rights, the racial culture as well as the political alliances of Rome unions were firmly in place. Although national labor leaders argued that support for segregationists was damaging to labor, Rome unionists had already learned to work effectively within the South's political system and were not persuaded that such an agenda was inconsistent with unionism as they knew it. Moreover, the general white southern alienation from the federal government in the 1960s was intensified in local union circles by the simultaneity of the government's effective local intervention on behalf of civil rights and its dismal failure to defend the rights of organized labor. What the labor movement had allowed as relationships of convenience in the 1940s and 1950s eventually became forthright local support of anti-government segregationists such as George Wallace in the 1960s.

Finally, this book concludes with an examination of how and when whiteness went underground. When the moral authority of segregation was destroyed by the civil rights movement, defenders of whiteness adopted a new rhetoric of seemingly race-neutral conservatism. Although it was not a direct expression of sympathy for white supremacy, its inversion of "rights" and its premise that current white advantages had been "earned" rather than granted by discrimination proved equally pernicious. A new rhetoric of "qualification," reminiscent of euphemisms for whiteness forged under the regime of the FEPC, soon replaced "whiteness" in the public opposition to nondiscrimination under the Civil Rights Act's Title VII. Rome's civic leaders, unions, and employers proved capable of adapting the race-neutral language of the post–civil rights era, but their communities remained anything but neutral on matters of race.

Prologue

The Politics of Whiteness

STEPPING UP to the microphone on September 8, 1934, in Rotary Park in Rome, Georgia, Governor Eugene Talmadge ceremoniously took off his coat to reveal his trademark red suspenders. A "tremendous cheer" arose from a record-breaking crowd of more than fifteen thousand people from all counties of northwest Georgia who had braved the broiling late-summer sun to hear the governor's famous "hair-in-the-face oratory." Those who could not squeeze into the treeless expanse of the park observed the spectacle from their cars, and still others listened to the governor's final northwest Georgia stump speech on Atlanta radio station WSB. Glenn Griffin, a prominent Rome labor leader and candidate for the state legislature, had just introduced Governor Talmadge as the "present, the best, and the next governor of Georgia." After quieting the shouting and applauding and the blaring car horns, the governor commenced his speech with a typical denunciation of his detractors, inside and outside the South. "They tried to make labor believe I was against them—that I was in favor of 5 cents per hour for labor and the men in overalls not getting over a dollar a day," he fumed, but the "working people of this state know that I am the best friend they ever had in the governor's chair."[1]

The Rome stump speech was typical Georgia political fare, complete with entertainment by "Fiddling" John Carson, appearances by quartets from Dalton and Rome, singing, shouting, and more likely than not, a few discreetly hidden jars of corn liquor. Although poll taxes, literacy tests, and other disfranchising schemes often made the mechanics of Georgia politics seem an elite affair, the stump speech was the pure embodiment of popular political culture, bearing the distinct mark of the plain white folk of the Georgia countryside. And Talmadge was a master of it. As described by an *Atlanta Constitution* reporter in 1934, Talmadge bristled with "enthusiasm" and sparkled with "wit" that drew more "hearers in two years than any other public speaker the state has ever had." In a cadence reminiscent of a Baptist preacher, Talmadge kept the crowds cheering with call and response, concluding with a roll call by county of who would vote for him. Modeling his style after Populist leader Tom

[1] *Rome News-Tribune*, Sept. 9, 1934; Talmadge quotes from *Atlanta Constitution*, Sept. 9, 1934.

Figure 1. Audience present at Eugene Talmadge's stump speech in Rome's Rotary Park, September 9, 1934. Talmadge has just begun to poll the crowd, asking attendants to raise their hand if they plan to vote for him in the primary.

Watson, the governor spoke to the common white man and woman in their own language, addressing their frustrations, disappointments, and resentments. He attacked their enemies—African Americans, city folks, northerners, and wealthy capitalists—with a confidence and haughty rebelliousness that defied the grim realities of rural poverty in depression-era Georgia. The stump speech incorporated all the emotionalism and mass delirium of an old-time revival, and at the end of the speech, as at the end of a camp meeting, many would leave the park as new true believers.[2]

In Rome in 1934, the governor took up a standard issue in early-twentieth-century southern politics—southern opposition to federal encroachment on white supremacy. That year, one of the most popular issues of the primary was the governor's opposition to the federal National Recovery Administration (NRA) wage scale for black workers in the state highway department. It was his opponents, Talmadge charged, who "tried to bluff

[2] *Atlanta Constitution*, Sept. 9, 1934; Calvin McLeod Logue, *Eugene Talmadge: Rhetoric and Response* (New York: Greenwood Press, 1989), 10–11, 53; William Anderson, *The Wild Man from Sugar Creek: The Political Career of Eugene Talmadge* (Baton Rouge: Louisiana State University Press, 1975), 42–43, 66–70.

me into having the highway department fix a minimum wage scale of 40 cents per hour for common labor on the highways." But, he continued, "I answered back and told them that it would be wrong for our white farmers and their families to be picking cotton in the fields in Georgia right beside the road and see a negro making 40 cents per hour shoveling dirt and rolling a wheelbarrow" when "good white men and white women working . . . alongside the same roads" hardly got that much. Few of the white workers and farmers in this northwest Georgia audience would have earned more than thirty-five cents an hour in 1934, and most would have agreed that tax dollars should not pay such a relatively extravagant wage for highway labor, "especially when the majority of those highway laborers are negroes." It was a "contention always cheered" among white Georgia audiences, according to the *Atlanta Constitution*. "It isn't right, it isn't fair, and it isn't honest," Talmadge protested to white workers.[3]

Amid the spectacle of food, music, and speechmaking, Talmadge's words represented much more than a straightforward attack on his opponents. As he shouted about "common labor," the governor evoked some

[3] *Atlanta Constitution*, Sept. 9, 1934; John E. Allen, "The Governor and the Strike: Eugene Talmadge and the General Textile Strike, 1934" (Master's thesis, Georgia State University, 1977), 101; James A. Hodges, *New Deal Labor Policy and the Southern Cotton Textile Industry, 1933–1941* (Knoxville: University of Tennessee Press, 1986), 32, 95.

of white Georgia's most basic, if seldom articulated, ideas about identity, race, and status. He appealed to deeply held notions about the meaning of blackness and whiteness, and defended the institutions and ideas that gave race meaning in the early-twentieth-century South. Work, as well as the wage paid, was a primary symbol of racial difference. Resting on the ideology of white supremacy and only secondarily on cultural taboos against having black men near white women, a rigid system of segregation separated the South's black and white workers. Even though the majority of northwest Georgia's citizens farmed or worked low-wage positions in factories, jobs were classified, defined, and compensated meticulously by race. The NRA wage scale threatened the alleged superiority of white workers, not only by proposing to pay black workers "too much," but, as Talmadge understood well, by seeming to diminish the relative value of white labor.

For the people in the audience—a combination of farmers, sharecroppers, planters, businessmen, and millhands typical of the Georgia upcountry—Talmadge's rhetoric also held a number of specific appeals. It is likely that small farmers and sharecroppers were the largest group in the crowd, since about one-quarter of the forty-nine thousand people living in Rome and Floyd County earned a living by tilling the soil. The self-appointed champion of the "poor dirt farmer" rather than the wealthy planter, Talmadge was particularly popular with the tenants and sharecroppers who operated over 70 percent of the farms in Floyd County. At a time when much of the rest of the nation looked upon them with scorn, Talmadge validated their lifestyle with his earthy talk about farm chores and fields, his enduring faith in hard work, and his unwavering defense of farmers as the backbone of Georgia society. In spite of his economic conservatism, as governor he had supported cosmetic, but popular, reforms such as lower utility bills, a freeze on taxes, and discounted automobile tags. The much more elite group of large planters in Floyd County, whose earnings were dependent upon a large, steady supply of cheap agricultural labor to work their land as tenants and croppers, probably felt an even greater sympathy for Talmadge's general position against federal minimum wages and relief. For identical reasons, Talmadge also enjoyed the support of Floyd County's "uptown crowd," the merchants, managers, businessmen, and civic leaders who owned the neat two-story stores, grand hotels, and cotton warehouses lining the wide streets of Rome's downtown grid. Many of Rome's elites also earned their fortunes on cotton and labor from the countryside, whether they supplied and serviced the farmer, marketed his goods, held a mortgage on a farm, or supervised the farmer's family members in one of the county's many cotton mills. Predictably, Talmadge did not bother to address Floyd County's small population of African Americans. Only 17 percent of the county's people, black citizens were probably wholly unrepresented in the crowd gathered for the stump speech, since Georgia's Democratic Party barred black citizens from voting in the upcoming primary and social convention barred them from any such white social gathering. They might cast a vote in the general election, but given the overwhelming dominance of the Democratic Party, the November general election was a mere formality in 1934.

One group in the audience, growing in size and electoral importance in the twentieth century, was the county's textile workers, who accounted for nearly half of all nonagricultural workers in Floyd County.[4] As white Georgians, beneficiaries of the segmented market for labor, and inheritors of the plain-folk culture of the countryside, workers also had an interest in the governor's defense of the white wage. Since textile workers were among the few Georgians who earned an hourly wage, Talmadge frequently singled out their earnings for comparison to the NRA wage rates in order to illustrate the absurdity of the proposal in meaningful terms. In Dalton, a town just forty miles northeast of Rome, Talmadge had asked: "What is the minimum scale of wages paid to the people in Georgia who make those beautiful bedspreads and tapestries. . . . Do these white women receive 40 cents per hour?" In Gainesville he protested to an audience: "You textile workers' minimum wage scale is not 40 cents per hour." As Talmadge was undoubtedly aware, the NRA minimum wage for textile workers was thirty cents an hour.

In Rome, Talmadge took "especial notice" of a large group of textile workers in the audience, many of whom were out of work because of the 1934 General Textile Strike. Ironically, even as textile workers cheered the man who was running against the NRA in the name of whiteness, many were on strike against textile managers for failing to meet the standards set by the NRA for their industry. "I want to say a word to you striking textile workers," he said. "Be cool and calm. Do not take part in any violence and you'll always have a friend as long as Eugene Talmadge is in the governor's chair." Since the strike had begun on Labor Day, Talmadge had repeatedly promised strikers that "no giant corporation or big interest will ever dictate to me what to do" while in office. "I resent anyone on earth saying they are closer to labor, or a better friend of labor than I," Talmadge had said in August. "You can look at my hands and the color of my skin and tell it." In Rome he again reassured strikers that

[4] Textile workers, with the "chemical" textile workers at Tubize Chatillon included, represented 5,176, or 43 percent, of the county's 12,066 white nonagricultural workers. In comparison, the next largest categories of non-farm employment for whites in the 1930s—foundry work, retail and wholesale trade, and building trades—accounted for only 5, 9, and 4 percent, respectively. Figures calculated from U.S. Bureau of the Census, *Fifteenth Census of the United States: 1930*, vol. 3, pt. 1 (Washington, D.C.: Government Printing Office, 1932), 514.

no governor, including himself, "desire[d] for it to be necessary" to call out the state militia.[5]

Although Talmadge frequently claimed to be a friend of organized labor, his general conservatism, his frequent defenses of white supremacy, and particularly his criticism of the New Deal made him anathema to many state and national United Textile Workers (UTW) leaders. Historians have similarly regarded him as "anti-labor." But given the context of general anti-unionism prevalent in Georgia in 1934, Talmadge's direct appeal to organized workers on the stump was actually rather remarkable. Moreover, many rank-and-file unionists as well as unorganized textile workers in northwest Georgia wholeheartedly supported Talmadge. At the Rome stump speech, union workers held banners announcing their textile local's support for the governor. In Cedartown, a small community just twenty miles south of Rome, workers staged a parade for the governor, and the president of the UTW local declared his fellow members for "Governor Talmadge 100 percent." Addressing Talmadge's labor critics, a local union candidate for the legislature had asserted, "there are many over the state who seem to have been misled by a few self-appointed spokesmen of organized labor. . . . I want to say here and now that no one can tell organized labor how to vote." He assured the crowd that he would "vote for every one of Eugene Talmadge's policies if I am elected."[6]

A week after Talmadge's Rome visit, a record number of Floyd County's citizens would go to the polls and deliver him an overwhelming majority in the white Democratic primary. Just three days after the governor won, despite all his promises, he declared martial law and issued over four thousand troops to quiet "insurrection" and protect the "right to work." Calling Talmadge "Georgia's Hitler," national UTW leaders accused the governor of deliberately deceiving strikers, who "voted for him . . . because he had not [yet] called out the troops."[7] Many labor leaders, liberals, and historians since have typically viewed the whole affair as yet another example of how race was used to trick white southern workers into voting against their interests as members of the working class.

[5] Anderson, *Wild Man from Sugar Creek*, 110; *Rome News-Tribune*, Sept. 9, 1934.

[6] *Rome News-Tribune*, Sept. 9, 1934; *Atlanta Constitution*, Sept. 9, 1934. Apparently, northwest Georgia's textile workers had elected to deviate from the Georgia Federation of Labor's endorsement of Talmadge's major opponent, Claude Pittman. The Georgia Federation charged that Talmadge had failed to support President Roosevelt's recovery program. Local accounts of the campaign in Floyd County indicate that northwest Georgia's workers supported Talmadge, and no union records survive to suggest otherwise. John E. Allen, "Eugene Talmadge and the Great Textile Strike in Georgia, September 1934," in *Essays in Southern Labor History: Selected Papers, Southern Labor History Conference, 1976*, ed. Gary M. Fink and Merle E. Reed (Westport, Conn.: Greenwood Press, 1976), 31–49.

[7] *Textile Labor Banner*, Feb. 2, Aug. 24, 1935.

But in some very real sense, Talmadge, like the Democratic standard-bearers who would follow him in the twentieth century, did represent the interests of the white working-class people in that audience, including those who belonged to unions. Race, poverty, and the shape of the Democratic Party in the South made southern workers' interests exceedingly complex. Whiteness was rarely a simple matter of white racism, though that was clearly a component. Rather, the 1934 primary and the NRA wage issue illustrated several recurring contradictions inherent in southern workers' twentieth-century experience. While federal policy often promised to improve their lot, it also threatened to undermine the real material and cultural advantages they derived from the status quo in southern economic and social relations. In this sense, white workers shared a real interest with employers and elites in maintaining existing elements of the South's social conditions. And this interest, as Talmadge understood, provided much of the ideological glue for the southern Democratic Party in the first half of the twentieth century. Although northwest Georgians could not have predicted the role the federal government would play in finally undermining the connection between work and race, the fact that working-class identity was so tightly bound to race ensured that the majority of industrial wage workers had a continued interest in the politics of whiteness.

One

Boosterism, Whiteness, and Paternalism in the New South: The Creation of Wage Work

"IT CANNOT BE DISPUTED," American Federation of Labor president Samuel Gompers asserted in 1898, that "the spirit of resistance of [New England's] textile operatives is much further and higher developed than that of their Southern fellowcraftspeople." Comparing textile millhands of the South to foreign and what he believed to be racially inferior competition for jobs, Gompers remarked that southern workers were "chinesising [*sic*] our people, our institutions and our civilizations." They worked for one-third less wages than New England workers, and for a multitude of reasons usually ascribed to their character, southern millhands would remain significantly underrepresented in textile unions, even as the nation's textile industry migrated south in the twentieth century. By 1925 the South had surpassed New England to become the nation's largest regional producer of textiles, and southern workers, labor and capital agreed, had been the primary lure. The South possessed the "greatest, best, and cheapest labor market in the United States," according to one northern industrial executive, and southern boosters were not shy about promoting their human capital. Well into the early twentieth century, southern workers were "offered on the auction block pretty much as their black predecessors were," one economist lamented, "their qualities enlarged upon with the same salesman's gusto." In Rome, Georgia, the chamber of commerce peddled local people—"the labor . . . of native Anglo-Saxon stock—loyal and efficient"—in the same objective terms it used to advertise water, mineral, and transportation resources. "From the nearby mountains there is always available a large supply of intelligent white help," the chamber advised potential investors in 1934, while the "mild climate and the low cost of living make for contentment of labor."[1]

It was true that southern workers and the southern textile industry were distinctive, but this had less to do with the intangibles of "character" than with the unique historical context of southern industrialization. Floyd

[1] F. Ray Marshall, *Labor in the South* (Cambridge: Harvard University Press, 1967), 80; George Brown Tindall, *The Emergence of the New South, 1913–1945* (Baton Rouge: Louisiana State University Press, 1975), 318; Broadus Mitchell, "Fleshpots in the South," *Virginia Quarterly Review* 3 (1927): 169; *Rome City Directory* (Richmond: R. L. Polk, 1934), 16.

County, like many other southern locales, joined the campaign to build cotton mills under the banner of the New South. Fueled by regional pride, white supremacy, and poverty, southern industrial development schemes and their accompanying ideology transformed the economic shift from agriculture to industry into a civic crusade and a source of white unity. Until the cotton mill campaigns of the 1880s, the urban, business-minded boosters in Rome had often been at odds with the poorer, subsistence-minded inhabitants of the surrounding countryside. While Rome's entrepreneurial founders envisioned the city's becoming a center of commercial agriculture and trade, and the first local historians of Rome recalled their history as primarily the struggle to bring that vision to fruition, many yeoman farmers in the county initially held quite different goals. After the Civil War and Reconstruction, however, poverty, segregation, and industry permitted Rome's founders to follow their entrepreneurial inclinations. Hawking the South's most abundant resources of land, labor, and cotton, boosters and businessmen, with the subsequent cooperation of a local historian, manufactured a new myth of common white interests that would influence generations of industrial wage workers and managers. The alternative of rural poverty often made it seem as if the notoriously low-wage industries that came to dominate the New South really were serving the interests of farmers-turned-workers. The absence of trade unions provided verification for the claims of southern boosters and businessmen that workers' and managers' interests were in fact identical.

Racial ideology, in particular, influenced the course of industrialization. To an impoverished South, manufacturing provided not only wages but also new props for white supremacy. Because the South's largest industry hired whites almost exclusively, it made a significant contribution to the differentiation of black and white by creating new categories of racial identity for the South's poor whites that were grounded in their wage-earning status. Although the textile industry was one of the lowest-paying industries in the nation, the wage, supplemented by mill village welfare, introduced dramatic improvements in employees' lifestyles that widened the gap between white and black southerners. Race, in turn, also shaped millhands' ideas about class, tempered adversarial relationships between workers and managers, and informed workers' choices in regard to politics and unions. By the 1930s, the experience of textile workers and the perception of industrial wage work in the South had become inseparable from whiteness.

Rome, Georgia, located in the heart of the former Cherokee lands, sixty-five miles northwest of Atlanta in the foothills of the Appalachian Mountains, lies at the confluence of two navigable rivers, the Oostanaula and the Etowah. Traditionally the town traced its roots to five Anglo founding fathers who had the foresight to speculate that the seven hills near the Indian settlement "head of Coosa," with their fertile soil and natural transportation links, would make a profitable site for a town and trading center. The story, as passed down directly by the town fathers themselves, was a tribute to both white supremacy and boosterism, recalling the ingenuity and glory of white frontiersmen who had the pluck and vision to seize commercially viable land from Native Americans and develop it to its full potential. And although the local legend of Rome's founding was probably as much myth as the tale of ancient Rome's Romulus and Remus, as an origin story it was particularly revealing of both the myth makers and the myth keepers who recorded it.

Romans tended to recall their history in terms of those white founders, or perhaps in terms of white planters and black slaves, but it began as a conflict between whites and Native Americans. The site in Floyd County, named for a South Carolina plantation owner and politician who had led a brutal 1814 invasion against the Creek Indians, fell into white hands by rather nefarious devices, even in the local telling. In the late 1820s and early 1830s, the state of Georgia, with the support of President Andrew Jackson, passed a series of proclamations enabling white Georgians to confiscate Native American land, distribute it among themselves, and banish all Cherokees from the land they had inhabited for generations. Cherokee leaders, already much assimilated into Anglo culture, mounted a well-organized legal and political resistance through official government channels, but to no avail. In the 1830s, white settlers—"like a plague of locusts," in the words of a local historian George Macgruder Battey—"alighted on the choice hunting grounds of the Cherokees," looting and stealing as they made claim to Cherokee land, cattle, household possessions, and even homesteads. One Cherokee leader, who served as the postmaster, owned two ferries, and lived in a handsome two-story house in what became Rome, returned from negotiations with the federal government to find his boats confiscated, a white family living in his house, and his sick wife confined to a single room. White Georgians were not content, however, with simply stealing the most valuable property. In the words of Battey, "peace and the social order [were] not be attained . . . until the Indians were sent west lock, stock and barrel." In 1838, federal soldiers rounded up all seventeen thousand Cherokees and forcibly marched them eight hundred miles to a less desirable and certainly less profitable land in Oklahoma on the infamous "Trail of Tears." Four thousand Cherokees perished on the grueling wintertime march.[2]

[2] George MacGruder Battey, Jr., *A History of Rome and Floyd County, Georgia* (Atlanta: Webb and Vary, 1922), 33–36. On land distribution in Georgia, see Stephen J. Hahn, *The Roots of Southern Populism: Yeoman Farmers and the Transformation of the Georgia Up-*

Although the site of present-day Floyd County had been an important trade and commercial center with a large trading post, roads, ferries, and many white squatters for some time before it was appropriated by whites and the state of Georgia, early local histories also tended to portray Rome's founding as a venture into literal wilderness—a "forest primeval," in Battey's words. Rome proper, as recalled by early Romans, owed its creation to five businessmen—two attorneys, two local planters, and the nephew of Governor Wilson Lumpkin—who happened upon the site and saw in the river junction and surrounding hills "exceptional opportunities for building a city that would become the largest and most prosperous in Cherokee Georgia."[3]

In the spring of 1834, at a nearby plantation, the five partners worked out the details of establishing their town. By the end of the year they had completed a survey, acquired the land, bought the ferry rights, and used their personal connections to the governor and the legislature to have the county seat—with its attendant population and business, of course—moved to their new town. The process of choosing a name spoke volumes about their ambitions, but the actual choice was pure serendipity. After each of the five "pioneers" selected a name for the town, wrote his choice on a slip of paper, and placed the slip in a hat, they conducted their own lottery. The five names they chose were Hillsboro, Pittsburgh, Hamburg, Warsaw, and Rome, the latter "recalling the seven hills of ancient Rome on the Tiber." When Rome was drawn from the hat, the five agreed that it would be the name of their new city.[4]

Although the whole area languished as a rural outpost for several years, the partners quickly provided the town with all the accoutrements and institutions of white society. By 1835 they had founded a Rome Bar Association and the Western Bank of Rome, constructed a toll bridge across the Oostanaula River, and raised funds and built a brick courthouse at the center of "town" between the two river feeders of the Coosa. Even at this early stage, the town fathers also began to look outside the county for opportunities to enhance Rome's prosperity. Using connections to the Georgia legislature, they lobbied, though unsuccessfully, to have a proposed state railroad stop in Rome instead of point farther west in present-

---

country, 1850–1890 (New York: Oxford University Press, 1983), 19. On Indian removal, see also Michael Rogin, *Fathers and Children: Andrew Jackson and the Subjugation of the American Indian* (New York: Knopf, 1975).

[3] Battey, *History of Rome and Floyd County*, 33, 38; Roger Aycock, *All Roads to Rome* (Roswell, Ga.: W. H. Wolfe Associates, 1981), 38; Hughes Reynolds, *The Coosa River Valley from DeSoto to Hydroelectric Power* (Cynthiana, Ky.: Hobson Book Press, 1944), 28–36.

[4] Battey, *History of Rome and Floyd County*, 25, 30, 33–36; quotes from 34, 30; Reynolds, *Coosa River Valley*, 28–36.

day Chattanooga. Not until the eve of the Civil War would investments and efforts of the town's patriarchs finally begin to provide the prestige and fantastic financial returns they anticipated. By 1850, stores, inns, churches, and a post office dotted the streets of Rome, and although local pigs and cattle mocked the little city's pretensions by roaming at will through downtown streets, many townsmen began to turn a tidy profit from supplying farmers with dry goods and acting as agents to market local produce of cotton, corn, and wheat.[5]

Local histories, by focusing primarily on town interests and large slave-owning planters, suggested, if only through silence, that all Romans shared the founders' vision for commercial development. However, the yeoman farmers inhabiting the countryside around Floyd County held more modest goals. The land in Floyd County was fertile and could in fact support cotton, the South's preeminent cash crop, but the higher altitudes, cooler climate, and hilly, broken terrain discouraged the introduction of plantation-style commercial agriculture. Distribution of land by lottery also made it possible for common farmers, provided they were white citizens, to set up homesteads. In the 1850s, as the plantation economy grew elsewhere in the South, the majority of Georgia's upcountry farms remained small, subsistence-oriented ventures operated primarily with white family labor. Extensive slave ownership of twenty or more was confined to only the wealthiest 10 to 25 percent of upcountry farmers, with one-half to three-quarters of upcountry farmers owning no slaves. Farm efforts focused on cultivating foodstuffs such as wheat, potatoes, and corn, though farmers might raise a few bales of cotton each year for cash to buy household necessities. Floyd County farmers, who had access to railways and markets in Rome, raised a little more cotton than their neighbors but generally remained aloof from the commercial markets and credit that would become so devastating after the Civil War. Most of the upcountry's white yeoman farmers worked their own land or lived in households that owned land. Tenancy, particularly for young families just beginning a farming career, was likely to be a temporary stage of a farming career rather than a permanent status. Given the absence of large-scale plantation slavery and the relatively light slaveholdings of northwest Georgians, the whole population remained predominantly white. Indicating the distance between northwest Georgians and their fellow countrymen further South in the plantation belt, many Floyd County residents proved reluctant to support secession.[6]

[5] Battey, *History of Rome and Floyd County*, 38–39, 91–95.

[6] Hahn, *Roots of Southern Populism*, 25–26, 45; figures on slave ownership are based on Hahn's figures for northwest Georgia.

Only the election of Abraham Lincoln and the growing perception among southern whites that Republicans were conspiring to inaugurate "a ruthless war of the blacks against the whites throughout the Southern States" finally convinced white Floyd County leaders to support secession. Interestingly, resolutions passed in a Floyd County citizens' meeting after Lincoln's election expressed as much concern about northern abolitionists' spies—"its vile emissaries [sent] to instigate the slaves to destroy our property, burn our towns . . . and spread distrust, dismay and, *death by poison*, among our people"—as they did about the right to maintain private property in slaves. Floyd County leaders often portrayed the struggle as one of black versus white. Long before the phrase derived real meaning from radical reconstruction's enfranchisement of freedmen, for example, the editors of the *Rome Southerner* routinely condemned the Party of Lincoln as the "Black Republicans." Given the ambivalence of many plain white folk toward disunion, secessionists relied heavily on appeals to sectional and racial loyalties. Beginning with accusations about increasing northern "hostility to the form of society existing in the *Southern states*," the citizens' meeting resolutions declared the farmers', merchants', and speculators' determination to put "past differences" aside for the "good of our native South" and concluded with an exhortation to the Georgia legislature to begin arming local forces. However, a fair amount of dissension remained among citizens of northwest Georgia. In January 1861, when white Georgians convened a secession convention, Floyd County's three delegates voted yes for secession, but other reports indicated that the county had a "heavy majority" opposed. Perhaps many of the plain white folk of northwest Georgia felt less invested in the South's "form of society."[7]

All Floyd County whites, even the most committed supporters of secession, would pay dearly for their shift to the Confederate cause. Given the level of Unionist support in the mountains and foothills prior to the war, the desertion rate was predictably high, but casualty rates were even higher. In the twelve companies of soldiers raised in Floyd County, approximately two thousand men, the casualty rate reached 25 percent. Even those who remained at home suffered heavy losses. Many of the town's more affluent citizens simply fled Rome in 1864 as fighting drew closer. Other white slave-owning Romans who remained behind were dismayed to discover that their slaves preferred to leave with the "Yankees" rather than remain in their masters' homes. Mrs. Robert Battey wrote to her husband of her distress that "all the negroes left me and went with to the Yankees. . . . They have treated me very badly, left me sick; Bessie to nurse; cows to milk, cooking to do, washing and everything else." White

[7] Battey, *History of Rome and Floyd County*, 130–34.

farm families who did not own slaves also paid a heavy and perhaps more bitter price. In November 1864, on his famous march through Atlanta to the sea, Union general William T. Sherman himself captured Rome and burned most of it to the ground.[8]

Local histories of Reconstruction, compiled in the early twentieth century, generally described the era from an elite white perspective. Diaries and reminiscences collected by local historians recall a time of impatience when white Romans "endured . . . until their country was once more restored to their keeping." Although Reconstruction failed to permanently alter the relationships of power between black and white, or yeoman and planter, white leaders of Floyd County bitterly resented occupation by Union troops and the short revolution in race relations effected by Reconstruction. Disgust with government agents and "carpetbaggers" led many of Rome's more prominent citizens, including Rome newspaper editor Henry Grady and the mayor, to join the Ku Klux Klan. Local accounts conveyed particular anger and disbelief at the new status granted the freedmen. A Rome merchant's diary, for example, recorded his fury over the "oppressive laws of Congress [now] disfranchising a great portion of the best men." When federal officers registered new voters in 1867, he was shocked to discover two black men in line, one "an old man I had around 15 or 16 years and who was still staying with me. . . . This man registered and will be allowed to vote," he fumed, when he himself was refused. Unfortunately, black Romans' perceptions of the changes were not recorded. Their history emerges, however, from the discursive margins of white complaint, as they deserted former masters, waited in line to register to vote, supported Republicans, and prevailed on the services of the Freedmen's Bureau.[9]

How poorer whites viewed the changes wrought by the Civil War and Reconstruction also escaped the attention of local historians, but it was clear that wartime destruction affected farmers of modest means more profoundly than it did large planters. Higher land values in the 1870s, pressures from creditors made nervous by Reconstruction, and declining prices for agricultural products made it much more difficult for farmers to hold onto their land and maintain or purchase material necessities. In the 1850s nearly nine of ten white farm operators had owned land, but by the 1880s only about seven of ten owned their own land. Loss of land and equipment, in turn, necessitated greater reliance on landlords and credit, which introduced a devastating cycle of debt and poverty in north-

[8] On desertions and casualty figures in the upcountry, see Hahn, *Roots of Southern Populism*, 124–32; Battey, *History of Rome and Floyd County*, 175–79, 204, quotes from 199–200; Aycock, *All Roads to Rome*, 107.

[9] Aycock, *All Roads to Rome*, 117, 122; Battey, *History of Rome and Floyd County*, 199.

west Georgia. The less equitable practice of sharecropping, an arrangement that gave landlords more extensive rights of supervision and allowed them to pay out rather than receive a share of the crop, increasingly replaced tenancy. Landlords and creditors usually demanded that farmers plant cotton, effectively committing farmers to the vagaries of the commercial market. When the price of cotton began to fall drastically in the 1880s, many farmers found it difficult to meet their obligations and found themselves in a position tantamount to debt peonage. One Floyd County landlord remarked in 1886, "All the hands I employ come to me poverty stricken and have to be found in all supplies—I have never yet . . . had a negro or white man I employed that ever came to me with anything but the cloths [*sic*] they had on their back." By the 1890s, fewer than half of the upcountry's white farmers owned their own land.[10] For freedmen, sharecropping may have represented a compromise between a lack of resources and their desire to operate a single-family farm, but for the former white yeoman farmers it was a distinct demotion in status.

Writing in the early twentieth century, local historians tended to blame the Civil War and Reconstruction for the farmers' descent into debt, but contemporaries who lived through the crisis understood the issue more accurately in terms of class—the business class versus the producing class. Angered by the cycle of debt and frustrated with the inadequacy of post-Reconstruction Democratic politics, many upcountry farmers looked for solutions in farmers' organizations and independent political action. For a brief moment in the late nineteenth century, farmers of declining fortune seemed to challenge the trajectory of Georgia's economic and political future by joining the producer-oriented Southern Farmers' Alliance and later the Populist Party. Arriving in Georgia in 1887, the Farmers' Alliance was a combination social club, political organization, and cooperative movement. To eliminate the middlemen who skimmed profits off produce sales and turned even greater profits from supplying farmers on credit, the Alliance created producer-controlled cooperatives. It also advocated political solutions, such as the coining of silver money and the "subtreasury plan," a marketing and credit system designed to give farmers more control over the sale of their crops and the price of staple items. Alliance members lobbied southern Democrats, who had decisively reasserted their power over Georgia politics by the late 1870s, to incorporate their demands for banking, credit, shipping, and tariff reforms into national politics. But frustrated by the cavalier treatment they received from the South's traditional party, many Alliance members turned in the 1890s to the emerging political arm of the Alliance—the People's Party, or Populists.

[10] Hahn, *Roots of Southern Populism*, 156–58, 161–62, 167.

The Populist Party provided a third-party voice to express the growing frustrations of many upcountry farmers. At times its rhetoric seemed truly subversive, challenging the elite leadership of the state, the boundaries between black and white, and the prominence of town and businessmen in economic and political affairs. Georgia congressman Tom Watson, for example, no doubt expressed the anger of many when he complained to farmers that although they far outnumbered other Georgians, townsmen "have been organized and have been your masters in every question of finance or state control." Georgia's first prominent Democrat to join the People's Party, Watson articulated the resentment of many yeoman farmers. "You cultivate the crop," he told farmers, but northerners, westerners, manufacturers, bankers, and financiers did "all the reaping."[11]

In perhaps an even more radical critique of southern society and politics, Watson laid bare the contradictions of poorer whites' commitment to white supremacy, particularly as expressed in allegiance to the southern Democratic Party. In spite of Reconstruction-era reform and the extension of the franchise to the freedmen, by the early 1870s a resurgent white Democratic Party had used race, the Republicans' assault on southern racial sensibilities, and the Republican identification with black freedmen and northern radicals to lure most of the defeated white southern coalition back to a single sectional party. Watson, however, exposed the fundamental fallacy of Democratic white supremacy in repeatedly pointing out the common plight of black and white farmers. The Democrats, he charged, had used race as a smoke screen to divert attention from their own misdeeds in national politics, allowing "the South to be plundered in the interests of the Eastern and Northern plutocrats." Race was what southern Democrats talk about "when they come back home after one of their big surrenders [to the East] at a national convention." White and black, Watson wrote in 1892, "are made to hate each other" by the very people who "enslave[d]" both. "You are deceived and blinded," he told farmers, "that you may not see how this race antagonism perpetuates a monetary system which beggars both [black and white]."[12]

Providing what might be described as an inadvertent testament to the radicalism of the People's Party, Battey's 1922 local history did not even mention the Populists in any of its 640 pro-business pages, even though a native Roman was a Populist candidate for governor. Perhaps Watson's critique could not be reconciled with the black and white vision reconstructed by Battey for local posterity. Though local statesman and "Black

[11] Numan Bartley, *The Creation of Modern Georgia*, 2nd ed. (Athens: University of Georgia Press, 1990), 87–102, Watson quotes from 89.

[12] Ibid., 87–102, Watson quotes from 90; C. Vann Woodward, *Tom Watson, Agrarian Rebel* (Savannah: Beehive Press, 1938), 248.

Republicans" appeared frequently, the Populists were evidently edited out of the depository for Rome's collective memory.[13]

Watson's rhetoric and Battey's omission, however, belied the real complexity of the Populist movement, which never exclusively represented the interests of Georgia's poor people or the ideal of interracial solidarity in the Georgia countryside. Other Watson utterances (particularly his disavowal of "social equality" of the races) and the Populists' minimal attention to the particular needs of the black community suggested that the party's attempt to gain black support—and votes—represented some significant amount of opportunism. Although most of the state's remaining Republican leaders supported Populist candidates, the constituency of the northwest Georgia Populists was primarily white. Nor did Populist Party membership necessarily indicate racial tolerance or a recognition of the shared problems of white and black farmers. Rather, in the words of historian Douglas Flamming, "the race issue mingled with class and politics in enormously complex ways." As former yeomen clinging to, or only recently removed from, their independent farmer status, many Populists embraced a common nineteenth-century understanding of virtue, political or otherwise, as contingent on one's status as an independent producer. As a result, they likely viewed freedmen, career sharecroppers, and tenants with suspicion and contempt rather than sympathy. Plain white folk were also implicated in other nineteenth-century movements that expressed unmistakably racist impulses, such as the vigilante Whitecappers and the Ku Klux Klan.[14]

Ironically, the success of the Populists' appeal to southern farmers contributed to its eventual demise, as electoral politics forced the People's Party to seek a broader coalition to win electoral success, and their success in turn forced the Democrats to co-opt the most mainstream elements of the Populist platform. In Rome, for example, the initial political efforts of Alliance members met heavy opposition, and in an effort to become more respectable, party leaders began to nominate candidates such as Rome's Seaborn Wright, Populist candidate for governor in 1896. A well-

[13] On the Southern Farmers' Alliance and the Populist Party in northwest Georgia, see Hahn, *Roots of Southern Populism*, 269–71, 276–89; Barton C. Shaw, *The Wool-Hat Boys* (Baton Rouge: Louisiana State University Press, 1984); and Douglas Flamming, *Creating the Modern South: Millhands and Managers in Dalton, Georgia* (Chapel Hill: University of North Carolina Press, 1992), 69–75. On Populism in Georgia and more generally see Bartley, *Creation of Modern Georgia*; Robert C. McMath, *Populist Vanguard: A History of the Southern Farmers Alliance* (Chapel Hill: University of North Carolina Press, 1975); Woodward, *Tom Watson*; and Lawrence Goodwyn, *Democratic Promise: The Populist Moment in America* (New York: Oxford University Press, 1976).

[14] Flamming, *Creating the Modern South*, 72; Hahn, *Roots of Southern Populism*, 284–97.

educated and well-heeled attorney, Wright owned one of the finest houses in the city, wore stylish, expensive linen suits, and was rumored to be extremely wealthy. He expressed sympathy for the Populists, particularly their stand on temperance, but he had never been a member of the party.[15]

The bankruptcy of Georgia populism by the turn of the century represented a significant turning point for farmers and merchants in the upcountry. The now irreversible shift from subsistence to commercial agriculture permanently linked the economy of the countryside to town, yoking farmers ever more securely to the fortunes of commercial cotton agriculture, making the dreams of Rome's founding fathers possible, and enriching Rome merchants in a multiplicity of ways. By the late nineteenth century, just as the town's founders had predicted, the town's convenient location on three rivers had made it a "natural hub" for the marketing of southern agricultural goods and the sale of supplies to surrounding farmers. Because the shorter seasons and hilly terrain of the upcountry necessitated fertilizer for cotton cultivation, commercial agriculture created a booming retail market for guano. With the shift from corn to cotton, farmers also depended upon retail markets for the food they had formerly grown for themselves. Even in the sparsely populated upcountry, Floyd County merchants found that the potential for profits, especially for goods sold on credit, was immense. In 1873, for example, one of the larger county distributors sold over $10,000 of commercial fertilizers. In these same years, local farmers began to buy double the amount of food provisions.[16]

Even greater returns came from the marketing and sale of cotton, and "probably no town in the South offer[ed] better facilities for shipping the fleecy staple" than Rome, according to local historians. A handful of cotton factors dominated the marketing, shipping, storage, pressing, and ginning of the region's cotton, and the men who established these businesses reaped enormous profits. In the 1880s, as increasing numbers of farmers were pressed into commercial production, the Rome area produced an average of 80,000 bales of cotton per year, worth an estimated $9 million, most of it financed by local credit and distributed through town factoring services. Cotton presses, which compressed bales in order to facilitate storage and shipment, operated near the depots where, on a busy day, as many as 1,500 to 2,000 bales left Rome on railcars bound for Chattanooga, Atlanta, and beyond. Many a local fortune was built in the process. One large cotton dealer, whose offices, warehouses, and compression machinery occupied an entire downtown block, used his Rome profits to expand his business over three southern states, becoming one of the re-

[15] Shaw, *Wool-Hat Boys*; 150–57; Goodwyn, *Democratic Promise*, 256–63.

[16] Hahn, *Roots of Southern Populism*, 146, 148.

gion's largest buyers in just a few years. Another large cotton factorage business in Rome, run by brothers J. W. and J. A. Rounsaville, handled about half of the cotton distributed through Rome. Their warehouse, fabulously well equipped by nineteenth-century standards, had automatic water sprinklers tied into the city's water mains to protect their investment from fire. The Rounsavilles also ran a grocery business from their warehouse that grossed half a million dollars a year. Cotton and trade also created profits for city folks in less direct ways. With the growth of related retail and factorage business, the value of town property skyrocketed. A downtown lot purchased in the early 1880s for $7,250, for example, was resold within a just few years for over $62,000. Anticipating future growth, the Rounsavilles entered the real estate business and diversified their investments. J. W. became the president of the Rome Land Company, chartered in 1887, with $1 million of local capital, dedicated to the further growth and promotion of Rome.[17]

As in other small Georgia towns, the merchants, planters, doctors, lawyers, bankers, and other professionals who formed the county's elite were also the central source of political authority. In Rome a professional class had long resided in and around town where they controlled city and county government. After 1870, Rome's growing population of three thousand was probably joined by many planters. Tenancy did not require constant supervision, and as postbellum planters discovered, town life afforded comforts and luxuries that the country did not. At the turn of the century, affluent Romans might attend the opera at Nevins Hall or attend cotillions in the formal ballroom at the celebrated Armstrong Hotel. Gracious homes, country clubs, and an ample supply of low-wage black servants to tend kitchens, homes, and yards also enhanced the comfortable lifestyle of Rome's white professional and merchant class. Since the late nineteenth century, male members of this small elite had traditionally controlled the county courts, city government, the local Democratic Party, and just as significantly, credit and employment. Planter and founding father William Smith, for example, served as sheriff and state senator but was also rumored to control at least half of the county's votes.[18]

Post-Reconstruction and turn-of-the-century "reform" made feats such as Smith's much easier. Despite the Fifteenth Amendment's extension of the franchise to freedmen, the revived Georgia Democrats found ways to eliminate black citizens, and consequently most Republicans as well, from the voter rolls. In the 1880s the Georgia legislature implemented a cumulative poll tax, one of the most effective means to disfranchise cash-poor

[17] Aycock, *All Roads to Rome*, 162–64, 215.

[18] Bartley, *Creation of Modern Georgia*, 104–5, 153; Aycock, *All Roads to Rome*, 200, 235.

blacks and whites. In 1900, Georgia Democrats adopted a white primary, effectively barring all black Georgians from any meaningful political participation. Finally, in 1908 the state introduced a literacy test that required that potential voters not only know how to read but also be able to explain and interpret portions of the state constitution. This might have excluded much of the plain white folk as well, but the law provided ample loopholes for Confederate veterans and their descendants (all white, of course) and gave registrars discretionary grounds to include whites and exclude African Americans. Although the extent of white inclusion and the significance of popular politics has probably been underestimated, a small minority of the potential electorate actually controlled Georgia politics for much of the early twentieth century.[19]

Rome's merchant and business class also profited from its prescient vision for selling Rome to local, northern, and foreign capitalists as an ideal industrial development spot. The booster spirit that allegedly arrived in Rome with the first white settlers had since been nurtured by none other than the leading propagandist for the New South, Henry Grady. Before Grady became widely known as the Atlanta spokesman for southern industrial development, he had a brief but immensely successful career in Rome as the editor and publisher of the *Rome Commercial.* Grady's florid prose, denunciations of Reconstruction, and sympathetic coverage of the Klan made his paper the most successful in the region. Although Grady was best known for his friendly solicitations to northeastern investors in the 1870s and 1880s, Rome offered an early proving ground for many of the ideas so central to his vision of the "New South." Fifteen years before Grady, as editor of the *Atlanta Constitution*, coined the term in his famous 1886 New England speech of the same name, he offered essentially the same vision to Romans. In 1869 he urged Romans to take advantage of the South's natural resources, diversify the regional economy, and enter into productive, profitable relationships with outside investors. Southerners, he advised, needed to put sectional politics behind them and "lend their efforts to the more laudable cause of developing the great wealth that nature had bestowed upon us . . . [a cause] of infinitely more advantage to our bankrupt people." All the South needed, he argued, was "for someone to make a start and induce men of means to come among, to aid in developing the same"—a plan much like that adopted by Rome boosters in the 1880s.[20]

[19] Bartley, *Creation of Modern Georgia*, 104–5, 153; Jasper Berry Shannon, *Toward a New Politics in the South* (Knoxville: University of Tennessee Press, 1949), 41; Aycock, *All Roads to Rome*, 200, 235; Battey, *History of Rome and Floyd County*, 224.

[20] Battey, *History of Rome and Floyd County*, 246–52, Grady quote from 246.

With one simple illustration—the profits of producing cotton versus the profits of manufacturing cotton goods—Grady captured the imagination not just of Romans, but of an entire generation of southern boosters. The South, Grady pointed out, produced approximately $300 million worth of cotton, but the North converted the value of the same crop to over $900 million through manufacturing. Clearly the real profits from southern products were made in the North by industry. After 1872, when Grady moved to Atlanta, his vision for a industrialized and prosperous New South became something of a crusade. In the late 1880s and 1890s, New South boosters across the region joined Grady in arguing that the South should bring manufacturing to the raw materials, or the mills to the cotton.[21]

If Grady initially found it difficult to persuade Georgia's fiscally conservative governors to use the state's resources to attract capital and diversify the economy, Rome's civic and business leaders had long envisioned such a New South. In the words of one Floyd County businessman, many Romans had long believed that their city "ought to be the great manufacturing, commercial and financial center of this northwest Georgia . . . the future of Rome must be upward and onward." Battey, as Rome's first historian and not so far removed from the New South generation himself, described Rome's development movement as a collective and consensual "awakening" to an apparently self-evident truth. By 1886, in his words, "the people" of Rome declared that "it is time Rome was going out and getting more people, more industries, more prosperous. Let us form an association which will herald to the world the glories and advantages of Rome and Floyd County!" The idea, Battey claimed, "spread like the measles. Everybody took it up, especially the financial leaders."[22]

After the formation of the Rome Land Company, town meetings, fairs, newspaper columns, and other activities well documented by Battey were consumed by plans for local development. In 1887 Romans published a prospectus of the "advantages . . . [Rome] offered for manufacturing industries and unsurpassed homes for the people," which also appended, revealingly, the full text of Henry Grady's famous New South speech.[23] The Rome Land Company and the city council financed a number of community improvements to make Rome more attractive to outside in-

[21] On New South ideology, see Paul M. Gaston, *The New South Creed: A Study in Southern Mythmaking* (New York: Knopf, 1970); Bartley, *Creation of Modern Georgia*, 83–86; Raymond B. Nixon, *Henry Grady: Spokesman of the New South* (New York: Knopf, 1943), 71–73, 85.

[22] Battey, *History of Rome and Floyd County*, 324.

[23] *Rome, Georgia* (Atlanta, 1887), Georgia Collection, Felix Hargrett Rare Book and Manuscript Library, Athens, Georgia.

vestors, such as a local street railroad, an elegant drawbridge across the Oostanaula River, granite streets, and electric lights. Local subscribers also underwrote the expansion of Rome's rail lines to link the city to points in all directions. Many of the early enterprises, however, were financed by locals, as Rome, unlike most small southern communities forced to solicit funds from northern and western investors, had local sources of capital. In 1887, for example, a local judge announced the city's plans to raise $75,000, from $5,000 subscriptions sold to citizens, to build an iron-smelting furnace. The Rome Land Company, representing eight of the city's wealthiest businessmen, donated the site, purchased $10,000 worth of stock, and guaranteed funds matching those raised by subscription. In 1888 the *Rome Tribune* editors, also dedicated boosters, commended the Rome Land Company and announced their pleasure at looking "forward to the time when ours will be one of the greatest cities in the New South, and when, by reason of our unsurpassed resources, Floyd County will support one of the strongest communities to be found in the country." But local boosters also courted northern capital. That same year, the Rome Land Company hosted a delegation of forty New England industrialists. By 1900, Floyd County industrial concerns manufactured stoves, furniture, bricks, nails, mattresses, and rubber packing material.[24]

Textiles, however, were by far the most important industrial development in Floyd County, and in the South as a whole. When a "cotton mill campaign" swept the South in the 1880s, powered by small-town editors and preachers clamoring to bring the mills to their own hometowns, Rome's ambitious business leaders had already converted to the Grady gospel.[25] Requiring relatively little start-up capital, textile factories were well suited to take advantage of the resources the South had in abundance—cotton and cheap, unskilled labor. Between 1880 and the 1930, local capital and town recruitment efforts brought several large textile mill payrolls to northwest Georgia. Among the first local efforts was the Trion Cotton Mill, constructed in 1888, about thirty miles north of Rome in Chattooga County, owned primarily by a Rome businessman. By 1902 the Trion Mill employed about twelve hundred people and used sixty bales of cotton daily. In town, local businessmen established several small factories, such as the Rome Hosiery Mill. County industrialists contributed to the construction of the large Anchor Duck (later renamed Anchor Rome) Mills and mill village in northeastern Rome, which employed over eight hundred people. Local cotton dealers also used their connections to

[24] Aycock, *All Roads to Rome*, 214–19.

[25] On the cotton mill campaign, see Broadus Mitchell, *The Rise of the Cotton Mills in the South* (Baltimore: Johns Hopkins University Press, 1921), 106–35.

the cotton manufacturing industry to recruit northern investment. In 1896 a Rome cotton dealer and the Lindale Company, a local promotion group for a town immediately south of Rome, persuaded Massachusetts Mills to build a new factory in Floyd County. Massachusetts Mills' Lindale plant became the county's largest employer, with over twenty-five hundred people on the payroll.[26] In 1926 town boosters secured another large factory from an Italian corporation, the Tubize Chatillon Company, manufacturers of "artificial silk" (rayon), which employed another two thousand people. By the 1930s, three of the largest textile mills in northwest Georgia—Anchor Duck Mills, Tubize Chatillon, and Massachusetts Mills—flanked Rome's city limits and provided a significant anchor to the local economy, employing over five thousand people.[27]

The financial incentives to "bring the mills to the cotton" were considerable, and it was no surprise that business leaders eagerly took up the idea of industrial development. In 1902, Rome cotton dealers charged $.50 a bale for brokerage services and $1.50 per bale for shipment. By World War I, a line of heavy mules alongside Rome cotton warehouses, each loaded with five bales of cotton ready to make morning deliveries to local cotton mills, had become a familiar sight.[28] Industry also enriched merchants, bankers, and the businessmen making up the Rome Land Company by infusing the town with much-needed cash. Long before New Deal economists applied the ideas about wages and consumption associated with John Maynard Keynes, Roman businessmen understood full well the value of wages to a community. At an 1887 town meeting, for example, J. W. Rounsaville appealed to Romans to support local development projects on the basis of what future wages would mean to the town. "Recent improvements" in Rome's economy, he argued, particularly the large payrolls generated by current manufacturing concerns and the thousands of dollars that eventually found their way back into the merchant's pocket, justified further development ventures. By 1920, Rome factory payrolls averaged $1 million per month.[29]

But key to the success of New South boosterism as an ideology was its claim that industrial development held motivations much more altruistic than profit. To a once defeated and demoralized region, industrial development promised regional independence, jobs for the region's large population of poor whites, a broad tax base to finance civic improvements,

[26] Aycock, *All Roads to Rome*, 162, 164; Evelyn H. Knowlton, *Pepperell's Progress: History of a Cotton Textile Company, 1844–1945* (Cambridge: Harvard University Press, 1948), 308, 320.

[27] *Rome News-Tribune*, Oct. 16, 1949, Oct. 4, 1953, Feb. 14, 1952, Oct. 18, 1953.

[28] Aycock, *All Roads to Rome*, 162, 164.

[29] Ibid., 214–17, quote from 216; figures from Battey, *History of Rome and Floyd County*, 451.

and payrolls to feed the cash registers of local merchants. In 1888 the editors of the *Rome Tribune*, in a special commemorative edition, marveled at the difference industrial development had made in Rome and commended local boosters for their "noble" work. "Hope looks forward with ardent joy to the time when ours will be one of the greatest cities in the New South," the editors declared with breathless enthusiasm. "Then will the Rome Land Company . . . reap the joys of an abiding consciousness of laudable effort and of the encomiums of a grateful people."[30]

Gratitude became a significant element of the lore of industrialization. The Massachusetts Mills officials, for example, claimed that local farmers "flocked in [to the mill], when they heard of the opportunity of steady employment for a cash wage, glad to leave the old plow handles," the uncertainty of cotton prices, the boll weevil, and the "hilly, stony farms" of northwest Georgia. According to a contemporary Lindale resident, most of the early recruits to the Lindale mill had "not yet recovered their losses from the Civil war, its being only 20 years past Reconstruction days." Whether or not these first millhands actually greeted the corporation with such enthusiasm, it was firmly incorporated into local memory. Longtime Lindale resident Polly Gammon, whose mother and aunts were among the first generation hired at the mill, remembered hearing such stories when she was growing up. "My mama and her sisters were living out in the country and they were starving to death," Gammon recounted. "They were just overjoyed to come [and] have a regular job with regular income." In fact, many white southerners seem to have internalized the belief that the creation of jobs was as much a public service as it was a profit-seeking venture—a belief that persisted long after the New South industries were in place. Reinforced by the town's commercial successes, boosterism and the accompanying dogma had become central tenets of secular belief among Rome's town elite by the twentieth century.[31]

New South boosterism and industrial development also provided important props to white supremacy. Southern boosters proclaimed that mills would be the "salvation" of the region's poor whites, and in the very years that Jim Crow segregated whites and blacks physically, industrial development introduced an equally rigid economic segregation. The cotton mill campaigns of the late nineteenth century, in particular, had been characterized by explicitly racial rhetoric and a civic zeal to aid the South's poor whites. At the same time Grady argued that "the white race must dominate forever in the South," his followers declared mill jobs the

[30] Aycock, *All Roads to Rome*, 219.

[31] Knowlton, *Pepperell's Progress*; *Rome News-Tribune*, Sept. 4, 1934; Jim Gibbons, ed., *A History of Lindale: The Research of Polly Gammon* (Rome, Ga.: Art Department of Rome, 1997), 8; Polly Gammon, interview with author, May 16, 1994.

"only avenue open to our poor whites." Industry would remove the South's whites from their recent degradation to "intimate competition" with newly freed blacks for the meager earnings and chronic debt of the South's tenant farms. Should the poor of both races be permanently reduced to competition and economic equality, the logic of white supremacy implied, social equality was but the next step.[32]

If boosters did not always bother to make the connection between economics and race explicit, most southerners understood that white supremacy had little meaning if blacks and whites were equally impoverished by the same economic system. Industrial development actually contributed quite a bit toward the kind of post-Reconstruction resolution of race relations that Grady and other New South whites envisioned. By eliminating black competition for the new waged jobs, cotton mills became another instrument for segregating the white population of Georgia's working poor. At the same time, cotton mills seemingly reunited the interests of all classes of southern whites, an interest sorely divided by credit, the crop lien, and sharecropping. Claiming to represent the concerns of both white workers and businessmen for the mutual benefit of each, boosterism, just as significantly, excluded blacks. As white leaders codified the segregation of fairs, libraries, streetcars, and virtually all public conveyances in meticulous detail, they observed an equally stringent color line in employment.

In Floyd County and other southern locales, the creation of industrial jobs did in fact differentiate the lot of black and white workers by institutionalizing racial difference in occupation and by creating segregated markets for labor. Since the postbellum period, when U.S. Army officials of the Rome Freedmen's Bureau office had placed newly freed slaves in the employ of white housewives and planters as maids, washerwomen, and farmworkers, most Floyd County African Americans had earned their living in jobs associated with blackness, such as domestic service or common labor. This was no accident, for jobs constituted an important aspect of racial identity. Undoubtedly, most white Floyd County citizens would have agreed with the turn-of-the-century Georgia governor who claimed that the field of agriculture, or perhaps domestic service, was "the proper one for the negro." The significance of occupation to the perception of race was especially clear in white southerners' considerations of black southerners. For example, when local historian Battey dedicated a few pages of his text to "old time darkeys of Rome," he identified them according to which white person once owned or employed them and what kind of work they did. Many of the accompanying blurbs commented in stereotypical fashion on a man or woman's work habits: "never known

[32] Cash, *Mind of the South*, 176–83; Mitchell, *Rise of the Cotton Mills*, 106–35.

to hit a lick of work"; "will not quit chopping wood except to go 'possom hunting or to eat a watermelon." An accompanying collage of photographs portrayed most of Battey's black subjects at labor. One woman wears a maid's uniform; another balances laundry on her head; a man at the center holds an ax.[33] Clearly, many white Georgians thought of black Georgians in terms of work, and they expected that work to be limited to a specific class of tasks. Excluding the handful of black professionals who serviced the African American community in Rome, the prospects for occupational mobility were practically nonexistent. The racial imperatives of industrial development boosterism quite naturally justified black workers' exclusion from the new industrial jobs, while racial taboos made the placement of black men alongside white female textile workers virtually unthinkable.

Even as Floyd County's economy diversified in the twentieth century, the number of occupations open to black workers remained extremely small. In the 1930s almost 40 percent of African American men worked in agriculture, and about half of these men were farm laborers rather than farm operators or tenants. Over 70 percent of African American women worked as domestics. The remaining third of the black population labored in furniture factories, foundries, retail stores, service industries, and area textile mills, but in a limited number of positions. In textiles, Floyd County's largest industry, the lines between black jobs and white jobs were especially sharp. Black workers made up only about 5 percent of the total textile labor force, where they labored as janitors, "outside" workers who cut cotton bales, or laborers who tended mill village grounds. All other textile jobs remained "white" jobs for most of the twentieth century.[34] In a state as poor as Georgia, white jobs were of course also primarily low-wage and unskilled, but occupational segregation introduced significant disparities in wealth. In 1909 a family of three working as tenant farmers, the most common occupation for black southerners, could expect to earn about $375 a year, whereas a family of three working in a textile mill could earn $900 a year.[35] For black workers, exclusion from manufacturing eliminated even the illusion of opportunity and the chimera of status granted to whites.

[33] Battey, *History of Rome and Floyd County*, 370–74; on the significance of labor market segmentation for black women in the New South, see Tera Hunter, *To 'Joy My Freedom: Southern Black Women's Lives and Labors after the Civil War* (Cambridge: Harvard University Press, 1997).

[34] Bartley, *Creation of Modern Georgia*, 148; Battey, *History of Rome and Floyd County*, 242–43; U.S. Bureau of the Census, *Fifteenth Census: 1930*, vol. 3, pt. 1, pp. 501, 534; ibid., vol. 1, p. 257 (unemployment returns by classes for states and counties).

[35] Marshall, *Labor in the South*, 80.

For most of the twentieth century, the hiring policies of Floyd County mill managements internalized and respected southern beliefs about white jobs and white lifestyles. No black millhands had been hired for machine work by any of Floyd County's textile mills since the late nineteenth century, even though black labor certainly would have been cheaper. Moreover, white workers themselves enforced the policy, making it clear that they would "not stand negroes in the mill." In 1896, when Massachusetts Mills managers hired a black man for machine work to replace a discharged white man at their Lindale cotton mill, the nonunion workforce staged an elaborately organized protest to enforce the color line. White workers circulated a petition announcing that they "did not want their wives and children working along side of the colored hands." The superintendent refused to read the petition, discharged the men who presented it, and replied that he "was going to run the business to suit himself." Lindale's white workers were outraged. According to newspaper reports, there was "much hot talk and . . . threats of all quitting." Finally, white workers walked out.[36]

Evidently, many town leaders agreed with the workers that this was unacceptable practice for employers. The editor of the current daily paper, *The Hustler of Rome*, editorialized, "I am not ready to admit that it is good policy for whites and blacks to be worked side by side in the factory. . . . It's wrong, and here in the South, at least it won't work." The whole idea was so abhorrent, the paper suggested, that the "less said about such experiments that new concerns in the South attempt, the better for all parties." In conclusion to the brief column, the editor declared that had the Massachusetts Mills superintendent been a local, he would have known better. "Experienced Southerners would never dream of—nor would they attempt it."[37]

The conflict lasted over a week, until the corporation sent a new agent to Lindale who claimed himself "quite in sympathy . . . with the general southern feeling against the introduction of the negro with white labor indoors" and soothed the ruffled sensibilities of the white workers. In a statement to the *Atlanta Constitution*, the company's agent assured readers that "no white man was discharged or displaced by our action and there was no motive except to keep the mill in operation." The mill agent explained the lapse in racial hiring policy as only an "emergency" expedience and proclaimed the plant's past and future policy of hiring blacks "only for menial work." Significantly, the agent's statement not only provided explanation but also seemed to vindicate white southern views that

[36] *Atlanta Constitution*, July 17, 1896.
[37] *The Hustler of Rome*, July 17, 1896.

only "certain tasks about a cotton mill . . . are delegated by general consent . . . to negroes."[38]

Paternalism, a highly personalized management style that included such expressions of shared sympathies, also enhanced white supremacy and the plausibility of boosters' claims that industry served its low-wage white workers. As wage work promised to remove whites from poverty on the farm, mill village paternalism promised to "take care" of white workers when they arrived at the mill by placing them under the custodianship of altruistic white benefactors and providing plenty of nonwage compensations. In Floyd County, as elsewhere in the South, the construction of textile factories at the turn of the century had been accompanied by the construction of mill villages to house, feed, and service the retail needs of cotton mill workers. At first the villages had been required for the factories' economic viability, because housing was necessary to attract and accommodate enough workers to fill the mills. In this sense mill village paternalism differed very little from the sort of welfare capitalism practiced throughout the nation in the early twentieth century.[39] But welfare, or paternalism, operated in a very different context in the South, where it become much more than a business strategy. By the twentieth century a generation of workers and managers had irreversibly fused the practice of welfare capitalism with southern notions of elite beneficence, white supremacy, and boosterism. In the context of Jim Crow and the racially charged rhetoric about industrialization, welfare capitalism inevitably merged with notions of whiteness, shaping the expectations of white workers and constructing highly personal relationships between white employers and white employees. White mill managers took care of "their people," subsidizing a lifestyle far beyond the means of most rural Georgians. In the twentieth century, necessities like housing and medical care were supplemented by schools, churches, community centers, movie the-

[38] *Atlanta Constitution*, July 27, 1896.

[39] Flamming, *Creating the Modern South*, 122, 121–40. Bryant Simon and Douglas Flamming have remarked that the notion of paternalism has been used so often and in so many contexts that it sometimes seems to have no distinct meaning at all. Some of the earliest scholars of southern mill workers argued that mill village paternalism stemmed from regional culture and Old South planter-slave relations. More recently, Flamming argued that mill village paternalism was merely a form of welfare capitalism. On the historiography of paternalism see Flamming, *Creating the Modern South*, chapter 6; Simon, "Choosing between the Ham and the Union," in *Hanging by a Thread: Social Change in Southern Textiles*, ed. Jeffrey Leiter, Michael D. Schulman, and Rhoda Zingraff (Ithaca: ILR Press, 1991). See also Dwight B. Billings, Jr., *Planters and the Making of a "New South": Class Politics and Development in North Carolina, 1865–1900* (Chapel Hill: University of North Carolina Press, 1979); Cash, *Mind of the South*, 204–6; and Allen Tullos, *Habits of Industry: White Culture and the Transformation of the Carolina Piedmont* (Chapel Hill: University of North Carolina Press, 1989), 76–77.

aters, and baseball teams. Even if these nonwage compensations had been introduced to create stability within textile workforces, by the 1930s such extra-wage benefits had become standard accoutrements of textiles, attributed to the generosity, rather than the business acumen, of mill managers. In Polly Gammon's words, "The mill officials saw to it that we were given the best."[40]

Within the race-conscious society of the segregated South, village welfare and paternalism, like the wage itself, became informal badges of racial privilege, providing workers and other southern observers with plenty of verification that managers and millhands shared a common racial and economic interest. Black workers may have tended the grounds of the village, but they did not swim in the village pool or play on the white baseball team. According to Massachusetts Mills officials, black workers who did the "heavy work" outside the mill in Lindale "lived in a different world from the other [white] workers—in a separated section where their children attended a separate school." In deference to southern workers' feelings, after the 1896 debacle Massachusetts Mills also made an effort to recruit southern managers because the company thought they "had an advantage over many of the overseers in the North, since they understood fully the problems of the workers with no racial or class lines to hinder." Although the initial motivation for mill village welfare might have been entirely economic, the impact of cotton mill paternalism cannot be understood without reference to the larger process of cultural reinterpretation by communities of white workers. Blacks and whites understood that mill villages were created for whites only.[41]

By the 1930s, the combination of racial imperatives underlying boosterism and mill recruitment strategies had created a homogeneous and distinctively southern workforce in textiles. Most workers were recruited to work in the mills from farms in northwest Georgia and nearby Alabama, and the first generations of Floyd County millhands, like their rural neighbors, were overwhelmingly white, native-born, and of Anglo-Saxon descent. As late as the 1930s many of them remained first- and second-generation wage workers. They did not form trade unions. Descendants of the yeoman farmers, tenants, and sharecroppers of northwest Georgia, most millhands brought to the mill villages the rural, religious, and profoundly family- and community-oriented, plain-folk culture of the farm.[42]

[40] Gammon interview.

[41] Quotes from Knowlton, *Pepperell's Progress*, 331; Gammon interview; Opal Scott, interview with author, Sept. 10, 1994.

[42] Knowlton, *Pepperell's Progress*, 315; Gammon interview; Walter Brooks, interview with author, July 7, 1994. A wealth of anecdotal evidence suggests that the majority of Floyd County mill workers, like most southern textile workers, came to the mills from the surrounding countryside or migrated from other cotton mills. In a detailed analysis of a first

The experience of living in the mill villages, where residents lived close to each other in company-owned houses, pursuing work, leisure, and worship together in company-owned facilities, reinforced that strong sense of community. Workers typically moved to the village as family units, and broader communal ties established by marriage and neighborliness led many workers to describe the mill village and its workforce as "like a family."[43]

Although the southern textile mill workforce as a whole was strikingly homogeneous in comparison with those of other mass-production industries, the common southern practice of hiring entire families to work in the mill preserved and transplanted traditional rural hierarchies of gender and status into the world of wage work. Because of an alleged housing shortage, Massachusetts Mills managers required mill village families to send family workers to the factory at the rate of one millhand per room in their village house. The policy was undoubtedly also motivated by profit, since the purchase of family labor as a package permitted mills to pay adults less than a living wage, offer supplementary wages through the employment of children, and still offer earnings much better than farming. Between 1880 and 1910, for example, about one-quarter of the Lindale workforce was under sixteen years of age.[44]

Children and women had also worked on farms, of course, under a male authority tied to land ownership or right of contract. In the mills, wages and jobs replaced land-based and gendered symbols of status within the white working-class community with new ones that similarly reflected and reified notions of social worth. Just as all machine jobs were socially defined as white, many positions within the mill workforce were defined by age and gender. Children earned the least, but mill managers also preserved male privilege by making distinctions between "men's jobs," "boys' jobs" and "girls' jobs" (there were no "women's jobs"). Because women were associated with child care and domestic work, the notion that they were "patient, neat, careful workers" with "deft, nimble fingers" encouraged mill managers to assign them to fast-moving, repetitive machines in spinning or weaving. Similarly, because men were associated with strength, authority, and permanent career work, male workers were assigned to physically strenuous jobs in the carding room, low-level supervisory positions, jobs that required the investment of training, or machine fixing. Even in shop departments that employed both men and

---

generation of mill workers at the Crown Mill in nearby Dalton, Georgia, Douglas Flamming found that cotton mill workers came from more diverse backgrounds. See *Creating the Modern South*, 30–35, 60–69, 155–59.

[43] Hall et al., *Like a Family*, xvii, 140–46, 151–52, 361–63; Flamming, *Creating the Modern South*, 145–49, 184, 216–17, 247.

[44] Knowlton, *Pepperell's Progress*, 315; Hall et al., *Like a Family*, 52, 162.

women, such as weaving, female workers earned 50 to 60 percent less than male workers.[45]

The assignment of children, younger workers, and apprentices according to gendered categories ensured the preservation of wage, skill, and status hierarchies. Entry-level jobs in the card room, for example, were reserved for boys because the positions served as an apprenticeship for higher-paying jobs as carders. Self-confirming stereotypes also barred women from the most highly skilled and highly compensated positions as machine fixers. A belief that boys shared a "natural" curiosity about machinery encouraged adult male fixers to train only male replacements. Likewise, the reluctance to give women supervisory power over men also prevented women from becoming fixers, section hands, or other supervisors. Long after the family system of labor disappeared, this designation of male and female jobs and wages persisted.

Although the first southern cotton mills relied heavily on the labor of children and women, the age and gender composition of the workforce shifted during the first three decades of the mills' operation to one that was predominantly adult and male. In the 1930s, for example, approximately 53 percent of Floyd County's wage-earning women worked in the textile industry, but men held twice as many textile jobs as women. The employment of women and children had first begun to decline in the 1910s and 1920s when southern mills eliminated child labor and women's night work. By the 1930s a decline in women's employment also reflected cultural assumptions about who should earn a wage. In the Lindale mill, the largest in the county, managers adopted a policy during the depression of employing men rather than women on the assumption that men were supporting families and women were not. In 1933, for example, the workforce included 1,189 men and only 558 women. Between 1930 and 1940, as the total textile workforce had increased by over 20 percent, women's share of the jobs decreased by 9 percent. Although many jobs in the textile mills continued to be strongly identified as "women's work," and the presence of white women continued to serve as a bar to black employment, the trend from the 1930s onward was toward a more masculine workforce. This was probably also due in part to the relative status of textile work in the South as one of the more highly compensated jobs available for unskilled labor. The shift also coincided with rising textile wages.[46]

[45] On wage difference between men and women, see appendix 23 in Knowlton, *Pepperell's Progress*, 429; Hall et al., *Like a Family*, 67–69.

[46] Knowlton, *Pepperell's Progress*, 431. Figures on textile employment calculated from a comparison of the 1930 and 1940 census from Floyd County. U.S. Bureau of the Census, *Fifteenth Census: 1930*, vol. 3, pt. 1, p. 514; and idem, *Census of Population: 1940*, vol. 2, pt. 2 (Washington, D.C.: Government Printing Office, 1942), 265.

In spite of Samuel Gompers's 1898 judgment about southern workers' wages, the original cotton mill campaign maxim that factories would be poor whites' "salvation" probably resonated with the experience of many first- and second-generation mill workers in Floyd County. Although critics of the cotton mills bemoaned what seemed to be a loss of independence as farmers traded in the natural rhythms and fresh air of the farm for the industrial discipline and confined spaces of the factory, in reality northwest Georgia's farmers had not had access to the yeoman ideal for a long time. If the Civil War, Reconstruction, and the credit system had initially been responsible for the impoverishment of the region's farmers, developments in the twentieth century had done little to improve their fortunes. Although World War I temporarily raised the price of cotton and the fortunes of many tenants, a precipitous drop in cotton prices and infestation by the boll weevil in the 1920s spelled disaster for Georgia's farmers. Economic downturns in the 1920s and the onset of the Great Depression only made the hard life on a Georgia farm even harder. By 1920 over 65 percent of Floyd County farmers were sharecroppers or tenants. Between 1925 and 1930, as cotton agriculture began to suffer early signs of the Great Depression, the rate of tenancy in Floyd County increased by another 18 percent. Dependent upon landlords and desperate for cash, Georgia's small cotton farmers, croppers, and tenants had precious little independence to lose.[47]

For all those who clung to nostalgia about farm life, there were many more who remembered that they had never been able to "get ahead" or out of debt. Oscar Allen, whose family moved from the farm to the factory in 1930, recalled farming, especially sharecropping, as working "almost like a slave." His family rented "on thirds," dependent on the landlord to supply virtually everything. "We didn't have anything but ourselves to work, we didn't have any mules or horses or plows or nothing. The man that owned the farm would furnish all that. Then when we'd gather the crop, he'd get two thirds and we'd get a third," he explained. "That's a good way to starve to death!" Allen also recalled the demoralizing cycle of debt: "We'd settle up at the end of the year and all during that year, we didn't have enough. End of the year, we'd still owe money at the store." His family could not grow enough food to carry them through the winter, so they "just had to buy on credit." Many years, he said, "we wouldn't even break even. A lot of years we'd still owe money." Any drop in cotton prices was devastating. Many former farmers distinctly remembered when cotton prices had dropped to two and three cents a pound. Even mill worker H. O. Yarbrough, who grew up on a relatively

[47] Bartley, *Creation of Modern Georgia*, 169–77: figures on tenancy calculated from U.S. Bureau of the Census, *Fifteenth Census: 1930*, vol. 2, pt. 2, p. 516.

large, family-owned farm, was convinced by the depression that he should find some other kind of work. He remembered that even on his father's three-hundred-acre farm "you just didn't make much." Such experiences often validated southern apologists' otherwise self-serving descriptions of people flocking to the mill gates "glad to leave" the farm. Allen, for example, vividly recalled when in 1930 his parents began working at the Tubize Chatillon rayon mill on the outskirts of Rome. "We moved in the village, into a brand new house, with lights in the bathroom. Boy, we thought we were rich and we was," he explained many years later. "We thought we were in hog heaven."[48]

In comparison to Rome's landowners, businessmen, and professionals, however, Floyd County textile workers held less social and political power than their skin color and the rhetoric of paternalistic benefactors and Democratic politics might lead one to expect. Although Floyd County workers had successfully defended a bar against black workers, they operated through the first third of the century without trade unions and had very little control over wages and working conditions. Mill villages provided some of the material comforts commonly associated with town life, but workers' lifestyles differed dramatically from that of their uptown neighbors. While the lavish hotels, the cotillions, the theater, and the opera were, in a legalistic sense, open to all whites, economic class prevented mill workers and most white farmers from occupying many places reserved for "whites only." Rome's elite attended the Episcopalian church, sent their children to the private Darlington school, and joined the country club; mill workers attended mill village churches and camp revivals, sent their children to village schools, and swam in the village pool. Local boosters might brag to outsiders that Floyd County workers came from the "finest Anglo-Saxon stock," but at home many townspeople disparaged cotton mill people as "lintheads" and "white trash."[49] Moreover, the poll tax was a race-blind mechanism that inhibited all working-class political participation until the 1940s.

Outside the South, the perception of southern textile workers, and the New South in general, was frequently even less charitable. The zenith of cotton mill construction in the South in the 1920s coincided with an outpouring of social commentary on the region from journalists, reformers, and scholars. As the rest of the nation entered the age of consumption, the South became widely associated with poverty-level wages, inadequate

[48] Oscar Allen, interview with author, Aug. 28, 1994; H. O. Yarbrough, interview with author, July 14, 1994; Bartley, *Creation of Modern Georgia*, 131; Knowlton, *Pepperell's Progress*, 315.

[49] Forrest Shropshire, interview with author, May 3, 1994; see also Tindall, *Emergence of the New South*, 210–11; Frank Tannenbaum, *Darker Phases of the South* (New York: Putnam, 1924).

education, and poor health. When this image of the "benighted South" came of age in the 1920s and 1930s, southern mill workers were often described as primary victims. The coexistence of rhetoric about white supremacy with the paltry wages, dependency, and almost universal lack of trade unions in southern textile centers like Rome, in particular, provided grounds for some of the most biting social criticism of the South. Contemporary economist Broadus Mitchell likened the emerging market for the region's cheap industrial labor to white slavery. In an article titled "Fleshpots in the South," Mitchell compared boosters' attempts to sell the South's white workers to slave auctions of the early nineteenth century. In sharp contrast to southern boosters' promise of good jobs and steady wages, critics of the southern cotton mill system warned that the mills were creating a hereditary helot class and a distinct "social type."[50]

Primed by a swell of social science tracts and journalistic exposés on the backwardness of the South, the labor movement often adopted a similar attitude toward the South. In the first decades of the twentieth century, union activists as well as scholars and journalists echoed Gompers's early assessment of southern workers as exceptional. According to conventional wisdom, southern workers were passive and compliant, the products of paternalism, oppressive conditions, bizarre religious beliefs, and a backward, individualistic culture. Until the 1920s, when the South's dramatic industrial growth forced the United Textile Workers to seriously consider the southern worker, there was considerable resistance in the union to recruiting them. Northern UTW officials perceived themselves, as organized and more highly paid workers, as members of a class above southerners.[51]

It was perhaps inevitable that northern workers form this impression, for descriptions of poor living conditions in the South regularly slipped into careless descriptions of southern millhands as an alien and inferior "breed." In 1929, Progressive reformer Sinclair Lewis described southern workers as "cheap and contented," sickly and anemic-looking, undernourished and living in hovels. In the 1940s, journalist W. J. Cash portrayed southern cotton mill workers as no less than physically and psychologically deformed. The southern cotton mill worker was a distinct physical type: "A dead-white skin, a sunken chest, and stooping shoulders were the earmarks of the breed. Chinless faces, microcephalic foreheads, rabbit teeth, goggling dead-fish eyes, rickety limbs and stunted bodies

[50] Tindall, *Emergence of the New South*, 324–25; Mitchell, "Fleshpots in the South," 169; Harriet Herring, "Cycles of Cotton Mill Criticism," *South Atlantic Quarterly* 28 (1929): 123.

[51] Hodges, *New Deal Labor Policy*, 22–28; Janet Irons, "Testing the New Deal: The General Textile Strike of 1934" (Ph.D diss., Duke University, 1988), 7–9.

abounded." Female workers, Cash contended, were ugly and unfeminine, "characteristically stringy-haired and limp of breast at twenty, and shrunken hags at thirty or forty." Even southern millhands' protests were dismissed as immature or accidental. A major obstacle to unions, Cash argued, was the "very carelessness of [southern textile workers'] psychology." Southern apologists, such as the mill managers who ardently defended the southern mill village and its workers, only reinforced this image by reducing millhands to seemingly stupid, carefree, grateful recipients of mill village welfare.[52]

Although early-twentieth-century writers indulged in vastly oversimplified generalizations and sensationalism, the tenacity of this image of southern workers was due in part to a slender correlation with reality. In Floyd County, Baptist and Methodist churches had a truly broad influence on all aspects of life. In the 1930s, for example, the local clergy were deeply involved in the political debate about state prohibition and, locally, a referendum considering a continued ban on Sunday movies. Each year, thousands of northwest Georgians would attend Rome's annual citywide revival, an emotional spectacle that was only technically nondenominational. While the revival was in progress, the *News-Tribune* editor would daily encourage all to attend, and often the paper would follow up with a story on the number of souls "led to the Lord."[53] Outside observers speculated that the prominence of the southern church acted as an important instrument of social control. However, religion was not an inherently conservative force. The church frequently became a source of both inspiration and collective identity for southern workers. Religion also fulfilled a modest but important role in the social lives of millhands who had little discretionary income for commercial leisure. All the mill villages supported a number of independent prayer groups and church-related social clubs, and usually workers attended churches as a group. Anchor Duck workers, for example, attended Summerpark Baptist or the Southside Methodist Church. In the Tubize village, workers established their own Baptist and Methodist congregations that took turns meeting in the city auditorium. In Lindale, managers urged workers to attend church, but workers also held church suppers and meetings in their own homes for their own pleasure.[54]

[52] Hodges, *New Deal Labor Policy*, 22–28; Cash, *Mind of the South*, 204; Sinclair Lewis, *Cheap and Contented Labor: The Picture of a Southern Mill Town in 1929* (New York: United Textile Workers of America and Women's Trade Union League, 1929).

[53] In 1934, for example, Floyd County commissioners, at the urging of the Rome Ministerial Association, banned a vaudeville show from the city auditorium because they deemed it obscene. *Rome News-Tribune*, Mar. 17, May 4, 17, 1937, May 30, June 22, 1948.

[54] Brooks interview; Vicky Vinson, interview with author, July 13, 1994.

Southern workers' positive associations with the mill and mill managers, although often mistaken for "contentment" or "apathy," also had some basis in fact. It was true that southern textile workers were among the lowest-paid workers in the nation, but mill village welfare subsidized what must have seemed to be a relatively prosperous lifestyle for white workers in the rural South. In Floyd County poverty was probably measured on more relative terms, of black and white, farmer and wage worker. Despite the contemporary emphasis on mill village poverty, the first generations of textile workers lived, ate, and dressed better than the majority of Georgia's rural inhabitants. In the 1920s, for example, about 90 percent of Floyd County farms did not have telephones, electric lights, or even running water. In dramatic contrast, mill village residents had electricity, indoor plumbing, iceboxes, movie theaters, baseball teams, swimming pools, and laundry services. In 1935 the Farm Security Administration estimated that the average Georgia family's net worth was only thirty-five dollars. Southern textile workers earned an average of forty dollars each month.[55]

Textile workers also undoubtedly gained the most from what contemporary scholar W.E.B. DuBois described in 1935 as "a sort of public and psychological wage" granted to all whites in the South. Although the South's textile workers earned very little by national standards, all white workers received intangible sorts of compensation merely for being white citizens of the segregated South. As DuBois observed, "They were given public deference and titles of courtesy because they were white. They were admitted freely with all classes of white people to public functions, public parks and the best schools. . . . Their vote selected public officials, and while this had small effect upon the economic situation, it had great effect upon their personal treatment and the deference shown them." Southern newspapers "specialized in news that flattered the poor whites," while "the Negro was subject to public insult." Mill village paternalism promised millhands "the best." DuBois speculated that white supremacy and segregation had defeated Reconstruction, populism, and, most importantly, the ability of white southern workers to understand their economic relationship to capitalists in terms of class rather than race. "The theory of race was supplemented by a carefully planned and slowly evolved method," he argued, that had driven a permanent "wedge between the white and black workers."[56]

If the wages of whiteness, or the prestige and status accorded whites under racial segregation, provided intangible compensation to all whites, textile workers enjoyed a singular claim to such psychic compensations.

[55] Bartley, *Creation of Modern Georgia*, 169–77.

[56] DuBois, *Black Reconstruction in America*, 700.

Given the role that race played in the formation of the industry, in time whiteness resided not only in the identity that workers brought to the job but in the job itself. Just as janitorial work was associated with blackness, textile work became associated with whiteness. The status that accrued to textiles through its original association with race remained as long as segregation and preferential hiring remained in place. Many millhands, encouraged at every turn to consider their managers as white partners rather than adversaries, probably did consider their jobs a privilege. Thus, as DuBois and historian David Roediger have argued, the wages of whiteness indelibly shaped the identity and the vision of white workers.[57] Whiteness divided, as they have argued, by preventing whites from seeing a common interest with black workers.

However, the role race played in the course of southern industrialization also ensured that whites and blacks would not in fact have identical class interests. In a very real way, whiteness actually determined the ability *to become* working class in the New South, and this was not necessarily a decline in status. Moreover, the benefits white workers derived from discriminatory hiring policy—wages, jobs, and welfare—encouraged them to define their interests as racial ones and gave them a material investment in the maintenance of white supremacy. For the first half of the twentieth century, whiteness may have been the conceit that allowed business leaders and industrial development boosters to claim, and workers to believe, that what the working class really needed were lower wages for black workers and more white jobs, rather than better jobs. But it also promised that any material benefits that did accrue would be granted exclusively to whites.

A century of white supremacy, Democratic politics, and industrial development had thus uniquely prepared white Georgians for Eugene Talmadge's 1934 tirade against National Recovery Administration wage scales. From the town's founding fathers to *Rome Courier* editor Henry Grady to the civic leaders of the 1930s, Floyd County's history had been shaped by the desire of white town leaders to achieve commercial success and maintain white supremacy. In Floyd County, as elsewhere in the South, local entrepreneurs and civic leaders had seized upon Grady's advice to bring the mills—and capital and wages—to the cotton. Promising a wage and steady work to destitute farm families, boosters had claimed that textiles, now the South's preeminent industry, would serve the interests of everyone by drawing capital southward, providing a livelihood for the region's poor whites, and stimulating the local economy. Paternalism, the highly personalized management style introduced in the South's mill

[57] Roediger, *Wages of Whiteness*, 12–13.

villages, enhanced and institutionalized that myth of common white interests. Thus industrialization had, by the 1930s, sharpened racial distinctions and deepened existing intraracial relationships of economic and social dependency.

Although southern textile workers would continue to earn less than industrial workers anywhere else in the nation, the introduction of new waged work as an exclusively white opportunity in the context of segregation had enhanced poor whites' status in complex ways. If white workers had always received intangible compensation merely for the color of their skin, the creation of jobs, mill village homes, and industrial wage-earning status exclusively for them further institutionalized the benefits of whiteness. At the very time that Georgians were codifying legal segregation, New South industry introduced the distinction of "white jobs" and "black jobs." By creating a de facto occupational segregation and a privileged pool of white labor, southern cotton mills paired racial identity with the new waged occupations, dividing the South's poor into classes of white and black, "inside" and "outside" workers, machine tenders and janitors. By the 1930s the pairing of whiteness and work had created a new category of racial identity, one that blurred lines of class between whites and intensified distinctions between black and white workers.

When the Great Depression began to undermine the profitability of cheap white labor and the mill village system, paternalism would, however, face its greatest test. For the first time in Floyd County workers' history, the appeals of the United Textile Workers and the New Deal would provide serious competition to the mill managers and traditional white southern leaders who had customarily held their loyalties. But the racial identity of textile workers established by the cotton mill campaigns, sustained by the 1896 Massachusetts Mills strike, and strengthened by the creation of mill village paternalism remained strong. Even in the 1930s, when the poverty of the South's low-wage, labor-intensive economic system was becoming painfully apparent, the ability of traditional southern leaders such as Governor Talmadge to manipulate race and conceal class would reveal just how deeply most Georgians had internalized the wages of whiteness.

Two

"Labor's Best Friend": Talmadge, Paternalism, and the 1934 Strike

On Labor Day, September 3, 1934, just a few days before Eugene Talmadge arrived in Rome, the *Rome News-Tribune* declared the arrival of "the zero hour of the greatest struggle between capital and labor in the nation's history." A general strike of the nation's textile industry had begun at midnight the night before, called by the United Textile Workers. That afternoon, as Rome's residents observed the holiday with segregated festivities—a downtown parade, political speeches, and barbecue on the banks of the Coosa River for whites, and a Labor Day program across town for "colored citizens"—speculation ran rampant about the extent of Georgia's participation in the 1934 General Textile Strike. Most of the mills were closed in observance of the holiday anyway, but with union and mill executives both claiming the "loyalty" of Georgia's sixty thousand workers, Georgians anxiously awaited Tuesday to judge the impact of the general strike. On Labor Day only one mill workforce in Floyd County, the millhands at Brighton Mills in Shannon, Georgia, had already voted to strike. Local union officials at Tubize Chatillon and Anchor Duck Mills reported that their local had not yet received orders from national UTW leaders. The unorganized cotton mill workers in Lindale, according to the paper, were "not affected," and they spent Labor Day "as usual" at their machines in the mill. The *News-Tribune* noted that there "were wide differences of opinion . . . over the possible effect of the textile strike in the Rome territory" but concluded that "the theory persists that the strike will not be general in this quarter."[1]

Although many Romans were surprised by the number of local textile workers who did walk out in the following week, the *News-Tribune*'s predictions actually proved a more accurate description of the character and scope of the 1934 strike in northwest Georgia than many subsequent historical accounts. Historians have generally described the 1934 textile strike as a massive, region-wide, militant general strike of as many as 200,000 southern textile workers who were fed up with southern managers and willing to cast their lot with the New Deal.[2] In northwest Georgia,

[1] *Rome News-Tribune*, Sept. 1, 3, 1934; *Atlanta Constitution*, Sept. 3, 1934.

[2] See, for example, Hall et al., *Like a Family*; Irons, "Testing the New Deal," especially chapters 5–6; Simon, *Fabric of Defeat*; and the film *The Uprising of 1934*.

however, the divisions among workers and the general confusion that characterized this limited local protest gave the whole conflict a very different character. As the authors of *Like a Family* have cautioned, the General Textile Strike, in spite of its alleged proportions, "cannot be understood as a single event."[3] Although many northwest Georgia workers were equally frustrated with managers and enamored of the New Deal, their many loyalties overlapped in complex and at times contradictory ways that never clearly represented a complete break with southern tradition or their paternalistic employers. This is not to say, however, that northwest Georgia workers misunderstood their interests. Rather, millhands at the three largest mills in Floyd County responded to the strike call in ways that were consistent with their unique experiences of paternalism and their own sense of fairness, whether they joined the union or not.

In particular, textile labor's simultaneous support of the UTW and Governor Talmadge complicates prevailing interpretations of 1934 as a major disruption in the history of southern textile workers. Although the depression had put pressure on the relationships between white Georgians of different classes, a core of shared beliefs about the southern economy, regional wages, and racial practices remained in place. Literally a few days after some workers struck to demand compliance with the National Recovery Administration's textile code, they joined parades and carried banners cheering Talmadge's assertion that the NRA had no right to pay black workers a higher wage. If, as historian Bryant Simon has argued, the 1934 strike represented a political protest in favor of an activist state, Georgia workers' simultaneous allegiances to the New Deal and Talmadge asserted their acceptance of federal activism on distinctly regional and racialized terms. As southern whites they also expected the state to reflect their understanding of an appropriate racial order, and these views persisted long after the events of 1934 faded in local memory.[4]

Until Franklin Roosevelt's New Deal ushered in an entirely new sort of politics and policy for American workers, any region-wide protest by southern textile workers would have been unimaginable. The American labor movement as a whole had taken a major beating in the 1920s, and its efforts to recruit southern workers in the years prior to the New Deal were limited at best. With the exception of workers involved in a few

[3] Hall et al., *Like a Family*, 340. The authors of *Like a Family* caution that "broad-brushed generalizations must await fine-grained local studies" (340) and offer comparisons of two communities, Durham and Burlington, North Carolina, to illustrate how community support of the strike could be unanimous, or bitterly divided.

[4] Simon, *Fabric of Defeat*.

scattered strikes between 1929 and 1931, one labor historian has speculated, the majority of southern millhands had probably never been touched by a strike or even seen a union organizer until 1934.[5] Then, Roosevelt's New Deal, and the National Industrial Recovery Act (NIRA) in particular, seemed to change labor's fortunes in the South, and more generally in the United States, virtually overnight. Although the Roosevelt administration envisioned the NIRA primarily as a piece of legislation to aid business and the economy, it did much to level the playing field between business and labor. A major component of the NIRA, the suspension of federal anti-trust laws in order to allow manufacturers to regulate production and prices through the implementation of industry-wide codes, was clearly pro-business in intent. Textile businessmen, for example, who were plagued by chronic overproduction and cutthroat competition in a diminishing market for their goods, used the opportunity to introduce reforms that industry leaders had recommended for over a decade. However, the NIRA, hailed by union contemporaries as labor's "Magna Carta," also subjected labor relations to an unprecedented amount of federal supervision under the NRA and included in the famed Section 7(a) the first federal recognition of labor's right to organize. As described by the NRA's chief, General Hugh Johnson, and understood by millions of American workers, it was legislation "to put people back to work." Moreover, by mandating that minimum wages, maximum hours, and the right to join a union appear in all industry codes, the NIRA really did seem to promise workers a new and better deal.[6]

Textile millhands greeted the NIRA with great enthusiasm, and their positive and optimistic assessment of this federal intrusion into their lives was due in no small part to the popularity of President Roosevelt. "He was a great man," one Floyd County mill worker explained simply. "That's why we loved him." Where Herbert Hoover, his predecessor, had been perceived as cold and uncaring, Roosevelt entered office with the reassuring announcement that there "was nothing to fear, but fear itself" and decisively introduced dozens of boldly experimental pieces of legislation to combat the Great Depression in the first hundred days of his presidency. Of equal importance, Roosevelt had a rare ability to speak to ordinary Americans and persuade them that the federal government was looking out for them. His regular addresses on the radio, his inclusive language, and his actions on behalf of working-class people endeared him to mill workers as if he were one of their own. Because Roosevelt had enough political savvy to avoid such divisive issues as race, southern workers incorporated his persona into the familiar and traditional white

[5] Hodges, *New Deal Labor Policy*.

[6] Simon, *Fabric of Defeat*, 84–88; Hodges, *New Deal Labor Policy*, 52–54.

southern Democratic culture they ordinarily endorsed with surprising ease. Even Talmadge, who bitterly opposed elements of the New Deal, attested to Roosevelt's popularity by adopting the 1934 campaign slogan "It's Roosevelt and Talmadge for Georgia." Roosevelt often encouraged people to write him about their difficulties, and amazingly, hundreds of ordinary southern mill workers did. When the UTW told workers that Section 7(a) meant that "the President wants you to join a union," southern millhands, including many in northwest Georgia, took it to heart.[7]

Workers also expected employers to live up to the promises of the NIRA, and many were outraged when textile employers subsequently refused to recognize unions, fired workers who organized, and undermined the code's intent by demanding outrageous increases in productivity. Most mills compensated for higher labor costs and decreases in production by doubling or tripling workloads. In the eyes of many southern workers, the "speed-up" and "stretch-out," as the increases were called, betrayed the spirit of the NRA. For the first time in their history, large numbers of southern workers, including several hundred in northwest Georgia, looked to the labor movement for justice. By August 1933, UTW president Thomas McMahon claimed that the demand for organizers was so great that it was now "impossible to meet it."[8]

Histories of the 1934 strike typically describe these events—the election of Roosevelt, the creation of the NRA, rising dissatisfaction over higher workloads, and resentment of southern managers' code violations—as a natural progression leading to the general strike. According to traditional accounts, southern workers, inspired by the New Deal and furious with textile managers' failure to live up to its promises, began pouring into the UTW in 1933–34. Then, frustrated by the union's and the NRA's inability to address their grievances, they staged a massive walkout in September 1934 to protest an industry-wide reduction in hours approved by the Textile Code Authority.[9] The UTW claimed to represent 340,000 workers nationwide, and the national press coverage corroborated this claim even as textile business spokespersons issued equally exaggerated and contradictory declarations about the course of the strike and who really controlled the South's workers. On the first day of the strike, for example, the Associated Press reported that over 110,000 southern workers, almost half of the South's 252,500 textile workers, had walked off their jobs. A

[7] Quote from Earl Fricks, interview with author, July 5, 1994; *Statesman*, July 3, 1934; Simon, *Fabric of Defeat*, 79–89.

[8] Hall et al., *Like a Family*, 290–308, 319–20; Hodges, *New Deal Labor Policy*, 53–61. On the significance of New Deal rhetoric and Franklin Roosevelt, see Simon, *Fabric of Defeat*, 79–108.

[9] Irons, "Testing the New Deal," especially chapters 5–6; Hodges, *New Deal Labor Policy*, 60–103; Hall et al., *Like a Family*, 304–7, 328–29.

week later the estimate had risen to 400,000 workers on strike, 200,000 of them in the South.[10] These numbers formed the basis for subsequent historical accounts. Perhaps because the rise, and fall, of the southern UTW was so sudden and dramatic, however, very few records documented who actually participated in the strike and why.

Published histories and documentaries of the 1934 strike have tended to focus on this national narrative, or the most dramatic moments of the strike such as the tragic encounter between unionists and company guards in Honea Path, South Carolina, or the exploits of the flying squadrons.[11] From that perspective the 1934 strike does indeed seem to be something of an anomaly in southern workers' typically anti-union history—a brief but nearly ubiquitous expression of class militancy that was quickly extinguished by the array of force marshaled by mill officials and southern political leaders. However, the history of textile workers in northwest Georgia in 1934 suggests that, despite national reports, southern workers' allegiances were not so simple or so easily categorized. The behavior of workers and managers at the three largest mills in the Rome area defied generalizations about union sentiment. Some joined the union, some participated in the walkout, but given the conventional wisdom on the strike, a surprising number did neither.

Some aspects of the traditional account, however, did ring true for northwest Georgia. The depression and the New Deal placed an enormous strain on paternalism and southern class relations. Between 1933 and 1934, for example, hundreds of workers at the Anchor Duck and Tubize Chatillon mills, inspired by the NRA or angry about the stretch-out, turned their back on their traditional benefactors and joined the UTW. At the same time, however, the overwhelming majority of workers in Lindale did not, proving just how potent the management strategy of paternalism and the ideology of boosterism continued to be. Although superficially every mill conformed to the standards of mill village paternalism with housing, recreation facilities, and the like, only management at the Lindale mill managed to sustain workers' faith in their managers' professed concern for them. The difference was considerable. All Floyd County mill workers had benefited from the southern textile industry's largesse in the pre-depression years, but the NRA and the stretch-out introduced a new tension into workers' relationships with their paternalistic

[10] Simon, *Fabric of Defeat*, 112.

[11] A documentary on the strike, *The Uprising of 1934*, a video project sponsored by the Research Consortium for the Southwide Textile Strike of 1934, which aired on PBS in 1995, argued that managers created such a legacy of fear that southerners en masse had repressed memories of the strike, but the documentary focuses primarily on union members and on locales such as Honea Path, South Carolina, and Newnan, Georgia, both major centers of union activity.

white patrons. The treatment meted out by managers during the depression became critical. How well managers coped with the simultaneous pressures of the economic depression and workers' expectations of paternalism proved to be one of the most important factors determining whether workers struck.

Perhaps no one in Georgia, or even the South, personified paternalism quite like the six-foot, four-inch, 240-pound "Captain" Harry Parrish Meikleham. The "agent" of the Pepperell factory in northwest Georgia, Meikleham was the uncontested patriarch of the Lindale mill village for thirty-six years. Arriving in Floyd County in 1901, he stayed on after the mill was purchased by the New England Pepperell Manufacturing chain in 1926 and remained there until his death in 1937. In those years he transformed the small village four miles south of Rome into the management ideal of mill village paternalism. Meikleham attempted to control every aspect of life in Lindale, from work to recreation to politics, and he did so seemingly with the complicity of workers. In the early years of the mill, the village had a reputation as a "rough" place, but by 1934 the tiny town—owned entirely by the company—with five thousand inhabitants was a "wonder" of "orderliness," housing over three-quarters of the cotton mill's workforce in uniformly painted white wooden houses, laid out in a neat formation immediately south of the factory. Because Meikleham believed "wholesome recreation [was] the antithesis of communistic agitators and labor disturbers," Lindale was equipped with an elaborate community center, an indoor pool, a local movie theater, and a year-round sports program supervised by E. R. "Slick" Moulton, a former Auburn University baseball star.[12]

Meikleham's paternalism wielded both carrot and stick, because a central aspect of his management philosophy held that only happy, healthy, virtuous workers were loyal and productive. Under Meikleham the mill established free health care, a kindergarten, and a company-subsidized school. Company nurses inoculated workers against smallpox and typhoid and supervised Lindale wives and mothers in the production of nutritious meals. The mill even took care of workers' pets, sponsoring an annual "dog-shooting" day to administer rabies shots. Meikleham also extended paternal supervision to the character and behavior of millhands. Because he believed that workers' after-hours pursuits could be potentially subversive, the mill established an elaborate range of "options" for workers' leisure time. To stop male workers from "seeking relief from

[12] Quotes from a typescript of article on Lindale and Captain Meikleham, allegedly written by a Lindale worker, ca. 1935 (copy in author's possession), personal papers of Polly Gammon; Evelyn Knowlton, *Pepperell's Progress*, 315; see also Gibbons, *A History of Lindale*.

the unaccustomed industrial monotony by gambling or by walking the railroad tracks to Rome for liquor," Meikleham organized a Lindale band, social clubs, and a military company of which he became "captain." Of course, Meikleham and the workers understood that mill village leisure was not entirely optional. "If you didn't do what he said," one mill village resident remembered, "it cost you your job. . . . He controlled whether you almost lived or died." Ultimately, Meikleham could not eliminate drinking in the village, but he did force workers to gather in hiding places like the old Lindale gristmill where he would not catch them.[13]

As the monitor of his workers' spiritual and political progress, Meikleham also regularly advised workers on matters of religion, politics, and unions. The speeches were widely attended, and to ensure a heavy turnout, Meikleham lured workers to the city auditorium with promises of free admission to the movies when he finished. "Things can't be right unless you find God," he reminded his workers at the conclusion of a typical speech in 1935. On this occasion, Meikleham, ironically, had postponed a local revival in order to preach on the evils of the New Deal, the unions, and President Roosevelt. In case workers got any wrong ideas, he told them that most articles in the newspapers were a "mess of lies." The NRA was "rotten and unconstitutional," threatening to "ruin the country." Congress was helping Roosevelt break the "laws of God and man" with his New Deal. "If you want it [the NRA] and communism," Meikleham warned employees, "alright. But God help you." For the unions, Meikleham reserved a particular fury. "They'll move heaven and earth to get you to join," Meikleham warned, "they'll tell you anything." To disabuse workers of the union's contention that mills were to blame for short time and low wages, Meikleham reminded workers that "everyone" was "in the same boat." The mill would do the "best we can . . . things [would] work out" as long as workers did not "lose their heads."[14]

Once described as a "republican who hates negroes," Meikleham also shared the typical southern white understanding of race, in spite of the fact that he was neither a southerner nor a Democrat. Massachusetts Mills hired Meikleham because the previous agent, implicated in the 1896 strike, was "not successful in dealing with 'southern' people." Although the Lindale village was somewhat unusual in providing housing for some of the mill's black workers, village leisure and the town itself were strictly segregated. Black workers lived in a separate section, and it was probably

[13] Knowlton, *Pepperell's Progress*, 312–17, first two quotes from 316; Opal and J. C. Allen, interview with author, Sept. 12, 1994; description of Meikleham from Scott interview; Gammon interview.

[14] Gammon interview; Grady Poole, interview with author, July 5, 1994; Scott interview; "A Talk by Captain Meikleham," ca. May 1935, personal papers of Polly Gammon (photocopy in author's possession).

no accident that this section lay in the less desirable area of the village on the floodplain.[15] The mill also contributed to white status by re-creating racial distinctions in the village. Hiring black domestic workers was not a luxury that all millhands could afford, but the mill village hired a crew of black laborers to tend to the maintenance of the homes and grounds, in effect supplying every white millhand with black help.

Although Meikleham had not completely eliminated undesirable behavior, he had succeeded in creating a stable workforce in an industry that historically had high rates of turnover. He also persuaded most workers, whether by carrot or stick, not to join the union. Meikleham's estimate, based on what was "deemed reliable authority from a union labor source"—possibly a company spy—counted only fourteen union members in 1934. By the 1930s, three decades of mill village paternalism and Captain Meikleham had already made many millhands anti-union "company men." The majority of Lindale workers had either worked under Meikleham during much of his tenure or grown up in his village. Many were direct descendants of the first generation of workers who had joined the wagon trains migrating to Lindale in 1894. Meikleham liked to brag in the 1930s that 65 percent of the workforce had been born and raised in Lindale. In 1933, of a total of 1,747 workers, 395 had worked at Lindale for ten or more years, and 135 had been at the mill for over twenty-five years.[16]

Although few workers failed to understand the real power Meikleham exercised over their lives, the Captain's association with welfare capitalism, his very personalized management style, and especially his "generosity" during the depression had impressed many residents and workers in the village. In 1932, to celebrate his sixtieth birthday, Meikleham treated the folks in Lindale to a feast that must have been truly awe-inspiring in depression-era Georgia—four thousand pounds of barbecue, over 150 cakes, and hundreds of gallons of lemonade.[17] Even among those who recognized Meikleham's arrogance in telling them what to do and what to think, he may have indeed seemed like a benevolent, if sometimes overbearing, patriarch. In addition to unmistakable evidence of corporate welfare on every corner of the village, Meikleham was known to help individual families. As Lindale resident Opal Scott, whose father and grandfather worked in the mill under Meikleham, explained, her father had always

[15] Letter to Polly Gammon, n.d. (photocopy in author's possession); Knowlton, *Pepperell's Progress*, 313–14.

[16] H. P. Meikleham to John L. Connor (Textile Labor Relations Board), Nov. 19, 1934, Pepperell Manufacturing, Lindale folder, E 402, RG 9, National Archives, Washington, D.C. (hereafter NA); workforce statistics calculated from table of Lindale employment statistics, appendix 24, in Knowlton, *Pepperell's Progress*, 430.

[17] Gibbons, *A History of Lindale*, 16.

been a "company man" because he "thought Captain Meikleham would just do anything for him." When Scott's father built their house, Meikleham provided several loads of cinders from the mill to fill in and level out their yard at no charge. Similar stories—of poor widows given a home, of sons bailed out of the Rome jail—abounded and contributed to the myth of Meikleham.[18]

The local lore about Meikleham also incorporated other elements of booster ideology. The Captain was regularly credited with good business sense and the benefits that accrued to the workers as a result of it. Undoubtedly, the impression was aided by the Captain himself, who frequently reminded people of Lindale of the many offers he had to work elsewhere. According to one Lindale resident, Meikleham found the Lindale mill "unsuccessful almost to failure" when he arrived, but within a few years "successful management had insured continued operation and steady employment; contentment had replaced uncertainty, and Lindale . . . became known far and near as a good place to live and work." The impression had some basis in reality, for Meikleham had spearheaded a number of improvements in the machinery and production of the mill. Remarkably, company outlays on new buildings and machinery had continued even after the onset of the depression.[19]

Although Meikleham liked to dwell on the importance of welfare, Pepperell mill policies during the depression actually proved the most significant in earning workers' collective loyalty. Unlike many other southern mills, Pepperell managed to successfully share the work. When the NRA textile code came into effect, the Lindale mill created two forty-hour shifts and doubled the number of people on the payroll to thirty-three hundred workers, employing about 55 percent of the population in the immediate Lindale vicinity. When the textile code cut hours more drastically in the summer of 1934—the action that precipitated the general strike elsewhere—the Lindale mill shifted to two shifts at twenty-four hours per week but compensated for the loss of hours and wages in meaningful ways.[20]

First, Meikleham took the case to the workers. In numerous speeches he positioned himself as the defender of Lindale workers, portraying himself as fighting the wage and hour cuts forced upon him by the corporation and the textile code. He agreed with them that "cotton mill people never got what they should" and assured them that he was doing the "best [he]

[18] Scott interview.

[19] Gammon interview; talk given at Lindale Bible class, Aug. 1, 1937, personal papers of Polly Gammon (photocopy in author's possession); Knowlton, *Pepperell's Progress*, 321–22.

[20] Knowlton, *Pepperell's Progress*, 328–29.

could" to keep the mills running and wages at current rates. The mill had even taken orders "at a slight loss," he claimed, "to give you people employment." More importantly, rather than trying to disguise pay cuts in the speed-up and stretch-out, Meikleham spoke to workers frankly about wage rates and short time. It was a good strategy, as workers were much less offended by honest pay cuts than the treachery of the stretch-out. When layoffs became a necessity, Meikleham applied the standard of seniority. Second, Meikleham understood how welfare was measured locally. Although Lindale workers worked longer hours for less money than northern Pepperell workers, Meikleham ensured that they always got "a little more wages" than other southern workers. Finally, and most important of all, when the textile code mandated the 1934 curtailment, Meikleham counterbalanced the impact on take-home pay and workers' loyalty by providing village services for free. Polly Gammon, who was just a child during the depression, remembered that in recognition of "hard times, [mill officials] did away with the rent." If Lindale managers introduced the stretch-out, which was practically ubiquitous by 1934, Meikleham's paternalism evidently mitigated the hardship in the eyes of workers. No complaints about workloads or wages were registered with the textile authority of the NRA from Lindale.[21]

Other mill managers in Floyd County, such as the Italian managers at Tubize Chatillon or Superintendent D. D. Towers of the Anchor Duck Mills, were less successful in sustaining the paternalistic ideal through the depression. In the Tubize mill village, paternalism seems to have had precisely the opposite effect on workers. Although the mill's construction in 1929 on the northeastern side of Rome's city limits had been heralded as another superb opportunity for workers, the Italian managers of the Tubize Corporation had a difficult time establishing a local management that Rome workers would respect and trust. Differences in language and culture alienated many of the Rome workers from the Italian managers and undermined any sense among Tubize millhands that they shared common interests with managers. Even the relative affluence of the Riverside mill village encouraged workers to conclude that they also deserved additional benefits that might be acquired through a trade union.

The Tubize Chatillon Corporation's rayon and acetate yarn mill, with its fine brick-home village, had long served as a tribute to local boost-

[21] Ibid.; "A Talk by Captain Meikleham," ca. May 1935, personal papers of Polly Gammon (photocopy in author's possession); *Rome News-Tribune*, Dec. 20, 1934; Gammon interview. The NRA did receive one anonymous letter from Lindale, which alleged that workers installing some new machinery in 1935 were not being paid the rate guaranteed to textile operatives, but these workers were not covered by the code. See anonymous letter to Franklin Roosevelt, Dec. 5, 1935, Pepperell Manufacturing, Lindale folder, E 402, RG 9, NA.

erism, if not paternalism. Built in 1928–29, the mill complex, which covered fifty acres and included 464 houses, was an important source of pride, as well as revenue, for civic leaders. Rome Chamber of Commerce heads and prominent civic figures "had worked long and hard to secure the new plant," a product of joint American and Italian capital, within county borders. The ground-breaking ceremonies for the rayon plant in 1929, according to a local historian, "outdid any public demonstration since the Armistice that marked the end of World War I." Meikleham was also there, leading the Lindale band, which played the Italian national anthem in honor of the many Italian dignitaries present, the "Star-Spangled Banner" in recognition of American and Georgian officials, and, appropriate to the South's recent eclipse of New England as the largest producer of American textiles, closed with "Dixie." Booster-editor J. R. Hornady devoted the entire front page of the Sunday *Rome News-Tribune* to the opening of Rome's "new industrial era."[22]

Superficially, the Tubize plant conformed to all the standards of mill village paternalism, though Italian managers could never re-create Meikleham's personal management style. Even in 1933, before the unfinished village had paved roads, many Romans boasted that the Tubize community, with its neat brick houses, school, community center, and winding roads all named for different trees, was one of the nicest mill villages in the South. But the workers, many of whom migrated to the area from textile mills and farms in Alabama, never felt especially close to the foreign managers or even southern-born managers promoted from within. Symbolic of the gulf between workers and managers, the mill operatives lived on one side of the mill while the Italian managers lived in large homes on the other side in "boss town." Millhands, however, came up with their own name for the bosses' neighborhood. "The workers called it 'what town,' " according to one longtime resident of the village, "because we couldn't understand what they said."[23]

Another misunderstanding of sorts also revealed the cultural distance between Italian executives and Floyd County residents. For many years, La soie de Chatillon of Milan, Italy, the Italian partners in the Rome plant, had used the Etruscan statue of the Italian Capitoline wolf, symbol of the Romulus and Remus myth, as a trademark of the corporation. When construction of the Rome plant began, corporate headquarters shipped, along with the machinery, a replica of the statue to be placed in front of the mill. When the statue—described by a local historian as "an ugly she

[22] Aycock, *All Roads to Rome*, 393–95; *Rome News-Tribune*, July 31, 1929; *Tubize Yarns* (company employee magazine), November 1945, Special Collections, Sara Hightower Library.

[23] Brooks interview.

wolf with her pendulous teats, and . . . the babies with all their anatomy exposed for everyone to see"—arrived in Rome, local managers hid it away in a storage room. Wary of the community's likely reaction and somewhat unnerved themselves, they informed Milan that they were sending it back. Italian executives of the Chatillon Corporation protested that shipping would be too expensive now. On the way to Georgia, the statue had come as part of the machinery, but now it would have to be shipped as a work of art, which entailed a heavy tax. Exasperated Georgia managers then threatened to throw the whole thing in the Oostanaula River.[24]

Finally, the Italian and American management "put their heads together" and worked out a clever "hocus-pocus," in the words of a local historian. To the statue they added a marble base and a bronze plate dedicating the statue to the city of Rome "as a forecast of prosperity and glory . . . from Ancient Rome to New Rome" from none other than the Italian premier Benito Mussolini. Now the statue became the center of a townwide celebration. The Rome City Commission organized a ceremony and invited the governor and Georgia congressmen to attend the unveiling on July 2, 1929. "Literally thousands" thronged the city auditorium for the unveiling, according to the *Rome News-Tribune*. But when the speeches concluded and the restraining ropes were taken down so people could get a closer look, "some of them were horrified and abashed," according to local accounts. Many citizens of the "insular and unsophisticated" Rome, one Georgian remarked, considered the anatomical detail of wolf's teats and the frontal nudity of the infant twins to be obscene, "shameful," "disgraceful," and a threat to the "moral standards of the community." Although some citizens immediately "pointed with pride to this evidence of the favor of the great," for some years afterward the twins were "diapered" with pocket handkerchiefs during city elections and other large public events. At times the statue sported more ribald accoutrements, as some mischievous Romans kept painting the teats of the wolf red. But signaling the town's final acceptance of the statue by 1934, the Rome Rotary Club had just commissioned a replacement twin for one stolen as a prank in 1933.[25]

The success of Tubize executives in gaining acceptance of the corporation among civic leaders was not as easily duplicated in the mill. Cultural insensitivity aside, Tubize managers had other serious problems with their workers. Although Tubize rayon workers did not labor under the notoriously overbearing management of the southern cotton mills or the industry-dominated Cotton Textile Code, the chemical transformation of cellu-

[24] Reynolds, *Coosa River Valley*, 273–77.

[25] Ibid.; Aycock, *All Roads to Rome*, 393–96.

lose into "artificial silk" was dirty, dangerous work under a management that could be equally arbitrary. A continuous-flow process involving caustic chemicals and high temperatures, rayon production could be extremely hazardous, even if everything worked as planned. "The acid out there was terrible," according to a longtime employee of Tubize. Without protective clothing, "it would eat your pants right off your legs. It'd eat your shoes off your feet." Change left in a pocket or locker turned black, a frightening indication of the unhealthy working conditions at Tubize. Because the chemicals were not totally contained in pipes or tanks, acid mist filled the air and workers' eyes. In the area around one spinning room, workers regularly contracted what was referred to as "fume eyes," a kind of temporary blindness. As a child in the village during the 1930s, Harold Waddell remembered "seeing many of our neighbors being brought home at the end of the shift blind." Mill security people would have to walk them home and "lead them in the house." The chemicals also emanated a distinct and unpleasant odor. Waddell's grandfather, who lived in Alabama, claimed that he could sometimes smell the Tubize plant at his house over forty miles away.[26]

Although they denied any pretensions of thinking they were better than "cotton mill people," Tubize employees did think of themselves, their village, and the work itself as a little better than others in Floyd County. Oscar Allen, whose family moved to the village in 1930, recalled, "It was a wonderful, wonderful place to work. We made good money. We made a lot more than . . . in a cotton mill." They expected to be treated accordingly. Their homes were in a "brick village, compared with wood structures in the other villages," Harold Waddell explained, which many believed "really was a cut above." Rayon workers also thought of themselves as more highly skilled, an impression encouraged by both the management and the union.[27]

Conditions in the mill and management's subsequent behavior, however, did not conform to workers' expectations and sense of entitlement. As in most unorganized mills, management exercised extraordinary power. "They'd just fire you at the drop of a hat," according to one Tubize employee. Another worker recalled managers regularly threatening, "If you don't want to do what I'm telling you to do, there's a barefoot boy out yonder from Alabama looking for a job." Tubize employees also resented the fact that this power was given to their former co-workers, who

[26] Harold Waddell, interview with author, July 23, 1994; Brooks interview; "Agreement between Tubize Rayon Corporation and Textile Workers Union of America," Apr. 16, 1945, Tubize Chatillon Agreements file, box 471, MSS 396, Textile Workers Union of America Records, State Historical Society of Wisconsin, Madison (hereafter cited as TWUA Records).

[27] Oscar Allen interview; Waddell interview.

used their promotions as an opportunity to show off "right in [the] face" of their neighbors and friends. Local managers, promoted from within the Rome workforce, made both petty and more serious demands. One manager, for example, required that his female employees bring him ham biscuits to work. Mistreatment of the plant's minority of female employees, many of whom were related to other employees by marriage or kin, particularly offended Tubize workers' sense of propriety. "It was bad," in the words of one employee; "honestly bad." It was what "you'd call harassment." So, in 1933, encouraged by the NRA's recognition of their right to organize and the growth of the UTW, Tubize employees formed Local 1826.[28]

Employees at the third major textile mill in Rome, Anchor Duck, followed a similar path to the union—driven, in a very literal sense, by their superintendent, Donigan Dean Towers. With 156 one- and two-family houses on the south side of Rome, the Anchor mill, one of the oldest in the county, had always had village-style paternalism, though it never approached the scale of Pepperell or Tubize. Anchor was a small mill, and the textile depression had forced the company to focus its energies on modernizing machinery and broadening its product line rather than village welfare. Nevertheless, Towers, like Meikleham, also made broad claims about the mill's benefits to workers and the devotion of "his efforts towards improvement of the plant and its community." A native Roman, born in 1882, Towers had received a degree in textile engineering at Georgia Tech. After a stint in Texas he moved back to his hometown to become superintendent of the Anchor Duck Mill in 1924. Towers was well known and respected within the industry and among Rome's uptown crowd as a leader of civic and social affairs, serving as president of the Rotary Club and director of the First National Bank. On "Towers day," a poor imitation of Meikleham's massive sixtieth-birthday barbecue, the editors of the trade journal *Cotton* and of the *Rome News-Tribune* personally paid tribute to Towers's business acumen and the mill's contribution in taxes and payrolls to the community of Rome.[29]

Towers was much less successful, however, in managing his workers. Like so many other southern managers, he tried to make up for the higher costs necessitated by the textile code by squeezing more work out of millhands. The mill deliberately violated the NRA codes, and—perhaps even worse from the workers' point of view—Towers consistently lied about

[28] Although the UTW did not keep records of how many women worked in the mills, the census figures from Floyd County confirm anecdotal accounts of the Tubize factory's employing a workforce that was over 60 percent male. Waddell interview; Brooks interview; Herman Anderson, interview with author, July 20, 1994; U.S. Bureau of the Census, *Fifteenth Census: 1930*, vol. 3, pt. 1, table 20, p. 514.

[29] *Rome News-Tribune*, Jan. 1, 1942, Oct. 8, 1934, Sept. 5, 1937.

it. When the NRA textile code went into effect in August 1933, Towers laid off two hundred employees and stretched out their work over the remaining six hundred workers. To avoid paying NRA minimum wages, Towers reclassified some of the experienced workers as "learners," or new workers entitled to only half the regular wage. Many millhands complained that they had to go in to work at least a half an hour early, off the clock, in order to prepare their machines, clean up, and get a head start on production. Workers who could not keep up were demoted to learners, and if they could not catch up they were fired without regard to seniority or their complaints about overwhelming workloads. An experienced spinner in the mill, Izora Kilgo, for example, reported to the Textile Code Authority that her workload had been almost doubled from running eight sides in an eleven-hour day to running twelve and fourteen sides in the new eight-hour day. Her co-workers who refused the stretch-out or could not keep up, she reported, were fired.[30]

Management's disregard of millhands' experience, competence, and seniority particularly outraged workers. Writing to Hugh Johnson at the NRA just two weeks after the code went into affect, Neesey Wooten explained, "I have been employed by the Anchor Duck Mill Co. for seven years and feel that I am competent to do the work laid out for me. But, since the eight hour schedule has been adopted, I am classed as a learner. . . . [I]f I don't make the required amount, I will be laid off." Wooten informed the NRA that "it is almost impossible for some of us to make the amount required with the kind of work furnished." Her daughter, Lou, who had been employed by Anchor Duck for five years, had also been classed as a learner. Wooten expressed the sentiments of many, concluding, "Now we don't feel that we have been treated fairly in this." Anchor management had coldly informed Wooten that she had to learn to run a "standard job." Just a few weeks after writing to Johnson, the Wootens apparently gave up and quit.[31]

Yet Towers continued to deny that the stretch-out existed, and whether he believed it or not, he also insisted that there was a "general satisfaction here among the workers." Speaking to a group of Rome ministers as a representative of "management's viewpoint," Towers informed the local clergy that the "so-called stretch-out" was simply a "misnomer." Belittling workers' good sense with a deliberate misunderstanding of their complaints, Towers claimed that work in the mill was not a "stretching process" at all but "a simple scientific division of labor." To make his

[30] See Textile Code Authority reports on complaints, Anchor Duck Mills, Oct. 13, 1933, Jan. 5, Mar. 13, 1934, and affidavit of Izora Kilgo, Nov. 24, 1933, all in Anchor Duck folder, series 398, National Recovery Administration Records, RG 9, NA.

[31] Neesey and Lou Wooten to Gen. Hugh Johnson, Aug. 12, 1933, ibid.

point, Towers assembled a set of "authentic figures" from the textile industry to invalidate workers' claims about stretch-out. The proof, he argued disingenuously, lay in the fact that an "identical amount of cloth yardage is produced as was produced previously." Towers neglected to mention that Anchor Duck was producing the same amount of cloth with only 70 percent of the former workforce in about 70 percent of the time. Echoing the traditional gloss on the southern mills, Towers continued to claim that the textile industry had "proven itself the best friend of the local laborer."[32]

However, the effects of the stretch-out were so severe and universally experienced in Towers's mill that angry and offended Anchor Duck workers organized half the workforce in a little less than a month. The president of the new UTW Local 1852, L. E. Oates, began collecting evidence of the stretch-out. The union also went to Towers, demanding recognition of the union and negotiation over the workloads. When Towers refused to negotiate with the workers' committee or rectify the stretch-out, half the workforce staged an independent walkout on August 29, 1933, a full year before the general strike.

Indicative of workers' frustration and their new sense of how politics might serve them, Oates sent a long telegram to Roosevelt, informing him of "what we have to take" and claiming that no one listened to the union's complaints about the stretch-out and the code violations. The Anchor union members wanted answers. "Where can we get lawful action," Oates asked the president. "When the NIRA Law is violated who has the authority to enforce same"? Why "can't we have the right to organize," Oates demanded, "without interference by mill officials here in Rome Ga."? The telegram was signed "Local 1852, The Forgotten Spot in Rome, Ga."[33]

The telegram, like so many other southern workers' letters, probably never reached the president. Instead, it was forwarded to the Cotton Textile National Industrial Relations Board (CTNIRB), or Bruere Board, as it was commonly known. Created in August 1933 by Hugh Johnson to handle the mountains of code violation complaints collecting in Washington, the Bruere Board was an all-purpose labor relations board for the industry, ostensibly handling code violations and investigating workers' complaints. Reflecting the administration of the textile code, however, the CTNIRB was dominated by business interests, and it never acted as an agency to protect workers' rights under the NRA. Typically. the board responded to a charge of code violation with a letter acknowledging the

[32] *Rome News-Tribune*, Oct. 8, 1934.

[33] Telegram, L. E. Oates to President Roosevelt, Oct. 21, 1933, Anchor Duck folder, series 398, RG 9, NA.

complaint accompanied by a mimeographed copy of the code. The board had only one full-time active member, Robert Bruere, who was by all accounts under the thumb of industry magnate and president of the Cotton Textile Institute, George Sloan. In effect, the textile industry was left to investigate itself.[34]

Although the Bruere Board typically moved slowly in dealing with workers' complaints, Anchor Duck workers got an immediate response when Johnson received a telegram about the strike on August 29, 1933. Conciliators from the Labor Department were rapidly dispatched to settle the conflict. The CTNIRB did not immediately intervene, although Bruere quickly wrote the Labor Department's director of conciliation a gentle reminder that according to Section 17 of the Cotton Textile Code, the board held final jurisdiction over textile disputes. A few days later a commissioner from the Labor Department visited Rome, assembled the 463 striking workers from Anchor Duck, and persuaded them to go back to work. Echoing Bruere, the commissioner argued that their differences with the company should be settled under the textile code and the Bruere Board. On September 8, Bruere telegraphed the president of Anchor Duck, "delighted to learn the settlement of the strike at your mill," and expressed his "desire to be of any possible service in cooperating with you and your employees in adjusting the controversy which was the occasion of the strike." Not Bruere, but his secretary later wrote the president of the Anchor Duck union to inform him that workers' complaints had been "referred to the proper authority."[35]

Oates followed the advice of the Labor Department conciliator and the textile code in good faith. Anchor Duck workers circulated petitions, dutifully collected notarized affidavits, and specified their complaints in letters that were submitted to the CTNIRB. Over the next six months, code authorities investigated three of the complaints and did find the mill in violation. Anchor Duck managers who met with code authorities, however, claimed to have misunderstood the code, or blamed millhands' troubles on their own inefficiency as workers. In regard to reclassifying experienced workers as learners, the management admitted that "everything contained in the . . . complaint was true" but offered the dubious excuse that they were under the impression that "they could make an inefficient

[34] The textile industry established its own labor board by amendment to the code, and therefore the textile industry was not under the jurisdiction of the National Labor Board, created by President Roosevelt under the NIRA. Irons, "Testing the New Deal," 224–29; Hodges, *New Deal Labor Policy*, 63–64, 68–72.

[35] Telegram, L. E. Oates to Gen. Johnson, Aug. 29, 1933; Bruere to Hugh Kerwin, Dept. of Labor, Sept. 2, 1933; telegram, Commissioner Dunnigan to Hugh Kerwin, Dept. of Labor, Sept. 5, 1933; telegram, Bruere to George H. Lanier, Sept. 8, 1934; "Analysis" of the strike, n.d.; all in Anchor Duck folder, series 398, RG 9, NA.

employee go through the six weeks apprenticeship for the purpose of avoiding the increased wage" until that employee "demonstrated to them the fact that he or she could handle a standard job." Investigator E. O. Fitzsimons did not inquire into what constituted a "standard job," nor did he ask why the company had, after tolerating an alleged inefficiency for seven years, suddenly reclassified Neesey Wooten as a learner. As if Towers really had misunderstood, Fitzsimons "explained to the superintendent and to the manager" what the code actually meant, and he was "assured that correction would be made." The company's representatives denied knowledge of any employee starting work before his or her shift, and suggested that was the employee's rather than the supervisor's misdeed. Management promised to "make every effort to apprehend the party guilty of this infraction." Despite the many promises made to Anchor workers, the board did nothing about the stretch-out or mill management's refusal to recognize the union. Local 1852 officials claimed that the company had retaliated against the union by cutting hours to less than ten per week, and that as a result "people [were] in very bad financial conditions." In desperation, Oates telegraphed Roosevelt and the U.S. attorney general, demanding, "If the NIRA is law show some enforcement."[36]

Anchor Duck workers' experience in 1933 foreshadowed hundreds of similar conflicts that led to the general strike call. From August 1933 to September 1934 the Textile Code Authority received more than four thousand complaints from southern workers. Throughout the spring and summer of 1934, short, spontaneous strikes broke out across the South in spite of advice to the contrary from UTW president McMahon. Frustrated by the failure of the NRA, new southern members of the UTW pressed union leadership closer to a confrontation. However, UTW leaders were reluctant to authorize a general strike for several reasons, including a basic insecurity about the union's strength in the South. Despite its phenomenal growth in 1933–34, the UTW was largely a union on paper, without dues, organizational experience, or institutional structure. Moreover, even southern AFL leaders possessed a deep skepticism about the prudence of such a walkout because they still had doubts about whether southern textile workers were reliable union material. AFL leaders in Georgia were "particularly nervous" because they had little confidence in the strength of the UTW or its ability to lead a successful strike. When

[36] Textile Code investigation reports, Anchor Duck Mills, Oct. 13, 1933, Jan. 5, Mar. 13, 1934; telegram, L. E. Oates to President Roosevelt, Oct. 21, 1933; petition, Oct. 29, 1933, signed by D. A. Fuman, Frank Smith, John R. Sims, Melvin Coheley; affidavit of Izora Kilgo, Nov. 24, 1933; L. E. Oates to National Labor Board, Oct. 30, 1933; J. Z. East and J. W. Plemons to "Gentlemen," Oct. 24, 1933; all in ibid.

the UTW called a special convention in August 1934, however, a group of southern delegates entered over fifty resolutions on the first day calling for a general strike. On the third day of the convention, UTW leaders finally relented. An emergency strike committee was established under popular UTW vice president Francis J. Gorman, who began to "furiously plan the strike."[37]

To bring out the workers who did not respond to the initial strike call on September 2, the UTW introduced a controversial new tactic to capture territory, the "flying squadron." The squads were to function as "shock troops," traveling in caravans from mill to mill. When the group arrived, union members would march around the mill, singing union songs and calling out the workers. When it worked, they closed the mill down. Georgia had only one large flying squad of 250 people, organized in Newnan, that traveled to mill centers across the northern part of the state in a caravan of cars. It was unclear if the tactic actually helped the union cause in Georgia. Although the flying squadron allowed the UTW to stretch out union manpower, the squad's circling band of unionists sometimes created the impression that the mill was under attack, frightening and alienating rather than enlisting recruits to the strike. A squad's arrival, UTW leaders admitted, "was often the signal for an exodus of workers through the back door." Mill owners also seized upon the squadrons as an excuse to arm the mills, which led to tragic accidents as well as strike-related violence in northwest Georgia.[38]

The initial reaction to the strike call among Floyd County textile workers, even UTW members, seems to have been confusion. With the exception of the one thousand Brighton Mills workers in Shannon, who were actually scheduled to work on Labor Day but struck instead, no textile workers in Floyd County responded to the strike in the first four days. Although southern AFL leader L. E. Brookshire sounded a UTW call *in person* at Rome's citywide Labor Day celebration and political rally on Monday for organized labor to "do its part" and "cooperate with the national textile strike," the union workers at Anchor Duck, Tubize, and Rome Hosiery went to work on Tuesday. Leaders of the largest group of union cotton mill workers in Floyd County at the Anchor mill announced curiously that they were waiting for further instructions. Technically, Tubize workers, although members of the UTW, were not included in the cotton mill strike, but other Floyd County cotton textile workers with ties to organized labor at Berryton Mills, Primrose Tapestry, and Strain

[37] Irons, "Testing the New Deal," 338, 360–73, 413–15; Hodges, *New Deal Labor Policy*, 98.

[38] Irons, "Testing the New Deal," 428–29, description of Georgia flying squad on 429; Hodges, *New Deal Labor Policy*, 111; *Textile Labor Banner*, Feb. 2, 1935.

Manufacturing also went to work. Local textile managers, however, apparently took Brookshire's call to heart. Even before any textile workers in Rome gave any sign that they planned to strike, managers at Lindale and Tubize installed corps of armed guards in anticipation of flying squadrons. The only other group of workers who heeded the strike call seems to have been Rome's foundry workers, who were already on strike and took up the textile workers' cause themselves.[39]

Although the UTW was not directly involved, the first reports of bloodshed in Georgia came from northwest Georgia on the third day of the strike. On Wednesday, an ad hoc flying squadron of foundry workers tried to shut down the Trion Cotton Mill in Trion, a town about thirty miles north of Rome in Chattooga County. Forty-six special Trion Mill deputies awaited them, and when the Romans arrived and tried to persuade guards to lay down their guns, a small battle ensued. A Trion deputy and a Rome foundry worker were killed, and more than twenty others were wounded by gunshots or clubs.[40]

When word of the Trion incident reached Floyd County later in the day, Captain Meikleham deputized members of the mill baseball team under Captain "Slick" Moulton and added two hundred guards to the regular mill security force in anticipation of a flying squadron. Snipers were placed on the roof behind bales of cotton, and fire hoses were connected to the mill's boiler room so that the squadron might be showered with boiling water. Guards armed with clubs—fabricated Tuesday in the Pepperell carpentry shop—stood inside all the plant entrances. The rumored flying squadron never showed up, but Lindale's miniature arsenal resulted in the would-be vigilantes' hurting many of their own people. On the "first evening of guarding," as an officer tried to take a gun away from a drunk deputy, one of the guns accidentally discharged. In the confusion that followed, nineteen guards and bystanders were sprayed with shot, including a young boy who was shot in the eye. Stories about both incidents appeared in papers across the state the next day. But Rome millhands again reported to work.[41]

[39] *Rome News-Tribune*, Sept. 1, 3, 1934.

[40] Ibid., Sept. 5, 6, 1934; *Atlanta Constitution*, Sept. 5, 6, 1934.

[41] There are very few manuscript sources on the Georgia strike. The UTW has very few records from this period, and nothing on Georgia except a list of southern locals after 1934. Sorting out what actually happened is difficult because the managers and the UTW gave the newspapers conflicting stories. To correct for this, although it was not always possible, I have relied on newspaper stories only to fill in the details of incidents that could be confirmed by NRA records (which include the correspondence of both workers and managers) or oral histories. On the other hand, I have taken the liberty of assuming that the *News-Tribune*'s pro-business editor would not have printed a story about drunk mill guards shooting each other unless it was true. *Rome News-Tribune*, Sept. 4, 5, 1934; *Atlanta Constitution*, Sept. 5, 6, 1934; Gammon interview; Poole interview.

Late Thursday afternoon, the 175 employees of the Strain Manufacturing Company cotton mill earned distinction as the first of Rome's textile workers to join the strike. The impact of the Strain walkout, however, was muted by the quick response of other local managers who seized the moment to claim workers' loyalty and their deep concern for the safety of "their workers." On the same day, John Berry, president of the Rome Hosiery Mills chain, announced his decision to close the company's three small factories in Rome and its small cotton mill in Berryton. The four mills employed about eleven hundred workers altogether. Although about six hundred of Berry's workers belonged to the union and it was likely that they were planning to follow Strain Manufacturing workers' example and walk out when Gorman issued the call to hosiery locals, Berry beat them to the punch. On Thursday Berry announced that mills would be closed "for a few days . . . at the request of mill workers who thought such course advisable to prevent trouble from outside strike agitators." Since no one had actually struck Rome Hosiery yet, Berry's lockout stole the opportunity for a large number of UTW members to demonstrate the union presence in Rome. Rome Hosiery's union workers, on "vacation" according to Berry, met throughout the strike but never established a picket at the mills. Berry insisted to the papers that "there's not any strike or anything like that," and with little evidence to the contrary, he issued a public statement claiming, "we simply acted at the request of our employees who didn't want to get in any trouble. . . . Our employees are perfectly loyal and we are going to do what we can to protect them." On the same day, commissioners of the Northwest Georgia Textile League announced the closing of the textile baseball season, "due to the unrest among textile workers and the fear that disorders might result among spectators at the games."[42]

After the first five days, two more textile workforces joined the general strike. On Friday, six hundred Anchor Duck employees finally walked out and established a "peaceful" picket in front of the mill. Towers, however, also tried to make it look like the walkout was a simply a matter of safety and thus no indication of disloyalty. Speaking to the *Atlanta Constitution*, Towers claimed, "Our workers have been intimidated to such an extent that they feared for their safety and they decided to walk out." Towers and the local boosters running the *News-Tribune* inexplicably seemed to have forgotten the Anchor Duck walkout in the fall of 1933. On the same day, Pepperell claimed that only eighteen employees of the Lindale mill belonged to the union, and that only eighty of thirty-three hundred millhands, an ordinary absentee rate, failed to report to work during the strike. Mass picketing continued in Shannon, where signs along the high-

[42] *Atlanta Constitution* Sept. 7, 1934; *Rome News-Tribune*, Sept. 7, 1934.

way to the mill warned, "Strike Zone, Scabs Keep Out." None of the mill managers, however, bothered to reopen local mills with strikebreakers. On Sunday, September 9, Tubize workers received a telegram from Francis Gorman ordering them not to strike, and just a few days later, with the assistance of southern AFL representative George Googe, Local 1826 and Tubize management signed a contract. The following Wednesday, September 12, the day of the Democratic primary, pickets persuaded the seventy-five workers at Rome's Primrose Tapestry factory to walk out. Primrose millhands brought the total number of workers on strike to its peak of 3,075, or about 40 percent of the County's 7,375 textile mill workers.[43]

In neighboring Chattooga and Polk Counties, the arrival of the flying squadron made the character of the strike much more volatile. The squad induced only a minority of union workers to come out, but those strikers were subsequently harassed, intimidated, and beaten by mobs of anti-union workers and mill guards. In Polk County the textile industry consisted primarily of five large mills, including three plants owned by Goodyear Tire and Rubber Company. Although all five closed, only about 715 of Polk County's 2,500 workers actually joined the strike.[44] In Rockmart, anti-union workers beat up the union's president and vice president and ordered them to leave town. A note left at their homes warned, "Move your furniture out of Rockmart and Polk County . . . we mean move now and not next month—get gone." Town officials had the union evicted from its meeting hall, and the chief of police personally prevented strikers from receiving federal relief.[45] On Saturday, a week after the initial strike

[43] Towers as quoted in *Atlanta Constitution*, Sept. 7, 1934; *Rome News-Tribune*, Sept. 7, 8, 13, 1934. I calculated the number of strikers from the total number of workers at Anchor, Strain, Primrose, Pepperell, Tubize, Rome Hosiery, Berryton Mills, and Brighton Mills, as reported to the NRA and newspapers. A union contact reported to the CTNIRB that the Lindale mill had 350–400 union workers, but other company records indicated that they did not strike. CTNIRB report Oct. 11, 1934, John L. Tower, CTNIRB investigator, to Textile Labor Relations Board, Nov. 22, 1934; H. P. Meikleham to John L. Connor, Nov. 19, 1934; both in Pepperell Manufacturing, Lindale folder, E 402, RG 9, NA.

[44] This figure is based primarily on local union reports and correspondence with the NRA after the strike. In all the Goodyear mills, union members charged that they were blacklisted from work and federal relief programs after the strike, and as a result, local leaders of the company and the union carried on an extensive correspondence with the Textile Code Authority and the NRA. See, for example, Textile Code Investigation Report, Jan. 14, 1935; J. M. Neel to Samuel McClurd, CTNIRB, Dec. 14, 1934; both in Goodyear Clearwater no. 1 folder, E 402, RG 9, NA. Textile Code Investigation Report, Oct. 6, 1934; Lillian Bailey to Franklin Roosevelt, Oct. 15, 1934; Gay B. Shepperson, Relief Administrator for Georgia, to Harry Hopkins, Oct. 29, 1934; all in Goodyear Clearwater, Rockmart folder, E 402, RG 9, NA.

[45] Textile Code Investigation Report, Oct. 6, 1934; Lillian Bailey to Franklin Roosevelt, Oct. 15, 1934; Gay B. Shepperson, relief administrator for Georgia, to Harry Hopkins, Oct.

call, several hundred millhands from another mill closed by management paraded through Rockmart with banners reading "We Want to Work," "We Want Militia Protection," and "We Are Loyal to Goodyear." Just a few days later, the flying squadron arrived in the small Polk County town of Aragon, where a group of "loyal forces" of anti-union workers and sheriff's deputies were armed and lined up for a fight. The squadron retreated, but officials of the Aragon mill closed the plant and declared a "holiday" to give the loyal workers an opportunity to "clean up the village" and expel all "disloyal workers." A mob of Aragon employees delivered notice to union members, who numbered only twenty-five, to leave town.[46]

In Chattooga County, local town and mill officials' alarm suggested that the walkout was at least partially successful. Just three days after the strike began, the mayor of Trion and vice president of the Trion mill, J. N. Murphy, wired the governor requesting National Guard troops to protect workers who were attempting to cross the picket line. Murphy claimed that the twenty-six hundred workers at the Trion mill and the thirteen hundred workers at a nearby Summerville mill "wanted to operate" but strikers and pickets had prevented the mill from opening. Talmadge wired Murphy a refusal, but reminded him that "the sheriff of your county has authority to deputize as many citizens over twenty one years old as he deems necessary to maintain order." Murphy did deputize hundreds, which had led to the early affray between Rome foundry workers and deputies.[47]

Murphy's wire to the incumbent governor was but one example of how managers and millhands looked to politics and the state to broker some solution. Because the strike coincided with the climax of the state Democratic primary and the general politicization of labor relations under the New Deal, labor assumed an unusually prominent role in Georgia politics that year. Union leaders in Rome, for example, sponsored a series of campaign speeches, incorporated discussion of the textile strike into political events, and used their position on the stump to rally local workers to participate in both the strike and the election. On Labor Day, the first day of the strike, Romans heard Talmadge's major, but much less popular, opponent, Judge Claude Pittman of neighboring Bartow County. But before Pittman took the podium, an AFL representative addressed the crowd and made a direct connection between the strike, current politics, and pa-

---

29, 1934; all in Goodyear Clearwater, Rockmart folder, E 402, RG 9, NA; *Rome News-Tribune*, Sept. 14, 1934; *Atlanta Constitution*, Sept. 14, 1934.

[46] Textile Code Investigation Report, Jan. 14, 1935; J. M. Neel to Samuel McClurd, CTNIRB, Dec. 14, 1934; both in Goodyear Clearwater no. 1 folder, E 402, RG 9, NA; *Rome News-Tribune*, Sept. 14, 1934; *Atlanta Constitution*, Sept. 14, 1934.

[47] *Atlanta Constitution*, Sept. 5, 6, 1934; *Rome News-Tribune*, Sept. 5, 6, 1934.

triotism. Adopting the rhetoric of Roosevelt and the NRA, he portrayed the strike as a matter of supporting the president and the fight against the depression, telling the audience that labor was "fighting to uphold the national [textile] code" and urging local labor to "do its part to strengthen the NRA in accordance with President Roosevelt's program."[48]

As labor leaders sought to link the current strike to the New Deal, both of the major contenders for the governor's race tried to demonstrate support for the state's workers. Although Georgia had, for all practical purposes, only the single party, the strike became an issue in Georgia's primary race between competing Democratic factions. Pittman's major issue was, above all else, opposition to Talmadge-style government, particularly the governor's heavy-handed domination of state government agencies, but he also challenged the governor's credentials as a New Deal supporter. He attacked the governor's opposition to the NRA wage scale for highway workers, claiming, as some state Federation of Labor leaders had, that defiance of this NRA rule was anti-labor, anti–New Deal, and anti-Roosevelt. Answering charges against himself that he represented corporations, Pittman told an audience of Romans that he did represent corporations, "but not the monied part." Rather, he claimed to represent "the workers in all the large utilities and corporations in the state." In comparison to the populist rhetoric marshaled by the governor, it was a less than inspired response, and folks in the Rome audience, most likely a combination of farmers and workers, were evidently unimpressed. Talmadge supporters jeered when Pittman was introduced, and they had to be "called down" at several points in his address.[49]

Talmadge also claimed to be a friend of organized labor, and a fair portion of his 1934 stumping was directed toward union workers. At one point in the primary, Talmadge claimed that 75 percent of organized labor would vote for him, and he was probably correct. In a state not traditionally identified with a heavy union influence, the governor took surprisingly strong stands in favor of organized labor, long before the strike actually began. In July, for example, in a headline story in his own political paper, *The Statesman*, Talmadge declared himself "labor's best friend" and laid out all of his labor credentials. The paper reminded readers how he had acted at the request of the state Federation of Labor to restructure the state Public Service Commission in 1933, and how he had refused to intervene in other strikes. He also informed readers that his wife was a union member when he married her, and "to this day has a union card in her trunk."[50]

[48] *Rome News-Tribune*, Sept. 4, 1934.

[49] Ibid.

[50] *Statesman*, Aug. 14, 1934.

To those who argued that Talmadge's stand on the NRA wage scale for highway workers was anti-labor, the governor countered with a logic that probably held greater sway with the white rank and file. Although a few Atlanta labor leaders, such as the president of the Georgia Federation of Labor, J. Sid Tiller, might have "appointed themselves to tell organized labor in Georgia how to vote," Talmadge retorted that he did "not think that the great mass of workers who compose organized labor disagree with me on the highway pay scale." On the stump he mocked Tiller as a fool "trying to look after the wages received by a negro rolling a wheelbarrow on the right-of-way, who has never joined the Union." To claim that this was a union issue was preposterous, Talmadge argued, when so few union members were either common laborers or African Americans. There was "not one man in five hundred in a Union who works on grading and paving roads," he noted, "and Organized Labor knows this." The governor, on the other hand, could assure the white people of Georgia that he was making sure that wage rates were "right and fair." Where there were "men and women working in the mills, in stores and other places of business, good steady white citizens who are not able to earn 40 cents an hour . . . I do not believe that negroes working on the highways should get it." When Talmadge shouted this on the stump in Gainesville, according to *The Statesman*, workers responded, "We don't either!"[51]

Moreover, Talmadge's past record in labor disputes offered some reassurance to the rank and file of union labor. Months before the textile strike, the sheriff of Floyd County had asked Talmadge to send troops to Rome to end a strike at a local foundry, and he refused. In August 1933, Talmadge had refused a petition to send the National Guard to Savannah during a textile strike. Though it would soon become clear just how much Talmadge sympathized with Georgia manufacturers, all his public speeches catered to labor's perspective. During the 1934 primary, in Rome and elsewhere, Talmadge had assured workers that he did not plan to send in the guard.[52]

Mill workers had not traditionally been a major electoral force in Georgia politics, but ordinary white folk, whether they labored on a farm or in a factory, had always been central to all aspects of Talmadge's strategy. Talmadge consistently claimed that working people lay at the core of his platform, even if his overall vision was a conservative one. His opposition to relief, for example, stemmed in part from his contention that it was unfair for common white folks to work so hard for so little and for others to get government handouts, especially because he usually assumed that the recipients of handouts would be black. "When I go over Georgia and

[51] Ibid., July 31, Aug. 14, 21, 1934.

[52] Ibid., July 31, 1934; *Atlanta Constitution*, Sept. 5, 1934.

see the thousands of people at work at a low starvation wage, it makes my heart bleed," he told an audience in northwest Georgia. But it was equally absurd for the government to pay highway workers forty cents per hour "and let the other laborers in the fields look on and see the injustice being done them by the State government." In effect, Talmadge insinuated, relief work devalued the good, honest work that Georgia farmers and mill-hands were doing, unless it earned wages comparable to the prevailing community scale. Perhaps even more significantly, Talmadge consistently affirmed and flattered Georgia workers' labors and their lifestyle. In Dalton he was moved to recite a poem on the subject: "Mother told me / Father showed me / Hard Labor makes a man." In the Talmadge vision, white workers and farmers were honest, hardworking, self-reliant folk who did not need government handouts or federally mandated minimum wages because virtue and backbone would see them through.[53]

Workers and farmers were also central to Talmadge's electoral strategy, even though the poll tax and literacy requirements clearly inhibited poor white political participation. Many white workers and farmers who attended the Rome stump speech probably did not cast votes in the primary. In 1934, a record year for voter registration and turnout at the Floyd County polls, the number of votes cast in the primary represented only one-third of eligible white voters. In the precincts representing the mill villages of Lindale and Tubize Chatillon, only 35 and 25 percent of eligible voters, respectively, would actually cast ballots in the 1934 primary.[54] Although Georgia editors and elites frequently commented that the poll tax was an extremely small price to pay for the right to vote, because it was cumulative the cost for a mill worker or a tenant farmer could be relatively exorbitant. In 1934 textile workers earned an average wage of about ten dollars per forty-hour week; the cumulative poll tax was one dollar each year. If a person at the age of thirty-one, for example, decided to register and vote for the first time in the Democratic primary, it would cost that person a week's salary to exercise his or her white privilege. But however marginal the vote of ordinary folks in the overall primary, many a Georgia county and many a state election had been won on such a margin. In fact, the whole Georgia electoral system operated in such a way as to give rural folks the greatest voice in state politics. Georgia elected its governor as well as its senators and congressmen on a county unit system, which assigned each county at least two unit votes and gave larger counties four or six. Because the units were not assigned proportionately, the county

[53] *Statesman*, Aug. 7, 1934.

[54] Voter turnout calculated from 1934 primary returns from the *Rome News-Tribune*, Sept. 14, 1934, and population figures for adults over twenty-one from U.S. Bureau of the Census, *Fifteenth Census: 1930*, vol. 3, pt. 1, pp. 493, 534.

unit system placed most of the state's electoral power in the smaller counties. Floyd County, for example, had as many unit votes as Atlanta's Fulton County, even though Fulton residents cast almost two and one-half times as many votes in 1934. Talmadge had already proven in 1932 that a gubernatorial candidate could win on the votes of the countryside alone. In 1934, his choice of issues also acknowledged how significant workers and farmers were to the upcoming primary.[55]

Georgia mill owners and industry leaders, however, kept up the pressure on Talmadge, and they were joined by some mill workers who demanded state "protection." At one of the governor's final campaign speeches, in the northwest Georgia town of Newnan, a group of mill workers held aloft a banner comparing the strike to the governor's 1933 battle with the state highway board: "It is more important to use the troops to permit us to work than to put out the highway board," the banner proclaimed. Given that thousands of workers were not on strike but locked out of their mills, it is perhaps not surprising that many wanted to go back to work. Georgia mill owners, however, seem to have had a more direct influence on the governor. Ted Forbes, secretary of the Cotton Manufacturer's Association of Georgia and a close friend of Talmadge's, arranged a secret meeting between the governor and about twenty of the state's leading manufacturers for Friday, September 7, the night before Talmadge was to speak in Rome. According to Forbes, the governor listened to story after story about the destruction of mill property in silence, then told the manufacturers that while he sympathized with their problem, he could not "do anything about it if I'm not re-elected." After the election, he promised, he would "take care of it." When the governor left, Forbes said, the manufacturers decided to make a $20,000 "campaign contribution," a considerable sum in 1934 dollars. Over the weekend, even as Talmadge made promises to northwest Georgia mill workers from the Rome stump, Adjutant General Lindley W. Camp was instructed to begin planning for the deployment of troops immediately after the election.[56]

On the morning of September 12, as a light rain fell on downtown Rome, a record number of Floyd County voters filed into the polls and delivered over 70 percent of their votes to Talmadge. Of approximately ten thousand registered voters, a record of almost seven thousand Floyd County citizens cast votes, delivering six county units to a statewide Talmadge landslide. Final Georgia returns on Thursday indicated that Talmadge beat his opponent, Claude Pittman, in the popular vote by a mar-

[55] On the county unit system see Numan Bartley, *From Thurmond to Wallace* (Baltimore: Johns Hopkins University Press, 1970), 14–15.

[56] *Atlanta Constitution*, Sept. 5, 7, 1934; Allen, "The Governor and the Strike," 115–17.

gin of nearly two to one, carried 155 of the states's 159 counties, and won 394 of 400 county unit votes. In Floyd County the governor amassed large majorities in both identifiably union and nonunion precincts. In the mill village districts of Tubize and Lindale, workers delivered 80 and 67 percent of their votes, respectively, to Talmadge.[57]

Almost immediately, Talmadge mobilized the guard. On Friday, just two days after the election, the governor received word that a flying squadron was headed for the Goodyear mill in Bartow County, immediately east of Floyd County. Three companies of troops were dispatched to northwest Georgia mills in Rockmart, Cartersville, and Aragon, where on the same day a mill guard was shot and killed. On Saturday, thirty-seven hundred soldiers, armed with machine guns, prepared for the greatest mobilization in the state's history. Troops were also ordered to Atlanta, Augusta, Savannah, and Macon. Talmadge issued a statement promising full protection to nonstriking mill workers and operators of the mills closed by "outside influence" on their employees. Across the state, mill owners prepared to open their factories. On Monday, September 17, Talmadge declared martial law and troops arrested forty-three members of the Georgia flying squadron in Newnan. Several hundreds more were arrested in the final days of the strike, and over a hundred prisoners were placed in an old barbed-wire prison camp from World War I. Talmadge claimed that he had been petitioned by "mill owners, sheriffs, judges, private citizens, strikers who were on strike, [and] mill employees who were at work in the mills." Martial law, he asserted, was to "protect the lives and property of all of the citizens of this state. This means strikers, union members, non-union members. laborers, executives and all."[58]

Undoubtedly, many striking workers were outraged by Talmadge's contention that he had "looked into the situation and found that the strikers themselves admit that the mills are paying the NRA scale" and thus "following the provisions of the National Recovery Act." Strikers, he argued, were "petitioning for a different code," which was a different kind of battle. It did "not require a strike, either forced or voluntary." By this time, President Roosevelt had appointed a mediation board to look into the petition of the millhands, and thus the governor concluded that the issue had been settled. Given the actual basis of millhands' complaints, it was an outrageous misdescription of the issues, but in reality it differed little from the statements that would be issued by the UTW national leadership. Gorman would also finally defer to the authority of the president, place the dispute in the hands of the board, and declare "that the union

[57] Local vote totals from *Rome News-Tribune*, Sept. 16, 1934.

[58] *Atlanta Constitution*, Sept. 16, 17, 1934; *Rome News-Tribune*, Sept. 16, 17, 18, 1934; Allen, "The Governor and the Strike," 125–29; Hodges, *New Deal Labor Policy*, 110–11.

has won an overwhelming victory, that we ought to terminate the strike as no longer necessary, and that we now go forth in a triumphant campaign of organization."[59]

Talmadge's electoral victory and his betrayal of union workers was a striking example of how a Democratic candidate in the segregated South could appeal to race and class interests at the same time in effective, and ultimately conservative, ways. Speaking in Rome just a few days before he deployed the guard, Talmadge had told workers that his sympathy for whites proved that he would look out for working-class interests. But this claim was also a remarkably successful strategy for addressing the broad range of interests of white Georgia in this conflict. He simply claimed that he was on the unambiguous side of all whites, and by doing so claimed to be on the side of *all* textile workers, even though they were bitterly divided among themselves over the UTW and the strike. Even calling out the guard had not truly undermined his promises because, in the light of Georgia millhands' uneven support of the strike, he had acted in what a large number of workers indicated to be their interests. There were hundreds of workers in northwest Georgia who supported Talmadge's defense of their right to earn more than black laborers, as well as their "right to work."

In Rome on Tuesday, September 18, as a North Carolina representative of the UTW belatedly presented organized labor's position to the Rome Ministerial Association, what support there had been for the Georgia strike had already begun to crumble. In Floyd County only Brighton Mills workers in Shannon and Strain Manufacturing millhands stayed out for any substantial period after the governor's announcement. That Monday, Primrose Tapestry opened with a full workforce, and a meeting of Anchor Duck workers voted to return to their jobs. The next day, union employees of the Rome Hosiery Mills voted to continue the strike, but by Thursday, Rome Hosiery president John Berry reported that he had spoken to about two hundred workers who informed him that they wanted to go back to work. By the end of the third week of the strike, most mills in Floyd County were operating with full workforces. In Shannon, where union members maintained their picket even as mill managers planned to reopen, three companies of state guards arrived "in order to forestall any rioting," in the words of the *Rome News-Tribune*.[60]

Although hunger and vigilante violence had already taken a significant toll on morale, UTW vice president Gorman blamed Governor Talmadge for the rapid collapse of the strike in Georgia. Two days after the declara-

[59] *Statesman*, Sept. 18, 1934; Irons, "Testing the New Deal," 471–77; Hodges, *New Deal Labor Policy*, 112–15.

[60] *Rome News-Tribune*, Sept. 17, 18, 20, 1934.

tion of martial law, Gorman issued a scathing attack on Talmadge, accusing him of "using the armed forces of your state to drive men back into starvation conditions and absolute subservience to mill owners." It was also clear that martial law had upset the already weak lines of communication between the UTW and mill towns, and probably encouraged many, such as the Anchor and Primrose workers, to go back to work before the UTW officially called off the strike. But hunger and a lack of relief, more than anything else, probably broke the strike in Georgia mills where the walkout was successful. The UTW just did not have the resources to sustain strikers. Revealing the desperation of many southern mill workers, prisoners in Georgia's makeshift internment camp invariably noted that they had "plenty to eat" in prison when interviewed by the newspapers. Although the UTW *claimed* that forty thousand of Georgia's sixty thousand textile workers were still "out of work," the strike had seriously faltered. When Gorman, at President Roosevelt's request, declared a "victorious end" to the strike only twenty days after it began, over 60 percent of Georgia's spindles were already in operation.[61]

Although the UTW never gave up the claim that it controlled most of the South's workers, the behavior of Floyd County workers in the strike and the election suggests a more ambiguous scenario. Clearly the strike was neither as "general" nor as well organized as many assumed. Strike tallies were particularly suspect. While newspapers reported on the number of mills closed and the number of workers idle, it was not always clear *why* workers were not at their machines. In Floyd County alone, at least 625 workers counted as "idle" were not on strike but locked out by management. With the 3,300 Pepperell workers in Lindale almost outnumbering strikers in Floyd County, a generous estimate places the number of strikers at 40 percent.[62] In Polk County, still greater numbers of idle workers had actually ignored the strike call. Even local unionists claimed a total of only 715 strikers among 2,500 workers.[63] National UTW claims, then, represented either a mass self-deception in the organization or an attempt to embellish what was already a large, but not general, strike. After all, the UTW also insisted on declaring a glorious victory,

[61] Ibid., Sept. 19, 23, 1934; Allen, "The Governor and the Strike," 125–29; Irons, "Testing the New Deal," 465–68; Hodges, *New Deal Labor Policy*, 110–11.

[62] This probably overestimates the number of strikers because I counted all six hundred workers at Rome Hosiery as on strike, even though there is evidence suggesting that the workforce did not unanimously support the union.

[63] *Textile Labor Banner*, Feb. 2, 1934; Textile Code Investigation Report, Oct. 6, 1934; Lillian Bailey to Franklin Roosevelt, Oct. 15, 1934; Gay B. Shepperson, Relief Administrator for Georgia, to Harry Hopkins, Oct. 29, 1934; all in Goodyear Clearwater, Rockmart folder, E 402, RG 9, NA; *Rome News-Tribune*, Sept. 14, 1934; *Atlanta Constitution*, Sept. 14, 1934.

even as textile workers returned to the mills a little poorer and under essentially the same conditions that prevailed before the strike.

From their initial expressions of disbelief to their implementation of lockouts, management also attempted to control public interpretation of the strike. Since textile industry leaders had long disregarded the UTW's claims to represent large numbers of southern workers, the first response of southern manufacturers had been a confident prediction that their workers would ignore the general strike. When many southern workers, such as those at Anchor Duck, failed to come out on the first two days of the strike, Cotton Textile Institute president George Sloan had announced to the press, "It looks as though the preponderance of workers in the south want to go on working." When thousands of textile workers struck, mill managements across the state hid their surprise and humiliation behind accusations of "outside agitators" and their desire to protect loyal workers. As the UTW estimates climbed upwards of two-thirds of the Georgia textile workforce, mill managements claimed "temporary" shutdowns at the request of their employees.[64]

Throughout the conflict, the uptown reaction to the strike in Rome was remarkably restrained. Although the UTW claimed that all Georgia papers "showed a marked bias on the side of the owners," Rome editors defied such a simple description. The *News-Tribune* editor devoted proportionately more space to management's comments, but the paper actually complimented local strikers on several occasions. Union pickets were repeatedly described as "peaceful," and a local columnist for the *News-Tribune*, the "Roaming Roman," reported that he had "not discovered a single instance in which a Rome textile worker has created a disturbance." The "great majority of textile workers hereabout," the Roaming Roman concluded, "are honest, hardworking, church-going men and women and their conduct in Shannon as well as in Rome shows their respect for law." In the second week of the strike the Rome Ministerial Association adopted a neutral resolution condemning "intimidation on either side" and pledged "utmost sympathy with all efforts toward such adjustments as would promote peace and Christian sentiment and fullest justice." When the Tubize Chatillon Company signed a contract with Local 1826 and removed the armed guards, it was "interpreted" by local manager R. C. Jones and the *News-Tribune* "as a decided improvement in the local textile situation."[65]

Despite the community's relatively friendly reception of strikers, the UTW presence receded quickly after the strike. Many Romans were undoubtedly bitter about the outcome of the strike and the union's subse-

[64] *Atlanta Constitution*, Sept. 3, 4, 1934; *Rome News-Tribune*, Sept. 1, 1934.

[65] *Rome News-Tribune*, Sept. 16, 7, 17, 1934.

quent inability to remedy the blacklist that was imposed almost immediately afterward. Although the strike settlement instructed managers to rehire strikers, workers in Shannon and Lindale charged that the mills had permanently banned those who struck. Frustrated workers soon discovered that the UTW had no power to get their jobs back. Although UTW records offer no explanation, the four textile locals in Floyd County stopped paying dues and dropped out of the International in 1935. In Rome, some workers claimed that locals failed because of the UTW, while others attributed it to the inability of workers to hold their unions together. One Rome worker reasoned that the millhands of 1934 "just couldn't get together . . . couldn't get unified." New Rome locals, according to another worker, "didn't have no support" from the UTW-AFL. Even during the strike, the UTW had "probably less than ten" full-time staff members in the entire South. When the dues of 170,000 southerners failed to materialize, only a few union organizers remained.[66]

The UTW's use of organizers who worked for commission undoubtedly strengthened the impression that the International did not support its southern locals. In Georgia the UTW did not install a full-time staff person in the early 1930s, relying instead on organizers who earned a commission on initiation fees for every worker they signed. While the use of commissioned staff stretched the small resources of the UTW over a wider area in the short term, it undoubtedly damaged textile unionism in the long term. Organizing campaigns encouraged workers to think that union dues purchased a service, but commissioned organizers typically collected dues and moved on. The UTW's inability to deliver aid generated resentment and confirmed the suspicion of many workers—and the accusations of many managers—that the union was only after dues money. Exacerbating the situation, some of Georgia's commissioned organizers did not make a "satisfactory accounting of funds collected." In Floyd County, one UTW member recounted how a union organizer set up a table in front of the Tubize mill, collected dues, and then disappeared. Although the UTW representative may have been a commissioned organizer who had simply moved to another mill, this worker was convinced that dues had been stolen, and in the end that belief was what mattered locally.[67]

The demise of Floyd County unions in the wake of the General Textile Strike reflected a decline of textile labor's fortunes across the nation. While the strike had dramatically revealed the weakness of the UTW rela-

[66] "Report of Local Unions for 3 months, Nov. 1, 1935–Jan. 31, 1936," financial reports file, box 674, TWUA Records; Hodges, *New Deal Labor Policy*, 129–30; John L. Connor to Textile Labor Relations Board, Nov. 22, 1934, Pepperell Manufacturing, Lindale folder, E 402, RG 9, NA; Pat and Ernest Burch, interview with author, Sept. 12, 1994; Brooks interview; Waddell interview.

[67] Irons, "Testing the New Deal," 317–18, 320–24; Oscar Allen interview.

tive to management, the new investigative boards proved an unsatisfactory substitute for real concessions from the industry. Consonant with the UTW's positive assessment of the strike, national union leaders advised workers through 1934–35 to be patient, but government investigations actually did little to change the post-strike balance of power between mill owners and the UTW. In the spring of 1935, the report of the Cotton Textile Work Assignment Board delivered the "crowning blow" to the UTW and southern workers by denying widespread existence of the stretch-out. By May 1935, when the Supreme Court declared the NRA unconstitutional, both labor and management had already abandoned faith in the industry codes. Meanwhile, UTW membership continued to dwindle. Less than three years after the strike, the UTW had only 37,588 members nationwide and 5,472 members in the South. In Georgia, union members numbered only 445.[68]

Although major changes in New Deal labor policy and the labor movement itself led to dramatic union growth in the latter half of the 1930s, the UTW never regained its footing in the South or in Floyd County. Even the 1935 National Labor Relations Act, or Wagner Act—a much stronger assertion of labor's right to organize and the federal government's obligation to protect that right—and revolutionary changes within the American labor movement failed to draw millhands to the union fold. When a group of industrial unionists bolted the AFL to form the Congress of Industrial Organizations, UTW leaders who had long favored CIO-style industrial unionism over AFL craft unionism eagerly followed. In 1937 the textile union, now reorganized as the new Textile Workers Organizing Committee (TWOC), launched another major organizing campaign. Although the union announced its intention to finally bring southern textile workers permanently into the union, the TWOC was headquartered in New York City, its highest committee had no southern representatives, and although its staff far exceeded that of the former UTW, only 112 of 600 organizers hired were to cover the entire South.[69]

Opposition to the textile unions from employers as well as workers persisted in the South in spite of union growth elsewhere in the nation. If the general textile strike had not been enough, the massive and dramatic sit-down strikes led by the CIO in 1937 alienated many uptown and working-class southerners from the cause of unionism. Rome's local editors, the chamber of commerce, and Floyd County mill managers redbaited the CIO in print and in public throughout 1937, especially after the TWOC opened an office on Rome's Broad Street in May. In one of

[68] Irons, "Testing the New Deal," 483–93; Hodges, *New Deal Labor Policy*, 124, 130–33.

[69] Hodges, *New Deal Labor Policy*, 148–51.

his "talks" to the workers, for example, Captain Meikleham informed Lindale millhands that the CIO "embodied communism and anarchy." If organizers came to Lindale, the Pepperell agent advised, employees should "treat them courteously, listen to their spiel, laugh at them, and send them on their way." He counseled against any "rough stuff" but added, "if the time came when the people of Lindale had their God-given rights threatened then the offenders would be handled accordingly."[70]

On the day the Rome TWOC office opened, the Roaming Roman responded with a column that reasserted much of the New South dogma behind boosterism and industrial development that became fixtures of regional anti-unionism. He recounted first the "personal injuries and the immense financial losses . . . in various communities in the North and mid-west" due to labor unrest. The South, he implied, was different, and he attributed its uniqueness to the shared interest among all classes of southern whites. The column asserted that "the record proves undeniably that when friction and fighting arises in a community, especially among the Anglo-Saxons of the South, it is the result of the deliberate efforts of outsiders who come in for the specific purpose of creating disturbances." Such interference, the article continued, was financed by none other than the communists in Moscow. On the same day, a prominent Rome physician, Dr. W. H. Lewis, blasted the 1937 sit-down strikes as "the result of the desire of a very few men, in control of the minority of workers in any plant, to exercise dictatorial power [and] to secure incomes which even a Morgan or Rockefeller might envy." In August, the Roaming Roman specifically acknowledged local organizers and accused them of selfishly "trying to swell the volume of cash flowing into the CIO treasury." He warned Floyd County workers to think soberly before "kicking in cash." Their union dues would be "sent away where it will do them nor any other Roman any good." In a tortured metaphor, Lewis had made the same argument in 1934. The textile industry was the South's "goose which laid eggs of gold." To get the golden eggs, he warned, "we must feed the goose, not strangle it."[71]

Whether or not Rome's workers were swayed by any of these anti-union arguments, the majority of workers in Floyd County and the state of Georgia refused to join the textile workers union. In October 1937 the TWOC nationally represented only about twenty-two thousand workers, in plants that accounted for only 2 percent of the region's active spindles. By the end of the decade, the TWOC, which formally became the Textile

[70] Paul David Richards, "The History of the Textile Workers of America, CIO, in the South, 1937 to 1945" (Ph.D. diss., University of Wisconsin, Madison, 1978), 43–67; Meikleham as quoted in *Rome News-Tribune*, Apr. 4, 1937.

[71] *Rome News-Tribune*, May 20, Aug. 1, 1937, Sept. 16, 1934.

Workers Union of America (TWUA) in 1939, had established what one historian has aptly described as only "a thin residue of permanent unionism" in the South. Floyd County workers would stand aloof from the TWUA until a better economy and a greater federal guarantee of their rights emerged during World War II.[72]

At the end of the decade, the lives of most Floyd County textile workers had been changed very little. Although the 1938 Fair Labor Standards Act placed a floor under southern mill conditions with a national minimum wage and maximum hours, New Deal labor policy and the UTW failed to introduce substantive changes in northwest Georgia's textile industry or its politics. The General Textile Strike had done little to diminish either the cult of paternalism or the ideology of business boosterism. Though Anchor Duck superintendent D. D. Towers certainly overstated paternalism's case when he asserted that the textile industry was the local laborer's best friend, the strike had given Floyd County workers many reasons to suspect at least that they did not have any other friends.

The depression may have actually added a degree of authenticity to the claims of boosters and paternalists. Three decades of mill village welfare had succeeded in minimally raising the standard of some southerners' living, even if Floyd County workers now had little choice but to accept what mill owners were willing to give. In terms of wages, Floyd County workers could not have helped but notice that they were in fact much better off than many of their white neighbors on the farm, and almost prosperous in comparison to black workers. Although textile workers earned low wages, poverty was not a mill problem but a southern problem. In the year after the strike, 8,241 people, almost one-third of the Floyd County population, received some kind of relief from the federal government. The overwhelming majority, 7,673, received emergency relief. Under such conditions, many workers undoubtedly internalized the claims of mill men and boosters that a healthy industry and "competitive" wages were in their favor. If individual textile workers questioned the value of a mill job, there were hundreds of unemployed, hungry farmers and workers willing to take their place. As one longtime Lindale worker informed a union worker at Tubize, "Why if they'd cut my pay in half, I'd go back in there, because they gave me a job all these years."[73] Northwest Georgia's workers may have resented being sold as "cheap, native-born" labor to the nation's industrial opportunists, but the need for more jobs and more wages was undeniable. In 1937, when Rome civic, business, and religious leaders lined up behind the chamber of commerce's

[72] Hodges, *New Deal Labor Policy*, 163; Richards, "History of the Textile Workers," 60–67.

[73] *Rome News-Tribune*, June 1, Sept. 21, 1937, Sept. 16, 1934; Brooks interview.

"Keep Rome Ahead" campaign, they were probably supported by many workers.[74]

If the severity of the depression produced only a temporary challenge to the conceits of boosterism and the states's low-wage economy, it had a similarly short-lived influence on Georgia politics. In 1936, when Governor Talmadge, who could not succeed himself in a third term according to Georgia law, ran for the U.S. Senate, his growing opposition to the New Deal relief programs finally became a significant issue. Against the incumbent, Senator Richard Russell, and symbolically against President Franklin Roosevelt, Talmadge could not win. That year, former Georgia House speaker E. D. Rivers replaced Talmadge on the promise to bring a "little New Deal" of state relief programs to Georgia.[75] But Rivers spent beyond his state's capacity to pay and the voting public's willingness to fund. Many people in Georgia apparently still clung to the belief that poverty and dependence on government relief were moral failings. State legislators refused to pay for the redistribution of state resources. When the legislature refused to raise taxes and his administration began to collapse, Rivers declared martial law. Under charges of incompetence and corruption, he left the governor's mansion in disgrace. Talmadge, who had never really left Georgia political life, stepped into the vacuum, promising fiscal conservatism and the elimination of Georgia's state debt. In 1940 Georgians placed Talmadge and his economic platitudes back in the governor's office, indicating, if not organized labor's forgiveness of Talmadge, its inability to resist Talmadge-style campaigning and hold a grudge.[76]

As Floyd County's workers settled back into the old patterns of paternalism, northern textile union leaders rediscovered the conventional wisdom about southern workers. In the eyes of many union leaders, the militant "170,000" strikers had dissipated into a sea of unresponsive and seemingly anti-union millhands. Echoing Gompers's pronouncement in 1898, the TWUA's research director, upon returning from a trip south, reported to union leaders in 1939 that the obstacle to organizing the South was still the southern worker. In his words, the southern millhand was "a small town, petty individual . . . extremely provincial, petty, gossip-mongering," and "most suspicious of every outsider." Evidently, millhands preferred "to be left alone and isolated." Despite the thousands of workers who actually had supported the 1934 strike, northern leaders of the

[74] *Rome News-Tribune*, Sept. 21, 1937.

[75] Bartley, *Creation of Modern Georgia*, 190–94.

[76] Ibid., 190–94; William F. Holmes, "The 1920s and the New Deal," in *A History of Georgia*, ed. Kenneth Coleman (Athens: University of Georgia Press, 1977), 312–18.

labor movement fell back into the old pattern of thinking that the absence of unions and the overwhelming presence of mill paternalism corroborated southern exceptionalism.

But if the 1934 strike confirmed southern difference to northern union leaders, it must have also confirmed the temporary expedience of accepting paternalism and racial privilege to many of the South's white workers. In the 1930s the union, the mill managers, and Governor Talmadge all made big promises to southern workers. Paternalism had delivered at least small concessions in the form of welfare capitalism and the recognition of whiteness. Talmadge had misled strikers, but he unfailingly defended millhands' right to higher status among Georgia workers and consistently recognized their way of life as noble and worthwhile. The UTW and the 1934 strike had delivered very little.

The effects of paternalism, however, were enormously complex. Welfare capitalism, like the NRA, raised a variety of expectations. While all white workers shared in the wages of whiteness and paternalism, not all Floyd County workers internalized its rules. When World War II and wartime federal labor relations machinery drastically transformed the balance of power between workers and employers in Georgia, many Floyd County workers demonstrated that indeed they were willing to join a union and assert their class interests, but they would do so on their own terms.

Three

"So-Called Fair Employment": World War II and Whiteness

After the outbreak of World War II, the demands of patriotism and total war created new ideological and cultural conflicts in the insular communities of Floyd County. The first Roman casualty of World War II was that local trophy of boosterism, Rome's replica of the statue of the Capitoline wolf. Once heralded as "evidence of the favor of the great," the statue began provoking anonymous telephone threats in 1940, when Italy joined the Axis invasion of France. In a special meeting, the Rome City Commission decided the statue had to be removed from its marble base in front of the city auditorium, and once again Romulus and Remus were secreted away to storage, this time in the county courthouse basement. The statue's removal, commissioners announced, symbolized modern American Rome's "protest against ancient Rome's entry in the war against the democracies." Besides, town officials explained, the commission was concerned that if the statue had been dynamited, it "might have caused damage to the municipal building." After the bombing of Pearl Harbor and the U.S. entry into the military conflict, the city commission began to consider stronger measures of symbolic patriotism. In 1942 city leaders considered junking the whole statue and turning it over to the War Production Board's salvage division as scrap metal. Interviewing folks on the street, the *Rome News-Tribune* found most Floyd County citizens in agreement that the statue "would serve a much better use as bullets." Some Romans had never entirely accepted the statue "as a thing of beauty" anyway. "Melt it down and shoot it back," a salesman at a local car dealership told the paper. Although some Romans questioned the appropriateness of using a gift made in goodwill and peace to later shoot the giver, "it was decided in all cases that, after the way Italy joined in the war against this country, it wouldn't be exactly unfair to use the gift as the people saw fit." Fortunately for town boosters, the multimillion-dollar Tubize village and rayon plant, now American-owned and turned to military defense production, did not seem to present a similar conflict of conscience.[1]

[1] *Rome News-Tribune*, Aug. 7, 4, 1942; Reynolds, *Coosa River Valley*, 278–79.

But World War II presented other extraordinary—and extraordinarily problematic, from the perspective of the white South—opportunities for economic development and boosterism. In the early 1940s, federal defense projects and military contracts became the new capital to court, but federal attention also exacerbated conflicts between the American and "[white] Southern way of life." For as the U.S. military fought for the preservation of democracy abroad, non-southern political pressures to increase democracy at home accelerated. In Congress, a broadened mandate emerged behind African American civil rights that advocated measures such as a federal anti-lynching statute and the elimination of the poll tax. All federal reforms to combat racial discrimination—especially what southerners called the "so-called Fair Employment Practice Committee"—provoked bitter denunciations from politicians and employers across the South. Elimination of the color line in employment, many southerners claimed, threatened the whole system of segregation. In Rome, traditional defenders of the South's low-wage white industrial workforce charged that the FEPC was created as a "sinister" means of "punishing the [white] South merely for the gratification of colored politicians in the North." Even as southern "patriots" grabbed federal defense production contracts, southern *Textile Bulletin* editor and Dixiecrat David Clark charged that the FEPC's real purpose was "to force Southern [white] people to accept Negroes as equals, to work side by side with them and to admit them to hotels and restaurants."[2]

In practice, however, federal fair employment mandates did not alter many of the basic hiring practices of northwest Georgia's textile factories. In truly remarkable and significant ways, traditional leaders in Floyd County were able to shape the modernizing pressures of total war and federal policy into devices that maintained important elements of segregation and the low-wage economy. Maintenance of an all-white workforce in textiles, for example, emerged as a primary, if seldom acknowledged, goal of manpower policy. With what amounted to a federally sanctioned blacklist, Georgia bureaucrats, local management-labor boards, and mill managers used federal policy to preserve their traditional workforce in spite of a wartime boom economy that ordinarily would have pulled many Floyd County workers into more highly skilled and remunerative pursuits.

The war did, however, open up novel opportunities for working-class organization and political expression. Real economic recovery, full production, labor shortage, and meaningful federal intervention into labor relations created ideal conditions for union organization, and workers in two of the county's largest mills formed permanent unions for the first

[2] *Rome News-Tribune*, Apr. 5, 1945; *Textile Bulletin*, Oct. 1, 1945.

time. The expansion of economic power was also accompanied by an expansion of the franchise. In 1945 Georgia eliminated the poll tax, clearing the way for a vastly expanded working-class voice in Georgia politics. But the South's success in preserving basic elements of the regional market for labor meant that workers' organizations and subsequent political activity also bore the imprint of segregation and racial privilege. Thus, although historians are accustomed to thinking of World War II as the "seedtime" of the modern civil rights movement, essential ideas about southern workers, whiteness, and blackness remained in place. Even as the basis of citizenship changed, the fundamental structures of Georgia society and the racial identification of the Floyd County working class remained the same.

In 1940, almost a year before Japan's attack on Pearl Harbor and the United States' declaration of war, *Time* magazine reported a "defense boom in Dixie" as training camps, plant construction, and a newly invigorated textile industry quickly banished the depression from the American South. New payrolls "bounced from one merchant's cash register to another," the magazine author noted, widening the effects of industrial recovery and growth. At the close of the depression decade, defense-sector spending, war preparations, and foreign demand for American goods stimulated basic industries and lifted the economy nationwide. Within the first two years of the war, the federal defense budget alone grew larger than the gross national product a decade earlier. From 1939 to 1940, American unemployment dropped from over ten million to about four million. "Suddenly," *Atlanta Constitution* editor Ralph McGill observed, "it seemed, by 1942, everyone had money."[3]

Southern leaders, sensing an opportunity to complete industrial development plans cut short by the Great Depression, quickly seized the moment to recruit federal defense spending southward. Although early-twentieth-century concentration of labor-intensive, low-skill industry had ill prepared the South to capitalize on the initial war production boom, as early as 1940 the Southern Governors' Conference called upon the federal government to utilize the South's "vast reservoirs of natural resources and available labor." Individual governors and development agencies pressed the federal government for their "fair share" of war contracts, airfields, training camps, and defense plants. In 1941, leaders of the Southern Governors' Conference appointed a committee to lobby the president and

[3] *Time*, Feb. 17, 1941, 75–80, quoted in Tindall, *Emergence of the New South*, 694–95; Robert Zieger, *American Workers, American Unions, 1920–1985*, 2nd ed. (Baltimore: Johns Hopkins University Press, 1994), 62–63; Ralph McGill, *The South and the Southerner* (Boston: Little, Brown, 1959), 168.

the Office of Production Management. The National Resources Planning Board, with support from President Roosevelt, argued that the war effort should exploit the "large numbers of workers" available in "low-income area[s]" such as the South, which needed "supplementary employment opportunity." By 1942, shipyards, aircraft plants, and ordnance plants had sprung up across the South, representing over $4 billion of government and private investment. In 1944, War Production Board chairman Donald M. Nelson told an Atlanta audience, "A bird's eye view of large-scale Southern industry makes you feel that the South has rubbed Aladdin's lamp." The war finally accomplished what millions of New Deal federal dollars and dozens of southern platitudes about hard work and moral living had always promised but never delivered. Between 1940 and 1945, southern incomes increased by about 250 percent and the region's manufacturing capacity rose about 40 percent.[4]

The impact of new factories radiated beyond the borders of immediate plant locations, drawing workers for hundreds of miles. Although the war did not bring a new defense plant to Floyd County, for example, hundreds of local workers took advantage of new opportunities in Georgia and Alabama when two of the country's largest defense factories located within a hundred miles of Rome. Bell Aircraft brought a huge bomber and modification plant to Marietta, Georgia, about forty miles southeast of Rome, and Du Pont built the largest combination powder and explosive plant in the nation in Childersburg, Alabama. In the early war years, federal manpower officials estimated that more than a thousand people left Floyd County for jobs in shipyards, government arsenals, and the powder plant. The crush for housing and expanded city services in defense boomtowns encouraged many to stay put and commute. Many of Bell Aircraft's employees, for example, lived in Floyd County.[5]

The South's, and Floyd County's, largest industry also experienced an incredible stimulus from war production, for as leaders of the Textile Workers Union proudly proclaimed, "no less than iron and steel and chemicals and rubber, textiles have gone to war." While hostilities in Europe rapidly widened the market for American textile products, the increasing likelihood of a general draft in the United States promised even greater demands for textile goods to supply the army. The task of provid-

[4] Tindall, *Emergence of the New South*, 694–95; Gavin Wright, *Old South, New South: Revolutions in the Southern Economy since the Civil War* (New York: Basic Books, 1986), 240, 261.

[5] "Local Labor Market Survey, Rome, GA," May 1, 1942, Rome labor demand and supply reports folder, series 12, War Manpower Commission Records, Region VII, RG 211, National Archives, Southeast Region, East Point, Georgia (hereafter cited as WMC Region VII Records); John Corson, *Manpower for Victory: Total Mobilization for Total War* (New York: Farrar and Rinehart, 1943), 73; Dean Wood, interview with author, Sept. 10, 1994.

ing basic uniforms and supplies for millions of soldiers created an extraordinary demand for textile goods. Per soldier, the TWUA reported, the textile industry supplied over 122 yards of cotton cloth and 29 yards of woolen cloth just for uniforms. In the spring of 1943, for example, the army ordered 18 million undershirts, 10 million blankets, 78 million pairs of socks, 60 million yards of mosquito netting, and 18 million sleeping bags. The textile industry also manufactured many non-apparel products for the military, such as parachutes, gas masks, and rubberized rafts. Just as northern auto factories converted to war use, Floyd textile firms converted to meet military orders. Locally, the Anchor Duck and Pepperell mills manufactured cotton duck (an industrial fabric) and the Tubize factory manufactured parachute cloth. In the first three years of the war alone, Pepperell's profits totaled more than those of the entire period 1925–39.[6]

As early as 1942, federal manpower officials estimated that military production had "doubled the payrolls" in Floyd County, and "practically all of the increase has been in connection with textile mills." After years of short time and layoffs, Tubize, Pepperell, and Anchor Duck were all running three full shifts and considering how to obtain reserve workers. Although the federal government categorized the Floyd County labor market as an area with a surplus of labor, local employers had already begun preparing for possible labor shortages in 1942. Tubize managers reported, for example, a loss of two to four hundred workers to the Childersburg plant. Because Floyd County's textile mills employed majority male workforces, most managers were also concerned about losing workers to the military. Managers at both Pepperell and Anchor Duck were considering the possibility of running two twelve-hour shifts per day instead of three eight-hour shifts in order to keep production up with fewer workers. Pepperell had also begun to train a reserve labor force of women and children from the village who could step into jobs vacated by men leaving for the armed forces.[7]

Once the United States entered the war, government interest in war production prevented local employers from simply crafting local and private solutions to manpower problems. The attention of the vastly expanded federal government now turned upon matters of manpower and production with unprecedented scrutiny and authority. With almost 70 percent of the nation's industrial capacity operating under defense orders,

[6] Flamming, *Creating the Modern South*, 234–35; Jack Blicksilver, *Cotton Manufacturing in the Southeast: An Historical Analysis* (Atlanta: Georgia State University, School of Business Administration, Bureau of Business and Economic Research, 1959), 151; *Textile Labor*, February 1943.

[7] "Local Labor Market Survey, Rome, GA," May 1, 1942, pp. 4–9, Rome folder, box 18, series 12, WMC Region VII Records.

a series of new federal agencies, such as the Office of Production Management, the War Production Board, and the War Manpower Commission (WMC), closely monitored industrial production, labor supplies, and labor relations in factories holding federal contracts. A War Labor Board (WLB) assumed the judicial and mediating functions of the National Labor Relations Board. The WMC, in particular, carried the burden of meeting the vast military and industrial demand placed on American manpower, undertaking the monumental task of guaranteeing adequate labor supplies in all essential defense industries. Nationally, WMC officials began a massive propaganda campaign to recruit women into defense jobs and elicit voluntary compliance from employers.

At the community level, the most important agency handling the day-to-day affairs of employers and workers was the United States Employment Service (USES), a series of offices created in 1933 to administer federal New Deal programs for the unemployed. As early as 1940, the USES's information-gathering operations were turned to military and defense needs. After U.S. entry into the war, President Roosevelt federalized state employment offices for the duration of the manpower emergency so that they would operate, in the president's words, as the "corner grocery stores of our manpower system." Local USES offices provided a number of services to the war effort. For the WMC, the USES offices gathered information on labor supply and demand in local markets and essential industries and coordinated labor exchanges between communities in order to direct migratory workers to places where they were most needed. Unemployed workers registered at the USES, where they were interviewed and referred to employers. USES offices also provided voluntary services to employers, such as advice on how to break down jobs so that fewer skilled workers would be necessary; offered assistance in filling vacancies; and, significantly, helped employers keep present employees on the job.[8]

Given its role in the administration of manpower, the USES provides an extraordinary source on otherwise undocumented experiences of industrial workers in Rome. Because it reported local employer concerns and traced migratory patterns among workers, it recorded the impact of opportunity on the labor market and the region's low-wage workers, thus revealing how local administrators responded to fair employment. The labor market surveys were typically fifteen- to twenty-page reports compiled by area WMC supervisors or USES staff that contained a wealth of

[8] In the 1930s, state USES offices registered the unemployed, referred them to private employers and federal relief projects, and administered social security and unemployment. Leonard P. Adams, *The Public Employment Service in Transition, 1933–1968: Evolution of a Placement Service into a Manpower Agency* (Ithaca: Cornell University Press, 1969), 23–29.

information on local industries, workers, the activities of local manpower offices, and manpower policy. Individual workers rarely appeared in office reports, but the reports do provide insight into the collective working-class response to the market and hints about possible motivations for such behavior. Because the local manpower offices operated officially as a voluntary "service" to employers and employees during the war, the USES staff in Rome were concerned about the attitudes of both business and labor. Monthly reports included the USES interpretation of labor needs and employment trends, such as turnover and morale, as well as indications of employer preferences and personnel procedure. As the pivot between federal policy, local workers, and employers, USES reports also revealed the goals and ideas that governed the local implementation of policy. Officials' race-, gender-, and regionally based assumptions about workers, as well as textile employers' preferences for what kind of worker would replace enlistees, for example, were evident throughout the reports.

Initially, the USES office in Rome, which administered the Floyd County labor market, worked primarily as an information gatherer. Unemployment in 1940 had been so high that textile manufacturers filled extra shifts without difficulty for at least two years, despite out-migration and additional local demand. The personnel manager at the Tubize mill, for example, informed the USES in 1942 that he had "more acceptable applicants in his waiting file than he [could] possibly use."[9]

Although early USES reports generally did not dwell on the racial implications of hiring policy, field supervisors' reports indicated that new hires respected the traditional racial market for labor, as "there are no Negroes used in manufacturing, except as common labor." The Brighton Mills in Shannon informed the USES that they had created a reserve force by training every unemployed resident of the mill village. Given the mandates of segregation, that reserve force was certainly all white. Most local mill managers, the office reported to the WMC, preferred to replace workers with "[white] women, physically handicapped, draft deferred and persons living in close proximity to their establishments." Anchor Duck, for example, was "replacing all men lost with women where possible." While employment in the textile industry increased by over a third between 1940 and 1943, women's share of textile jobs increased from 38 to 43 percent. Black women, however, were still excluded. By 1943 the textile industry employed a total of 8,972 people, 3,834 of whom were white women.[10]

[9] "Local Labor Market Survey, Rome, GA," May 1, 1942, pp. 4–9, 13, Rome folder, series 12; State Office field supervisor's report, April 1942, pp. 1–3, Rome folder, series 19; both in WMC Region VII Records.

[10] "Local Labor Market Survey, Rome, GA," May 1, 1942, pp. 4–9, 13, Rome folder, series 12; state office field supervisor's report, April 1942, pp. 1–3, Rome folder, series 19;

Although mill managers assumed that women could easily fill their needs as a surplus workforce, wartime work was a mixed blessing for many working-class women in Floyd County. Even when the war opened up new opportunities for waged work or promotion, the heavy workloads and hours that accompanied defense production represented a substantial burden, particularly for women with responsibilities outside the workplace. WMC officials usually assumed that recruiting women was a matter of making the right kind of appeal. Recruiting efforts centered on flyers, direct mail, and publicity, but not until 1943 did the USES consider day care a "community problem." Local mills did not establish nurseries or any arrangement for child care until the end of 1943, and even then existing facilities were sorely inadequate. Tubize established a twenty-four-hour day-care center that provided care for forty children of working mothers on each shift. A government-run nursery school under the supervision of the Floyd County schools in southwest Rome, also established in 1943, provided care to children of working mothers at the Anchor Mill. Pepperell provided only kindergarten, and management reported that although the "problem was being studied," employers had reached "no conclusion." Local WMC authorities reckoned that accommodation for as many as five hundred children would be required but took no further action. Many working mothers were forced to find individual solutions, as they had before the war, such as leaving a child with a family member, a teenager, or sometimes a black baby-sitter or housecleaner.[11]

For younger or single white women displaced from other jobs or taking their first "outside" job, the wartime boom in textiles provided opportunities for advancement ordinarily closed to them. Dean Wood, for example, walked out on her job as a sewer in a garment factory and found a better and higher-paying job almost immediately at the Tubize mill. Before the war, Tubize had refused to hire Wood because managers thought she was too frail for the work, but during the war she got a permanent job that she kept for many years afterward. Other women took their first waged jobs or left work on the family farm for the first time. Claudie Knowles, for example, took her job at the Lindale mill in 1940 at the age of nineteen. The oldest daughter in her family and, in her words, her "Daddy's oldest son," Knowles had always worked on her father's small dairy farm. Before she went to the Lindale mill, Knowles had done a little of everything—cut wood, plowed with a tractor, "cut hay, raked hay,

---

both in WMC Region VII Records. Increase in employment calculated from a comparison of the 1940 census with the WMC's 1943 report. U.S. Bureau of the Census, *Census of Population: 1940*, vol. 2, pt. 2, p. 265; Rome labor market report, June 15, 1943, p. 7, Rome folder, series 12, WMC Region VII Records.

[11] Labor market report, Aug. 18, 1943, p. 14, Rome folder, series 12, WMC Region VII Records.

helped bale hay, hauled hay . . . you name it." Since the age of fifteen she had driven her father's delivery truck. But in 1940, she said, "things were beginning to look bad about World War II, so I went to work in the mill." Knowles was "the first woman they ever taught on a man's job" in the Pepperell mill spinning room. Although she found a "full job" (the ordinary amount of work assigned to a man) "too heavy," she recalled that "sometimes . . . I was the best they had, and I did what I could with it." She also remembered that women got paid less than men for doing the same work. While an average male textile employee earned 49.1 cents an hour, an average female textile worker earned only 44.8 cents an hour, almost 10 percent less.[12]

In the first three years of war production, enough women like Knowles took jobs to prevent serious textile labor shortages, but Floyd County's other major industry, cotton agriculture, experienced the flip side of the defense industry boom as temporary farm labor was the first job abandoned. After 1940, cotton growers who had traditionally relied upon the availability of an underemployed, low-wage workforce experienced novel and serious annual shortages of agricultural labor, especially during the cotton cutting and picking seasons. Farm employers relied heavily on the services of the USES to find tenants, croppers, and common laborers.[13] Between October and December 1942, for example, the USES reported a demand for sixteen hundred temporary workers to pick cotton. In Cedartown the shortage became so serious that farmers feared crops would rot in the fields until the USES recruited twenty-two Boy Scouts to work for a local farmer. Although the Rome USES continuously processed applications and made referrals, records indicated a chronic deficit of registered job applicants willing to do farm labor against unfilled "orders" from employers. On other occasions the USES would bring an employer and worker together but the worker would refuse the job.

In the case of male manpower, all officials agreed on the source of the problem. The "difficulty" filling farm labor orders, the Rome USES field supervisor explained to the state employment office, was "due to the low rate of pay." As it had been in the 1930s, common labor on the farm, even white labor, earned paltry wages. In 1942 farm labor paid only "$1 a day and as low as $15 and $21 dollars per month" for long hours and more physically taxing work than most factory jobs. The daily farm wage, which did not have a minimum specified under the Fair Labor Standards Act, was less than one-third of the lowest average textile operator's wage of forty cents per hour. Moreover, farm employees were often expected to work from sunup to sundown. Some farm tenants also complained

[12] Claudie Knowles, interview with author, June 28, 1994; Wood interview.

[13] Administration of farm manpower was removed from USES jurisdiction in 1943.

that even with such meager monthly salaries, planters who promised fuel, house rent, water, wood, and other supplies tried to charge them two to three dollars a month for these necessities.[14]

A more sensitive and permanent problem for WMC and USES officials, however, was race. President Roosevelt and members of the war mobilization committees had always supported the principle of fair employment, and it became official policy in 1941 with Executive Order 8802, the first major piece of federal civil rights action since Reconstruction. A response to pressure from African American labor leaders concerned about discrimination against black workers in defense industries and the armed services, President Roosevelt's order declared that job training programs, manufacturers holding government contracts, and government agencies were not allowed to discriminate on the basis of race. In other words, federal policy specifically forbade the kind of employment discrimination that was standard practice in southern textile mills. The executive order also created the Fair Employment Practices Commission to investigate complaints.[15]

In spite of federal antidiscrimination mandates, the Rome USES office managed to operate throughout the first half of the war without disturbing the racial market for Floyd County labor or violating federal policy. In 1942 the field supervisor advised local employment office workers to "be careful not to encourage race discrimination." Staff members taking employment orders were directed not to "indicate [racial] preference unless explicitly expressed by the employer." In practice, however, employers usually did request employees by race and sex, and in actuality the USES referral program operated around a whole system of racial and gender classification. While noting practical information on workers' skills, labor market surveys of available workers also always broke down the supply into categories of male, female, black, and white. Georgia USES officials regularly estimated the demand for workers according to what sort of workers were deemed appropriate for each job. In 1943, for example, the director for the Georgia USES wrote the regional director of the WMC to inform him that Rome would need a total of 960 more workers—319 white men, 327 black men, 238 white women, and 76 black women. The Rome USES also broke down the supply of labor, for

[14] Field supervisor's report, Rome, May 18, 1942, p. 4, Rome folder, series 12; local labor market survey, Rome, May 1, 1942, p. 15, series 12; field supervisor's monthly report, Cedartown, Georgia, Aug. 11, 1942, Cedartown folder, series 19; all in WMC Region VII Records.

[15] Merle E. Reed, *Seedtime for the Modern Civil Rights Movement: The President's Committee on Fair Employment Practice, 1941–46* (Baton Rouge: Louisiana State University Press, 1991), 12–16.

example, as "2,850 white male, 400 negro male, 2,003 white female and 200 negro female."[16]

Technically, Georgia supervisors of the WMC and USES manpower efforts did not explicitly violate federal procedures governing race and employment. Supervisors conscientiously issued the appropriate reminders about nondiscrimination, and Rome's reports to the state office dutifully reported on local racial practices. However, Rome manpower officials observed only the most superficial aspects of fair employment, and supervisors' positive reports relied upon only the most shallow measures of equal treatment. In July 1942, for example, a field supervisor visiting the Rome office for an annual report informed the regional WMC that he "saw no evidence of race discrimination." As proof, he noted that "both negroes and whites enter through the front door and each receives the same treatment and service from the office." The office did not "refrain from the referral of qualified Negroes," the supervisor reported.[17]

Fairness, however, always received less priority than established patterns of segregation. Staff reports always assumed that plants would hire either blacks or whites, but never employ the two together. In 1943, for example, the Rome USES reported to the WMC that "the employment of nonwhites . . . is relatively small and practically consists of common labor jobs, such as cotton truckers, bale openers, truck driver helpers, etc. There are 2 reasons for this—one is custom and the other is the non-availability of colored labor in sufficient quantities to use nonwhites in more advanced work." The smaller number of nonwhite workers, who represented only about 15 percent of the total workforce, frequently served as an excuse for the WMC and employers to recruit whites only. Ratios of whites to nonwhites, the USES explained, "encouraged employers to concentrate on white labor due to it being available in greater quantities." USES officials also implied indirectly that the reason they did not refer African American workers was that they were unqualified, explaining on another occasion that "most [of] the nonwhites are unskilled." In reality most workers of all races in Floyd County were unskilled, but the USES did not feel it necessary to make the same observation about the hundreds of white women recruited for textiles.[18]

[16] Rome labor market surveys, May 1, 1942, Apr. 15, 1943; Thomas. H. Quigley to B. F. Ashe, May 22, 1943; both in Rome folder, series 12, WMC Region VII Records. For an example of textile employer preferences, see P. D. Ostrander, Superintendent, Goodyear Clearwater Mills, to Frank Constangy, Deputy Regional Director, WMC, May 17, 1944, Cedartown folder, series 12, ibid. Ostrander informed Constangy that his Cedartown plant needed sixty white men, three negro men, seventy-two white women, and no black women to meet maximum production.

[17] W. B. Klugh, "Annual Report," July 11, 1942, Rome folder, box 4, series 19, ibid.

[18] Labor Market Report, Apr. 15, 1943, p. 8; and Labor Market Report, Oct. 18, 1943, p. 12; both in Rome folder, series 12, ibid.

The reluctance of national USES officers to cooperate with the FEPC to enforce federal fair employment policy undoubtedly contributed to noncompliance in Floyd County. Although the USES national director, John J. Corson, adamantly supported nondiscriminatory use of all manpower in theory, he was also averse to making the local USES offices the policemen for fair employment. Corson feared that if state USES offices tried to enforce FEPC policy, many employers would stop using the placement services and perhaps hinder the war effort. Moreover, many local employment officers, including those in Rome, identified and sympathized with employers and were reluctant to antagonize them. Under pressure from other, more idealistic USES and WMC officers, Corson finally issued a notice to all USES personnel defining discrimination and urging staff members to discourage employers from prejudice. However, unless local USES staffers were interested in eliminating discrimination or were compelled in any way to do so by national staff, a memo was worthless.[19]

Local manpower policy and practice in Floyd County also reflected customary white southern ideas about race and gender because WMC bureaucracies in Georgia drew upon traditional sources of authority in the South and men close to the textile industry. One regional director of the Georgia WMC, for example, was Atlanta corporate attorney Frank Constangy, one of the most notorious anti-union lawyers in the South, whose practice represented several mill managements in northwest Georgia. In Rome, the Floyd County USES cooperated with an area management-labor board that was entrusted by the WMC and USES with carrying out the "governing actions" for the Rome manpower area. It included four local mill managers and *Rome News-Tribune* editor and former chamber of commerce president J. R. Hornady. Despite the fact that textiles overshadowed all other industries in terms of importance to the war effort, labor representatives included no textile workers. The industry's principal representative was Donigan Dean Towers, general manager of the Anchor Duck Mills. Not surprisingly, board decisions respected the traditional norms that had historically shaped local labor relations, such as the preponderance of low-wage jobs and the racial market for labor.[20]

Board member J. R. Hornady, for example, was a staunch booster and defender of such southern traditions as white supremacy, the North-South wage differential, and paternalism. As described by his successor to the

[19] Reed, *Seedtime for the Modern Civil Rights Movement*, 63–65; Corson, *Manpower for Victory*, 135–40.

[20] Rome Management-Labor Committee membership list, ca. November 1944; minutes of first meeting, Management-Labor Committee, USES, Rome, Georgia, July 12, 1944; both in Rome Area Mgt.-Labor Committee folder, series 14, WMC Region VII Records.

presidency of the chamber of commerce, Hornady was a man who "loved his section of the country more than life itself." As editor of Rome's only daily newspaper and a prominent member of the community, Hornady attempted to shape both public opinion and his community. He spearheaded industrial development through the chamber of commerce and the Coosa-Alabama Rivers Improvement Association, serving as a leader of each and rallying public support through his newspaper columns. In the 1940s, Hornady became perhaps the most visible and outspoken defender of the white South in northwest Georgia via his *News-Tribune* editorial page, frequent public lectures, and a daily commentary on Floyd County radio station WLAQ. He tirelessly denounced the FEPC, civil rights "agitators," unions, and all critics of the South. "So-called" fair employment policies particularly nettled Hornady. Oblivious to the contradictions, Hornady declared the FEPC especially pernicious in the context of World War II. The FEPC, he argued "means the introduction of racial warfare upon thousands of fronts in this country at the very time when the Nation is exerting itself to bring peace to the World and securely establish the principles of democracy." The Rome Area Management-Labor Board's actions, guided by the principles of meeting production goals while preserving segregation, indicated the representative nature of Hornady's views.[21]

In spite of the USES's ability to circumvent federal policy in practice, civil rights measures, especially the FEPC, provoked a vociferous opposition and an increasing defensiveness from white southerners and employers. Old resentments of federal intrusions into social and employment matters festering among southern Democrats since the New Deal erupted in opposition to any measure that seemed to threaten, or even alter, the segregated status quo. Virtually all southern congressmen stood solidly in opposition to war-inspired attempts to widen democracy at home. Georgia senator Richard Russell, for example, built a strong reputation on his opposition to anti-lynching measures and the FEPC. Rather than oppose civil rights per se, white southern opposition was often couched in principled defenses of state's rights or "constitutional" government. Rome's Hornady, for example, who was an outspoken opponent of lynching, also opposed anti-lynch law proposals as an effort "to fasten a larger measure of Federal control over law enforcement in the South." Southern senators used the filibuster to defeat both anti-lynching and anti–poll tax bills introduced during the war. Resistance to civil rights measures in employment was particularly fierce, provoking a virtual "anti-FEPC gab fest in the Senate," in the words of author and activist Stetson Kennedy.[22]

[21] *Rome News-Tribune*, Mar. 2, 1948.

[22] Stetson Kennedy, *Southern Exposure* (New York: Doubleday, 1946), 130–32, quote from 325.

Opposition to the FEPC on the ground level in Georgia was also intense. When *Atlanta Constitution* editor Ralph McGill warned the FEPC director that he feared the opening of the regional FEPC office in Atlanta might cause a riot, he was only slightly exaggerating the extent of white anger. In 1942, when the office opened, the city council protested that the agency "planned mixed employment of the races in one of the office buildings" and called upon southern congressmen to "insist upon the removal of said office from the city of Atlanta." Senator Russell obliged and made an attack on the FEPC in the U.S. Congress, for which he received laudatory recognition from the council. When the regional office hired a black secretary, white female employees protested to the building owner and the governor about sharing a bathroom with her. The Southern Industrial Trades Association sent a letter to the FEPC that maligned the stenographer as a "brazen Negress" and condemned Georgia FEPC director Bruce Hunt as a "carpetbagger."[23]

Eugene Talmadge likewise made tremendous political capital out of opposition to fair employment. Attacking the policy on the stump and in print, Talmadge also published a series of cartoons in the *Statesman* that graphically displayed the basis of white opposition. In these figurative editorials, white Georgians were shown exactly what the logical consequences of fair employment would be: a world turned upside down, with blacks, *as whites saw them*, in positions of authority and control. One *Statesman* cartoon, for example, portrayed a scene that would have been almost unimaginable for white Georgians in the 1940s. It depicts a black man as an FEPC officer giving dictation, in dialect, to a white woman. On his left, an African American woman portrayed in blackface and a servant's uniform berates a much shorter white man. As the white man stands humbled, hat in hand, she shouts, "Don't 'm'am' me! You's *fired*!" Although drawing them in blackface, wearing zoot suits and maid uniforms, and speaking in dialect would have made it clear to any reader which were the black characters, the artist, underlining the absurdity, often wrote "White" on the white figures. The cartoons also indicated how important jobs were to white Georgians' conceptions of race, as black and white figures were usually portrayed in "uniforms" appropriate to their race. White figures—at least those who were not identified as part of the FEPC, and presumably representative of the good white folk of the South—were drawn with nondescript office clothes, suits, ties, and dresses. Black male figures lording it over their former bosses smoked cigars and were portrayed in the symbolically unpatriotic zoot suit or otherwise clownish attire. Black women were always drawn as maids. One cartoon of a black and a white man conspiring in an FEPC office

[23] Ibid., 318–20; Reed, *Seedtime for the Modern Civil Rights Movement*, 222–26.

Figure 2. Cartoon appearing in Eugene Talmadge's newspaper, *The Statesman*, September 28, 1944. The FEPC as Talmadge saw it—a world turned upside down, where black maids fired white male executives, and black office men dictated to white secretaries. Note how cartoon figures are dressed.

made it clear that the white man was not a southerner by equipping him with a carpetbag labeled "F.E.P.C."[24]

Resistance to the FEPC in Rome was equally fervent and public. In July 1942, when Alabama governor Frank Dixon made a heavily publicized refusal to accept government contracts at state-owned textile factories because of a federal contract clause on discrimination, Rome leaders and other southerners immediately came to his defense. Earning praise from Talmadge, Dixon charged that the clause concerning discrimination made a "clear intimation . . . that unless the Southern [white] people change their way of living and abandon the principle of segregation, they would be forced to do so by Federal Government." Should Alabama sign the contract to produce almost two million yards of cloth for the army, Dixon warned, they must also expect "fair employment practice committee immediately to descend upon the State and demand that Negroes be put in positions of responsibility." About two weeks later, the *Rome News-Tribune* published a photograph of the members of the FEPC on the front page, and in case readers failed to inspect the photograph closely, pointed

[24] See, for example, *Statesman*, Sept. 21, 29, Oct. 12, 19, 26, 1944.

Figure 3. Eugene Talmadge commentary on the Atlanta FEPC office, where a cigar-smoking black man and race-mixing "carpetbagger" lord it over the southern white folk. Note the carpetbag labeled "FEPC" and the blackface. *The Statesman*, October 12, 1944.

out in the cutline that "the person second from the left is a 'Chocolate Drop' from Chicago, while the one fifth from the left is a big 'Tar Baby.' " A *News-Tribune* editorial, rerouted to the front page, commended Dixon for "one of the noblest defenses of white supremacy that has resounded throughout the South for many a moon" and proclaimed his statement a "bold utterance, worthy of the best that ever fell from the lips of great Southern leaders like Robert Toombs, Alexander Stephens, John B. Gordon, Henry Grady and other immortals." Dixon, the *News-Tribune* noted approvingly, "realized the evils that might result from having members of both races working in the same weaving department."[25]

The FEPC made front-page news in Rome again when garment makers in Floyd County and elsewhere in Georgia received notice from a "government agent" in August 1942 that they were expected to *comply* with the antidiscrimination clause in their current contracts. Perhaps because southern employers had a history of selectively "misunderstanding" federal policies, the letter explained exactly what the clause meant, including the elimination of references to race on employment applications and of

[25] *Rome News-Tribune*, July 23, Aug. 10, Sept. 4, 1942.

Figure 4. Cartoon appearing in Eugene Talmadge's newspaper, *The Statesman*, October 26, 1944. In case the exaggerated blackface and dialect were not enough to clue white readers in to the depiction of race, the boss is named "Rastus Black" and the "white secretary" is labeled as such.

any sort of racial bias in recruitment, promotion, and hiring. Rome employers and the local USES, of course, were guilty of every single offense. Local supporters of Governor Talmadge reassured the white public, however, that they did not expect enforcement to "be undertaken in earnest until after the September primary" because "the racial issue" was so central to the 1942 gubernatorial campaign. Lest any white readers miss the significance of the federal government's announcement to segregation and southern racial taboos, the *News-Tribune* reminded them that the garment factories in question "at present employ white women."[26]

[26] In October 1942, USES personnel also received a memo from the national director defining discrimination specifically, at the urging of the FEPC. Reed, *Seedtime for the Modern Civil Rights Movement*, 65; *Rome News-Tribune*, Aug. 30, 1942.

Despite the typical Talmadge ballyhoo, the governor and his challenger, Ellis Arnall, were essentially in agreement on the necessity of maintaining segregation. It was actually Talmadge's handling of a race-related incident in the state university system that had become a divisive, but not necessarily popular, issue in 1942. Talmadge had taken it upon himself to purge the University of Georgia system of "foreign professors trying to destroy the sacred traditions of the South," namely, segregated education. Among the "foreigners" Talmadge targeted for removal were professors educated in the Midwest or identified with the Rosenwald Fund, which Talmadge labeled "Jew money for niggers." In May 1942 the governor spearheaded a move among the university's board of regents to fire the president of the Statesboro Teachers College, the dean of the University of Georgia College of Education, and eight other university employees. He forced several members of the board of regents to resign. While Talmadge held highly publicized and inflammatory hearings in Atlanta, a state committee searched for "subversive" books among the public school textbook list and the university libraries. In response, the Southern Association of Colleges and Secondary Schools and other educational organizations removed accreditation from ten schools in the University of Georgia system for "unprecedented and unjustifiable political interference."[27]

The reaction from the Georgia public spanned the spectrum from outraged protest by university students, their parents, and Atlanta liberals to congratulatory letters from Talmadge's rural wool-hat boys and other white supremacists. The *Rome News-Tribune*, for example, sided with Talmadge, dismissing accreditation organizations as "bumptious and presumptuous highbrows." Mocking the organization's authority with a decidedly racial dig, the *News-Tribune* suggested that "shoe shine parlors" and "colored bus boys who handle dishes in restaurants" had the same power to "form an association to 'accredit.' " As the 1942 primary approached and criticism of the governor mounted, Talmadge refused to compromise, insisting that the purge had been necessary in the larger battle to defend segregation. In his opening campaign speech, Talmadge warned voters of "carpetbaggers" and of "subtle influences" trying to "creep in" and destroy southern tradition. On the campaign trail Talmadge played up the issue as he had in 1934, informing an audience in Moultrie, for example, "before God, friend, the niggers will never go to a school which is white while I am Governor."[28]

Notwithstanding his equally outspoken opposition to integration, Talmadge's major opponent in the 1942 primary, Georgia attorney general

[27] Bartley, *Creation of Modern Georgia*, 193–95; Anderson, *Wild Man from Sugar Creek*, 197–201.

[28] Anderson, *Wild Man from Sugar Creek*, 200, 207; *Rome News-Tribune*, Aug. 2, 1942.

Ellis G. Arnall, seized upon the university scandal. To those who might be swayed by Talmadge's race-baiting, Arnall gave assurance to voters that he did not believe in "racial coeducation." However, in some minor but qualitative respects, the character of Arnall's racism did differ from that of Talmadge, even in the eyes of Georgia's black community. The African American newspaper *Atlanta World*, for example, noted that the "mere fact that he [Arnall] does not carry on an active campaign of hate toward them [African Americans] is a real improvement over his predecessor." Nevertheless, Arnall did find it necessary to defend his credentials as a white supremacist, telling an audience in Coweta County that "any nigger who tried to enter the [white] university would not be in existence [the] next day." Arnall attempted to persuade voters that the choice was not between segregation and integration, but between accredited and nonaccredited segregated schools—and between honest, respectable government on the one hand and Talmadge demagoguery on the other.[29]

The strength of the Talmadge argument, and the foundation of much of the governor's support in Rome and elsewhere in Georgia, lay in his ability to persuade white Georgians that the influence of "foreigners" in the state university system was but another symptom of a widespread assault on segregation. On the campaign trail, Talmadge linked opposition to any encroachment on segregation, such as the FEPC or the integration of the armed services, to his candidacy. As he argued to an audience in northwest Georgia, many "outsiders" were interested in "breaking down" the South's racial traditions. "The negro people up north," he informed another audience, "are accusing Governor Dixon of Alabama and Talmadge of Georgia of being the champions of white supremacy. I am proud of it and I accept the title." He applauded Dixon's refusal of the government textile contract and promised, "as long as I am governor of Georgia, no negro foreman is ever going to give orders to our white girls and boys." The *News-Tribune* agreed, endorsing Talmadge and specifically citing the threat of the FEPC. How could Arnall dismiss the "racial equality drive" as "spurious," the local editorial page fumed, when "every cotton mill whether in Rome or Richmond, that has a war contract is told to subscribe to the famous racial equality cause"? The governor's responsibility, the paper asserted, was to meet "this problem of today face on . . . combatting a widespread interracial movement that, unless checked can only lead to repetition of the chapter of American history known as 'Reconstruction Days.' "[30]

[29] *Rome News-Tribune*, Aug. 2, 5, 1942; Harold Paulk Henderson, *The Politics of Change in Georgia: A Political Biography of Ellis Arnall* (Athens: University of Georgia Press, 1991), 140–41.

[30] *Rome News-Tribune*, Aug. 2, 7, 9, 1942.

In spite of Talmadge's association with white supremacy, many white voters in Floyd County and the rest of Georgia were apparently unconvinced by Talmadge doomsday rhetoric about segregation. Moreover, the governor had other political liabilities in 1942. Whether or not working-class folk cared about the accreditation of the university system, "the better element," an emerging coalition of white urban elites, formed the core of a growing opposition to Talmadgism. Some Georgia observers speculated that Talmadge overplayed the race issue and "soured" his candidacy. Though Arnall had also taken pains to show his commitment to the segregated "Southern way of life," he did so without appearing as mean-spirited or embarrassing to the state of Georgia.[31]

In September, Arnall was elected with 261 unit votes, winning almost all of the midsize counties, including Floyd, all the large urban counties, and half of the small, two-unit counties. Most political commentators credited the university issue for Talmadge's defeat, but in a place like Rome, where a minority of people had personal ties to the university and less than 2 percent of the population attended college, Arnall's victory may have also indicated a movement away from Talmadgism. Even in the mill village of Lindale, always a Talmadge stronghold, many working-class voters felt that Talmadge had embarrassed the state of Georgia. Claudie Knowles remembered "a good bit" of support for Talmadge in Lindale. "A lot of people thought he should have been president." Knowles herself did not care for Talmadge, who, in her opinion, bore a dangerous resemblance to Louisiana demagogue Huey Long. In 1942 most voting residents of Lindale apparently agreed with Knowles. Talmadge received only 163 votes to Arnall's 277 in Lindale. Just as white southerners argued throughout the 1940s that an anti-lynching bill made the South look bad, evidently many also believed that Talmadge's meddling in the university system made Georgia look bad. To the uptown crowd or the "better element," Talmadge demagoguery must have seemed particularly egregious at a time when the state was desperately trying to catch up with the rest of the industrialized nation. Arnall's victory cannot, however, be interpreted as any indication of racial liberalism. Arnall himself repeatedly denounced rumors that he favored integrated education as "the biggest lie and the most bunk and baloney that has ever been thought up." Raised in a north Georgia merchant and textile family, Arnall was an avid proponent of economic growth and industrial development and simply the kind of segregationist that white Georgians felt more comfortable with in the 1940s.[32]

[31] Henderson, *Politics of Change*, 42–50.

[32] Knowles interview; Henderson, *Politics of Change*, 49.

The persistence of rural support for Talmadge, in combination with a generally low turnout, also indicated the limited nature of the shift from Talmadge ruralism to Arnall respectability. Indeed, the 1942 Floyd County gubernatorial vote closely followed a straight urban-rural split within Floyd County's nineteen voting precincts. For example, six of the seven voting districts surrounding Rome, including the Lindale and Shannon districts, cast majority votes for Arnall. Nine of twelve rural districts, with predominantly a rural-farm population, went to Talmadge (see table 1). Overall, Arnall received more than two-thirds of the vote, winning 2,809 to Talmadge's 1,766, and the bulk of his majority came from town voters in Rome, who cast twice as many votes for Arnall as for Talmadge. The difference between urban and rural voters is particularly striking when the county vote is considered without the returns from Floyd's most populous and "urban" districts. With the mill and town votes excluded, for example, the Floyd County farm population favored Talmadge 586 to 489. Given the high rate of rural support for Talmadge and the generally low turnout (only 55 percent of the eligible population actually cast ballots), Arnall's victory could not be interpreted as a clear defection from Talmadgism.[33]

Although Arnall had not been elected with a mandate for any major social changes, he was an astute politician. By clever combinations of public relations and outright manipulation, his administration, the first in Georgia history to serve the new four-year term, presided over a series of changes that vastly expanded the state's notoriously restrictive franchise. First, in 1943, Arnall overcame heavy opposition and persuaded the legislature to make Georgia the first state to lower the voting age to eighteen in order to enfranchise soldiers. Then, in 1945, Arnall persuaded the legislature to do away with the poll tax. Evidently many Georgia Democrats did not see the poll tax as an exclusively racial issue, and many leading Georgia politicians in the U.S. Senate and House, as well as Talmadge, had already come out in favor of repeal. Arnall tried to make the issue one of southern pride, telling Georgia's state legislators that he was tired of seeing Georgia "kicked about in Congress" over the poll tax. He assured the legislature that he saw "no danger" of blacks voting as long as the state maintained the white primary, and he finally threatened that if they did not repeal, he would do so by executive order. The bill passed and Georgia became the fourth southern state to eliminate the poll tax.[34]

[33] By rural districts I mean those with a majority farm population according to the 1940 census. Figures on voting were calculated from a comparison of the 1940 census and the 1942 primary returns from *Rome News-Tribune*, Sept. 11, 1942; U.S. Bureau of the Census, *Census of Population: 1940*, vol. 2, pt. 2, pp. 219, 237, 328–29.

[34] Henderson, *Politics of Change*, 84–85, 90–92; Ellis Arnall, *The Shore Dimly Seen* (Philadelphia: Lippincott, 1946), 51; Ellis Arnall, interview by James F. Cook, Mar. 25, Apr. 17, 1986, Georgia Government Documentation Project, Southern Labor Archives, Atlanta.

TABLE 1.
Distribution of Urban-Rural Votes in Floyd County 1946 Gubernatorial Election (Talmadge districts in bold)

Militia District (precinct)	*Total Population*	*Percent Rural Farm*	*Talmadge Vote*	*Armall Vote*
Armuchee	**1,191**	**63**	**79**	31
Barkers	1,390	99.9	15	15
Cave Springs	**2,075**	**54**	**45**	37
Chulio	**1,758**	**87**	**47**	40
Etowah	**1,751**	**87**	**38**	28
Everett Springs	**465**	**92**	**51**	7
Floyd Springs	**452**	**99.7**	**43**	20
Fosters Mill	**543**	**98**	**37**	4
Glenwood	1,022	18	29	52
Howells	**1,405**	**67**	**60**	20
Lindale	5,470	2	163	277
Livingston	**749**	**100**	**24**	9
Mt. Alto	1,852	43	50	69
North Carolina	1,520	99	36	60
Riverside [Tubize)	1,972	9	43	134
Rome	26,282	0	876	1,809
Texas Valley	482	98	21	22
Van's Valley	1,887	29	11	25
Watters [Shannon]	3,875	33	98	100
			1,766	2,809

Sources: U.S. Bureau of the Census, *Census of Population: 1940*, vol. 2, *Characteristics of the Population*, pt. 2, *Florida-Iowa*, 328–29; Election returns, *Rome News-Tribune*, Sept. 11, 1942.

Meanwhile, the U.S. Supreme Court heard a case with an even greater bearing on southern democracy. In the spring of 1944, the Court's decision in *Smith v. Allright* declared the Texas white Democratic primary in violation of the Fifteenth Amendment. Across the South, white Democrats responded with bitter criticism and hastily concocted schemes to circumvent a similar ruling in their home states. Georgia's legislature, for example, considered removing any reference to the primary from the state constitution, which would theoretically remove it from the jurisdiction of the Fifteenth Amendment. While Arnall initially responded with silence, even Florida senator Claude Pepper, one of the most liberal supporters of the New Deal in the South, proclaimed defiantly that "the South will allow nothing to impair white supremacy." In the meantime, Georgia's white Democrats expeditiously and conveniently decided that *Smith v. Allright* did not apply to Georgia, and ruled that despite the Court, the 1944 Georgia primaries would also be white.[35]

Most Georgia Democrats had not believed that the white primary would be affected by *Smith v. Allright* when they eliminated the poll tax, but in 1945 a black resident of Columbus challenged Georgia's white primary in federal court and won. Although the state of Georgia appealed, with Arnall's support, the lower federal court was upheld again. When the U.S. Supreme Court declined to hear the case, Arnall made an announcement startling to many white Georgians. In a public statement in 1946, Arnall declared, "I will not be a party to any subterfuge or 'scheme' designed to nullify the orders of the courts," and he threatened to veto any legislation repealing laws by a self-convened session. Although Arnall believed that "the great mass of Georgia citizens" supported his decision to abide by the courts, other white Democratic leaders believed it was a serious mistake. Arnall admitted that among the "heavy" amount of mail he received on the subject, some of the letters were "mildly abusive in nature; a few were more violent."[36]

Georgia was now the only deep South state without a poll tax or a plan to circumvent *Smith v. Allright.* When Arnall became governor, there were about 500,000 qualified voters. By the end of his term, the Georgia electorate had doubled to over one million voters. Of the state's new voters, 150,000 were black. Just two days after Arnall made his announcement, Eugene Talmadge announced his candidacy for governor yet again, this time on the promise of restoring the white primary.[37]

In contrast to Arnall's relatively quick and easy successes at democratizing Georgia's franchise from 1943 to 1945, fair employment continued to

[35] Henderson, *Politics of Change*, 141–42.

[36] Ibid., 141–44; Arnall, *The Shore Dimly Seen*, 59–60.

[37] Henderson, *Politics of Change*, 90–92.

be stymied by the hands of local WMC administrators. As the manpower shortage and WMC warnings about discrimination seemed to become more serious, however, the struggle against fair employment did become more complicated. By the spring of 1943, the construction of a new U.S. Army hospital in Rome finally created a real labor shortage in northwest Georgia, and local USES officials and employers scrambled to prevent major shifts across the color line. Textile defense contracts already had local factories employing well over the normal number of workers when the USES determined that the army's Battey hospital would require about twelve hundred additional workers, a significant figure for a town of just about thirty thousand. In June 1943 the USES office estimated that the Rome area would need 1,185 more workers by August, 2,885 by November, and 4,835 by May 1944. It seemed more likely than ever before that Georgians would witness "the evils that might result from having members of both races working in the same weaving department."[38]

Similar shortages of manpower across the nation in 1943 led the national leaders of the WMC and USES to take more serious steps toward nondiscriminatory use of manpower, but the impact of more vigorous fair employment policy was semantic rather than substantive in Rome. Supervisors who inspected the Rome USES operations in June 1943 reported that "job specifications and standards for referrals asking for only white labor have been practically eliminated." Moreover, the "majority of the employers," supervisors claimed, "are now participating in the program without showing any racial discrimination." In September the USES monthly report even claimed that "one large [textile] mill has recently begun to employ Negro men and women." However, the Rome offices' records of new hires and employment at local factories revealed that employment practices remained essentially the same. The average percentage of African American employees in all manufacturing remained around 4 percent. Although one historian has recently claimed significance for the "doubling" of the black textile labor force during World War II, such a measurement is surely misleading. In Floyd County textile mills, the number of black workers did increase in a strictly numerical sense, as the number of shifts increased, but black workers never comprised more than about 2.5 percent of the wartime labor force, roughly equivalent to the prewar percentage. Moreover, the real meaning of the shift was revealed by the USES admission that black workers were hired by the textile mills for "certain jobs, such as cleaners."[39]

[38] Labor market report, June 15, 1943, p. 7, Rome folder, series 12, WMC Region VII Records.

[39] Timothy Minchin, *What Do We Need a Union For? The TWUA in the South, 1945–1955* (Chapel Hill: University of North Carolina Press, 1997); labor market report, June

Nor did cosmetic rules about the designation of whites and nonwhites on employment forms eliminate stereotypical biases against certain types of workers. Racism, sexism, and a thinly veiled disdain for workers regularly informed WMC actions and interpretations of local manpower problems. In October 1943, a USES staff member reported that in spite of their estimate that 275 black women should be available to work, "colored female labor" was "becoming increasingly hard to secure." Without any particular evidence, he attributed the shortage to an "indifference to work among the colored female workers because of allotments from relatives in the Armed Forces." It was in euphemistic fashion repeating what white employers had long chosen to believe about black workers: that their lack of enthusiasm for the jobs designated as appropriate for them was a sign of laziness; black workers labored only when forced by economic necessity. In the same fashion, another USES report added, "the fact that their male relatives at home are making increased amounts of money over previous times" explained why black women could not be recruited for jobs as maids and laundresses. In 1944, USES reports began to refer to the phenomenon with even stronger language, describing alleged black attitudes as "undoubtedly an indifference" to employment among northwest Georgia's "colored persons."[40] Although local officials had recognized that low pay and poor conditions had contributed to farm employers' difficulty securing adequate manpower, WMC officials, satisfied with stereotypes rather than solutions, never considered that the problem filling "colored female" jobs might lie in the jobs rather than the women.

However, the collective refusal of women to take these jobs, paired with other anecdotal evidence, suggests that the USES may have inadvertently stumbled upon an explanation for black women's motivations, even if they drew the wrong conclusions. The USES never offered better-paying clerical or other white-collar jobs to black women, so their interest in other kinds of work unfortunately cannot be measured. But given the low pay, low prestige, and segregated nature of the jobs, African Americans would have understandably been reluctant to take the jobs that whites allocated for their race and sex. Since private individuals had been com-

15, 1943, p. 7, series 12, Rome folder; field supervisor's analysis of Rome office, Sept. 8, 1943, p. 7, series 19, Rome folder; final quote from labor market report, Aug. 18, 1943, series 12, Rome folder; all in WMC Region VII Records. The average percentage of black workers was calculated from the USES reports on the employment of nonwhites in September 1943, as reported in the field supervisor's analysis of Sept. 8, 1943.

[40] Field supervisor's analysis of Rome office, Sept. 8, 1943, p. 7, series 19, Rome folder; labor market report for Rome, Oct. 18, 1943, p. 7, series 12, Rome folder; estimate of in-migration into the Rome labor market, Mar. 1, 1944, p. 3, series 12, Rome folder; all in WMC Region VII Records; McGill, *The South and the Southerner*, 168–69.

plaining since 1942 about the "shortage" of cooks and maids, and even the *Rome News-Tribune* recognized a "servant problem," it was not surprising that industry was having a difficult time convincing women to perform the same jobs in industry. Excluding laundry and custodial positions, the USES estimated the demand for black women workers in essential industries at zero. In contrast, the demand for white women at the same time called for an additional 1,023 workers. Manpower staff had simply assumed that black women would take their place in the traditional labor market. However, black women in Floyd County, by refusing the same old jobs, proved just how much the war had threatened the racial market for labor despite USES machinations.

Ironically, it was this alleged "indifference" among black women and not a shortage of textile labor that struck the only major blow to the color line during World War II in Floyd County. As northwest Georgia manpower planners tried to predict the staffing requirements for the new Battey hospital in the spring of 1943, they estimated, according to the "skill, race and sex breakdown," a need for 319 white men, 327 black men, 238 white women, and 76 black women. By the USES's estimate of the labor supply, there were 384 potential "negro female" workers in the area, which the USES planned to place in laundry and maid service jobs at Battey. Proceeding on these racially rationalized assumptions, manpower officials accordingly designated a federal housing project currently under construction for "colored occupancy." When local black workers failed to materialize, the USES began planning to "in-migrate" (recruit) black workers from outside the area rather than shifting efforts to recruit the supply of local white labor. By October the USES was forced to inform the WMC that "it is thought that even then [with in-migration] it will not be possible to meet the service demands with colored labor, and white labor will have to be used on certain shifts."[41]

But the racial typing of jobs in the South proved exceptionally tenacious. In spite of the failure to recruit black workers, the commanding officer at the Battey hospital insisted on pursuing the original plan to hire "a considerable number of negroes" for at least eight more months, a virtual eternity in the context of the war emergency. Not until January 1944 was the officer finally "convinced by the Rome USES manager that negroes will not be available . . . and that white workers will have to be used to enable the hospital to reach full employment." Although the hospital would hire both white and "colored" labor, USES reports suggested

[41] B. F. Ashe, Regional Director, WMC, to Thomas Quigley, Georgia Director of USES, May 22, 1943, Rome folder, box 18, series 12; "Estimate of In-Migration into the Rome GA Labor Market" Apr. 2, 1943, Rome folder, box 2, series 12; Labor Market Report, Oct. 18, 1943, Rome folder, box 8, series 12; all in WMC Region VII Records.

that their shifts would be separate, and segregated. Separation of the races, however, got even more complicated than filling shifts at Battey. The Rome USES director also had to worry about fitting workers into the segregated community. Fortunately for the WMC and USES, the federal housing project intended to accommodate the new hospital workers had not become permanently associated in the community with "colored housing." The Rome director of the USES contacted the regional WMC director in time to have "all of the housing programmed for negroes" reallocated, or renamed, "to allow white occupancy." "Negro in-migrants," the director declared, could find housing in a slum- clearance housing project also under way, which apparently had already been designated "colored."[42]

Race was not the only bias indicated among WMC staff. USES reports also revealed the persistence of other common stereotypes about women. Recounting conversation between staff and employers, the USES often betrayed a real contempt for workers and a particular devaluation of female workers. While managers expressed concerns about losing male workers to the armed services, for example, they also assumed that they would lose as many women to pregnancy. In a labor market of several thousand women, it is difficult to imagine enough women simultaneously becoming pregnant to upset production schedules. What managers and WMC officials were really insinuating was that women workers were unreliable. Managers also indicated a persistence of the belief that women were casual workers who took jobs only for "pin money." As Christmas approached, USES staff and managers expressed fears that large numbers of women would quit after the holidays. Despite the textile mills' historic reliance on women workers, the war did not alter preconceived notions about women workers as naturally, indeed biologically, less dependable.[43]

USES and management reports also indicated a uniquely southern management bias against wage workers and a chronic miserliness among textile employers in spite of the wartime production boom. On several occasions, the managers and USES officials in Rome complained that wages were too high. When Anchor Duck Mills, for example, could not meet government orders for one million yards of cotton duck per quarter, management blamed wages. Although the Anchor Mill did have real technical problems of imbalance because the yarn department was unable to pro-

[42] B. F. Ashe, Regional Director, WMC, to Thomas Quigley, Georgia Director of USES, May 22, 1943, Rome folder, box 18, series 12; labor market report, Oct. 18, 1943, Rome folder, box 8, series 12; both in ibid.

[43] Spot surveys of Anchor Duck Mills, Dec. 5, 1944, WPB Appeals, Anchor Duck Mills folder, series 21, ibid. On the assumptions about women embedded in wage and labor policy, see Alice Kessler-Harris, *A Woman's Wage: Historical Meanings and Social Consequences* (Lexington: University Press of Kentucky, 1990).

duce enough raw material to supply the departments manufacturing cotton duck, management also asserted that the "fact that the workers are earning more money than ever before contribute[d] partially" to the mills' inefficiency. The A. D. Julliard Mills' overseers similarly argued that "too much money" was causing absenteeism at their Rome plant. Echoing the pronouncement on black women, the War Production Board, called in to study the problem, concluded that older and female textile workers demonstrated an "indifference" to work. Since most millhands were earning a piece rate and a relatively high minimum wage of forty cents, management concluded that workers did not have enough incentive to work hard or even to report for work when they did not feel like it.[44]

Assuming that motivation was the answer to "indifference," local USES staff and employers cooperated in extensive community propaganda campaigns to inspire northwest Georgia textile workers. Although other problems, such as poor working conditions and a lack of child care, were at least as likely causes of absenteeism, the USES focused most of its energies on propaganda. The Rome office sent seventy-one hundred letters and distributed over two thousand handbills in Floyd County. Nor did the USES let up on workers once they took their place manning the machines at local factories. In the spring of 1944, the USES office manager, Nevin Patton, delivered a lecture to workers at the Trion mill over the mill's public address system. In the event that workers could not hear Patton's speech over the ordinarily deafening noise of the textile machinery, forty-two hundred mimeographed copies were distributed. In April 1944 the USES reported plans for an even larger advertising campaign to "raise" workers. The local office planned to place articles in all newspapers in northwest Georgia and northeastern Alabama, distribute twenty thousand circulars, mail ten thousand USES form letters, and make regular broadcasts over northwest Georgia's three radio stations.[45]

Floyd County mill managers felt that high wages were contributing to absenteeism, yet most other observers, including the TWUA, the WLB, and the national WMC, suspected that low wages paid in textiles were responsible for shortages in the industry. Southern textile wages had always lagged behind wages for other American industrial workers. As early as 1943, when a shortage of textile production first appeared, the WMC reported that the "underlying cause" of high turnover and insufficient labor was "low wages." On these grounds, the TWUA pressed the

[44] Spot surveys of Anchor Duck Mills, June 16, Dec. 5, 1944, WPB Appeals, Anchor Duck Mills folder, series 21; spot survey of A. D. Julliard and Company, Inc., Oct. 3, 1944, A. D. Julliard folder, series 21; Labor Market Report, Apr. 15, 1943, p. 8, Rome folder, series 12; all in WMC Region VII Records.

[45] Field supervisor's analysis, Mar. 24, 1944, Rome folder, series 19, ibid.

WLB and individual employers throughout the war to raise the minimum and eliminate the North-South wage differential. "We do not feel . . . that God has ordained the textile workers to be forever the lowest-paid worker in our nation," TWUA president Emil Rieve told a special WLB panel in April 1944. With 77 percent of the textile industry in the South, the TWUA argued, there was no reason to believe that southern mills could not compete while paying the northern wage. Southern employers and politicians, including Georgia senators Richard Russell and Walter George, just as ardently defended the regional differential as necessary to preserve the "area economy" and southern competitiveness. Any regional wage raise, southern employers warned, would result in inflation and "disturb" the southern economy. Southern textile workers earned an average of $19.82 per week, which was $9.41 a week less than the average American industrial worker and $2.61 less than a northern textile worker. Even in comparison to southern war plants, however, textile mills paid miserable wages. These low wages, the TWUA argued, encouraged southern textile millhands to leave for "higher paying jobs in shipyards, munitions plants, machine shops and aluminum plants inside and outside the 'area economy.' " "Would $22 a week tempt the public members of the WLB to take a job in a cotton mill?" the TWUA asked the special wage panel in 1945. Between 1942 and 1944, the TWUA estimated, the textile industry had hired nine people for every ten who quit, and the industry had permanently lost 250,000 workers by December 1944.[46]

Despite protests from employers and limits imposed by government anti-inflation controls, the combined effect of pressure from the TWUA and the shortage of textiles raised textile wages considerably during the war. In August 1942 the TWUA won approval for an increase of 7.5 cents per hour. After the WLB's "Little Steel" formula and other federal policies limited wage increases in order to control inflation, the TWUA was forced to argue that southern wages were "substandard." It was not a difficult argument to make, for despite the 1942 raise, southern wages still remained significantly lower than wages in northern textile mills because across-the-board increases did not disturb the regional differential. In a series of WLB hearings in the final two years of the war, the TWUA argued persuasively that southern workers needed higher wages and, moreover, that low wages were hindering the war effort. In February 1945 the WLB approved a minimum wage of fifty-five cents per hour for all textile workers north and south. Although the regional differential persisted between average rates and skilled workers, WLB decisions narrowed the gap between northern and southern earnings to a historically small margin. The TWUA continued to argue that wartime inflation rendered textile earn-

[46] *Textile Labor*, November 1943, May 1944.

ings a poverty wage, but the extent of wartime change was actually quite remarkable. In just ten years, southern textile workers' minimum wages had almost doubled, from thirty to fifty-five cents per hour. Much higher wages in munitions and bomber plants, however, continued to draw workers out of the textile mills.[47]

The USES and Floyd County employers finally solved their labor problem not by raising wages, lowering wages, or widening the pool of acceptable applicants, but by introducing the WMC's "labor stabilization plan" to northwest Georgia. Mocking the TWUA's protests to the WLB that the textile industry "cannot freeze poverty," the labor stabilization plan did essentially "freeze" Floyd County's white labor in the lowest-paying jobs of the defense industries. In essence, the stabilization plan discouraged turnover and out-migration by imposing penalties on workers who quit. With the cooperation of area employers and strict adherence to a referral system, the USES could enforce stabilization by limiting workers' access to all other employers holding military contracts, which was essentially every major employer in 1943. Unless a worker received permission to change jobs, he or she could not take a new position, even in another war plant or essential industry, because all employers using the USES were compelled not to hire workers without an official "release" from the employment service.

The WMC first introduced the employment stabilization plan in 1942 to solve manpower shortages in western nonferrous metal mines and the lumber industry. Western lumbering and mining jobs, like seasonal farm labor in Georgia, apparently were the first low-wage jobs to be abandoned as better opportunities attracted the traditional workforce to new pursuits. Just as many of Floyd County's wage workers had migrated to better jobs at the bomber plant in Marietta or the powder plant in Childersburg, western miners had left the mines for higher wages and better working conditions in the construction, shipbuilding, and aircraft industries. In USES director Corson's words, stabilization introduced "indirect or disguised compulsion" to force workers to stay on their jobs. Apparently the compulsion for many workers to leave the mines was even stronger. To boost production in western copper mines, employers finally had to have some five thousand miners released from the armed services and even more workers recruited from Mexico to take jobs in the mines.[48]

The USES and the Rome Area Management-Labor Board officially introduced the stabilization plan to Floyd County in May 1943, when labor

[47] According to the WLB's "Little Steel" formula and the orders of Roosevelt, wage increases were limited to cost-of-living increases relative to prewar levels unless wage increases were needed to eliminate substandard living, aid the war effort, or correct gross inequities. Richards, "History of the Textile Workers," 184–88; *Textile Labor*, February 1945.

[48] Corson, *Manpower for Victory*, 32–33, 273.

demands for the construction of the army's Battey hospital exacerbated an increasingly serious shortage of textile labor. A similar plan was also introduced to "stabilize" Floyd County farmworkers. Employers and the local USES had been "voluntarily" trying to effect the plan for several months before the area board made Floyd County a "closed area." In practice the Floyd County stabilization plan worked like a blacklist—a traditional remedy for southern labor trouble. Employers cooperated with each other to deny employment to persons who broke the stabilization plan's rules.

In theory the plan was not completely authoritarian, because all workers under the stabilization plan had the right to appeal to the USES and the area board for a "release," or permission to take a new job. In practice, however, the plan did compel workers to stay in their present jobs. Releases were almost impossible to secure, and the punishment for quitting without a release was a mandatory thirty-day—and later sixty-day—layoff from all war industries. Even during the war, it was unlikely that many textile workers could afford two months of unemployment, particularly since the USES office also presided over unemployment benefits.[49] Because the stabilization system was set up expressly with the intent of keeping workers on the job, the USES staff and employers had little incentive to grant releases, and standard office procedures developed around the goal of discouraging appeals in the first place.

Enforcement assumed various forms. USES staff members alternately used patriotism, arbitration, rejection of appeals, and finally punishment by layoff. To avoid the excessive paperwork and energy of appeals, staff tried to simply limit the number filed. According to a USES supervisor, "workers seeking releases are firmly but courteously handled and appeals have been kept down." Two months after the plan went into effect, the only appeal filed by the Rome office was subsequently refused. Workers unfamiliar with the workings of the WMC bureaucracy were easily discouraged from filing appeals. When Dean Wood, for example, left her sewing job she wanted to apply for a better-paying position at Bell in Marietta where her father worked. "I hadn't ever been there [the USES office] to put in for another job," she remembered, but she was informed that she "had to have that little card" from the USES before she could apply for work at Bell. When Wood went to the USES office, the staff simply told her, "We can't give you one [a release] to go out of town. We need you here real bad." Instead they gave her a release to work at the

[49] According to the TWUA, the state USES could deny unemployment compensation to workers who refused to take jobs. *Textile Labor*, October 1946.

Tubize rayon mill. It was a better job, but not as highly paid as a job in Marietta might have been.[50]

The stabilization plan almost always worked in favor of employers because managers had more authority with USES staff and the appeals board than workers. When the USES's persuasion failed to cajole workers into staying with their present job, the employees were "required to give a full statement as to why they should have a release." Perhaps because employers frequently claimed that workers deliberately broke the rules to get releases, USES staff members processing the statement "checked with the employer" to verify or refute the workers' claim. The next step for those workers denied releases was to appeal to the area management-labor board, which was also heavily biased in favor of management. According to the Rome office's reports to the regional WMC, only *one* release was authorized in the two years the plan was in effect, and that release was given to a male worker who, because of the shortage of housing, was forced to move his family of three into a four-room house with eight other people.[51]

Stabilization also aided the fight against fair employment by tying white workers to white jobs. In the South's "free" market for labor, black workers had historically taken the jobs that whites did not want, such as cutting open cotton bales or cleaning the mill. If whites had been permitted to move on to better-paying jobs and the shortage had intensified, textile employers might have been forced to hire black labor as workers moved up the employment ladder. At first employers had successfully held off integration of textile jobs with requests for "white males" and "white females." Then, after they were directed to drop racial designations, employers requested "experienced textile hands," which just as effectively meant whites. Now with stabilization they had the means to compel their white workers to stay. For example, when the entire contingent of loopers at Rome Hosiery threatened to quit, the USES finally persuaded them to stay by warning them that they could not find employment elsewhere for sixty days. With federal limits imposed on the right to strike for the duration of the war, workers had little redress but to quit. In Floyd County, stabilization seemed to deny even that right.[52]

Not surprisingly, the USES reported that employers were "sold on" and "well-pleased" with the stabilization plan. Apparently, Floyd County managers were not bothered by the plan's violation of that sacred cow of

[50] Labor market reports, June 15, Jan. 3, 1944, Rome folder, series 12, WMC Region VII Records; Wood interview.

[51] Labor market report, Jan. 3, 1944, Rome folder, series 12, WMC Region VII Records.

[52] Labor market report, Oct. 18, 1943, p. 16, Rome folder, series 12, ibid.

southern employers, the "God-given right-to-work." Ever the defenders of the "free" contract between employer and employee and of individual rights against unions and the federal government, southern textile manufacturers suddenly abandoned their ideological attachments to individualism in favor of federally enforced compulsion. Board member Hornady, for example, who deemed union security measures "one of the most flagrant departures from Constitutional freedom that has arisen in this Country" and considered the FEPC a "contemptuous disregard or the rights of American citizens," expressed no such disgust for federally compelling textile workers to stay on their jobs. Nor did many textile employers seem to resent enforced cooperation between managers as they had under the 1933 textile code and the NRA.[53]

In contrast to the limitations imposed on workers, no equivalent coercion was placed on employers. The area management-labor board, for example, discovered in 1944 that there were hundreds of idle and experienced textile workers in nearby Summerville, but the two mills in that small city refused to employ them. WMC officials expressed their disbelief that "so many people" could be "undesirable," and investigators discovered only that "the mills have something against them [which they did not specify in the report] and won't rehire them." Evidently, Rome mills did not want Summerville's "undesirables" either. Rather than compelling the Summerville mills, which were simultaneously reporting a "short[age] of help," to employ those blacklisted workers or arranging for these experienced textile workers to move to Rome, the area board made plans to "send them on" to Bell Aircraft. Stabilization penalties only operated in one direction.[54]

Besides compelling workers to stay on their jobs, stabilization gave employers virtual ownership of local labor for the duration of the war and provided new ways to discipline workers. The "right to work" in one of the lowest-paying defense industries in the nation was now a sentence for the duration of the war. Some Floyd County employers wanted to make the rules governing stabilization even stricter. The USES reported that most managers "felt that the thirty-day lay-off period should be ninety days." Thirty days, evidently, was not deemed long enough to punish workers who broke the rules. In 1944 the USES and the area management-labor board increased the layoff penalty under the stabilization plan to sixty days. Stabilization thus permitted employers to chasten recalci-

[53] Labor markets report, Aug. 18, 1943, Rome folder, series 1, and minutes of the Mgt.-Labor Committee, Dec. 7, 1944, Rome folder, series 14, both in ibid.; *Rome News-Tribune*, Mar. 12, 1945.

[54] Minutes of the Mgt.-Labor Committee, Dec. 7, 1944, Rome folder, series 14, WMC Region VII Records.

trant workers by long layoffs at the same time it effectively forbade the workers from taking another job.[55]

Although the interests and concerns of textile workers rarely appeared in the daily records of the USES, subsequent reports suggested that workers were in fact attempting to resist the stabilization plan. Textile workers determined to undermine stabilization rules forced the USES to "use extra diligence," according to supervisors, because they were not "sticking strictly to the reasons for separation." Denied the right to quit, many millhands apparently fell back on their right to get fired. As job applicants became "more familiar with [stabilization] regulations . . . and ways of getting around the reasons for denying releases," the USES reported, "it has become more exacting and has required a great deal of careful study in the majority of cases in regard to releases." Employers argued to the USES that "a discharge should not be a ground for release in all instances, as many persons will deliberately infract a rule in order to be discharged." Wages must have been a significant motivator, for most of the dissatisfied textile workers who applied for releases requested transfer to Bell Aircraft.[56]

Although the TWUA did not directly represent unorganized textile workers in Floyd County, union spokespersons leveled major criticisms of the stabilization program on behalf of all textile labor. The TWUA criticized the plan as an "effort to rule manpower by edict, and without regard to democratic procedures." In response to pressure from the TWUA and other unions, the federal government approved a modification of stabilization that would permit workers to move from one essential job to a higher-paying essential job when "such a move would aid the war effort."[57]

In practice, however, machinery for exceptions proved much less democratic in action than on paper. The lack of experience or "essential" skills among textile workers in anything but textiles almost always prevented release. Although training classes had been provided since the beginning of the war, only about sixty Floyd County residents were attending them in 1942. The WMC and USES relied mainly on employers to refer workers for training based on "their past experience, first and aptitude, second." Employers, of course, would have had little incentive to refer their workers, skilled or otherwise, given their concerns about labor shortages. The basis for referral—experience and skill—likewise worked against offering

[55] Labor market report, Oct. 18, 1943, pp. 14, 18, Rome folder, series 12, ibid.

[56] Labor market reports, Aug. 18, 1943, Jan. 3, Oct. 18, 1944, all in Rome folder, series 12, ibid.

[57] "Textile Workers at War," TWUA Executive Council Report, May 1943, Third Biennial Convention of the TWUA-CIO proceedings, TWUA Records.

training on a fair basis. Trainees included only six white women and no black workers, for few people other than white men had past experience in fields such as pipe fitting, welding, diesel mechanics, machine fixing, or sheet metal. Nor did enrollment in training classes significantly expand for whites, blacks, or women as the manpower shortage became more serious. In August 1943 the USES discovered that "employers [were] not encouraging their personnel to attend [vocational] training courses" because "they state it tends to make [workers] dissatisfied with their present employment." Class enrollment was "only one-third of capacity." Even if textile workers completed a training course, the stabilization program would not permit them to leave unless they had on-the-job experience, which of course they could not obtain because of the stabilization plan. After 1943, most of the local people taking advantage of vocational training were the unemployed. The USES attributed the composition of the classes to a "great interest" expressed by the unemployed, but it was also true that under the stabilization plan, unemployed persons were the only northwest Georgia workers given a genuine opportunity to train for new jobs.[58]

Although local manpower agencies and employers forestalled wartime challenges to the white and low-wage market for textile labor, World War II did improve the conditions of Floyd County textile workers by creating an ideal climate for union organization. Long plagued by underemployment, low wages, and the threat of a reserve workforce waiting to take over their jobs, Floyd County textile workers now enjoyed something close to full employment, a shortage of labor, higher wages, and a sense of security. The stabilization plan, while imposing limits on labor, also indicated the relative value of textile labor in northwest Georgia between 1943 and 1945. During the depression, textile workers had been forced into inordinate dependence upon textile jobs and paternalism. World War II, in just a few years, had significantly altered the direction of economic dependency. To continue to receive government contracts, employers had to meet production and abide by federal labor laws. And while federal agencies failed to enforce nondiscriminatory employment practice, the War Labor Board did enforce the Wagner Act. While the prewar National Labor Relations Board (NLRB) had been forced to depend upon the lengthy and uncertain enforcement powers of the courts to administer NLRB-ordered remedies, the WLB had the authority to withhold federal contracts.[59]

[58] Local labor market surveys, May 1, 1942, p. 16, Rome folder, box 18, and Apr. 15, 1943, box 8, both in series 12, WMC Region VII Records.

[59] Richards, "History of the Textile Workers," 164–71.

Although federal labor policy had, since 1935, protected the right of American workers to organize, the WLB made it much easier. The WLB established a pattern of settling labor disputes quickly and completely in order to aid war production, which also aided the unions. Moreover, the WLB's policies were often pro-union in practice. For example, in recognition of organized labor's no-strike pledge for the duration of the war, and federal limits on strikes such as the Smith-Conally Act of 1943, WLB policy supported union security measures such as maintenance of membership and the dues checkoff. Both assured stability in union membership by requiring that all union members covered by the contract pay dues, which were automatically withheld from their paychecks for the duration for the contract. For newly formed union locals in the South, such measures could be especially critical to the union's future.

Recognizing the significance of wartime federal labor policy, the TWUA seized the opportunity to launch yet another major southern organizing campaign from 1941 to 1945. In the light of the TWOC's dismal record from the late 1930s, the wartime drive achieved some remarkable immediate successes, especially in the upper South states of North Carolina and Virginia. Resistance in the deep South states, however, remained intense, and union gains came only in the final years of the war at the height of WLB authority. In Georgia, TWUA organizing efforts concentrated on the more heavily industrialized northern region of the state, especially around Rome and Atlanta. Ten mills in four northwest Georgia counties would sign with the TWUA between 1945 and 1950, including four in Floyd County.[60]

Although Tubize workers had resisted the efforts of the TWOC in 1937, Rome rayon workers became the first Floyd County workforce to sign with the textile union. According to accounts of the earliest members, there were no major complaints with the company—"just plain grievances"—and "almost everyone at the Tubize plant in Rome had one in the summer of 1944." Tubize workers actually sought out the TWUA for organizing assistance, and when the union arrived, Tubize "people were ready," remembered Walter Brooks, union member and longtime resident of the Tubize village. "They were ready because of the way they were treated, and the way they were working," he explained. "Most of them joined." While the war brought textile workers additional prestige, it had not corrected workplace problems such as favoritism, dangerous conditions, arbitrary workloads, and the more demeaning aspects of paternalism. The union now promised to rationalize workloads, provide mill-

[60] Ibid.

hands with some control over matters on the shop floor, and permit workers to command the respect of managers.

Brooks, for example, had grown up in the mill village and first started working at Tubize in 1941, a year before he enlisted in the Marine Corps. Before the union, he said, local management treated workers as if they owned them: "They thought you were theirs." For Brooks, the dignity and respect attached to union membership was the most important part of joining the TWUA. "The best thing I ever got out of the union—it wasn't money—it was just my right to stand up and tell the boss that I was not going to, you know, [be pushed around]. They'd stand up for you, protect you."[61] Similarly, union member H. O. Yarbrough recalled, "We worked hard to get that union. But we finally got it, and it was just all the difference in the world." Before Tubize workers organized, managers "could tell you to do anything—you had to do it." Tubize managers did not cease efforts to get more work out of millhands, Yarbrough said, but in his department "if they come up there and put another . . . trick [more work duties] on that [assignment] sheet, we didn't do it."[62]

Within a few months of their initial contact, the local organizing committee was prepared to petition for a union election. In November 1944, Tubize workers delivered a decisive victory to the TWUA, casting 1,043 votes for the union and only 546 against. In May 1945, the Georgia director and TWUA organizer Joe Pedigo, now permanently assigned to the Rome area, helped the new TWUA Local 689 negotiate the first union contract in the mill since the early 1930s. Tubize officials had not been "exactly keen on the union," in the TWUA staff's words. In fact, managers even wrote to one soldier who was serving overseas and asked him to vote against the union. But TWUA officials were pleasantly surprised by the "harmonious relations" that unfolded between Tubize and the union during negotiations. TWUA representatives and *Textile Labor* "commended" Tubize "on its responsible position . . . unique in the history of Georgia industry."[63]

Tubize paternalism, as much as World War II, had probably contributed to the formation of Local 689. The sense of entitlement and prestige fostered by the company and by mill village paternalism among the first generation of Tubize workers in the 1930s persisted among former members of UTW Local 1862, the children of mill workers, and second-generation Tubize workers in the 1940s. Tubize management and personnel poli-

[61] Brooks interview.

[62] Yarbrough interview.

[63] *Textile Labor*, June 1959, May 1945; Decision and Direction of Election, Final Vote Tally, Nov. 8, 1944, in NLRB Case 10-R-1307 (1944), National Labor Relations Board Papers, RG 25, National Archives II, College Park, Maryland (hereafter NLRB cases are cited by number and year).

cies, as well as the significance of textiles to the war, reinforced that collective feeling. Tubize was one of the only mills in northwest Georgia, for example, to give paid vacations, though workers were only eligible for three days after fifteen years of service. However, by insisting on a higher education level among its workers, paying more, and maintaining the most expensive and expansive village in the area, Tubize management reinforced a sense of skill, stature, and distinction among the workforce. Tubize workers felt that they should be treated accordingly, and most workers now believed that joining the TWUA-CIO was the way to receive the treatment they deserved.

Becoming the first workforce in their community to organize permanently enhanced Tubize workers' sense of themselves as different. In retrospect, union member Harold Waddell explained, "We were, I guess, more willing to sacrifice than a lot of the local plants around here. We realized . . . a little sooner, that if the company was making a profit, we were making that profit for them and we were entitled to a fair share of it." Often, he said, "people at the cotton mill, most of them, said 'Hey, I need more hours in order to make more money.' But we saw that we were making profit for this company, and we felt like we deserved it [too]. So we just, you know, organized ourselves. We got behind the officers of the union. We were just a strong group of people."[64]

By changing not only the economic position but also the perspective of workers, World War II facilitated TWUA organizing at Tubize and indicated that workers had internalized much of the rhetoric about democracy. Army-Navy production awards, wartime propaganda, and the WMC stressed the importance of textiles to the nation and the war effort. As WMC propaganda continuously reminded the community, "One end of that [battle] front starts on the production lines right here in and near Rome." Textiles were now not only important to the economic base of the community, but critical to the nation.[65] Not only had the war revived the textile industry, increased job security, and encouraged management cooperation with the union, but the military conflict itself heightened a sense of entitlement among working-class veterans. The soldier who received a letter from management soliciting a "no" vote on the union explained, "I was fighting in a war to make people free, and if they [workers] figured they wanted a union, I figured it was their business." He told management as much in a letter back to the company. Military veterans who returned to their jobs in 1944 and 1945 just as the TWUA completed

[64] Waddell interview.

[65] *Rome News-Tribune*, Apr. 24, 1945; Flamming has noted the increased respectability that the war and war production brought to Dalton's textile workers and the TWUA. See *Creating the Modern South*, 234–61.

the organizing campaign and began negotiations brought to Local 689 a new sense of their rights as American workers. "It was as different as night from day when I got back," one veteran explained. Walter Brooks recalled that when he came back from the Marine Corps and learned of the union, he "jumped right in it." When a manager tried to revert back to the pre-union days and order him around unnecessarily, Brooks quickly let him know in no uncertain terms that he was offended and that he would not tolerate it anymore. His attitude toward managers had changed, Brooks explained, "because I was older and because I'd learned better. I came back and I wasn't . . . going to let them talk to me that way. No way, no way." Veterans like Brooks who returned to Tubize with a perspective of the world and the nation beyond Floyd County sustained and strengthened the union. Several veterans assumed leadership positions in the local as stewards and elected officials.[66]

Tubize workers also benefited from the expert assistance of TWUA staff member Joe Pedigo, who was transferred to Rome in 1945 to continue the TWUA's organizing campaigns in northwest Georgia. Born in Roanoke, Virginia, in 1908, Pedigo was a former rayon worker who took his first job at the age of nineteen at the American Viscose synthetic fiber plant. In his words, he was raised by "sort of a unique family back there in the mountains." His father was a carpenter, a Republican, a racial liberal, and a union member.[67]

In 1931, when the precocious twenty-two-year-old Pedigo was working at American Viscose, he and a couple of his friends organized the plant's forty-five hundred employees by themselves, without even consulting with an international union. When their union had less than a quarter of the workforce signed, the plant manager called Pedigo to the mill office. Pedigo, who described himself as "sort of a budding Socialist," bluffed the manager and led him to believe that the whole workforce was organized. The plant manager capitulated and agreed to recognize the union.[68] Pedigo's remarkable union success in Roanoke at such a young age, his continued activism in local labor affairs, and his friendship with TWUA vice president George Baldanzi eventually led him to the textile union staff. In 1939, the newly organized TWUA-CIO hired him as an organizer at twenty-five dollars per week, ten dollars a week less than he had earned in the spinning department in Roanoke. Between 1939 and 1945, Pedigo helped the TWUA organize the first mill of the Cone chain in Greensboro, North Carolina, and win the largest NLRB election ever held to that date

[66] *Textile Labor*, June 1959; Brooks interview; Yarbrough interview.

[67] Joseph Pedigo, interview by Bill Finger, Apr. 2, 1975, transcript, Southern Oral History Project, Louis Round Wilson Library, Chapel Hill, North Carolina.

[68] Ibid.

at the Dan River Mills in Danville, Virginia. By the end of his career, Pedigo had organized "more plants in the South than any other individual" and earned a confidential ranking as the best organizer on the southern staff, according to southern CIO official Boyd Payton.[69]

Pedigo's theory on organizing held that "no organizer really organizes a plant." Rather, he believed that "you organize a few key people," and they do it. The trick, Pedigo said, was to find people in critical departments who were well respected among the workforce and "educate the hell out of them." Just taking the first guy who came along "with a chip on his shoulder," he warned, was a big mistake, because "chances are that he is mad at the company and the chances are that he should be fired if he hasn't been fired and will be fired the first time he sticks his neck out for the union." If the organizer's groundwork was done too quickly, Pedigo believed, "you wind up with people on your committee that nobody has any respect for." Once you recruited that "1 percent," the "kind of people that other people respect," they would "carry the ball for you." Pedigo "always stuck with that formula together with another formula . . . developed down in Georgia."

That other formula involved Tubize union members and union education. When Pedigo arrived in Rome, Tubize had just organized and "they came into a lot of money when they started collecting dues." He persuaded them to use some of Local 689's funds to put out a newsletter to all post office box holders—not just workers but virtually everyone in the county. "And I didn't push organizing, I just cited all the good things that I could in passing, all the positive stuff," he explained. Pedigo kept up the newsletter for about six months, trying to "saturate . . . the whole area around Rome." Then, he said, "I got a nibble from one plant, that they wanted somebody [from the union] in." From that point on, Pedigo said, "It was like shooting rabbits sitting." With the assistance of volunteers from Local 689, Pedigo began actively organizing the entire area. In May 1945, for example, he was leading leaflet distribution at the Julliard mills, the Pepperell plant in Lindale, and the Goodyear plant in Atco. Fortunately, no one in Rome ever discovered Pedigo's socialist past, and with a well-honed strategy he "knocked off nine plants in this Rome, Georgia area in a year and a half's time."[70]

While the rapid successes of the TWUA at the end of the war and Pedigo's enthusiasm seemed to belie the myths about regional resistance

[69] Ibid.; "Confidential Rating of Southern Organizing Staff Members," n.d., box 1, Boyd Payton Papers, J. Murrey Atkins Library, Charlotte, North Carolina.

[70] Pedigo interview; Pedigo to Horace White, May 20, 1945, Horace White correspondence folder, box 2; and Pedigo to Miles Horton, July 19, 1945, box 3; both in acc. 85-10, TWUA Northwest Georgia Joint Board Papers, Southern Labor Archives, Atlanta (hereafter cited as Joint Board Papers).

to unions, some mills and towns offered up the same old-time southern obstacles to unionism that the TWOC had encountered in the late 1930s. In Atco, for example, a small town about twenty miles east of Rome in Bartow County, Pedigo and the Tubize volunteers "had an argument with the Company Police and the Sheriff" about their right to hand out leaflets. Finally, when Pedigo convinced the sheriff that the "only way he could stop me was to put me in jail," the sheriff "backed down." Other mill managers, however, were more persistent and resourceful in fighting the union. Anchor Duck Mills managers, for example, waged a "particularly vicious" and "provocative racial campaign" when the TWUA began organizing their Rome cotton mill. The major tools Anchor management chose to fight the union were a radical right-wing, fundamentalist paper distributed out of Chattanooga, Tennessee, and the TWUA-CIO's own liberal racial policy.[71]

In the months preceding the election, Anchor Duck millhands began receiving letters from a "mysterious post office box" and free subscriptions to the "special labor edition" of the *Militant Truth*. Like its counterpart, the *Trumpet*, published in Columbus, Georgia, *Militant Truth* used a combination of fundamentalist rhetoric and race-baiting to discredit organized labor and convince readers that the CIO was anti-Christian, anti-southern, and anti-segregation. Indicating the white supremacist leanings of *Militant Truth*, one of the regular advertisers was Joe Kamp of the Constitutional Educational League, "one of the nation's most outspoken anti-Semites" and an open admirer of Adolph Hitler. Both papers were heavily bankrolled by southern textile manufacturers and trade groups such as the Southern States Industrial Council. In 1945 employers could purchase "subscriptions" to *Militant Truth* at a "group rate of 35 cents each, per year, [which] includes mailing direct to the homes of the employees." According to CIO staff, the paper "usually appeared mysteriously in workers' mailboxes . . . com[ing] to them free, 'with the compliments of a friend.' " Between 1945 and 1946, the paper was distributed to the millhands at eighteen textile mills in Georgia alone, including workers at Anchor Duck and A. D. Julliard in Rome.[72]

The editor, Sherman Patterson, defined his paper's objectives as promoting "fundamental Christianity and constitutional Americanism," but it was also true that he saw unions as incompatible with both. To support anti-unionism, the *Militant Truth* regularly cited the biblical injunction "Be ye not unequally yoked together," which Patterson interpreted as for-

[71] Pedigo to Horace White, May 20, 1945, Horace White correspondence folder, box 2, Joint Board Papers.

[72] Kennedy, *Southern Exposure*, 232–38; Lucy Randolph Mason to Billy Graham, Oct. 27, 1950, John Ramsey Papers, Southern Labor Archives, Atlanta; *Textile Labor*, July 1946.

bidding Christians from joining any organization that included people of other religions. Patterson got even greater mileage out of the passage because he could argue that the Jewish leaders of the labor movement, including the TWUA, were not only Jews and "foreigners" but supporters of racial integration.[73]

Militant Truth's particular brand of Bible-thumping and labor- and race-baiting, however, was not unique to Patterson. It was a fairly common rhetoric among leading spokesmen in the textile industry. The business journal *Textile Bulletin*'s editorial page, for example, was not above citing biblical and regional authorities to argue against unions and civil rights. In a typical editorial, the *Bulletin* argued "God made three races, the white the yellow and the black. . . . In fact in Leviticus 19–19 it is said 'Thou salt not let thy cattle gender with a diverse kind. Thou shalt not sew thy field with mingled seed.' " On the heels of this not-so-subtle sexual imagery, *Bulletin* editor David Clark argued that if God had intended the races to "amalgamate," he would not have made them different in the first place. "Proof" of the fact that "nature has a way of controlling such matters," he continued, was the fact that "*white men do not marry Negro women*" [his italics]. The reason, he speculated, was the "same racial instinct which keeps a canvasback drake from mating with a mallard duck." Clark did admit that "a few white women" married "negro men." Thus followed the danger of mixing whites and blacks in the mill, which Clark regularly posited as the secret and invidious plan of the CIO.[74]

Although Clark usually avoided toting out biblical injunctions to bash the union, he regularly attacked TWUA leadership as outsiders, communists, carpetbaggers, and promoters of racial equality with foreign-sounding names. In 1945, as Pedigo and TWUA members were organizing in northwest Georgia, the *Bulletin* opined, "this *Baldanzi* [his italics] who assumes the right to dictate to the Joneses, Smiths, Browns and Robinsons in the textile mills of the South is a racketeer who is living upon money taken from their pay envelopes." TWUA-CIO leaders, he warned, may "attempt to deny that they are communists, but they dare not deny that they are advocates of social equality of Negroes with whites." In fact, he continued, "most of them had just attended a C.I.O. convention at Atlantic City which unanimously voted approval of a FEPC law which would make it a crime for southern cotton mill girls to refuse to work with, or under the supervision of, Negroes." The (color) line "has been drawn," he warned. The "white mill operatives of the South" would have to take

[73] John A. Salmond, *Miss Lucy of the CIO: The Life and Times of Lucy Randolph Mason, 1882–1959* (Athens: University of Georgia Press, 1988), 135–36; Kennedy, *Southern Exposure*, 232–38.

[74] *Textile Bulletin*, Feb. 1, April 1948.

their place on one side or another. If the textile mill employees of the South, "who have pure Anglo Saxon blood," were willing to affiliate with an organization advocating that whites work alongside blacks, Clark scolded on another occasion, "they are different from their fathers and grandfathers."[75]

Racial liberalism was indeed a weak point in the TWUA's southern organizing campaign, and Floyd County managers tried to take advantage of it. Anchor Duck managers, for example, got their hands on some CIO literature on racial equality and "used [it] as incitement," in the words of a TWUA staff member. Rumors about union advocacy of integration and photographs of white TWUA leaders with black labor leaders, such as the snapshot of CIO official John L. Lewis's white daughter seated between African Americans A. Philip Randolph and John Davis of the National Negro Congress that appeared in the *Textile Bulletin*, also began to circulate around the mill. One of the Anchor Duck employees who helped organize in the mill and later became the local's president, Ottie Argo, recalled that company officials "played the race issue to the limit." Argo said the plant superintendent and the superintendent of his department came to him several times on the job and "told me that if the union came into the plant that they would put negro help on any job in the plant and that the white people would just have to work with them." A third supervisor tried to dissuade Argo from unionism by arguing that "the union would have negroes living side by side with us in company owned village houses." The race-baiting campaign was so intense that the Georgia director of the TWUA wrote the FBI requesting an inquiry, feeling that "a race riot as a result of the campaign is a definite possibility."[76]

What is interesting about managers' use of race was precisely how and why it failed to block organization of Anchor Duck's white workers. It was not because the war had prompted a growing tolerance among whites or revealed the inherent contradictions between war aims and segregation. Indeed, it is far more likely that the war's major impact had been to confirm the rigidity and permanence of segregation in the textile industry workplace. For example, union members repeatedly complained that the plant supervisor and the personnel manager at Anchor Duck "helped to keep rumors that the CIO was a Communistic, negro-loving outfit." When workers discussed management's tactics against the unions, they repeatedly referred to it as simply the act of spreading "*rumors*," by implication unsubstantiated, or complained that race was simply a confusion tactic. As another worker complained to the NLRB, "race was used to

[75] Ibid., Sept. 15, 1945, May 15, July 1, 1946.

[76] Kenneth Douty to FBI, Sept. 25, 1945, Kenneth Douty correspondence folder, box 2, Joint Board Papers; sworn affidavits of Ottie Argo, July 1, and Henry Farmer, Eugene Ingram, and James E. Forsyth, July 2, 1947, all in NLRB Case 10-CA-84 (1951).

keep the people confused about the real issues in the [union] campaign." The dismissal of race-baiting by Rome's textile workers was also revealing of the terms upon which they approached their union. As Argo pointed out to the NLRB, "They [managers] knew I would not want my children going to school with negroes and playing with negroes and later having to work side by side by negroes." Argo implied that he shared his white manager's distaste for integration. However, in the eyes of Argo and many other white southern unionists, the threat was so distant, and so removed from their all-white local, that he and his counterparts could easily dismiss it as an empty one.[77]

Even as Anchor Duck management raised the specter of integration, workers' concerns over what they perceived to be "real" issues in the mill helped the TWUA staff sign enough millhands to create a second TWUA local in Rome, Local 787. Although ten years had passed since Anchor workers had organized their first union in 1933, the stretch-out remained an important issue for Anchor workers. Just as Towers had placed the burden of the NRA wages on workers in 1933, he compensated for the wartime raises by demanding increased productivity. One Anchor worker complained to the WLB that he was actually working more for less money than prior to the raise. By the end of the summer, the union had signed over two-thirds of Anchor's 931 production workers. Superintendent Towers now tried other means of thwarting the union, first questioning Pedigo's right to represent workers, then simply stalling, neither refusing nor agreeing to meet with Local 787's committee. Pedigo believed that Towers was preparing a "strong fight against the union," and he suggested that the state director "file immediately for certification." In an October 1945 NLRB election, TWUA members won a solid union victory, with 518 ballots cast for the union and 251 against. With the addition of Anchor Duck workers, two of the largest mills in the Rome area now belonged to the TWUA. Election victories at Rome Hosiery and A. D. Julliard's Floyd County mill followed soon after. Union staff and volunteer organizers also began working on the largest cotton mill in the county and the final outpost of paternalism, the Pepperell workforce in Lindale. The TWUA had made significant progress toward "winning the peace" in northwest Georgia.[78]

[77] Sworn affidavit of Ottie Argo, July 1, 1947, NLRB Case 10-CA-84 (1951). The fact that race did not present an obstacle to organizing was also repeatedly substantiated by union leaders and workers I interviewed in Rome. For a discussion of rumors as cultural expressions, see, for example, Bryant Simon's introduction to Howard Odum, *Race and Rumors of Race: The American South in the Early Forties* (Baltimore: Johns Hopkins University Press, 1997), viii–ix.

[78] Horace White to Joe Pedigo, June 14, and Joe Pedigo to Horace White, July 9, 1945, both in Horace White correspondence folder, box 2, Joint Board Papers; NLRB Tally of Ballots, NLRB Case 10-R-1544 (1945).

Paradoxically, the failure of race-baiting campaigns to discourage union organization actually confirmed how little had changed during World War II and provided the ultimate proof of the strength of the prewar racial status quo. Historians have debated the sincerity of CIO racial policy, but in this case the important point is that Floyd County workers were confident that it would not affect them. Moreover, their subsequent experiences as union members in the 1940s and 1950s confirmed that original assessment. Segregation in employment permitted white southern workers to organize white unions. Although a handful of black employees of the mills did join Floyd County TWUA unions, they joined on essentially the traditional terms of the segregated white South. As maids, cafeteria workers, or cotton cutters, they were entitled to membership, but they were not entitled to white jobs or white salaries. Although union maids might earn more in the union shop than elsewhere in Floyd County, TWUA locals did not challenge the hierarchy of race, labor, and wages that existed long before the arrival of the CIO.

The experiences of black and white labor during World War II, from the failure of federal fair employment policy to the success of TWUA organizing campaigns, had indicated both the limits of the war's liberalizing influence and the potential for change in postwar Georgia. Once again, the power of local mill paternalists had been threatened by the entrance of the federal government, first by WMC fair employment policy, then by the pro-union supervision of the WLB. The extent of government-led change, however, was exceedingly small. In the hands of local white southern officials, manpower policy and federal agencies managed to preserve the status quo. Although the gender labels of jobs shifted somewhat, permitting women to temporarily fill men's jobs, the cultural race-typing of jobs such as "textile worker" and "maid" remained firmly intact. Though the local USES officials may have been forced to replace racial designations with ruses such as "experienced" textile workers, they easily avoided the intent of FEPC directives.

The brouhaha over the regional FEPC's toilet arrangements in its Atlanta office, for example, or the outrage expressed by the *Rome News-Tribune* at FEPC directives to Floyd County garment employers revealed a significant element of white resisters' fear of fair employment and ultimately the reason why the FEPC failed. Truly fair employment practices by necessity challenged segregation and contemporary conceptions of blackness and whiteness, but the FEPC did not. Most officials of the WMC, even in Washington, D.C., had no intention of doing so. "Segregation, per se, is of no concern to my committee," the last wartime chief of the FEPC declared in 1944, and indeed the FEPC did not press the issue of fair employment at the expense of segregation or fundamentally altering the color line in the South's largest industry. Thus the USES was able to get away with positive assessments of "fair" employment with observations that blacks had been hired for "certain jobs" and that both races used the front door. An end to southern segregation in employment, housing, education, and public life was practically inconceivable to most white Americans in 1945, especially in the deep South. Even the Arnall administration never seriously considered dismantling Jim Crow. Arnall was for equal economic opportunities, but as a defender of segregation, he never advocated that blacks and whites work together in Georgia factories.

In subtle ways, however, the war had changed some members of Georgia society irreversibly. Although the wages of whiteness and segregation remained secure for the time being, the impact of the organization of several mills in Floyd County, the liberalization of Georgia suffrage, and the internalization of wartime rhetoric by ordinary white and black Georgians would soon be apparent. Real change percolated through Floyd County during the war years as ordinary blacks and whites, politicized by their experiences during World War II, began to envision a new postwar Georgia. Southern employers and civic defenders of white supremacy, however, also had an idea of how the postwar world needed to change. From 1946 to 1948, whites, blacks, employers, and union members would square off, sometimes in overlapping coalitions, in a series of pitched battles for nothing less than the definition of the modern South.

Four

"Still a White Man's Georgia": PAC, Operation Dixie, and the Resurgence of Talmadgism

In May 1946 when the county police found two bright, untarnished copper stills in the Wax community of Floyd County, the *Rome News-Tribune* interpreted the discovery as a sign that "the war is definitely over."[1] Marking the end of one particular local war-induced shortage, the Wax raid also symbolized an important aspect of what would become the South's peculiar transition to postwar "normalcy." Though the war had been a major watershed, the South had demonstrated a remarkable ability to incorporate and absorb change within its existing culture, customs, and social relations. Segregation, single-party politics, whiteness, and blackness remained firmly rooted in southern institutions, politics, and culture. Only the struggles that emerged after the war to influence politics, exert control over workplaces, and modify southern traditions revealed the more subtle effects of World War II on Floyd County's people. The experience of military service and the nationalizing influence of wartime democratic rhetoric shifted the South at the grass roots, empowering ordinary citizens, casting doubt on customary practices, and placing many of the traditional elite on the defensive. The 1946 contests over unions, labor politics, segregation, and white supremacy also represented the opening battles in the major conflicts of the postwar period. For many southerners the end of the war signaled an unusual opportunity to shape the future, to refine and redefine the modern South.

What the modern South should be, however, was highly contested. Many of the region's traditional leaders envisioned a postwar South that maintained its boosters' appeal to business, cut short the nationalizing influence of the war, and resisted the northern and liberal impulse to reform the region's racial practices. Others, including Floyd County's new union members, saw the postwar period as an opportunity to extend the influence of organized labor and New Deal–era politics. Given the success of electoral reform during the war and the unprecedented level of prosperity, Floyd County TWUA leaders had many reasons to feel optimistic about winning the peace. The postwar South presented perhaps the greatest potential in history for political transformation and organization. Full

[1] *Rome News-Tribune*, May 2, 1946.

employment and working-class organization disrupted paternalism's hold on white workers and opened a novel opportunity for a new politics based on class. For a brief period, textile workers and other white Georgians seemingly endorsed a shift away from the outright racial demagoguery of Eugene Talmadge, and they gained support from the state's new black voters.

However, rejection of Talmadge did not necessarily mean that a majority of Georgians endorsed significant changes in segregation or southern culture. White workers and elites still shared a general commitment to preserving a "white man's Georgia," in the words of one Roman, and Floyd County unions re-created many aspects of the traditional racial order within their new organizations. Despite local labor's generally conservative stance on racial matters, however, increasing outside pressures on southern economic, political, and racial practices coupled with the general identification of the CIO and its Political Action Committee (PAC) with northern liberals and civil rights activists ultimately intensified local opposition to the TWUA. A fierce reaction set in across Floyd County in 1946 that placed further limits on the immediate postwar potential of organized labor.

In January 1946, the *News-Tribune* proudly reported that Rome's Broad Street was "fairly bursting at its seams" as local businesses made ready for a much anticipated "public spending spree." The front-page story probably confirmed what individual Romans had already figured out on their own. With wages and hopes high, the times were good. World War II had nearly eliminated unemployment and contributed to an almost boundless optimism about the South's economic future. Not a single Broad Street building stood vacant. In fact, there were "few to be had anywhere in town," according to the paper, as new chain stores, restaurants, car showrooms, and garages put up their shingles and merchants prepared for the arrival of the cars, appliances, radios, and restaurants with curb service that soon became emblems of the postwar period. Labor also joined the boom, providing physical form to the CIO's postwar aspirations in the center of town, right on Broad Street. Just blocks away from the offices of the chamber of commerce and the favorite meeting place of Rome's business elite, the Forrest Hotel, the TWUA opened a downtown office, symbolizing organized labor's new foothold in Rome. Here postwar TWUA leaders would coordinate local organizing activities with the CIO's Operation Dixie, organize a PAC for the Seventh Congressional District, and lay other plans to consolidate labor and liberal gains in Georgia.[2]

[2] Ibid., Jan. 25, 1946, Aug. 16, 1945.

The fact that textiles provided the anchor to Floyd County's economy proved to be a strength. Given the absence of any industries that were strictly "war babies," local War Manpower Commission officials predicted a smooth reconversion to a peacetime economy. Although memories of the depression were fresh enough to give many Americans pause, labor and business leaders predicted that the South's largest industry would continue to prosper and provide high levels of employment. In 1945, Georgia's textile mills employed over 100,000 people, and the state director of the WMC estimated that pent-up demand for civilian goods would create 10,000 or more new jobs statewide. In Floyd County, persistent labor shortages at the largest mills seemed to lend credence to his predictions. Rome's United States Employment Service officers reported throughout 1945 and 1946 that available jobs outnumbered the jobless in Floyd County.[3]

Although textile businessmen, no less than local merchants, were anxious to meet the postwar rush for consumer goods, delays in conversion indicated how important traditional culture remained to employment practices. A brief reconversion crisis resulted in 1945 and 1946 from Floyd County managers' inability to resolve the conflict between, on the one hand, their desire to hire workers of the race and sex that had customarily worked each job, and, on the other hand, the realities of what sort of workers were available. Ironically, as WMC officials across the country labored to remove women workers hired during the war, Floyd County employers and USES officials reported a serious shortage, not simply of workers, but of "womanpower."[4] Throughout the early months of reconversion, local USES manager Nevin Patton pleaded with women to take jobs just as he had during the war. As he did so, interestingly, he made it clear that his real concern had less to do with women than with the maintenance of traditional gender lines in the mill. In an interview for the local paper, he stressed—without any irony—that one serious consequence of the unfilled women's jobs was the "fact that many men—both war veterans and non-veterans—are being denied job opportunities" as mills were forced to curtail third shifts. The shortage had become so dire, Patton reported in all seriousness, that one local mill was forced to use

[3] Ibid., Aug. 21, 13, Dec. 9, 1945.

[4] Most accounts of women's labor after World War II have stressed employer efforts to eliminate women from nontraditional jobs and the many social pressures on women to return to women's jobs or unpaid labor in the home. See William Chafe, *The American Woman: Her Changing Social, Economic, and Political Roles, 1920–1970* (New York: Oxford University Press, 1972); Alice Kessler-Harris, *Out to Work: A History of Wage-Earning Women in the United States* (New York: Oxford University Press, 1983), 273–99; Ruth Milkman, *Gender at Work: The Dynamics of Job Segregation by Sex during World War II* (Urbana: University of Illinois Press, 1987).

skilled male weavers as battery fillers (a job historically held by women or children). Why men could not fill the jobs in question, Patton did not say. But of course he did not have to, because most Romans probably understood the point, as he did. These were *women's jobs*. Only one large plant provided a possible explanation, by requesting that the USES refer short men, those under five feet, seven inches tall and 130 pounds, who could "stoop easily." Predictably, no one suggested hiring black women in the crisis. By that time, the mills had already reverted back to traditional personnel policies, as illustrated by postwar advertisements soliciting "colored help" and "male and female help."[5]

USES officials and the *News-Tribune* attributed the womanpower crisis to a movement from "mill to kitchen" as men returned home from the service. However, given the USES officials' history of selectively misunderstanding workers and their dogged determination to see what they wanted to see, these assumptions merit a heavy dose of skepticism. Perhaps the end of labor stabilization encouraged women to seek opportunities in the new restaurants, retail stores, and offices popping up all over Rome. Or, since WMC officials had never solved the problem of child care or the double day for working mothers, perhaps many workers welcomed an opportunity to return to a single job. In any case, this crisis, one uniquely of the mill managers' own making and at the same time uniquely revealing of their return to business as usual in personnel policies, persisted for much of the year.[6]

If full employment created frustrations for managers and some local workers, it also created an ideal situation for the recently established TWUA locals to put down institutional roots and extend the union's wartime gains. Nationally, the TWUA had made incredible strides during the war years, winning 436 representation elections covering 101,967 workers, and using the War Labor Board to raise wages 36 percent. In the Rome area alone, the TWUA had organized eight new union locals. In recognition of the region's importance as a textile union center, in August 1946 the TWUA created the Northwest Georgia Joint Board, an elected body to govern and serve locals in that area of the state.[7] Led by an executive committee of elected officials and managed by Pedigo, the Joint Board soon became the primary source of TWUA policy, political strategy, union

[5] *Rome News-Tribune*, Aug. 12, 1946.

[6] Ibid., Dec. 9, 1945, Jan. 17, 1946. Unfortunately, detailed records of USES surveys and placement activities that might explain more about the womanpower crisis do not exist for the postwar period. When the war ended, the agency reverted back to the state of Georgia, and that office did not save records.

[7] *Textile Labor*, May 1946; Joe Pedigo to Emil Rieve, Jan. 19, 1950, box 6, series 2A, MSS 129A, TWUA Records; Joe Pedigo to Horace White, May 20, 1945, Horace White folder, box 2, acc. 85-10, Joint Board Papers; Pedigo interview.

education, and volunteer organizing staff in the region. Members of Rome locals at Tubize and Anchor Duck assumed important positions of leadership and support behind the new regional body. C. N. King, the president of Tubize Local 689, was elected the Joint Board's president, and Ottie Argo, a member of the Anchor Local 787, became the vice president.[8]

In the spring of 1946, northwest Georgia TWUA members also organized the first CIO Political Action Committee in the Seventh Congressional District. The local PAC, like the Joint Board, also reflected larger CIO and TWUA plans. Specifically, PAC aimed to keep sympathetic senators and congressmen, who had been so critical to the CIO's tremendous growth between 1935 and 1945, in office. Creating an elaborate structure to organize workers from the national to the state to the local precinct level, PAC solicited voluntary campaign contributions and sought to mobilize a labor movement that now included over five million members. Although the leaders of the CIO PAC, like its predecessors within the AFL, aimed primarily to elect candidates friendly to organized labor, PAC also represented a significant departure from past union political activism. While the AFL had focused primarily on trade union issues, the CIO adopted a much broader agenda of working-class social welfare, including support for civil rights and the solicitation of support from a larger non-CIO public.[9]

TWUA leaders in particular realized how important the federal government, via the War Labor Board, had been to recent organizational and wage gains. Moreover, the TWUA's ambitions for the South gave leaders a compelling interest in regional politics. Southern Democrats had long been major obstacles to labor politics. In Washington, they allied more frequently with Republicans than with their own party on labor issues, and on the local level anti-union southern officials could make organizing campaigns much more difficult. In 1946, when a business-driven backlash began to chip away at the Wagner Act and threaten labor's wartime achievements, international union leaders deemed political action even more essential. "Never," TWUA president Emil Rieve informed union

[8] Richards, "History of the Textile Workers," 176–77; *Textile Labor*, August 1946.

[9] For a history of PAC and a comparison of AFL and CIO political policies, see James Caldwell Foster, *The Union Politic: The CIO Political Action Committee* (Columbia: University of Missouri Press, 1975), especially 3–49, 202. On PAC, see also Robert Zieger, *The CIO, 1935–1955* (Chapel Hill: University of North Carolina Press, 1995), 181–87, 306–12 passim; idem, *American Workers*, 114–34; David Brody, *Workers in Industrial America: Essays on the Twentieth-Century Struggle* (New York: Oxford University Press, 1986), 215–55; Nelson Lichtenstein, "From Corporatism to Collective Bargaining: Organized Labor and the Eclipse of Social Democracy in the Postwar Era," in *The Rise and Fall of the New Deal Order, 1930–1980*, ed. Steve Fraser and Gary Gerstle (Princeton: Princeton University Press, 1989), 122–52.

members in July 1946, "has the need for working men and women to concern themselves with politics been more forcefully presented than now."[10]

Headed by Hugh R. Gammon of Local 689, the Seventh District PAC organized around the upcoming Democratic primaries and, more generally, the future of the TWUA in Georgia. In speeches broadcast over a Rome radio station live from Local 689's union meeting, national labor leaders encouraged Georgia union members to think of PAC as an important part of building the union. The TWUA, the Georgia TWUA director Kenneth Douty told Romans, had "an organization job both inside and outside the unions." As union members, he continued, "we are part of the community and must see that the people's representatives in the legislature vote in the interests of the people." Although the northwest Georgia PAC did not issue endorsements of specific candidates, resolutions supported labor issues such as extension of price regulation and raising the minimum wage to sixty-five cents, and the group called upon all the state's union members, and members of union families, to register to vote.[11]

The character of TWUA announcements suggested the Rome unionists had internalized many aspects of the CIO's democratic liberalism. At the TWUA state convention in June 1946, for example, Rome unionist Pete Millican introduced a resolution denouncing the recent resurgence of the Georgia Klan as "incompatible with the democratic aims of the labor movement." Although condemnation of the Klan by the "better sort" became more common after World War II, the TWUA critique portrayed it as a union issue. In the past, Millican noted, "the Klan has served as an anti-labor force and has beaten and killed labor organizers, wrecked union halls and acted as vigilante groups in times of strikes." White Georgian delegates at the convention agreed unanimously.[12]

To thus align white labor's interests with those of African Americans was superficially quite extraordinary, but in significant ways, organized labor's new presence in northwest Georgia continued to be shaped by traditional ideas about race and gender. Because of the strict color line in southern textile employment, Rome's TWUA locals bore the characteristics of many other segregated organizations in the Jim Crow South. Blacks and whites may have paid their dues to the same organization, but segregated meetings and union functions meant that they effectively belonged to two different sorts of unions. Although the handful of black workers

[10] *Textile Labor*, June, July 1946.

[11] *Rome News-Tribune*, Mar. 25, 1946; *Floyd County Herald*, Mar. 4, 1946; *Textile Labor*, June 1946.

[12] *Textile Labor*, July 1946; *Rome News-Tribune*, June 17, 1946.

who labored in the mills gained some of the material benefits of union membership, race prevented them from becoming members of the white working-class community that developed on the shop floor and in the mill village.

In part, Rome workers were simply observing established customs for recognizing racial difference. In virtually every facet of southern life in the 1940s, blacks and whites observed and conformed to the dictates of race every day, as segregation compelled everyone to re-create, contest, or affirm the "reality" of race in countless ways. A worker who traveled to the mill on city streetcars, dined in a segregated cafeteria, or attended a movie downtown, for example, would by necessity observe the conventions of segregation. In the postwar era, white managers provided black help to wait on white workers in the Tubize cafeteria or to do their wash at the Lindale mill village laundry, re-creating relationships of racial hierarchy within mill institutions. The Tubize mill community even had two baseball teams—the white "Tubize Rayons" and the "Black Giants"—and segregated seating for spectators.[13]

How segregation might have affected white workers' ideas about race, the union, or class is more difficult to determine. However, as numerous scholars of race and class have argued, the ideas, attitudes, and practices associated with race continuously cross the boundaries between workplaces and communities, reinforcing notions of racial difference in both spheres.[14] Rome union members sometimes endorsed racial difference and white privilege in subtle but revealing forms. Without explicitly authorizing discrimination, for example, Local 689's contracts replicated the language and the intent of distinctions between black and white jobs. Although whites and blacks employed in cleaning jobs at the rayon plant earned equal salaries, contracts identified white cleaning staff as "sweepers" and black staff as "janitors" and "janitresses." The workers' plant newspaper, *Tubize Yarns*, granted space to the "colored personnel" as well as white-only departments, but also reproduced the privileges of whiteness. Racially insensitive humor at African Americans' expense, so at odds with the image of racial liberalism emanated by the CIO, appeared in several issues.[15]

[13] *Rome News-Tribune*, June 11, 1946.

[14] See, for example, Earl Lewis, *In Their Own Interests: Race, Class, and Power in Twentieth-Century Norfolk, Virginia* (Berkeley: University of California Press, 1991); Robin Kelley, " 'We Are Not What We Seem': Rethinking Black Working-Class Opposition in the Jim Crow South," *Journal of American History* 80 (June 1993): 75–112; Hunter, *To 'Joy My Freedom.*

[15] Local 689 wage scales, Jan. 20, 1947, and Nov. 27, 1950, box 471; Local 689 contract, Feb. 12, 1962, and Minnie Knox to W. M. Pollock, Sept. 8, 1964, box 437; all in MSS 396,

In July 1945, for example, *Tubize Yarns* included a cartoon portraying a local fish fry that starkly illustrated the culture of whiteness as seen through workers' eyes. In a manner not unlike Talmadge's *Statesman* cartoons, it also revealed the symbolic connections existing between jobs and race. The cartoon, drawn by a white worker in the plant, portrayed dozens of his white male co-workers lining up at a southern-style standing buffet. At the center of the drawing was a single black man wearing a server's cap and holding a fish on the end of a serving fork. The cartoon lampooned the large appetites of workers, but it also mocked the black server who spoke to the diners in dialect: "Gemmen dis is de lass one on de foth go round—is yo is or is you ain't." "Uniforms" provided visual clues to readers about the components of racial identity, but they also reflected and reinforced contemporary perceptions of racial difference. This particular white worker chose to portray his counterparts in ties and dress shirts. The artist also made a choice in this case about including the black figure, who really was not necessary to the ostensible subject of the cartoon. The function the black man served here was perhaps comic relief, but he also seemed to serve another important function of contributing to white workers' portrayal of themselves as they might have wanted to be seen—as "Gemmen" (gentlemen)—served by men lesser than themselves.[16]

The common racial identity shared by textile workers undoubtedly also facilitated the creation of the close, familial community of white workers that developed around the Tubize local. In a practical sense, the union's many social activities—dances, picnics, barbecues—would not have been possible in an interracial union. Nor would southern workers' identification of the mill village with family. Describing Local 689, a black Tubize worker and union member expressed it succinctly: "They [the white workers] was just one big family I guess, and that's what makes a union."[17]

In many ways, textile unions also sustained traditional hierarchies of gender in the textile industry. The Tubize artist also portrayed the workforce in male terms—all the cartoon figures were men—but it was unlikely that the fish fry was sex-segregated. Union contracts identified male and female jobs, and union rates institutionalized the practice of paying a woman less even when she performed the same job as a man. Nor did the TWUA challenge the assumptions fueling the "womanpower" crisis of

TWUA Records; see also, for example, *Tubize Yarns*, February 1947, Special Collections, Sara Hightower Library.

[16] *Tubize Yarns*, July 1945.

[17] Lewis Shelton, interview with author, Aug. 14, 1994.

1946. Leadership of the Joint Board and Rome TWUA locals, with a few notable exceptions, was also predominantly male.[18]

However, women workers and female family members played a significant role in the daily maintenance of the union and formed the core of the union community. Union social activities such as box suppers, beauty contests, cakewalks, covered dish suppers, and dances frequently depended upon the labor, participation, and support of women. Local 689, in particular, welcomed into the union's circle many wives, husbands, parents, and children who were part of the white working-class community but not on the payroll at Celanese. An active women's committee, a women's auxiliary, and a number of frequent family-oriented activities enhanced the membership base of the local and created a close-knit group. Women workers also extended the familial and gendered culture of the mill community into the shop. When one of five male employees in the predominantly female coning department announced his engagement, for example, his fifty female co-workers threw him a "bridal shower." Although women's roles in the union often conformed to traditional notions of gender, male and female members of the TWUA did not necessarily devalue feminine styles of participation. When describing the strong community that developed around the TWUA, male union members often recalled that their wives "had a lot to do with it." Local 689 member Harold Waddell recalled that his wife, who never worked at the rayon mill, was unfailingly supportive of his union work, even when his position as a shop steward required receiving frequent phone calls from the women working in his department.[19]

In addition to holding social functions for the membership, union wives participated in the local's union activities, walking picket lines, working with PAC, and helping the Local 689 volunteer organizing committee hand out leaflets. "[My wife and I] went out when it was snowing, ice cold weather, you know," Waddell recalled. "We'd carry us a thermos bottle with us. Jump out there when shift change came. Yeah, she'd be right out there with me." Pat Baker, whose father and husband worked at Tubize, distributed leaflets and walked picket lines, even though she, like Waddell's wife, never worked at the rayon mill herself. Although Baker described these activities as potentially dangerous, she also recalled her determination to participate, even when she was pregnant. "We'd go out to these little old cotton mills handbilling," Pat explained, "and I

[18] "Hourly Job Descriptions," ca. 1946, Tubize tables, wage rates, earnings folder; and "Wage Schedule," January 1947, Tubize 1947 negotiations folder; both in box 471, MSS 396, TWUA Records.

[19] Activities in the Tubize mill village regularly appeared in the "Tubize Rayon News" column of the *Rome News-Tribune* (see, for example, May 28, 1946); Waddell interview.

wouldn't tell my mother. But I thought, 'Shoot, I'm pregnant, there's nobody going to hurt me.' " Union wives also contributed to the mill village community during hard times. Pat, who worked as a hairdresser, donated her services to union members and their families for free when her husband's co-workers were on strike.[20]

The fact that Floyd County TWUA locals conformed to many of the postwar South's traditional social hierarchies, however, did not insulate them from a resurgence of regional anti-unionism. Many textile employers and Floyd County boosters had never accepted the CIO or New Deal labor policy, and just as the TWUA viewed the end of the war as an opportunity to press organized labor's agenda forward, the South's traditional leaders hoped to roll back the gains of "big labor." The CIO's announcement in the spring of 1946 of its plans to conduct a massive southern organizing campaign, "Operation Dixie," intensified the struggle. In Rome, Operation Dixie rallied union opposition by adding a source of constant irritation and creating an easy target for local employers and boosters. Negative publicity about the CIO also seriously undermined Pedigo's strategy of public education.[21]

The intent of Operation Dixie's leaders, of course, was quite the opposite. In the minds of CIO leaders, Operation Dixie held the promise of protecting locals, North and South, by eliminating the region as a haven for runaway union businesses, by changing the South's political climate, and finally by eliminating the perpetual supply of nonunion, low-wage workers that undercut the CIO's working standards elsewhere. Although CIO unions made significant organizing progress during the war, federation leaders also realized that "organized workers in the North, East and West [would] remain insecure until the South [was] solidly organized." In May 1946, armed with the dues of fifteen million members and the conviction appropriate to a holy mission, the CIO deployed 250 organizers across the South. Not surprisingly, textiles were considered vital, and Operation Dixie placed its greatest emphasis on the southern textile belt stretching from Alabama to Virginia. State CIO director Charles Gillman assumed leadership of CIO campaigns in Georgia, where he was assisted by Floyd County textile workers and the staff of the Joint Board.[22]

[20] Waddell interview; Pat and Frank Baker, interview with author, July 12, 1994.

[21] As historian Barbara Griffith observed, the very name "Operation Dixie" angered southerners. Griffith, *The Crisis of American Labor: Operation Dixie and the Defeat of the CIO* (Philadelphia: Temple University Press, 1986), 166–67.

[22] CIO, "Recommendations of the Executive Officers to the Meeting of the Executive Board," Aug. 30–31, 1948, box 12, Lucy Randolph Mason Papers, William R. Perkins Library, Durham, North Carolina; on Operation Dixie, see Griffith, *Crisis of American Labor*, 376–77; Marshall, *Labor in the South*, 255–56; Art Preiss, *Labor's Giant Step: Twenty Years of the CIO* (New York: Pioneer, 1964); Michael Goldfield, *The Decline of*

Textile employers, who had historically depended on a large supply of inexpensive labor and now had a substantial investment in regional wage differentials, were uniquely hostile to Operation Dixie. In the early twentieth century, textile businessmen had been pioneers in cutting costs and raising profits by moving operations to the unorganized South. Corporate decision makers at the head of the Pepperell mill chain, for example, had been gradually transferring production facilities south ever since their purchase of the Lindale plant in 1926. From the point of view of corporate officials, this was not exploitation, but good business strategy. Pepperell managers, for example, expressed regret that "the chief losers in this shift were the mill operatives and the citizens of the mill cities in the North," but ultimately they also believed that it was the workers' fault. Strikes and demands for higher wages, Pepperell's corporate history argued, drove the company into the "beckoning hands of workers, cities, and States in the South." Southern mill executives understandably viewed Operation Dixie with alarm, and for the duration of the campaign the opinion pages of business journals such as *Textile World* and *Textile Bulletin* were filled with anti-CIO propaganda, campaign updates, and strategic advice to combat union organizers.[23]

Industry leaders did not, however, publicly oppose the efforts of Operation Dixie on such self-interested grounds. Rather, textile business spokesmen concentrated on portraying the union as anathema to white southern workers' interests. Cloaking their comments within an expression of paternal concern for their white employees, textile industry leaders warned that Operation Dixie's real mission was to double-cross naive southern whites by pilfering their paychecks, then dismantling the Jim Crow system. Operation Dixie leaders' "blatant talk about spending $1,000,000 and organizing all the mills of the South," *Textile Bulletin* editor David Clark fumed, amounted to nothing more than "hopes of reaping a golden harvest from dues" to be spent on causes southern whites surely would not condone. "The cotton mill employees of the South have the purest Anglo-Saxon blood in the United States," Clark asserted in September 1946, and it was a "certainty" that they would not support an organization that advocated "social equality with negroes."[24]

Organized Labor in the United States (Chicago: University of Chicago Press, 1987), 238–40; Michael Honey, "Operation Dixie: Labor and Civil Rights in the Postwar South" *Mississippi Historical Quarterly* 45 (Fall 1992): 439–54; and Michelle Brattain, " 'A Town as Small as That': Tallapoosa, Georgia, and Operation Dixie," *Georgia Historical Quarterly* 81 (Summer 1997): 395–425.

[23] Knowlton, *Pepperell's Progress*, 341; Richards, "History of the Textile Workers," 195–96; Barry E. Truchil, *Capital-Labor Relations in the U.S. Industry* (New York: Praeger, 1988), 41–85.

[24] *Textile Bulletin*, Aug. 15, Sept. 1, 1946.

The CIO's simultaneous support of proposals to maintain the FEPC in the postwar period furnished easy targets for textile businessmen's anti-union propaganda. The CIO, Clark told textile men, supported laws that would "force their daughters to work with Negro girls . . . and would subject them to fines if they refused to work under Negro overseers and second hands." Comparing CIO supporters to traitors of southern lore, Clark recalled "those terrible days of the reconstruction period, when the carpetbaggers where [*sic*] trying to force social equality upon the South, and no white woman was safe from attacks by Negroes, there were some Southern men, who, for pay, turned against their sections and their people and assisted the carpetbaggers." He concluded, "any man who works for the C.I.O." was doing the same thing by supporting "an organization which openly admits, in fact, boasts . . . that it seeks to place Negroes upon the basis of social equality with whites."[25] Finally, Clark asserted on numerous occasions, the CIO's success in organizing black workers, when compared to elections "in textile plants, where the employees are almost 100 percent of Anglo Saxon blood . . . show[s] very clearly that as far as the South is concerned, . . . the CIO is an organization for Negroes."[26]

In Rome, the inauguration of Operation Dixie marked the opening of a hostile and prolonged community struggle over the legitimacy of CIO unions in Floyd County. At the forefront of the opposition stood the traditional leaders of local opinion—the uptown business interests personified by J. R. Hornady's *Rome News-Tribune* and County Commissioner W. H. Lewis. Drawing on local boosterism, anti-communism, white supremacy, and regional identification in particular, Lewis and Hornady tirelessly denounced the CIO in print, on the radio, and at the local stump throughout 1946.

William Howard Lewis, a prominent local doctor, chairman of the Floyd County Board of Roads and Revenue, and county commissioner, became the most public and vociferous critic of the CIO. A colorful editorialist prone to hyperbole and sensationalism, Lewis had long been a civic leader and a vocal booster of industrial development. In the 1940s, Lewis delivered regular addresses to Rome civic clubs, gave speeches over Rome's radio station WRGA, and made frequent editorial contributions to the local newspaper. At the war's conclusion, for example, Lewis wrote several columns of "advice to the worker" to disabuse Floyd County workers of the notion that unions, social security, and unemployment insurance were good for working people. The Wagner Act, he claimed, was "as foul as loaded dice." In the first year of Operation Dixie, Lewis

[25] Ibid., Oct. 15, 1946.

[26] Ibid.; see also Oct. 1, Nov. 1, 15, Dec. 15, 1946, and Jan. 1, 1947.

stepped up the pace and the dimension of his printed attacks on the CIO. Though Lewis's editorial pieces had often appeared in regular newspaper columns, his 1946 "articles" began to appear in full-page formats, with sensational banner headlines in huge letters. One headline greeting the CIO Southern Organizing Committee, for example, announced: "Operation Dixie: The Iron Curtain Descends." In the six months after the announcement of Operation Dixie alone, Lewis published fourteen full-page and five half-page attacks on the CIO.[27] Borrowing a famous phrase from the UAW-CIO's Walter Reuther, he claimed to be "opening the books" on the CIO "to show the worker the malignant forces which are operating within labor organizations," which he believed were "seeking to gain absolute control, to paralyze our great industrial system and eventually to make good the prophecy of Lenin." American workers, he asserted, "and particularly our Southern workers must have the facts." With these "facts," he claimed, southern workers were "intelligent and loyal enough to defeat the forces of Red Revolution."[28]

Although Lewis developed an obsessive dislike for prominent CIO leaders such as John L. Lewis and Walter Reuther, he reserved some of his most vicious rhetoric for the CIO's Southern Organizing Committee, comparing the campaign alternately to a Russian invasion or a second Civil War. "The South stands again at Vicksburg," he charged, as a "siege [was] laid to it by a Northern invasion." When the CIO announced a campaign to organize Rome's retail and public workers, Lewis only half-jokingly suggested that the sixty-six thousand residents of Floyd County "might brush up on the Russian language" in their spare time, for "Joe Stalin plans to come to [Rome's] Broad Street."[29] In spite of the fact that many CIO leaders, including the international leadership of the TWUA, were avowedly anti-communist, Lewis rarely bothered to make such distinctions. He frequently cited the wave of postwar strikes in the coal, steel, and automobile industries as evidence that the CIO was attempting to disrupt the economy in order to foment communist revolution. In fact, Lewis informed local residents on another occasion, Rome, Georgia, was "Communist Party headquarters" of the South. When the CIO began to expose and expel Communist Party members, Lewis merely took it as confirmation of his suspicions about the CIO.[30]

[27] "Loaded dice" and final quote from *Rome News-Tribune*, Oct. 2, 1946; see, for example, the six-week series of "articles" in ibid., Sept. 24, 27, Oct. 1, 4, 5, 18, 1946.

[28] Ibid., Sept. 27, 1946.

[29] In order of appearance, quotes are taken from Lewis columns in the *Rome News-Tribune*, May 27, 4, 1946, June 23, 1947, and Oct. 2, 1946.

[30] Ibid., Oct. 2, 1946; on the CIO's alleged links to Moscow, see also radio address by Dr. W. H. Lewis, ca. January–May 1946, in series VII, Floyd County Official, subseries A, box 37, Richard Russell Papers, Richard B. Russell Memorial Library, Athens, Georgia.

Although Lewis preferred red-baiting to race-baiting, he adopted some novel positions on race and the CIO. For example, one Lewis column compared the CIO to the Ku Klux Klan. Both, he claimed, were extralegal, totalitarian organizations that sowed "hatred, violence and anarchy." Though Lewis condemned both in the process of drawing the comparison, he intimated that the Klan was the more respectable of the two. Evidently, Lewis believed that the old Klan, as opposed to its recent reincarnation in 1946, had been a legitimate expression of southern loyalty and law and order. He warned that the CIO might be responsible for the resurgence of that Klan. To the vice president of the TWUA specifically, he announced: "Mr. Baldanzi, you do not know the South. The Klan can rise again, the Klan of the old South, to restore to our people their rights and again drive out the carpetbaggers. You do well indeed to fear the Klan because you cannot destroy its spirit."[31]

Defending the South against the CIO was nothing less than a white southerner's patriotic duty, Lewis implied. "Do you [Floyd County workers]," he asked, "value your independence as a Southern American?" The "unsophisticated Southerner," he warned, "never having seen nor experienced the North, may listen to this alluring propaganda not realizing that he is surrendering the independence and personal freedom for which his ancestors [the Anglo-Saxons] fought for six hundred years." Southerners, after all, had never seen the "slums of the great cities of the North with people crowded like insects, breeders of social[,] moral and economic degradation." The basic difference, he claimed, rested on the fact that the "South is Anglo Saxon" and the "North is mixed races."[32]

In perhaps his soundest attacks on the CIO, Lewis employed his authority as a county leader. Though the doctor's dire warnings of communist takeovers, anarchy, and racial violence may have struck many Floyd County residents as hyperbole, appeals to local boosterism were more difficult for the union to address. It was in fact true that county leaders had lured industry to Floyd County with cheap, unorganized labor. Now, Lewis cautioned workers, the CIO asked Floyd County workers to jeopardize all that the South had accomplished and turn their backs on paternal benefactors. If workers "looked at the books" in Floyd County, he argued, they could see that industry had made Floyd County prosperous—more prosperous than other counties in Georgia. The employer, he argued, provided a service, taking "savings of years . . . to make jobs and to serve his fellow citizens." During the depression, he reminded workers, "Did the mills close, did they turn employees out? No, they sweat blood to keep their plants going that their employees would not be destitute."

[31] *Rome News-Tribune*, Oct. 15, 1946.
[32] Ibid., Oct. 4, 1946.

And not only did employers take care of workers, Lewis argued, they also supported the welfare of the entire county. In 1945, he noted, textile employers paid over two-fifths of the county's total tax revenue. They also supplied four-fifths of the county's school services. Floyd County leaders, and southerners generally, had been working on these kinds of assumption for half a century.[33]

Initially, Joint Board manager Joe Pedigo had felt that "such an hysterical, unbalanced attack as that of Lewis should not be dignified by an answer." Members of Local 689, however, persuaded Pedigo "that in allowing Dr. Lewis to go unchallenged we are admitting that what he has said about us is true." In November 1945, just after Lewis inaugurated his series of advice columns for "Mr. Working Man," Pedigo composed a five-column letter to the editor of the *News-Tribune* in which he answered several of Lewis's charges. To balance the bad press, Pedigo and other prominent CIO leaders, such as Baldanzi and CIO public relations representative Lucy Randolph Mason, also answered Lewis's invective in speeches over local radio. But the TWUA and the Joint Board simply did not have the budget or the time to answer every attack, which by September and October averaged two full pages of abuse per week. Although most people in Rome, according to Pedigo, believed Lewis to be something of a crank, "overbearing and dictatorial," he also believed that "too many people are falling for this red-baiting to shrug it off lightly and forget about it." Describing the situation to George Baldanzi, Pedigo claimed that "these ads are doing some harm. You can feel the reaction when you get out around town." By the spring of 1946, the rivalry between Pedigo and Lewis had gained such notoriety that a local illustrator for the *Floyd County Herald* chose the feud as subject of a political cartoon on the editorial page. The drawing portrayed Lewis and Pedigo standing in front of an operating table with the CIO as the "patient." Lewis, holding a large knife, smiles and says, "Now I'll see what's making him crow!" Pedigo, on the right, holding a large club behind his back, answers, "O Yeah!"[34]

In real life, however, it was difficult for the TWUA to address Lewis's attacks because the doctor simply refused to confront the union outside of print and radio. Pedigo challenged Lewis to a public debate "before any audience which he might select—whether it be the Lions Club, the Chamber of Commerce or what not." On another occasion, Pedigo

[33] Ibid., May 27, Oct. 2, 1946.

[34] Ibid., Nov. 1, 1945. See also ad for a radio speech by Pedigo, sponsored by Local 689, "The Doctor Doesn't Know," ibid., Jan. 1, 1946; Joe Pedigo to Lucy Randolph Mason, Jan. 28, and Joe Pedigo to George Baldanzi, Oct. 17, 1946, both in box 2, acc. 85-10, Joint Board Papers.

offered to arrange a debate with Operation Dixie director Van Bittner. C. L. Ross, the business agent of the Joint Board, also offered to debate the doctor on the radio, with the TWUA paying for the time. Lewis declined every invitation. Baldanzi wanted to sue Lewis for libel, but the CIO's legal counsel advised that it would be difficult to "make it stick . . . [because] it seems that there is plenty of room for those who wish to defame the character of those who represent labor."[35]

Lewis's attacks were particularly harmful because they coincided with the most ambitious organizing campaign undertaken in Floyd County, the effort to organize the huge Pepperell plant in Lindale. The 1,850 textile workers added to the TWUA rolls in the northwest Georgia area in 1946 paled in comparison to the prize represented by the 2,400 workers employed at the Lindale cotton mill. In Pedigo's opinion, the Pepperell workforce was "key to organizing the rest of the unorganized plants in this section of Georgia." Lindale, however, had one of the most notorious records of anti-unionism in the state. Lewis's anti-CIO tirades, especially his accounts of employer goodwill and beneficence, articulated what were already deeply held beliefs among many Pepperell workers. In fact, TWUA leaders claimed that Pepperell management was responsible for the "financing of the advertisements and the advertisements themselves of Dr. W. H. Lewis" on at least two occasions.[36]

By the summer of 1946, local unionists had already invested a year of groundwork in Lindale. Volunteers from the Anchor and Tubize mills handed out leaflets and talked to workers at the Pepperell plant gates, while Pedigo continued the public education effort. Operation Dixie organizers also assisted, although this campaign was carried out primarily by TWUA staff in Georgia.[37] In late 1946, when enough Lindale workers—"a good representative group," in TWUA representative Truman Henderson's words—showed interest, the union began to give out membership cards and start a concerted "drive" at the Lindale mill.[38] Unlike concurrent campaigns in northwest Georgia, however, the inauguration of a card-signing drive at the Pepperell plant would not advance the TWUA toward victory. Reports to the International throughout 1946 and 1947

[35] Joe Pedigo to George Baldanzi, Oct. 17, and Baldanzi to Pedigo, Oct. 21, 1946, both in box 2, acc. 85-10, Joint Board Papers.

[36] Kenneth Douty to John S. Woods, July 2, 1947, ibid.

[37] The CIO drive staff, according to Georgia director Kenneth Douty, were "good fellows," but were incapable of assuming full responsibility. Although Douty did not elaborate, presumably they were committed to work elsewhere. Unfortunately, the precise role that CIO drive staff played in Floyd County is difficult to measure because Operation Dixie papers from Georgia were not preserved.

[38] Truman Henderson to Lindale organizers, n.d., and Pedigo to Horace White, May 20, 1945, both in Horace White correspondence folder, box 2, acc. 85-10, Joint Board Papers.

indicated that organizing continued but made only slow progress. Support for the Lindale union had originated among the more highly skilled fixers and weavers in the plant, but it became clear that the mill had a larger group of anti-union employees who could not be moved by union education. In April 1947, just a couple of months before the TWUA had scheduled an NLRB election, Douty could only report that although the Lindale situation was not "on fire," it "look[ed] hopeful."[39]

Pepperell management employed many of the same anti-union tactics the TWUA had encountered during the Anchor campaign. Douty claimed that mill agent R. Donald Harvey raised "racial issues between white and negro Americans as well as between Americans of varying racial origins." Although Douty did not elaborate, it was probable that Harvey, like Anchor manager Towers, had informed workers of the CIO's support of a permanent postwar FEPC and noted that the TWUA was led by men with foreign-sounding names like "Baldanzi." Employees in Lindale also received copies of the anti-union *Militant Truth*. In protest, Douty wrote Georgia congressman John S. Woods, requesting that Woods take action in his capacity as a member of the House Un-American Affairs Committee. "We feel sure that an investigation will disclose Un-American activity on the part of Mr. R. D. Harvey, manager of the mill and other agents of the company . . . to prevent the proper exercise of the rights of the employees." Union officials also claimed that Lindale teachers, merchants, and ministers became active agents against the union.[40]

Employer paternalism and local boosterism, however, posed the most significant obstacles to the organizing campaign. Most workers expressed their opinion of the union not in terms of dislike for the CIO, but in terms of their positive feelings about the company. Many had apparently internalized textile employers' claim that supporting the TWUA meant disloyalty to the company. Claudie Knowles, for example, undoubtedly spoke for many residents of Lindale when she described herself as having "no use for unions" and the Pepperell plant as "a good place to work." That was "just the way I was brought up," she explained, "that you—whoever was your boss—you were supposed to do the best you could with them." Although she remembered organizers coming around to the plant gates and handing out leaflets, she was "just dedicated to the company and I thought if they were paying my wages and I was working for them, they had a right to tell me what to do." Earl Fricks, who had worked at the mill since the early 1930s, provided a similar explanation

[39] Kenneth Douty to Emil Rieve, January 1947, and Kenneth Douty to Emil Rieve, Apr. 15, 1947, both in Georgia folder, box 1, series 2A, MSS 129A, TWUA Records.

[40] Kenneth Douty to John S. Woods, July 2, 1947, Douty correspondence folder, box 2, acc. 85–10, Joint Board Papers.

for anti-union feeling in Lindale. Although he was not opposed to the union, he explained, most people in Lindale "grew up on that." Since Lindale millhands had no experience with a working union local, they relied on what they had been taught. Fricks recalled that co-workers tried to talk him into joining, and although he was sympathetic, he also refused to join.[41]

Many workers cited what the mill had done for the community and their anger when people criticized it. "There's been a lot of children that have grown up from proceeds of working in that mill," Knowles explained. The company also "helped out the churches . . . put on new roofs for them," and provided even more for the workers. They had "an auditorium put up in memory of men who died in World War I" where the company provided relative luxuries such as a pool room and a swimming pool. Another longtime resident of Lindale, Grady Poole, explained it more cynical terms: "Management had people thinking they was their god and savior—that they couldn't get along without a job down there."[42]

In the small community of Lindale, the generational passage of respect and gratitude for the company was difficult to overcome. Typically, union organizers could turn frustrations and resentments against managers into support for the union, but this strategy failed in Lindale. Pepperell had a number of older workers who recalled firsthand Meikleham's generosity during the depression. Others remembered what the mill had done for their parents. Poole, for example, grew up in the mill village and eventually became a staunch supporter of the TWUA, but he opposed the union in the 1940s. At the time he thought the union would eliminate the advantages of Pepperell paternalism. Two generations of his family had worked in the mill, and because of their long personal relationship with managers, in his words, they "had pull down there." A personal word with a supervisor, for example, had gotten Poole his home in the village. TWUA promises to replace favoritism with more objective measures, such as seniority, would also do away with such favors.[43]

Although mill agent R. Donald Harvey was less flamboyant than Meikleham, Pepperell workers had also "grown to trust" and respect him. Born in Rome, Harvey had begun his textile career in Lindale under Meikleham after graduating from the Georgia School of Technology in 1920. He started "at the bottom," working with Pepperell operatives in each of the mill's departments in order to gain experience, until he was he was promoted to assistant superintendent, to superintendent, and finally to assistant agent. He took over when Meikleham died in 1937. According

[41] Knowles interview; Fricks interview.

[42] Knowles interview; Poole interview.

[43] Poole interview.

to Pepperell historian Evelyn Knowlton, Harvey held "a deep fatherly affection for his employees" that endeared him to the millhands. Carrying on Meikleham's tradition of public addresses, Harvey also reminded millhands himself on many occasions that he had workers' "interests at heart—first, last, and always." In a well-timed Christmas speech about midway through the union's organizational drive, Harvey announced a holiday bonus and characterized the union as an unnecessary, expensive assault on the right to work. Speaking over the Lindale public address system, Harvey made workers a self-serving promise that as long as he was manager, "it will never be necessary for anyone to pay money to any individual or to any organization for the right to work in Lindale."[44]

In June 1947, after a diligent but humdrum campaign by TWUA staff and volunteers, the sympathies of Lindale millhands were put to the test of a union election. Not only did the union receive a solid thumping in the election, but the whole event backfired on the TWUA and became a mass demonstration of anti-unionism. Pepperell employees voted 1,982 to 438 against the union, then erupted into a spontaneous celebration of the union's defeat. Pepperell managers, who traditionally refused millhands even the right to take off Labor Day, indulged celebrating workers by allowing them to shut down the mill. As news that the CIO was losing four to one spread through the plant, "machine after machine in the mill was shut down by the workers." The Lindale correspondent of the *News-Tribune* reported that when the final votes were tallied, "the men and women flowed out of the mill to Lindale's main street where yells and laughter vied with the blare of automobile horns and the wail of sirens." Outside the plant, in a heavy downpour, a mass of celebrating workers hung an effigy of the CIO from an improvised scaffold by the Southern Railroad Station. "Hundreds of motorists moved slowly in a continuous stream by the spot," the paper reported, "with a hand pressing each horn button."[45]

The next morning, the crowd reassembled and staged a mock funeral to bury the effigy of the CIO, complete with casket, hearse, pallbearers, flower girls, undertakers, and a grave. Three workers served as mock "preachers," delivering "stinging remarks," greeted by large "amens" from the spectators. A sign behind the grave announced: "Died June 20, 1947 . . . C.I.O. This is to signify that the American citizens of Lindale, GA., do not approve of the C.I.O. and its communistic element." Accounts of such an elaborately organized display among unorganized workers, of course, smacked of management interference, but the subsequent participation of much of the town must have lent the whole affair

[44] Knowlton, *Pepperell's Progress*, 324–25; Gibbons, *A History of Lindale.*

[45] *Rome News-Tribune*, July 1, 1947; *Textile Bulletin*, July 1, 1947.

a veneer of legitimacy. At least one Lindale resident documented the amazing demonstration on film, and according to newspaper reports, the walkway in front of the local Knight's department store "was crowded all . . . afternoon by Lindaleans viewing picture of the funeral" placed in the store window. Photos and the text of the *News-Tribune* report were submitted to the *Textile Bulletin*, which devoted a full-page spread to the celebration titled "Stone Cold Dead in Lindale." Appearing in the *Bulletin* was a photo of Lindale children standing around the "body" in a casket, and another photo documented a mass of workers standing by the grave under a funeral tent, shouting and waving. In the foreground of the second photograph stood a small boy with a sign mocking the manager of the Joint Board personally, which read "FUNERAL, 10 AM, PEE-DA-GO." The whole event, from the mob to its grisly symbolism, recalled a traditional southern lynching. In the evening after the hoopla died down, the *Bulletin* reported, the merchants of Lindale sponsored the broadcast of a "Lindale Victory Jamboree Program" over the *News-Tribune*'s radio station, WLAQ.[46]

The spectacular defeat and the even more extraordinary outpouring of anti-CIO feeling in Lindale was truly a singular event in the annals of southern anti-unionism, but it also reflected Operation Dixie's misfortunes elsewhere. By 1947 the optimism characterizing the initial stages of the CIO drive gave way to a series of sound losses. The CIO southern organizing campaign continued officially for another six years, but the CIO's inability to create a transforming victory in the larger southern textile mills centers like Lindale at the start of the campaign undermined efforts to make the CIO an accepted southern institution.[47] By invigorating employer opposition and confirming truisms about southern anti-unionism, early and large losses derailed Operation Dixie. At the same time, election defeats seemed to confirm that southern workers preferred their employers and the perquisites of paternalism over the CIO.

The participation of local workers in the antics of public anti-unionism lent an air of authenticity to the traditional claim that southern workers had no interest in unions. It also made the subject of southern workers unavoidable in any assessment of Operation Dixie's defeat. Interestingly, Rome unionists often seized upon the same generalizations about Lindale workers that national CIO organizers made about southern workers. Local unionists described Lindale workers as "uneducated," "afraid," and conditioned by generations of paternalism. "Their Mothers and Daddies worked there, and their Mothers and Daddies before them, and the company would tell them . . . they didn't need a union. And most of them

[46] *Rome News-Tribune*, July 1, 1947; *Textile Bulletin*, July 1, 1947.

[47] Griffith, *Crisis of American Labor.*

believed it," Local 689 member Walter Brooks speculated many years later. Fear was a problem even among those who sympathized with the union, he remembered, because "they were scared to be seen coming in to the union hall, because they knew them people in Lindale would be watching them." Lindale millhands, another unionist agreed, were simply afraid that "they'd lose their jobs" if they supported the union.[48]

TWUA efforts to organize the Lindale plant continued well into the postwar period, but the hard-line anti-unionism nurtured by the company and other workers in 1946 and 1947 remained. Many union members described what amounted to an absolute refusal by some nonunion workers to listen or discuss the merits of the union. Harold Waddell and other volunteer organizers recalled being spat upon and berated by nonunion mill workers. Waddell remembered, for example, that when one of his companions offered a handbill to a woman coming out of the plant at shift change, "she took it and she wadded it up and she threw it down, and she spit on it and she dug it with her foot. And she said, 'Why don't you get you a job and go to work?!' Well, there we were, employees at [Tubize], out on our own trying to help these people realize that they could do better and she thought we were people that didn't work."[49] Anti-union propaganda that portrayed CIO members living high on the hog from union dues probably contributed to the misunderstanding. Pat Baker attributed anti-unionism to a simple but almost insurmountable fact. "Either you are, or you're not [union], and that's the way most people were. You're all the way or you're not all the way," she explained.[50]

Floyd County unionists faced an equally formidable challenge on the second front of the TWUA's and CIO's postwar struggle—politics. PAC, like Operation Dixie, held the potential to dramatically change the postwar balance of power in the South. If PAC could make the South more amenable to the New Deal Democratic sort of liberalism favored by the CIO, it would eliminate, in a single move, some of the most obstreperous enemies of organized labor. Although the formation of southern PACs subjected southern unionists to the same sorts of attacks elicited by Operation Dixie, the 1946 Georgia primary, as the first major election to be held with the participation of African American voters and no poll tax, also held enormous potential for change. The 1946 primary also provided a unique opportunity for TWUA PAC members to demonstrate the union's new presence in state politics and take a crack at ousting the

[48] Brooks interview; Waddell interview.

[49] Waddell interview.

[50] Pat and Frank Baker interview.

Seventh District's entrenched ten-term "anti-labor" congressman, Malcomb Tarver.[51]

In Rome, the TWUA's formation of the Seventh District PAC immediately drew condemnations from the traditional county leaders. Although PAC announced only its intention to raise registration among union members, the prospect was characterized by Lewis, the *News-Tribune*, and several Georgia candidates as the dirtiest of tricks. The *News-Tribune* greeted the formation of the local group in the spring of 1946 by raising an alarm that "new conditions have arisen in Georgia" necessitating a united response. The way to defeat PAC, editor Hornady suggested, was "through wholesale registration on the part of citizens who are interested purely in the welfare of the State and not in the ambitions of minority groups that are financed largely by outside elements." Of course, the editorial page opined, the "Political Action Committee has a perfect right to attempt to control the politics of Georgia, but, on the other hand, the people have a perfect right to defeat the purpose if they are so disposed." For the benefit of "those who may not know," Lewis informed readers, the "C.I.O. Political Action Committee operates to control and guide state and national governments and to remove from office Senators, Congressmen and others who oppose them." Soon the CIO would "drop the mask and seize control of the South."[52] Despite the determined efforts of most Georgia unionists to remain independent, PAC became a red herring in several state primaries. Ben T. Huiet, the Georgia commissioner of labor, for example, urged citizens to vote for him precisely because he was opposed by the "CIO's radical PAC."[53]

Political observers across the state alternately speculated upon and denounced the probable influence of labor on state politics. As race came to dominate the governor's contest between Eugene Talmadge, James Carmichael, and E. D. Rivers, in particular, the CIO was repeatedly branded as an organization working hand in hand with communists and civil rights advocates. Although Talmadge reasserted his traditional platitudes supporting both the right to organize and the right to work, political observers assumed that memories of 1934 made him anathema to many unionists. Talmadge supporters and the Atlanta papers speculated that the CIO supported Talmadge's major opponent, James V. Carmichael.

[51] *Rome News-Tribune*, Mar. 25, 1946; on the southern Democratic Party, see Numan Bartley and Hugh D. Graham, *Southern Politics and the Second Reconstruction* (Baltimore: Johns Hopkins University Press, 1975), 1–24, or the classic V. O. Key, *Southern Politics in State and Nation* (New York: Random House, 1949), 106–29, 309–10; on southern labor and PAC in 1946, see Flamming, *Creating the Modern South*, 249–62.

[52] *Rome News-Tribune*, June 4, Sept. 24, 1946.

[53] *Floyd County Herald*, July 5, 1946.

Widely perceived as the moderate, progressive candidate, Carmichael was nevertheless the first gubernatorial candidate to launch a major attack on Georgia PAC. In May, the United Furniture Workers–CIO filed charges of unfair labor practices with the NLRB against a Carmichael-owned furniture plant, claiming that he closed it down because his employees voted to affiliate with the CIO. Carmichael declared that the charges were a purely political move and launched a blistering attack on the CIO.[54]

Although he offered excuses for the plant closure, Carmichael actually directed more of his energies toward discrediting PAC than denying the accusations before the NLRB. Charging that PAC meant to "run Georgia's election" by making him appear anti-labor, Carmichael announced, "I do not recognize and I will not recognize the right of the Political Action Committee from up East to come down into Georgia and try to run Georgia's elections." It was a popular position with many of Georgia's boosters, who feared the growing influence of organized labor in the state. As the editors of the *Rome News-Tribune* reported approvingly, Carmichael called upon "thoughtful workers of the state . . . to rise up and show the PAC that the People of Georgia are going to elect their own Governor without dictation from any organization and particularly from one whose avowed purpose is to take over the politics of Georgia." If there was to be a "fight in Georgia between democracy on the one hand and arrogant leadership of the CIO-PAC on the other," Carmichael blustered from the stump in Americus, "I welcome the opportunity to lead the fight for the cause of democracy and helping in crushing to earth once and for all in Georgia, the arrogant, dictatorial leadership of CIO-PAC."[55]

Georgia PAC had not in fact endorsed Carmichael, but at least some Talmadge supporters, obviously believing that it would hurt Carmichael, attempted to portray him as PAC's candidate. Just a couple of weeks after Carmichael denounced PAC, a political advertisement in the *News-Tribune* charged that the CIO-PAC's close association with Carmichael supporters such as Ellis Arnall and the *Atlanta Journal* was tantamount to endorsing Carmichael over Talmadge. "Yes, the CIO-PAC endorsed Ellis, and they have endorsed Jimmie," the ad warned. "The CIO-PAC are backing Jimmie Carmichael, the 'Niggers' candidate." If Carmichael and PAC had their way, the ad continued, "He will do as Ellis did, i.e. just what the CIO PAC tells him to do." And what PAC aimed to do, once they had power, was "to abolish the 'Jim Crow' laws."[56]

Although Talmadge did not personally attack PAC, the charges meshed well with the former governor's general platform of protecting white su-

[54] *Rome News-Tribune*, May 29, July 8, 1946.

[55] Ibid., May 3, 29, 31, 1946.

[56] Ibid., July 8, 1946.

premacy from outsiders such as the American federal government. Talmadge also charged that "alien and communistic influences from the East" were "agitating for social equality in our State," even if he did not identify PAC as one of them. Speaking to a crowd of fourteen hundred people in the Rome city auditorium, Talmadge identified the villains seeking to overthrow Georgia traditions as Ellis Arnall and his "Moscow-Harlem zootsuit crowd who now seek to consolidate a wedge in the color lines through the candidacy of James V. Carmichael." Across the state he railed against those outsiders who "desire Negroes to participate in our White Primary . . . to pass the F.E.P.C. Law and to defeat our Southern Congressmen and Senators who have opposed the F.E.P.C.." And, as gubernatorial candidates passed around the stigma of an imaginary CIO-PAC endorsement like a hot potato, Talmadge accused all his opponents of courting the black vote.[57]

While Talmadge traveled the state proposing hackneyed legislative solutions to circumvent the Supreme Court's ruling against the white primary, his major opponents—Carmichael and former governor E. D. Rivers—competed for votes of the "better sort" that ousted Talmadge in 1942. Although Arnall was ineligible to run again, he threw his support behind Carmichael, who ran against the tarnished images of Rivers and Talmadge as the candidate who could restore honest, efficient, "good government." Rivers simply recycled his promises for a "little new deal." Though both Carmichael and Rivers defended their credentials as white supremacists, they allowed Talmadge to make the white primary his own issue. Advising Georgians that the Court's ruling was law, Rivers and Carmichael both contended that the governor had no power to reverse the decision.[58]

The congressional race between Malcomb Tarver and his primary opponent, Henderson Lanham, though certainly less colorful, similarly revolved around the issue of Georgia's past and future. The incumbent, Tarver, was a classic southern anti–New Dealer who described himself as a "staunch Democrat" in spite of the fact that he had "in some instances differed with programs promulgated by party leaders." An advocate of fiscal conservatism, Tarver nevertheless brought millions of federal dollars to his district as a member of the House Committee on Appropriations. He procured over $60 million for a pet project of Seventh District boosters—the construction of dam and power projects on the Coosa, Oostanaula, Coosawattee, and Etowah Rivers. His opponent, Rome native Henderson Lanham, on the other hand, described himself as "progressive, without being radical" and announced his intention to solicit the

[57] Ibid., Apr. 7, June 30, May 19, 1946.

[58] Ibid., May 13, 1946; see also Bartley, *Creation of Modern Georgia*, 202–3.

support of young voters, veterans, and "every forward looking person" in Georgia. On the issue of labor and PAC, Tarver held his tongue in Floyd County but raged against PAC actions in his hometown of Dalton. Lanham announced his vague intention, to the approval of the *News-Tribune*, of supporting "fair but firm legislation to prevent strikes which paralyze the industries of the entire country, while preserving the right of labor to organize and bargain collectively."[59]

Rome unionists supported Lanham, but perhaps because PAC's participation in the congressional race had become so controversial in Tarver's own Whitfield County, they kept any local politicking out of public view. In Floyd County it was actually a group of veterans who spearheaded a campaign to defeat Tarver. In June the *Floyd County Herald*, a paper run by World War II vets, revealed that Tarver had voted against an appropriation for veterans' housing in Rome. Tarver flatly denied that he had voted to withhold the funds and pointed to his support of another housing bill. The *Herald* promptly pointed out that the bill Tarver claimed to have supported (there was no roll call) was passed six years ago. In the final weeks of the campaign, the *Herald* put every Tarver utterance to the test of the *Congressional Record*. When Tarver attempted to claim responsibility for support of rural electrification, for example, the *Herald* reported the claim "at variance with the vote by him against a rural electrification bill" in 1943.[60]

The *Herald* staff also opposed Talmadge in the name of local veterans. Endorsing Carmichael, the editors announced, "it [was] extremely gratifying to veterans (who have associated for years during their army life with non-Georgians and learned the low opinion they had of our state in the pre-Arnall days) to know that there is, with the election of Carmichael, assurance that the progressive enlightened days of Georgia are not over." In the last four years, the *Herald* claimed, Georgia had "passed from being the laughing stock of the nation, trotting meekly along behind a strutting, bespectacled, red-gallused dictator into a modern, progressive forward-looking governmental unit." The white primary issue, the *Herald* advised potential voters, was merely a smoke screen, but it would not "cloud the issue [Talmadge's past record] quite enough."[61]

Even as Talmadge railed about resuscitating Georgia's white primary, another political group new to the Floyd County political scene, African American members of the Rome NAACP, began to organize black residents to cast their ballots in the upcoming primary. Canvassing door-to-

[59] *Rome News-Tribune*, May 27, 1946.

[60] On PAC and Tarver in Dalton, see Flamming, *Creating the Modern South*, 251–53; *Floyd County Herald*, June 7, 14, 1946.

[61] *Floyd County-Herald*, Mar. 12, Apr. 26, 1946.

door, Rome's black ministers, the editor of the black community's newspaper (the *Rome Enterprise*), and several women active in the NAACP persuaded thousands of black citizens to go to the county courthouse and add their name to the "colored" registration book. Callie Martin, a resident of Rome who voted in 1946 for the first time, attributed the success of their efforts to the impact of World War II. "When the fellows began to come back from the war," she explained, they began to think, "I served my country, I deserve more freedom, I deserve more rights." Martin and "quite a few other women activists" agreed. In 1946 she and other volunteers organized 1,295 black voters, tripling the number of black registrants on the books. In a county with a black voting-age population of 4,907, it was quite an achievement.[62]

Talmadge supporters in Floyd County met African American voter registration with alarm and a concerted effort to purge the books. In mid-July, Talmadge's local campaign chairman, Vaughn Terrell, Rome attorney and solicitor of the county court, announced his intention to file petitions challenging black registrants' qualifications at the rate of 150 per day until the books were entirely white. The "better Negroes," Terrell claimed, "do not want political equality and I doubt if ever they are capable of meeting the responsibility." Even in the 1940s, Georgia's voting qualifications were highly subjective, requiring not only strict residency specifications but "good character," an "understanding of the duties and obligations of citizenship," and a literacy test. Such criteria were used to disqualify hundreds of black voters in Fulton, Sumner, and Muscogee Counties. Whiteness and not literacy was the real test applied by Talmadge supporters. If followed to the letter, one Floyd County registrar noted, the state's literacy laws could also be used to disqualify as many white voters. Terrell essentially agreed, telling the *News-Tribune* that race, rather than literacy, was "the only real issue in this campaign."[63]

Floyd County officials, however, joined the side of reason and reform, or at least the side of James Carmichael, serving notice that Floyd County was no longer a rural stronghold of Talmadge allies. Terrell had assumed that the county would bear the expense of serving the challenge papers and that black voters would bear the burden of proof. However, when Terrell filed his challenges with the board of registrars, they ruled that Terrell would have to pay the court costs of serving and processing the challenges. At $3 each, the cost would have been over $3,600, the equiva-

[62] Callie Martin, interview with author, July 28, 1994. In 1945, only 691 black voters appeared in county registration books. Figures calculated from Rome "Colored" voter registration book, 1934–1948, Floyd County Voter Registration Books, Floyd County Records Retention Center, Rome, Georgia.

[63] *Rome News-Tribune*, June 14, 9, 1946; on Georgia voting laws, see Bartley, *Creation of Modern Georgia*, 159.

lent of an average year's earnings for many Georgians. Terrell dropped his challenges, but a month later he returned to the board claiming that all black voters were illegally registered because "no oath was administered at the time of the registration." Terrell's attorney, who accompanied him for the hearing before the registrars, argued that the registrant "must give some indication that he recognizes the oath." When pressed to elaborate, it was clear that he and Terrell had not thought out the legal angles. The attorney finally conceded that the registrant "need not raise his hand, but must make some sign." At one point a frustrated member of the board of registrars leaned forward and demanded of Terrell: "Would you please tell me what we're trying to do here?" An attorney representing black registrants argued that the oath had been administered because registrants signed below it. As the hearing continued, it became clear that honoring Terrell's claim would disqualify virtually every voter in the county, black and white. Terrell explained that he intended to apply the law only to black voters, but the board, evaluating the evidence in private, returned a decision in favor of black registrants.[64]

Other white Floyd County residents, via the *Herald*, came to black voters' defense, suggesting that the war had forced many whites to reevaluate southern democracy in the light of their World War II experience. Glen McCullough, a white veteran writing in the *Herald*, scolded Terrell, "I shudder to think of the circumstances we might now be living under had [your] above theory been applied to the Negroes when the Draft Law was effected." If the "red-suspendered farmer isn't elected, you won't have gained a thing," he scolded; "on the other hand you shall have spent your own money and made an ass of yourself generally." Another white citizen writing to the *Herald*, W. M. Glad, asked, "Are not the colored doctors, lawyers, preachers, teachers and business people, as well as their high school graduates, as well qualified to vote as the many white people who vote without being able to recognize their own names . . . and have to sign their names with an X?" Glad described himself as not "one of Talmadge's nigger haters, nor am I what some call a nigger lover," but someone who "earnestly believe[s] in fair play." Rev. Thomas W. Anderson, writing on behalf of black voters in Floyd County, took it upon himself to "here and now inform Mr. Terrell that all intelligent and law-abiding blacks want the privilege of voting any time and anywhere public officials who are to have the slightest authority over them are to be elected." The *Rome News-Tribune* did not respond to the debate in the *Herald*.[65]

[64] *Rome News-Tribune*, June 14, 16, 20, 1946; *Floyd County Herald*, June 21, July 12, 1946.

[65] *Floyd County Herald*, June 21, July 12, 28, 1946.

Organized labor also remained silent, refraining from comment on the black registration drive or Terrell's attempted purge. PAC's own voter registration drive had elicited so much controversy that perhaps unionists opted to remain on the sidelines of this particular conflict. While International TWUA staff probably granted black registration much higher priority in the union's long-term plans for the South, it was also true that black registration was only peripherally connected to the TWUA's immediate political goals in Floyd County. Black voters were likely to have the greatest impact in the governor's primary, a race where PAC did not officially endorse a candidate. Union voter returns from the Tubize district, for example, later confirmed that organized workers did not share a united opinion on Talmadge, Carmichael, and Rivers. Other union political actions, however, suggested that union labor, if not hostile to black registration, did not grant it very high priority. Just two years later, Vaughn Terrell himself appeared on a Seventh District PAC memo as a "Georgia candidate favorable to labor."[66]

On election day, the largest number of voters in Floyd County history filed into the courthouse in segregated lines to cast their ballots in boxes labeled "white" and "colored." With a wide base of support from every precinct but one, Lanham won the popular vote in the congressional race by nearly two to one in Floyd County.[67] In the gubernatorial primary, Carmichael won a clear victory in Floyd County with 5,117 votes to Talmadge's 4,253. Across the county, citizens' preferences in the gubernatorial race followed what now seemed to be predictable patterns. Carmichael's support came from Rome residents, organized mill workers, and African Americans. Newly registered African American voters, in particular, had provided a critical edge. Over 1,000 votes, or one-fifth of Carmichael's total vote in Floyd County, had been cast by black voters, according to the *News-Tribune*. In Riverside, the Tubize mill village district, which was the only clearly identifiable union district, PAC had increased voter registration 11 percent and voter turnout from 19 percent in 1942 to 51 percent in 1946. Though village residents cast a strong vote for Lanham, the district divided in the governor's race. Riverside citizens cast 288 votes for Carmichael, 99 for Rivers, and 195 for Talmadge. In Lindale and rural districts, Talmadge's support remained strong, replicating a pat-

[66] "Georgia Candidates Favorable to Labor," n.d., in "Georgia 1948" folder, box 479, MSS 396, TWUA Records.

[67] Lanham received 7,022 votes to Tarver's 4,065 in Floyd County, winning in every precinct except the rural district of Etowah. Elsewhere in the congressional district, however, Tarver faired better. In fact, Tarver won more popular votes within the Seventh District, but Lanham won the election by winning the most county units. *Rome News-Tribune*, July 19, 1946.

tern across the state.[68] The defeat of Talmadge in Floyd County and other more urban areas of the state, however, could not overcome Talmadge's strong showing in Georgia's rural counties. As Georgia historian Numan Bartley observed, the 1946 primary election may have proved that "the forces of reaction could not attract a majority of voters," but it also indicated that "the forces of 'progress' could not achieve a county unit majority." Although Carmichael won a plurality of the popular vote, Talmadge won most of the smaller counties, thus winning the majority of county unit votes and the election. White supremacy had been put to the test, the *Rome News-Tribune* pronounced, but it was "still a white man's Georgia."[69]

Ultimately, Talmadge would not have an opportunity to make good on his promises to fight for the restoration of the white primary. His death in the brief period of time between the general election and his inauguration introduced a contentious crisis over succession to the governorship. Also elected in 1946, M. E. Thompson, the state's first lieutenant governor under the recently adopted new state constitution, claimed the office as rightfully his own. But Talmadge supporters, anticipating such a contingency, had organized a write-in campaign for Eugene's son, Herman, and claimed that the candidate with the largest number of write-in votes should take the office. With both Thompson and the younger Talmadge claiming the seat, the legislature met and counted the ballots. At first it looked like Carmichael, with 669 write-in votes, might take the seat, until Talmadge managers "found" an additional 56 write-in votes for Herman in the Talmadges' home county. Allegedly misfiled during the election, the votes were written in a single hand and mysteriously cast in alphabetical order by residents of a Telfair County graveyard. Nevertheless, the legislature named Herman Talmadge the new governor. When Arnall refused to surrender the post, Talmadge forces physically took over the governor's office and mansion. Arnall retaliated by proclaiming Thompson his suc-

[68] *Rome News-Tribune*, July 19, 1946; Floyd County Voter Registration Books. Figures for registration and voter turnout are based on an analysis of voter registration books for the Riverside district (the Tubize mill village) in Floyd County and a subsequent comparison with voting returns published in the *Rome News-Tribune*. Using the city directories from 1934 to 1950, I identified workers and their family members and excluded office, lab, and supervisory staff, who would not have been union members. From this I determined the number of registered workers, excluding those who were twenty or younger in order to measure deliberate registration rather than newly eligible registrants. Registration totals were then compared with the number of votes cast in the Riverside district to determine turnout. However, the Riverside district represents only a sample of Local 689's voters because not all millhands lived in the village. This method is the basis for all subsequent discussions of voter registration and turnout, unless otherwise noted.

[69] Bartley, *Creation of Modern Georgia*, 203.

cessor, and Thompson also declared himself governor and set up a rival office in downtown Atlanta. Finally, the state supreme court declared Thompson the legitimate governor and announced a special gubernatorial election to be held in 1948.[70]

In the realm of ideological succession, however, there was never any contest. Herman Talmadge immediately took up the mantle of his father as the most vigilant protector of the white "Southern way of life," defending Georgia's racial practices against the FEPC and other civil rights measures propagated by the national Democratic Party. Although Herman Talmadge's simultaneous reputation as a business-minded booster for Georgia industrial development sometimes allowed him to be portrayed as a moderate in comparison to his father, he soon emerged as one of the foremost defenders of segregation. In 1948 he won the governorship back on a platform defending white supremacy that was not unlike Eugene's 1946 campaign. Thus the controversy that emerged after the 1946 elections did not necessarily refute the *Rome News-Tribune* editor's assertion. Eugene Talmadge may have ultimately failed to restore Georgia to the state of pre-Arnall reforms, but the 1946 elections cleared a path for an equally vociferous defense of white supremacy to be mounted by his son in the 1950s.

Eugene Talmadge's narrow victory through the county unit system, however, disguised a real, if temporary, departure in popular Georgia politics. For a brief period, African Americans, organized labor, veterans, and other "progressive" citizens of Floyd County inadvertently formed an unprecedented political coalition. The results in Floyd County suggested a glimmer of what the CIO had envisioned for the postwar South—an organized, informed, active electorate of black and white Georgians supporting change, even if they supported candidates independently and for different reasons. It is perhaps a case of historical irony that political change did not arrive in the name of, or under the authority of, PAC actions. Rome unionists' subsequent alliance with Terrell also indicated that labor's interests would be pursued within the traditional boundaries of southern Democratic activism.

The extent to which Floyd County's textile workers remained a part of the white South, however, did not ease mounting anti-union pressures against organized labor. The outpouring of local anti-unionism and the TWUA's failure to organize the largest workforce in Floyd County suggested that organized labor had reached a plateau in northwest Georgia. Despite all evidence that Rome unionists' had internalized, indeed repli-

[70] Ibid., 204–5.

cated, traditional racial hierarchies within their unions, the CIO's high profile elsewhere as a defender of civil rights made it difficult to deflect charges that they had allied with "outsiders."

As the immediate period after World War II drew to a close, organized labor's future in Floyd County remained uncertain. While federal labor policy and government contracts in the first half of the decade had held anti-union aggression in check, the South's traditional leaders served notice in 1946 and 1947 that the TWUA-CIO would not so easily win the peace. In Congress, Georgia's representatives, with the exception of Lanham, joined Republicans to pass the Taft-Hartley Act. Placing new stringent restrictions on organized labor's activities, Taft-Hartley also broadened employers' freedom of speech, delivering a decisive blow to Operation Dixie. In Georgia, legislators passed a state right-to-work law that eliminated maintenance of membership, thus eroding the beachhead the TWUA had created in textiles during World War II. Southern boosters and businessmen liked to claim they did not question labor's right to organize, but in reality they had put labor on the defensive.

Five

"Some Romans Have Red Faces": The 1948 Strikes

DESCRIBING THE CITY "in unbiased terms" in a special preface to the 1947 city directory, the Rome Chamber of Commerce highlighted northwest Georgia's abundant supply of white labor as just one of the advantages their city offered "as a place of residence, as a business location, [or] as a manufacturing site." With convenient transportation, a wealth of mineral resources, "miles of good factory sites," and "all the advantages . . . possessed by a Northern climate, without the disadvantages," the hills of northwest Georgia were rich in labor of "native Anglo-Saxon stock." Elaborating on the local workforce, the chamber added the words "99.9% native-born," "efficient," and "loyal." To outside investors, perhaps wearied by the wave of strikes that followed World War II in the Midwest and Northeast, the chamber beckoned with the promise that a "splendid spirit of cooperation exists between employer and employee." Rome's workers were not only skilled, easily transportable, white, and experienced, but also devoted to their employers. As a result, the chamber boasted, "very few labor disputes" had arisen in Floyd County in the past twenty years.[1]

The following year, however, Romans experienced one of the most intense years of labor strife in the county's history. In spite of the promises of southern boosters, the pact between "benevolent" managers and "content" workers gave way to full-scale modern industrial disputes at two of the county's largest mills. Until World War II, poverty and unemployment had compelled workers to accept what mill managers offered. But unions now provided workers with new tools to renegotiate the terms that had initially drawn employers south, and not surprisingly, employers and boosters proved reluctant to give up Rome's advantages in the politics of business location. Armed with new legislation and the power of anti-union sentiment in the South, employers struck back. As the strikes unfolded at the Anchor and Tubize mills, latent concerns about "big labor," industrial recruitment, and regional pride emerged, permeating the rhetoric of the unions, managers, and community leaders. Managers recycled

[1] *Polk's Rome (Floyd County, GA) City Directory, 1947* (Richmond: R. L. Polk, 1947), 1–10.

all the regional arguments against unions as northerners, outsiders, and general meddlers in the affairs of like-thinking southerners. All sides looked to the authority of the state and traditional ideas in southern culture to resolve the conflict.

Although the strikes were essentially confined to the white community of millhands, managers, merchants, and county elites, race played an important, if seldom articulated, role in the conflicts of 1948. The strikes, initially triggered by contractual issues, also called into question some of the central tenets of southern boosterism and the collective white interests it purported to represent. Management's complicity in strike-related violence, in particular, seemed to discredit industry's avowed mission to "serve" the community and protect white workers. Finally, workers themselves forced the white community to confront the contradiction between the logic of boosting the South's allegedly superior workers and employers' determination to maintain a wage scale far below the rest of the nation's. In the end, the power of the ideas behind southern boosterism provided the critical leverage that allowed one group of workers to win legitimacy for their union and their strike.

Although each conflict stemmed from local disputes, Floyd County's 1948 strikes were intimately shaped by postwar changes in federal labor policy. In the summer of 1947, exasperated union textile workers had seen the Wagner Act, which had been so critical to early CIO gains, "cut to pieces" (in the words of *Textile Labor*) by a coalition of congressional Republicans and southern Democrats. The resulting Taft-Hartley Act liberalized restrictions on employers and set new limits on organized labor.[2] Because the TWUA had relied heavily on the machinery of the NLRB and federal policy to bolster southern efforts, Taft-Hartley placed a formidable burden on the textile union in the South. It attacked the security of locals by outlawing the "union shop," or in the parlance of southern legislators, by guaranteeing an anti-union employee the "right to work" under a union contract without joining the union. The act also sanctioned an employer's "freedom of speech" against unions. While the changes ostensibly did not eliminate the Wagner Act's guarantee of the right to organize, the resulting Georgia "right to work" law had important symbolic meaning. In the words of one Georgia labor historian, it sent "a signal to business leaders—and to workers—that unions in Georgia were too weak to wield any political clout and that unions were not welcome in the state." As the TWUA's 1948 contract negotiations opened, it quickly became

[2] *Textile Labor*, June 21, May 3, 1947.

clear that employers in Floyd County, and across the South, aimed to press their new advantage.[3]

Meanwhile, the cotton textile industry's immediate postwar boom in 1946 had given way to a serious slump by 1948 that undercut workers' economic leverage. When the domestic market for American cotton goods fell from the immediate heights of unleashed wartime demand and foreign producers began to provide new competition in international markets, textile industry leaders responded with a variety of cost-cutting strategies that had an immediate impact on labor. As boosters frequently noted, cost reduction had historically encouraged textile capital to make greater use of unorganized and cheaper labor in the South. However, increasing competition placed a particular strain on the smaller textile mills, such as the Anchor plant, that were concentrated in the South. Many of these firms, unable to compete in the volatile postwar textile market, liquidated their assets for sale, closed down permanently, or sold plants to larger textile corporations. Nationwide, hundreds of textile mills changed hands in the postwar years, mostly in the South. In Floyd County, for example, the ownership of three of the five largest mills, including the Anchor and Tubize plants, changed at least once between 1945 and 1950.[4]

TWUA leaders claimed that textile industrialists exaggerated the extent of corporate suffering, but the effect on northwest Georgia's textile workers was indisputable. Although the impact on payrolls was often disguised by layoffs or short time, textile industry cost-cutting measures led to a "slow, steady increase in (Southern) industrial unemployment," according to Georgia State Employment Service officials. By early 1948, Floyd County merchants and textile managers were calling it a "textile depression." A survey by the Georgia Department of Labor revealed that the chenille and cotton industries had reduced production in 1947–48 by 75 and 40 percent, respectively. The largest local textile producers in Rome, Lindale, Cedartown, and Shannon responded to this perceived depression with speed-ups, layoffs, and drastic reductions in the workweek. As a result, the "feeling about jobs these days," the *Rome News-Tribune* reported in 1948, "is they're hard to get." When the textile industry reached its lowest ebb at the beginning of January 1949, Georgia State Employment Service representatives in Rome reported that among area workers, eleven hundred millhands were permanently laid off from their jobs and another twenty-five hundred were receiving only part-time wages. Making economic matters worse, the number of farmers displaced

[3] Quote from Flamming, *Creating the Modern South*, 288; Zieger, *American Workers*, 108–14.

[4] Truchil, *Capital-Labor Relations*, 41–44; Blicksilver, *Cotton Manufacturing in the Southeast*, 153, 166–67.

by machinery and new agricultural practices in the postwar period had continued to increase, creating even greater competition for the dwindling supply of textile jobs. Just a few years after the war, southern textile communities faced conditions not unlike those in the 1920s and 1930s, with high levels of underemployment, diminished markets for southern goods, and heavy competition for industrial jobs, even within the racially segmented market.[5]

The workers employed at the Anchor mill had already begun to experience the impact of economic uncertainty and labor policy changes in early 1947. Rumors surrounding the possible liquidation or sale of the Anchor mill had been circulating for months when, in the spring of 1947, the mill was sold, then immediately put back on the market for resale.[6] The security of jobs at the Anchor plant remained uncertain for about a year until the president of Alabama Mills Corporation, P. A. Redmond, a native son of Rome and a former Anchor manager, took over the mills in the spirit of "local boy makes good." Announcing plans to expand and continue operation in the plant, Redmond made his son, P. A. Redmond, Jr., president of the mill and installed a veteran textile manager and former employee of Alabama Mills, L. H. Rice, as the plant manager. On Rice's advice, the corporation began to remodel the plant, now "Anchor Rome Mill," and installed new machinery to convert from production of industrial cotton duck to novelty textiles.[7] The mill also renewed its commitment to community welfare, donating significant sums to local churches and village activities. But more importantly from the larger community's standpoint, Redmond saved hundreds of white jobs and millions of community dollars.[8]

Although Anchor's old managers had never been particularly cooperative with the union, TWUA leaders were apprehensive about the sale.

[5] The *News-Tribune* reported regularly on trends in the industry, unemployment rates, and local employment conditions as monitored by the Georgia Department of Labor and the USES. Altogether they confirm the assessment by local textile businessmen that cotton textiles had "been in a bad way for the past three years"—1946–49. Quote from USES officials in *Rome News-Tribune*, Aug. 21, 1949. See also ibid., Feb. 8, 15, May 16, 1948, Feb. 3, 25, Apr. 3, June 16, July 10, Aug. 21, Oct. 7, 1949; *Textile Labor*, July 5, 1947; see also Minchin, *What Do We Need a Union For?*

[6] Testimony of Joe Pedigo and L. H. Rice in U.S. Congress, Senate Subcommittee on Labor and Labor-Management Relations, *Labor-Management Relations in the Southern Textile Manufacturing Industry: Hearings before the Subcommittee on Labor-Management Relations*, 81st Cong., 2nd sess. (Washington, D.C.: Government Printing Office, 1950), 175, 295–96 (hereafter cited as *Labor-Management Relations*).

[7] McCarthy, "Mill Background," n.d., folder "Celanese Strike, Rome, GA" box 6, series 10A, US MSS 129A, TWUA Records; Pedigo and Rice testimony in *Labor-Management Relations*, 173–75, 295–96.

[8] *Rome News-Tribune*, Feb. 15, June 25, 1948.

"We knew we were in for trouble," Joe Pedigo explained, because the "antiunion policy" of Rice and Alabama Mills "was well known." The TWUA had organized three of ten Alabama Mills' southern factories, and in each case the company had fought the union with the kind of tactics that the TWUA had identified in early 1947 as a southwide conspiracy. Alabama Mills managers fired union members, campaigned against the union in the shop, or simply closed the mill down. Rice himself had been plant manager in two of Alabama Mills' factories at the very time that the management had waged successful campaigns against TWUA locals. Local union officials in Rome braced themselves for a fight.[9]

When Alabama Mills took over in the fall of 1947, Local 787 was particularly vulnerable. In TWUA jargon, it was a "sick" local, where both enthusiasm for the union and membership had declined. Turnover and layoffs had whittled away the base of union supporters who had voted in the TWUA just two years before. Although Anchor Rome was still under contract when the sale was finalized, that contract, in order to comply with Georgia's new right-to-work law, had eliminated union security clauses and now permitted workers to withdraw membership during the contract year. As soon as the first sale of Anchor Rome had been announced, local management and some workers had begun campaigning to persuade individual millhands to withdraw from the union.[10] The company office furnished blank typewritten forms that read "Anchor Rome Mills, Inc.: Please do not take out any more union dues on me." When a union member protested to an overseer that he did not think managers should do this on company time, he was told "it was a free damn country and that they had a right to do it if they wanted too [*sic*]."[11]

The withdrawal campaign was but a foreshadowing of what became, in the words of Joe Pedigo, "an open all-out drive to smash the Union." Anchor management strategy in 1948 was a formidable mixture of both old and new anti-union tactics. Freed by Taft-Hartley to proselytize, managers revived the traditional southern arguments against giving money to outsiders and suspected communists. Emboldened managers attempted to erode the local's membership base, worker by worker, at a time when the current economic conditions must have made workers feel particularly vulnerable. Local supervisors who had quietly opposed the union since 1945 expressed open animosity against the TWUA-CIO and singled out workers in order to verbalize their disapproval. Union member L. P.

[9] Pedigo testimony, *Labor-Management Relations*, 173, 176–77, 296; McCarthy, "Mill Background."

[10] Quote from Pedigo, *Labor-Management Relations*, 175; Kenneth Douty to Emil Rieve, Apr. 15, 1947, Georgia folder, box 1, series 2A, US MSS 129A, TWUA Records.

[11] Union exhibit B and Pedigo testimony, *Labor-Management Relations*, 175–81; sworn affidavit of Henry Farmer, July 2, 1947, NLRB Case 10-CA-84 (1952).

Vassar remembered a night at a local beer tavern, for example, when a supervisor invited him over to a booth, bought him a beer, and then seized the opportunity to tell Vassar that the union was a communist outfit that originated in New York. The supervisor suggested that Vassar investigate the union before he had "anymore to do with it." When Vassar asked his supervisor what a communist was, the supervisor "could not tell [him]." Evidently the fact that the TWUA was from New York was bad enough.[12]

A more insidious management strategy consisted of sabotaging the union's role in the plant. Management simply made it impossible for the local to carry out its daily functions in the mill. At the very time that the company was instituting major production changes as it converted to a new product line, managers began to ignore established procedures for changes in workloads. Although Local 787's contract provided for three steps in the grievance procedure, or three opportunities to settle union complaints at successive levels of authority, supervisors began to ignore contract procedures and refer all grievances to the highest level of management, personnel director Robert Bachman. Meanwhile, Bachman, "never the most friendly individual to do business with," according to Joe Pedigo, became "unbearably overbearing and disdainful" of the union, refusing to meet with union officials and then threatening to throw grievance forms in the mill village creek. The company's policy for settling union grievances, according to Pedigo, became "a policy of settling nothing."[13]

Management intransigence not only frustrated union officials, it quickly drained the resources of the local. By ignoring normal grievance procedures, managers left Local 787 no other option than to seek outside arbitration, which was much more expensive and labor-intensive. The Northwest Georgia Joint Board had to employ an additional full-time staff member just to service Local 787. Moreover, the behavior of company representatives led union officials to believe that Anchor Rome was deliberately wasting union time and money. Pedigo claimed that management would allow grievances to reach the arbitration stage, let the union spend "days and nights" preparing for the hearing, then abruptly concede cases the moment before arbitration began. Finally, when arbitrators delivered decisions favorable to the union, Anchor Rome stalled implementation, badgered the arbitrator for a reversal, or disingenuously claimed that managers could not understand the decision.[14]

[12] Affidavit of L. P. Vasser, NLRB Case 10-CA-794 (1952); Joe Pedigo to Robert Armory, July 15, 1947 (copy), NLRB Case 10-CA-84 (1952).

[13] Pedigo testimony, *Labor-Management Relations*, 175–81.

[14] The arbitration process, a sort of mock court proceeding before three arbitrators, required the union to put its most valuable resources—time and money—into the preparation of the case, negotiate the selection of the arbitrator with the company, and pay arbitrator fees. Joe Pedigo to Robert Armory, 15 July 1947 (copy), sworn affidavit of William Shiflett,

Anchor Rome managers' ability to thwart the orderly function of the local soon undermined the rank and file's confidence in the union. Workers became frustrated when the union failed to remedy stretch-outs, the replacement of hourly wages with piece rates, and layoffs outside the seniority system. Union president William Shiflett blamed the breakdown of the grievance procedure for what became a steady decline in union membership. "When you don't get grievances settled for the employees, then they withdraw from the union," Shiflett explained. "They want to know why their grievances were not settled and it is very bad on the membership." Basically the company acted as if there were no union, operating as the mills had for forty years prior to the establishment of Local 787.[15]

In February 1948, when union officials met representatives from Alabama Mills at the bargaining table for the first time, with Local 787's contract two weeks away from expiration, it became clear that Anchor officials sought more than a protection of managerial prerogatives or a more favorable contract for themselves. Anchor Rome chose Frank Constangy, an Atlanta attorney notorious among TWUA staffers as a union buster, as their primary representative. Pedigo claimed that Constangy "devoted most of the meeting to castigating the union" and that "the effect upon the bargaining session was not good." Constangy questioned virtually every clause in the contract. At first the company even objected to the clause that permitted the union to bargain "in respect to rates of pay, wages, hours of employment and other conditions of employment."[16]

In subsequent meetings the company became "adamant, refusing to make any concession," according to Pedigo, on four union matters—the checkoff, union liability for strikes, and leaves of absence and superseniority for union officers. Furthermore, the company wanted to substitute individual for collective bargaining, to eliminate clauses providing for arbitration, piece rate, and incentive rate guarantees, and to give the company contractual power to increase workloads at will. In effect the company was demanding a union that existed in name only. Within their rights under the new federal and state legislation, company representatives also told the union that "under no circumstances" would Anchor Rome Mills include provisions for a revocable checkoff. "We think the union should collect its own dues on its own time and off of our property," Rice wrote in a letter to employees, without explaining that "our

NLRB final investigation report, all in NLRB Case 10-CA-794 (1952); Pedigo testimony, *Labor-Management Relations*, 182–84.

[15] Pedigo and William Shiflett testimony, *Labor-Management Relations*, 183–89, 221; William Shiflett v. Anchor Rome Mills, complaint filed in Rome Division of the District Court of the United States, copy in NLRB Case 10-CA-54 (1951).

[16] Pedigo testimony, *Labor-Management Relations*, 191–92.

property" included their mill village homes, parks, and community buildings. Union officials protested that without some sort of checkoff or at least the opportunity to collect on village property, dues collection would be impossible.[17]

Pressing a timely and sensitive issue, company representatives fixated especially on the liability clause, insisting that the union accept all responsibility for any kind of work stoppage, even if it was unauthorized by the union. In public addresses to employees, letters, and statements to the press, Redmond claimed that the union's refusal to accept a liability clause was the crux of company-union differences, and protested that management was merely asking that the union be held accountable to the contract in the same manner as the company. Although Redmond misrepresented the actual dispute, it allowed the company to take advantage of contemporary resentments toward postwar strikes and played upon people's suspicions that unions placed unfair burdens on companies. In fact, Local 787's officials were prepared to accept some modification of Redmond's demand, but the company rejected every offer to negotiate the clause. Finally, Constangy reported to the union that the company "would never agree" to any of the union's compromises and it would be useless to discuss the issue further.[18]

Given the weakened state of the membership and the union finances, as well as the general backlash against organized labor, Local 787 was not in the best position to call a strike, but Anchor Rome management left TWUA members little choice. Union leaders believed that "acceptance of the [company's] demands would have been suicide for the union." On March 18, 1948, when a last-minute meeting with the Federal Mediation and Conciliation Service in Atlanta brought the company and union no closer to settlement, members of Local 787 walked out and the union established picket lines around the plant. The *Rome News-Tribune*, a stalwart editorial defender of the "right to work," noted with approval that the demonstrations were "orderly" but also reported that "police protection will be provided to anyone wishing to work in the mill." With a veiled threat, Plant Manager Rice informed the union that he intended to operate the mill despite the strike, announcing, "We are going to run the mill unless we sell it." The Anchor plant remained open, and many nonmembers of the union did choose work over the walkout. By the end of the next day, according to local newspaper accounts, "rumors were

[17] NLRB, "Intermediate Report and Recommended Order," Feb. 25, 1949, NLRB Case 10-CA-84 (1951), 20; Pedigo testimony and Rice to Employees, Mar. 17, 1948, union exhibit K, *Labor-Management Relations*, 190–95; *Rome News-Tribune*, Mar. 21, 1948.

[18] NLRB, "Intermediate Report and Recommended Order," Feb. 25, 1949, NLRB Case 10-CA-84 (1951), 20; Pedigo testimony, *Labor-Management Relations*, 190–95; *Atlanta Journal*, May 19, 1948.

flying from both sides . . . as to the number of workers in the mill, with the Union claiming not over 100 were in the mill and the company claiming that 75 percent of the mill is in operation." Company estimates, unfortunately, were closer to the truth.[19]

The lack of support for the strike in the plant not only subverted the economic effect of the work stoppage but also undermined the union's ability to win public sympathy for the strikers. Support for the strike was broad among members of Local 787, but union members—even by the TWUA's generous estimate—made up only 450 of 850 eligible Anchor Rome workers in 1948. On the first day, 100 workers remained at work. Within the first week of the strike another 40 crossed the picket line. Just five days after the strike began, before the TWUA had even set up its commissary, the president of Anchor Rome Mills reported to the press that the mill was "operating at almost 100 per cent in all departments" on two shifts. He was probably exaggerating, but as long as Anchor Rome could keep the mill open it was unlikely that the company would compromise.[20]

As a public demonstration, however, the strike provided Local 787 with other potential means to place pressure on Anchor Rome management. The 450 members of Local 787 may have been a relatively small majority in the plant, but their presence around the mill village, located within the city limits of Rome proper, had a significant impact on the community. By placing the struggle literally on the streets and their complaints on placards on their backs, union members broadcast their grievances with Anchor management to a larger audience. If strikers could win the sympathy of townsfolk and local businessmen and convince them that the strike was hurting the community, union leaders hoped, mill officials might be shamed into negotiating with the union. Many of Rome's civic and business leaders, although wholly unsympathetic to organized labor, did have an interest in ending the strike.

Ironically, the logic of boosterism compelled such a stance. Almost everyone—merchants, businessmen, chamber of commerce leaders, workers, even the pro-business editor of the *Rome News-Tribune*—would have been glad to see the strike end by any means, for in the logic of boosterism the practical effect of a strike was first and foremost the loss of wages. The strike removed wages from community circulation and therefore the pockets of community businessmen. Moreover, strikes and the accompa-

[19] First quote from Pedigo testimony, *Labor-Management Relations*, 190–95; NLRB, "Intermediate Report and Recommended Order," Feb. 25, 1949, Case 10-CA-84 (1951), 20; Northwest Georgia TWUA Joint Board pamphlet, "Who Is Responsible for Violence?" ca. 1949, and "Fact Sheet on Anchor Rome Mills," both in "Anchor Rome Mills, Anchor Duck, 1948–49" folder, box 2, series 10A, US MSS 129A, TWUA Records; *Rome News-Tribune*, Mar. 19, 1948.

[20] *Atlanta Constitution*, Mar. 19, 1948; *Rome News-Tribune*, Mar. 23, 1948.

nying publicity also had a negative effect on industrial recruitment efforts, a project with nearly unanimous support in Rome.

Winning public sympathy was no small task, however, and Local 787 entered the conflict at a disadvantage. At every step the union had to contend not only with mill management but also with fallout from Operation Dixie and a growing public irritation with unions and strikes nationwide. In 1946 alone there had been 4,630 work stoppages that pulled 4.9 million workers off the job. Conservative civic leaders in Floyd County, such as Dr. W. H. Lewis and the editor of the *Rome News-Tribune*, had long viewed such strikes—particularly the nationwide shutdowns in the basic industries of mining, steel, and auto manufacturing—with anger and alarm. Throughout the late 1940s, editorial articles and radio addresses by Lewis publicly condemned postwar strikes, blaming them on "greed, indifference, disregard of law, and utter selfishness," while editor J. R. Hornady put forward more and more urgent arguments for the right to work.[21] During the strike, the *News-Tribune* observed only the most superficial modicum of impartiality in reporting "news" about the Anchor Rome conflict, providing plenty of opportunities for company spokesmen to charge that the union struck in the interest of big labor's greed, not in the true interests of ordinary workers.

In this facet of the struggle, Anchor management had an advantage. The less heroic part of the union's struggle against the corporation—the ugly fight among former co-workers—was immediately and eminently visible. There were "a lot of hard feelings," one Anchor Rome millhand remembered, and these feelings soon erupted into physical confrontations. Just two days after the strike began, a fistfight broke out between a striker and a strikebreaker in front of the mill. In a front-page story, the *News-Tribune* reported that the union member was arrested and charged with "assault with intent to murder." In response, Anchor Rome managers went to court and obtained a strict court order limiting picketing, a remedy sanctioned under the new Taft-Hartley Act. The injunction, issued by Floyd County Superior Court judge Claude Porter, drastically restricted the size and scale of Local 787's protest by prohibiting pickets from the streets beside the mill or anywhere within one hundred yards of the plant. All pickets, Porter ruled, were limited to groups of three, and groups had to remain at least one hundred yards apart, thus circumscribing the contact between strikers and scabs and minimizing the union's already limited means of swaying potential recruits. One union official

[21] On postwar strikes, see Brody, *Workers in Industrial America*, 173–211; Zieger, *American Workers*, 100–108; and Melvin Dubofsky, *The State and Labor in Modern America* (Chapel Hill: University of North Carolina Press, 1995), 193–94. *Rome News-Tribune*, May 5, June 6, Aug. 6, Sept. 24, Oct. 9, 25, Dec. 5, 6, 27, 1946.

protested that the injunction had placed strikers "so far from the gate that they couldn't throw a stone and hit the building."[22]

On the same day, Anchor Rome Mills issued "A Statement to the People of Rome," signed by mill president P. A. Redmond, Jr., outlining the mill's position in a full-page newspaper ad. Addressing "fellow citizens," the younger Redmond expressed his desire to correct any mistaken impression that the strike indicated that "management [was] unfair." Big labor, he charged, actually deserved the blame. "Only a few realize," he complained, "that strikes . . . are weapons of the great Labor Organizations against management, to secure advantages for themselves—not for the employees they represent—in which in fact these employees as well as management are the victims." The union's demands were characterized as unreasonable, selfish, and contrary to the interests of Rome workers. "The issues of the strike," Redmond attempted to explain, "are not demands for the benefit of our employees, but . . . so far as we can judge them, solely for the benefit of the Union itself." Company officials "sincerely hoped" that there would be no disorder, and they assured Romans that "if there should be violence, rest assured we will hold the Union, and those participating in it fully responsible." In conclusion, Redmond expressed the company officials' respect for the employees' right to strike and their "hope" that striking employees would accept their "welcome" to come back to work.[23] In the critical realm of community relations, members of Local 787 lost the first round.

In spite of the principled stand Redmond adopted in regard to strike violence and the concern he professed for "our employees," the company itself provoked a much more serious conflict between strikers and strikebreakers a few days later. On March 23 the personnel director, the plant engineer, the plant superintendent, and other supervisors led a pitched battle for strategic control of the mill's most vulnerable point—the railroad entrances to the mill—which had been blocked by pickets since the first day of the strike. By picketing the rail entrances, Local 787 ensured that even as strikebreakers crossed the picket line to work, the mill would eventually run out of raw materials and fail to deliver finished products. The ability of pickets to stop boxcar traffic in the first week of the strike thus gave strikers some control over production and some economic leverage over the company. Command of the rail entrance also held psychological value for both sides. If Anchor insisted on running the mill through the strike, Local 787 could at least claim that they were not turning out

[22] Vinson interview; *Rome News-Tribune*, Mar. 21, 1948; McCarthy, "Anchor Rome—Political Background," "Celanese Strike, Rome, GA" folder, box 6, series 10A, US MSS 129A, TWUA Records.

[23] *Rome News-Tribune*, Mar. 21, 1948.

products. Moreover, the siding was strategically important because the union held an advantage. The unionized Central of Georgia Railroad engineers would not cross a picket line on the tracks. In the first week of the strike, pickets had turned back freight cars on two occasions already.[24]

Just two days after mill president Redmond issued his statement, the railroad siding became the scene of a violent confrontation between managers, strikebreakers, and striking workers. On March 23, a group of three female union members and a male shop steward, in strict observance of the injunction, were, as usual, picketing the railroad tracks. Shortly before noon, when a railroad engine and freight cars approached the warehouse, a large group of nonunion workers armed with sticks, hammers, wrenches, and blackjacks, and led by mill officials, arrived on the tracks. The plant engineer ordered the group to "spread out over the track" and motioned for the train engine to proceed. When the conductor hesitated, the same supervisor ordered strikebreakers to "knock them off the track." One hundred people surrounded the four members of Local 787 and literally "beat, black-jacked and clubbed them" off the tracks. A handful of union members ran over to the tracks to defend the women, and within moments the confrontation turned into a kicking, shouting, fist-fighting, and hair-pulling brawl. The engine proceeded into the warehouse. In the course of the fight, several strikers were knocked down the twelve-foot embankment beside the tracks and many were seriously injured. Apparently, mill officials only cared about the safety of nonunion workers.[25]

Union members were outraged not only with the behavior of the mill officials and the strikebreakers but with what seemed to be the virtual silence of the community and the newspaper. "But where are the headlines?" Joe Pedigo protested. "If a union official led a mob to beat the workers the newspapers would scream their heads off." Local 787 members were shocked in particular that the mill had dared to attack "defenseless women." The *News-Tribune* did report that several workers were arrested, but it did not say who was responsible for the fight. Thereafter, the strike update provided a dramatic description of strikers surrounding carloads of scabs at shift change later in the day, jerking open car doors and attempting to pull the occupants from the vehicles. Union officials reported the railroad incident to the NLRB, but because the investigation and order took years to administer, federal authority provided little in the way of immediate satisfaction to the union.[26]

[24] NLRB, "Intermediate Report," Feb. 25, 1949, NLRB Case 10-CA-84 (1951), 24.

[25] Sworn affidavits of John T. Parris and Inez McCord, May 12, 1948, and NLRB, "Intermediate Report," Feb. 25, 1949, all in NLRB Case 10-CA-84 (1951); *Textile Labor*, Apr. 3, 1948.

[26] *Rome News-Tribune*, Mar. 24, 1948.

However silent it may have seemed in Rome, company officials' strong-arm tactics did not go unnoticed. In fact, silence in the press was probably a good indication of how seriously the community disapproved of the company's vigilantism. In the 1934 strike, managers' attempts to "guard" the mills had been proudly reported to the public. In 1948, as Floyd County boosters touted modern, amicable industrial relations as a regional selling point, Anchor Rome managers' behavior did not fit the community's desired self-image. Nor did it fit the mill's claim to be the workers' best friend. Even though the *News-Tribune* editor and city and county leaders did not condemn managerial aggression, just as significantly they refused to defend it. In fact, the railroad siding incident and a complaint from one of the mill's business associates even drew the brief attention of Georgia governor M. E. Thompson. Two days after the altercation on the tracks, the governor made a surprise trip to Rome to meet with company and union officials, contending that "these and other differences in Georgia [could] be settled peaceably." At the meeting, union officials offered to stop picketing and put workers back on the job immediately "if the company would agree in writing to arbitration." Anchor Rome managers, however, refused to discuss a compromise because their attorney was not present.[27]

Perhaps because they realized the company had lost some of the moral high ground in the railroad incident, Anchor managers tried to repair the company's reputation by tarnishing the union's. TWUA and company officials had been in conference with the governor for about an hour when the phone rang. "Mr. Bachman, who was sitting on one side of the bed away from the telephone," Pedigo recalled, "practically fell across the bed to answer the telephone." Bachman listened, shook his head, and said, "It is awful. Somebody has just driven past our plant and shot through it," breaking the windows. All the windows had, in fact, been broken, but police investigation later revealed that all the broken glass was discovered *outside* the mill, indicating that windows had been broken by someone inside the plant. Thompson left the following day, but not before the mill provided a tour of the alleged "vandalism." That night union pickets appeared at the main mill gate with two large American flags.[28]

In the following weeks, increasing and unrelieved tensions between strikers and the company and scabs frequently erupted into violence. A constant stream of petty vandalism, anonymous phone calls, threats, and stray bullets was punctuated periodically by more serious incidents of

[27] Ibid., Mar. 25, 1948.

[28] Pedigo testimony, *Labor-Management Relations*, 210; *Rome News-Tribune*, Apr. 1, 1948.

gunplay. Before the strike ended, two supervisors were arrested for drunken gun-wielding, a strikebreaker shot a striker on a public sidewalk, a strikebreaker was shot through the windows of his living room, and innumerable gunshots were exchanged between carloads of strikers and scabs. Bullets riddled union commissary headquarters, a village café, and several mill village homes.[29]

Despite the company's bungling of the broken-window incident and the arrest of several strikebreakers on criminal charges, other publicity efforts demonstrated a much higher degree of sophistication. Early in the strike, Redmond offered $1,000 rewards to anyone supplying information on crimes committed thus far in connection with the strike or "any future occurrences." Pressing the right-to-work angle, a few days after the railroad siding incident the mill purchased a full-page advertisement in the *Rome News-Tribune*, ostensibly produced by nonunion workers breaking the strike, which appealed for police protection. Above the names of hundreds of strikebreakers the ad declared, "We, the undersigned employees of Anchor Rome Mills, Inc., believe that under the law we have the right to work, and . . . we ask that the law enforcement officers of the City and County give us the necessary protection."[30]

Mill officials also tried to put the community's traditional perception of paternalism back to work for the company. Emphasizing their common interests and the alleged appreciation of employees, the mill bankrolled a second full-page appearance by their faithful workers in the *News-Tribune*. In this public statement the workers allegedly expressed their allegiance and gratitude to the new managers. "We, the workers," the statement declared, "have considered our employment a pleasure instead of work." Workers also thanked the people of Rome and Floyd County for "their interest and work in helping preserve peace and order." In subsequent statements the plant manager returned his employees' sentiments, portraying his fight against the union as one waged in the interests of his loyal workers. When Anchor Rome Mills filed charges against the union for violating the injunction, Rice expressed his regret that the company had to resort to this action, but "matters were getting out of hand as far as the safety of our workers was concerned."[31]

In spite of Rice's public posturing about safety, mill supervisors had actually been preparing to use force for some time. Although the union and the public were unaware of it until several weeks into the strike, plant

[29] *Rome News-Tribune*, Apr. 4, 6, 11, 19, 25, 30, May 5, 1948; *Atlanta Journal*, Mar. 22, 1948; *Athens Banner Herald*, Apr. 25, 1948; *Cedartown Standard*, Apr. 27, 1948; *Textile Labor*, Apr. 3, May 8, 1948.

[30] *Rome News-Tribune*, Mar. 28, Apr. 15, 1948.

[31] Ibid., Mar. 28, Apr. 15, 25, 1948.

officials obtained pistol permits nearly a week before the strike began. Rice, in fact, bought two .38s, earning himself the nickname "Two-gun" among unionists. Within the first two weeks of the strike, forty-one managers, supervisors, and nonstriking employees obtained "pistol-toter's licenses," as they were called in Georgia. The plant superintendent, the personnel manager, the maintenance foreman, and the cloth room overseer stood as surety for almost all the applicants, and the union charged that the company also paid for most of the licenses. Strangely enough, the officials who refused to check off union dues allowed strikebreakers to buy guns on time through company deductions from their paychecks.[32]

Although the union attempted to publicize the violence directed at the union's female members and the revelation that the mill had secured guns for strikebreakers, TWUA officials feared that the community held the union responsible. In late April, when a strikebreaker was shot in the eye through the windows of his home, Pedigo claimed that "public opinion placed the guilt on the union" even though another strikebreaker had actually fired the shot. Scattered violence on the night of the shooting apparently taxed the final reserves of community tolerance for the strike. Two days later a group of local civic associations called upon the police to "see that immediate steps are taken to avoid any further violence." An "open letter" published in the paper and signed by the presidents of the Rome Chamber of Commerce, the Junior Chamber of Commerce, the Rome Retail Merchants Association, and several service and social clubs, as well as the commander of the local American Legion Post, appealed to public officials: "Lives and property must be protected. . . . If the present scope of unlawfulness becomes beyond the control of our officers . . . then it becomes their duty to insist that the Governor of Georgia take the necessary steps to protect the rights of our people." In response, Rome police added three men to the force and the chief of police requested aid from the Georgia Bureau of Investigation.[33]

The next day, Dr. Lewis, in his capacity as a county commissioner, issued a public statement demanding that the governor send troops to Floyd County to restore order. Lewis made a halfhearted attempt to be neutral, but he subtly took sides by beginning with a recognition of the union's right to strike, the mill's right to continue operations, but "over and above these rights . . . the paramount right that every employee who so desires

[32] Testimony of Joe Pedigo and William Sword; union exhibit L, both in *Labor-Management Relations*, 190–99, 238–39; NLRB, "Intermediate Report and Recommended Order," Feb. 25, 1949, NLRB Case 10-CA-84 (1951), 23; Northwest Georgia TWUA Joint Board pamphlet, "Who Is Responsible for Violence?"; McCarthy, "Mill Background"; *Textile Labor*, May 8, 1948.

[33] "Rome, GA, Report of JGR," May 22, 1951, box 1563, folder 99, Ramsey Papers; *Rome News-Tribune*, Apr. 25, 1948.

can continue at work." Above all, Lewis argued, officials had a responsibility to maintain "law and order." The doctor charged that "riot and anarchy" prevailed in the mill village and that "women and children live in nightly terror." The statement was carried in several Georgia papers, although an *Atlanta Journal* correspondent dispatched to Rome on the story reported sarcastically that he had found no " 'reign of terror' nor any signs of 'anarchy and riot.' " The *Rome News-Tribune*, ignoring the *Journal*'s report, boasted that their staff had located Governor Thompson in Douglasville on the day the statement was issued and advised him of the doctor's charges.[34]

Initially the union had also hoped that the state would intervene in the strike. A week before Lewis demanded troops, TWUA officials called on Governor Thompson to appoint a fact-finding board. Running short on time and money, the union still might be able to force settlement, a TWUA International representative suggested, if they could "embarrass the hell out of the officials, get the governor off his flat fanny, and have the townsfolk get in on our side a little more vociferously." A fact-finding board would "at least show the people something is happening," the official advised. Thompson, however, was apparently more interested in politics than fact-finding. Pedigo reported that the governor would "not perform until we put the dough on the line—in this case the promise of CIO support in the fight for the governorship in the Fall." But Thompson continued to vacillate. Refusing to send troops, he also refused to investigate.[35]

TWUA officials then tried to recruit local businessmen to put pressure on Thompson for them. Local 787 officials knew that some business and community leaders were embarrassed by Anchor Rome managers' behavior in the strike. According to Pedigo, "there was private criticism among some of the better element of people in Rome." Moreover, the union's link to the courthouse crowd, attorney Graham Wright, informed union officials that other mill managers in particular were critical of Anchor Rome management. Wright found out from his brother, who was a Rome attorney representing Pepperell, Brighton, and other local mills, that "other companies are down on Anchor for the crudeness with which they are acting and have advised them to hire a public relations counsel or lay-off the rough stuff." With this in mind, the TWUA sent letters to some of Rome's leading citizens.

The Redmonds, however, were well connected in town, and it undoubtedly helped their case that they had saved a local mill once slated for liquidation. The mill had supervisory employees on the city council and the grand jury, and friends who could more effectively prevail on Gover-

[34] *Rome News-Tribune*, Apr. 26, 1948.

[35] *Atlanta Constitution*, Apr. 18, 1948.

nor Thompson. Evidently the governor was finally swayed to the mill's side by Judge Porter, who was a personal friend of the younger Redmond as well as "the Thompson man in this area," according to union officials. Since the strike began, the mill president and the governor had both been overnight guests at Judge Porter's summer home. Porter apparently persuaded Thompson against an investigation by selling "the governor the idea that he will lose votes if he steps in here and appoints the board."[36] In Pedigo's words, "there was a fight between the ruling class" and Rome's rulers decided "they must stay with the people that owned the mill."[37]

Meanwhile, the actual protest faltered as the number of strikers and pickets steadily declined. By early April a large percentage of the third shift had crossed back over the line. Even among those who remained loyal to the union, morale—and, consequently, interest in the strike activities—diminished. Attendance at daily strike meetings was "steadily dropping off," a TWUA official reported. Even though the court injunction compelled only a minimal showing on picket duty, the same official reported that "repeaters on the picket line [were] beginning to carry the burden." As the union's collective spirits lagged, complaints sprang up "about petty things" such as rations from the commissary. One striker grumbled to a TWUA International representative that the " 'little ol' boys were getting gas to go messin' round with little ol' girls' and that you could never find them for strike duty." Most damning of all, a TWUA official reported, was the fact that the mill continued to run, "knocking the hell out of morale even though the workers keep telling themselves that nothing is being produced." When the mill did finally produce something, he predicted, "they'll have to dig the strikers' spirits out of the mud on the bottom of the Coosa River."[38]

Local 787 had entered the strike under less than opportune circumstances, so the frequency of strikebreaking was perhaps not surprising to TWUA officials. Although the Joint Board never conceded that Local 787 held less than a majority in the plant, its records indicated that only 275 of roughly 850 workers paid 1947–48 dues in the Anchor plant. Since Alabama Mills had taken over the plant many new people had been hired, and the new contract did not compel them to either become or remain members of Local 787. "The workers in the mills [were] not the ones who

[36] Mac to Larry, n.d., ca. April 1948; "Recommendations," n.d., ca. April 1948; "Anchor Rome-Political Background" n.d., ca. April 1948; all in "Celanese Strike, Rome, GA" folder, box 6, series 10A, MSS 129A, TWUA Records.

[37] "Anchor Rome-Political Background"; Pedigo testimony, *Labor-Management Relations*, 182–84.

[38] NLRB, "Calendar of Important Events," NLRB Case 10-CA-903 (1956); McCarthy, "Mill Background."

fought to make the union," a TWUA official explained, and thus "they have never been really sold on its necessity."[39]

Given the poor state of the textile industry in northwest Georgia and the perception that the postwar boom was already giving way to a recession, the incentive to cross the picket line must have been great. Anchor Rome had no problem recruiting strikebreakers, even in a labor market circumscribed by race. Union members claimed that the mill had gone all over the northwest Georgia countryside to recruit labor, but a fair number of local workers were persuaded to cross the picket line. Lindale resident Opal Scott, for example, remembered that her husband, Arthur, an experienced textile worker and the son of a former mill boss, had not been able to find any job openings until the strike. At a time when "jobs were hard to find," she said, Scott crossed the picket line, applied for a job, and was hired right away. Although it was a long time before Scott got a "regular job," he worked more hours than most textile employees in 1948. The mill employed Scott just to escort strikebreakers in and out of the plant. At one point during the ten-month strike, Scott's wife remembered, he stayed in the mill "100 hours without coming home. He stayed night and day . . . guarding people. He would sleep there and then drive people back and forth" to work.[40]

A few weeks into the strike, union officials reported that "more and more workers are drifting into the plants from nearby towns." By the end of April, the mill had recruited two to three hundred workers from outside Rome to take over mill jobs. Sixteen-year-old Vicky Vinson and her family, for example, moved fifty miles to take jobs at Anchor Rome. Her father had worked at the American Thread mill in Tallapoosa, Georgia, but "wasn't getting many hours" so he decided to move. "Back then it was hard, jobs you know, you couldn't get a job hardly anywhere," Vinson remembered. The strike at Anchor Rome also provided Vinson and her brother with positions. "That's how we got the job. They were out on strike and they were looking for people to go to work, and so all I knew about the union was going through [the picket line]. . . . When we came to Rome we just went in and went to work and back." The mill constructed a new walkway so workers would not have to confront pickets as they entered the mill. Vinson remembered that working during the strike was sometimes rough, but as teenagers, she and her brother "didn't realize how serious it was, because when you're 16 years old you don't think that you could get shot. . . . You get a payday and that's all you're thinking about."[41]

[39] Pedigo testimony, *Labor-Management Relations*, 184; McCarthy, "Mill Background."

[40] Scott interview.

[41] NLRB, "Calendar of Important Events," NLRB Case 10-CA-903 (1956); McCarthy, "Mill Background"; Vinson interview.

Although the strike continued in an official sense until January 1949, the union was all but defeated in less than two months. On May 18 Rice announced the addition of a third shift, declared that he had permanently replaced those "who quit," and "flatly refused" a final plea from the TWUA for arbitration. The mill "would not agree to these provisions voluntarily, nor will we agree to them through the medium of arbitration," Rice told the press. "The matter is not arbitrary." The fact that six hundred people were now working in the plant, he continued, "clearly indicates to us that the position we take meets with their approval." These workers, he declared, and not the strikers, were now the mill's "primary concern."[42]

Surveying the Anchor Rome situation, a TWUA International representative mused to a colleague, "I may be getting over dramatic, but I think this is the beginning of a new era in strikes. Not only Anchor, but all of the other strikes which are now occurring." Other contemporary textile strikes in Tarboro, North Carolina, and Athens, Georgia, mirrored the situation in Anchor Rome, with management adamantly refusing key union contract clauses and forcing TWUA locals to strike.[43] Union officials blamed the Taft-Hartley Act. Many corporations with operations in the South, such as Alabama Mills, had never accommodated themselves to organized labor, and after 1947 they took a lead in aggressive testing of the new federal labor laws. Pedigo, for example, believed that Anchor Rome was "carrying the ball for all of the textile interests" in refusing the checkoff to set an industry-wide pattern. The permanent replacement of strikers, permissible under the act in "economic strikes," also became increasingly common. After 1947, critics of the new labor policy claimed that Taft-Hartley provisions for "right to work" laws and injunctions against mass picketing encouraged employers to open their plants during strikes, making violent conflicts between workers much more likely. Post-1947 strikes, union sympathizers observed, also tended to be "bitter and long."[44]

In July, the Floyd County court system delivered the final indignity to Local 787. The grand jury, with the secretary-treasurer of Anchor Rome Mills serving as its secretary, dismissed charges against several of the strikebreakers. When other strike-related cases came to trial in superior court, a strikebreaker who shot a member of Local 787 in the chest on a public sidewalk was acquitted, while in the same session a union member who started a fistfight on the picket line was sentenced to a year in jail.

[42] *Rome News-Tribune*, May 18, 1948.

[43] On other postwar TWUA strikes, see Minchin, *What Do We Need a Union For?*

[44] McCarthy, "Mill Background"; Harry A. Millis and Emily Clark Brown, *From the Wagner Act to Taft-Hartley: A Study of National Labor Policy and Labor Relations* (Chicago: University of Chicago Press, 1950), 639–42.

In the words of *Textile Labor*, it was a " 'Grand' Jury for Bosses." Pedigo bitterly expressed the union's anger, exasperation, and disillusionment in the summer of 1948. "We realize now that there is nothing to be gained by trying to be fair with these people," he said. From now on, "we will fight them right down the line, legal and otherwise."[45]

At the end of the summer, as the union at Anchor Rome Mills was collapsing, Rome's largest TWUA union, Local 689, was also compelled to strike. Although Local 689's strike reflected the impact of changes in national labor law, it was also intimately shaped by the fact it took place in Georgia. Managers tried to press the advantage of location in the lower-wage deep South, and Local 689 members were forced to defend their rights not only as union members, but as southern workers. Applying the bitter lessons of the Anchor strike, Local 689 put regional pride, boosterism, and the power of their payroll to work for them.

Negotiations between the Celanese Corporation, which had acquired the Tubize rayon mill after the war, and Local 689 began quite amicably, with both sides agreeing to postpone wage negotiations until other TWUA locals and larger rayon producers set a nationwide "rayon pattern" for wages. The TWUA held contracts in approximately 65 percent of the rayon industry, most of which expired in June or July. Since Rome's TWUA representatives shared an interest in the national pattern, they agreed to wait.[46] The International, meanwhile, made some ambitious demands on other rayon producers. Arguing that the process of turning out rayon yarn was a highly technical and profitable operation, TWUA negotiators felt that rayon workers deserved wages comparable to those paid by other basic industries under contract with CIO unions. Since the rayon corporations, unlike producers of cotton and chenille, continued to enjoy a heavy market demand and considerable profits, TWUA officials contended, there was no reason for rayon workers to earn twenty to fifty cents per hour less than other CIO workers. When rayon industry representatives suggested the pay increase that had been granted in the steel and auto industries—eleven to thirteen cents per hour—TWUA leaders countered that a flat increase would simply perpetuate the wage gap between rayon workers and other CIO workers. TWUA logic prevailed, and the nation's largest rayon producer, American Viscose Corporation, signed an agreement raising the wages of twenty thousand rayon workers by fifteen cents an hour. In short time, another major rayon producer

[45] *Textile Labor*, July 17, 1948; *Rome News-Tribune*, May 18, 1948; TWUA-CIO, "Fact Sheet on Anchor Rome Mills," "Anchor Rome Mills, Anchor Duck, 1948–49" folder, box 2, series 10A, US MSS 129A, TWUA Records.

[46] John Kabler to Herbert Payne, 26 June 1948, "#689 Negotiations—1948" folder, box 474, US MSS 396, TWUA Records; "A Report on the Celanese Strike," box 1563, folder 100, Ramsey Papers; *Floyd County Herald*, Sept. 16, 1948.

raised TWUA member wages by an average of eighteen cents an hour, and even granted an additional increase to its southern workers in recognition of the North-South differential within the textile industry. Following the pattern, Celanese granted its employees at Cumberland, Maryland, an increase of fifteen cents per hour.[47]

When Local 689's negotiation committee went back to Rome management and requested the same fifteen-cent raise, however, it was flatly rejected. Despite their earlier agreement to wait for the rayon pattern, company negotiators offered instead the southern *cotton mill* pattern, an 8 percent increase, with the argument that this "Southern pattern" suited the Rome Celanese plant better. Although Celanese had maintained a North-South wage differential in its plants in the past, managers at neither Tubize nor Celanese had ever argued that Rome rayon workers' wages should follow cotton mill wages. Rayon workers had always earned more. Local 689 officials pointed out that 8 percent on the base wage at Celanese constituted an increase of only seven and one-half cents an hour, half of the appropriate pattern—the *rayon industry* pattern, which had already been put in place in Maryland. International representatives stuck to their original argument: rayon yarn production was a technical and dangerous process that merited much higher wages. When the Federal Mediation and Conciliation Service scheduled a meeting in Rome between local management and union officials, the TWUA attended but Celanese officials stood them up. Plant manager W. Y. Brown's curt replies to the workers and the press indicated that the mill was willing to hold out for its own interpretation of the "Southern pattern."[48]

After six weeks of negotiation, on August 12, Celanese managers in Rome made the union its "first, last and only offer" of 8 percent. Local 689 members were outraged that the company dared to offer them less because they worked in the South. It was, in the words of more than one striker, "an insult to Southern workers." That evening 1,300 day shift workers met in the Rome city auditorium, and the following morning 350 night shift workers gathered for a strike vote. According to the *Rome News-Tribune*, the members of Local 689 "returned a unanimous decision" to strike.[49]

In spite of stubborn determination on both sides, the strike began with many signs of goodwill. Union officers met with Celanese officials and

[47] "Some Romans Have Red Faces," radio script, n.d., "Celanese Strike, Rome, GA" folder, box 6, series 10A, US MSS 129A, TWUA Records.

[48] C. L. Ross, WRGA radio script, Sept. 19, 1948, "Celanese Strike, Rome, GA" folder, box 6, series 10A, US MSS 129A, TWUA Records; *Floyd County Herald*, Sept. 16, 1948.

[49] *Rome News-Tribune*, Aug. 15, 1948; McCarthy, "There's a New War Being Fought . . . ," "Celanese Strike, Rome, GA" folder, box 6, series 10A, US MSS 129A, TWUA Records.

worked out some basic agreements on the conduct of the strike. The union agreed to allow supervisory and office staff into the mill and to permit some workers to operate the water plant, which served the mill and the mill village. In return, Celanese officials allowed the union to set up a picket tent on company property. More importantly, the company agreed not to attempt operation with strikebreakers. On August 14, Celanese workers "carefully shut down the plant," in the union's words, saving the company from losses that would have resulted from a more hasty walk-out. Because the Celanese plant was a "continuous operation" plant, the machinery had to be "closed with care so that the liquid which become rayon [did] not solidify in the pipes and machinery."[50]

The Celanese union, in contrast with the Anchor Rome local, turned out for the strike in an enthusiastic and overwhelming majority. The union held over 1,650 members in a plant with 1,800 production workers. Strike activities drew large crowds, and union meetings packed the city auditorium to capacity on several occasions. Local 689 officers and TWUA officials organized several strike committees and registered members for picket duty. Before official strike duty even began, sixty workers led an informal picket along the street opposite the main gate. Local 689 and company officials continued to meet, although superintendent Brown remained adamant about the mill's 8 percent offer. TWUA representatives offered to "call workers back to the plant immediately" if Celanese would agree to arbitration. Brown's terse public reply informed the union that the company did not "arbitrate wage decisions. It is not our policy to allow another party to spend our money."[51]

The Celanese Corporations's actions elsewhere, however, cemented an even stronger resolve among Local 689 members. After Rome mill officials released an elaborate explanation of the company's position on the "Southern" wage to the press, Celanese plants in Virginia and Texas granted wages well above what Brown had offered Rome employees. Rome unionists might have expected textile industrialists to defend a North-South wage differential, but in the light of wages at other Celanese mills, Brown's refusal to negotiate the fifteen-cent increase now seemed even more outrageous. "Some Romans," a TWUA radio program scolded, ought to "have red faces. . . . How would you feel if all the arguments upon which you based your drive were suddenly swept away? I think you would feel a little foolish and I am sure the local officials of the company feel that way too."[52]

[50] *Floyd County Herald*, Sept. 16, 1948; *Rome News-Tribune*, Aug. 15, 1948; McCarthy, "There's a New War Being Fought . . ."

[51] *Rome News-Tribune*, Aug. 16, 20, 1948.

[52] "Some Romans Have Red Faces," radio script, n.d.

The revelation about other Celanese raises also implied that a more sinister motivation lay behind Brown's offer of 8 percent. First, Celanese issued "an insult to all Southern workers," former Local 689 business agent and Joint Board official C. L. Ross fumed, and now the company expressed an explicit disrespect for Rome workers simply because they happened to live and work in Georgia. Celanese strikers responded quickly and indignantly to what they called this "Georgia-wage-scale-below-the-rest-of-the-world philosophy." Celanese, union officials protested, must think that "local people will be willing to live forever as second class citizens of the empire controlled by Celanese." The collective sense among strikers that this was deeply unfair suddenly raised the stakes much higher than the disputed seven and one-half cents an hour. Primed by industrial development rhetoric and ubiquitous expressions of regional pride, Celanese workers now demanded, as workers and as citizens of Georgia, their right to be paid a good wage.[53]

The rhetoric of strike speeches and meetings quickly incorporated the typical jargon of southern boosters about "first class workers" into the TWUA's denunciation of "third class rates." Union workers transformed the well-worn argument of southern boosters and put a new spin on it appropriate for the strike. Higher wages for Celanese workers, they argued, meant more spending, and better wages for the rest of the community. Speaking to a radio audience in September, C. L. Ross conceded that while the going was "rugged right now, it is better for us, better for the City and better for the State that we make this fight now . . . to protect ourselves and our children from unjust and undue exploitation by these forces from beyond the borders of the South or the Nation." To businessmen who might counter that the strikers nevertheless were currently losing money and depriving the community of their spending, union officials argued that merchants should not be shortsighted. To accept an increase of seven and one-half cents rather than fifteen cents, union leaders argued, would deprive the community of much more in the long term. Union officials calculated the difference at almost "$300,000 a year which will not find its way into the tills of the storekeepers and merchants of this town." The strike was no less than a defense of "our states's welfare," Ross informed listeners. Echoing Ross, one union member explained to the *Floyd County Herald:* "The mill company needs the yarn we ought to be making, and the local merchants need the money we're spending."[54]

Local 689's charges against Celanese laid bare the contradictions inherent in both the South's low-wage economy and the anti-union arguments motivated by boosterism. If wages were good for the community, the

[53] C. L. Ross, WRGA radio script, Sept. 19, 1948.

[54] Ibid.

union countered, then higher wages were even better. Other southern employers, of course, had a personal interest in keeping area wages low. Maintaining regional differentials in wages meant that they paid their own workers less by eliminating competition for labor with better-paying employers. The southern differential also served as a significant lure for industrial recruitment. In the past, regional wages had been defended on such grounds of maintaining regional balance and competitiveness.

However, defenses of low wages seemed benign only when it appeared that southern workers consented to them. In the past, southern workers hungry for steady work had readily jumped on the booster bandwagon for any work at any wage. But in this particular case, a defense of Celanese's position, even if it were based on the goal of maintaining regional competitiveness, would have come dangerously close to admitting the worst implications of boosterism. Even if boosters happily accommodated low-wage employers, they could not admit that they approved of exploiting Rome's own white citizens in the interests of keeping workers' standards low and collecting corporate taxes. The premise of boosterism, after all, was its claim to enrich everyone, including the South's "efficient and loyal" workers. The company's position, therefore, was a difficult one to champion. "No worker—no business man—no good Georgia citizen can bow down to a Georgia-wage-scale-below-the-rest-of-the-world philosophy," Ross chided Rome radio listeners.

Moreover, a disdain for the strikers' demands risked permanently offending a well-organized block of 1,650 consumers, as well as thousands of Local 689 family members and friends. Textile boosters had been arguing for decades that workers, industrialists, and merchants held a common interest, and the 1948 strike gave Local 689 an opportunity to put those interests to the test. Local 689 leaders realized the collective spending power they commanded, and they used it well. If businessmen wanted the benefits that accrued from textile wages spent locally, they would have to support the union's members in their time of need. Whether or not businessmen were sympathetic to the union's strike goals, when workers threatened to withdraw future wages from circulation, they got attention. As one union official explained: "Many of the merchants were willing to wait and the others readily saw the unfavorable position they would be in if they pushed repossession proceedings."[55]

If creditors feared losses resulting from millhands' inability to meet financial commitments, the union made it clear that they risked even greater long-term losses by offending a well-organized group of thousands of consumers. Union member H. O. Yarbrough, for example, was paying for a stove purchased on credit at Sears when the strike began.

[55] J. J. West to George Dillman, Jan. 6, 1959, folder 14, box 1609, Joint Board Papers.

Realizing that he would not be able to make the payments, he went to see the manager. At first the manager simply demanded that he make the payments or forfeit the goods. Yarbrough did not argue, but casually mentioned that he was on the way down to the union hall, and that he would inform everyone of Sears' policy. The manager suddenly had a change of heart. " '—Oh no, no, no, no.' he said, 'naw, just forget about it, don't do that. We don't want you to [do that].' " If Yarbrough would come into the store every week, the manager continued, they might be able to extend the payments. Yarbrough refused to be humiliated or treated as a reprobate because he was on strike. "I said, 'I ain't a coming in every week.' I said, 'When I go back to work, I'll pay you. But until I go back to work I'm not coming back up here.' " From the strikers' point of view, this was only fair. Union members would pay as soon as they could. After Yarbrough and other strikers pointed out the union's willingness to boycott those who did not work with them, he said, Sears and other local retail merchants "settled down. They didn't say any more. . . . A lot of people, a lot of places pushed [strikers], but they found out that the union would back them, then they quit pushing."

Yarbrough recalled that most businesses were sympathetic to the strikers as customers. "Most of the places they recognized it, and they carried them and they were real good about carrying them. And when they went back to work, people went and you know, paid it up. So they didn't have no trouble. It helped afterwards, because they found out people would pay them when they could." Although some businessmen maintained their opposition to organized labor, Yarbrough said, "we learned a lot and they learned a lot" from the strike.[56]

As the strike approached the one-month mark, morale remained high among Local 689's members. Secure in the belief that Celanese workers were not asking "for one thing unreasonable when we ask for the same wage increase the Company has granted employees in other Celanese plants," Local 689 members served notice that they were "in favor of continuing the strike, no matter how long." Three weeks into the strike, one worker told the local press, "We have a good solid strike and intend to keep it that way until the company quits treating us like third class workers." In different words but with similar conviction, Local 689's leaders issued a statement declaring, "We are first class workers and citizens and feel that we are worth just as much per hour" as Celanese employees elsewhere.[57]

[56] Ibid.; Yarbrough interview.

[57] "Some Romans Have Red Faces," radio script, n.d.; *Floyd County Herald*, Sept. 16, 1948.

The peaceful manner in which the Celanese strike unfolded undoubtedly won the strikers some support from the community. Even the *News-Tribune* was curiously silent about the strike, beyond describing the walkout as "orderly" and the strike scene as "serene." Union officials applied the lessons of the Anchor Rome strike and remained guarded in their comments to the newspaper, but they did not have to counter the negative attention of the police and the courts. Despite terse exchanges between company and union officials and aborted union attempts to bring mediation or conciliation, the company left the union alone. Without the daily confrontations between strikers and strikebreakers, picket lines were relatively untroubled at the Celanese plant. While the plant sat, closed down tight, with no threat of strikebreakers, the strike became what the union described as a contest "of attrition, the corporation waiting for the union members to get hungry for food and the union waiting for the union members to get hungry for the profits that the rest of the industry was making at that time."[58]

Local 689's officers repeatedly stressed that the strike represented a sacrifice for the future of their children, and within a few weeks, as the strike settled into an almost comfortable pattern, Celanese workers transformed the strike into a reaffirming family and community event. Just a few days into the strike, union officials replaced their small picket tent with one large enough to accommodate table tennis, dartboards, checkers, and card games, inviting members, after "your picket duty is done," to come by and "play a few games with the other boys and girls." Strike committees organized picketing and publicity, but more importantly, they organized activities that drew the entire mill village community into the struggle. Husbands, wives, and children of workers who shared the task of picketing participated in virtually all the union's strike activities. A weekly movie, dance, bingo, and other social activities filled what would otherwise have been long, frustrating weeks. In October, union president J. S. Whithurst announced that religious services would also be added to the picket line on Sundays, courtesy of a Baptist minister who worked in the upstroke twisting department.[59]

It was perhaps natural that the union made family so central to the day-to-day events surrounding the strike, because families, even more than individual workers, were deeply affected by the strike's lasting much longer than anyone expected, into the Thanksgiving holiday and then toward Christmas. Children of strikers recalled experiencing the strike with a mixture of excitement and fear. Although Pat Baker, who was seven

[58] "A Report on the Celanese Strike," box 1563, folder 100, Ramsey Papers.

[59] Local 689 TWUA-CIO, *Comment*, Oct. 6, 25, Nov. 6, 13, 20, 1948, box 1614, folder 70, Joint Board Papers; *Textile Labor*, June 1959.

years old at the time, remembered that it was the "worst Christmas ever," she also recalled going to the union hall and receiving a box of fruit and raisins from the TWUA. The union usually provided a toy or gift for union children, but in 1948, Pat remembered, "that's all we got." Pat's family lived on a farm, so she also remembered the novelty of receiving store-bought food from the strike commissary. "We had hominy—canned hominy," she explained, "and that was a treat for us because my mother always canned it. We had it in a tin instead of a glass jar and we really thought we were rich instead of poor." Pat also recalled her mother's fear. "It was frightening," she explained. "We didn't have anything, I mean we had *nothing*. We were renting our house. We couldn't get milk." Her mother was unable to nurse her little brother and had to rely on receiving milk from the commissary. Her father worked on the side hauling lime to a nearby cotton gin to earn extra money, but Pat also remembered that while her father sought extra work, she and her mother and her siblings had carried on the work of the farm.[60]

Women's customary role in the local as sustainers of the union's social and cultural life assumed new importance during the strike. The traditional work of feeding and caring for family members now extended over the union community. Mother—workers themselves or wives of strikers—set up a parties for their teenagers in the City Clubhouse and formed a children's chorus. The union's weekly mimeographed newsletter reported that "our strikers are so proud of the talent shown by their children and fellow members" that they proposed the publicity committee set up a Strikers Radio Talent Show. As the holidays approached, the women's activities committee set up special programs for the children. When one union member was asked how his wife felt about the strike, he said, "Why she wants us to win of course. She is a good cook and you would be surprised what she can do with those commissary groceries."[61] In contrast to the violence of the Anchor Rome strike, the friendly, family atmosphere created by members of Local 689 prevailed through most of the Celanese strike.

The strike also received enormous support from the International union and other TWUA locals. The union's national officers, as well as its other rayon locals, understood Local 689's strike as vital to the labor movement not only in the South but nationwide. Raising southern wages not only benefited southern workers but promised to eliminate the South as a non-union haven for other American manufacturers. As a member of a TWUA local in a Maryland plant told members of Local 689, if Rome workers

[60] Pat and Frank Baker interview.

[61] Local 689 TWUA-CIO, *Comment*, Oct. 6, 25, Nov. 6, 13, 20, 1948, box 1614, folder 70, Joint Board Papers; *Floyd County Herald*, Sept. 23, 1948.

accepted one-half of the increase his local received, "it will only be a matter of time until all union standards are broken down in every one of the organized Celanese plants." Members of union locals in other Celanese plants traveled to Rome, served picket duty, and became active participants in Rome's strike. West Virginia rayon workers at an American Viscose plant installed a weekly checkoff system to collect donations for Local 689. Industrial Rayon Corporation workers in Ohio pledged donations of five dollars per member. In addition to covering the costs of feeding 1,650 workers and their families, union donations provided money for newspaper ads, radio addresses, and health care. On Thanksgiving, strikers received a turkey dinner.[62]

Ten weeks after the strike began, however, Celanese managers suddenly became much more aggressive. In spite of their promises, they began distributing sign-up cards and trying to recruit residents of the village to go back to work. In a public statement, Celanese reminded strikers exactly how many dollars they had lost in wages and announced plans to open the mill on October 25. But the company's actions also indicated that they were not so sure of their ability to coax workers to cross the picket line. Without any warning to the union, Celanese managers followed the example of Anchor Rome and obtained a court order against pickets. The injunction, issued by superior court judge H. E. Nichols, who had only recently replaced Judge Porter as an appointment by Governor Thompson, was even harsher than Porter's. The 1,650 members of the union were now limited to a mere two pickets at each gate, at all times remaining twenty-five feet apart.[63]

At an overflow meeting held at the city auditorium on the night of the company's announcement, union leaders reiterated their argument that the goals of the strike served the South and the city of Rome. Union members passed a resolution to remain on strike. Pedigo, in a radio address the night before the mill was scheduled to open, stressed that the union was "interested in the kind of settlement that will benefit our community, ourselves, and our children, now and in the future." He condemned Celanese officials for refusing over the past ten weeks to discuss the issues of the strike and accused the corporation, which had British ownership and corporate headquarters in New York, of "complete disregard for the eco-

[62] Local 689 TWUA-CIO, *Comment*, Oct. 6, 25, Nov. 6, 13, 20, 1948, box 1614, folder 70, Joint Board Papers; speech by Playford Aldridge (president of Local 1874, Cumberland, Maryland), and radio script, n.d., both in "Celanese Strike, Rome, GA" folder, box 6, series 10 A, MSS 129A, TWUA Records.

[63] *Rome News-Tribune*, Nov. 2, 3, 14, 1948; Ex Parte Injunction, and Petition, October 1948, in *Carroll et al. v. Celanese Corporation of America*, Case File 16582, box 433, loc. 148-07, Georgia Supreme Court Case Files, Georgia Department of Archives and History, Atlanta.

nomic well-being of the community." Co-opting the language textile mill owners and southern boosters used against unions, he noted, "In 1776 we fought a war to get rid of a king; and the time has long-since passed, too, when carpetbaggers from the North and their hirelings can dominate the lives of the people of the South." He challenged the company to accept the union's offer of a "rational, American way to settle the strike—through arbitration." The company's apparent determination to break the strike, he concluded, compelled all workers to turn out even stronger. In closing, Pedigo reminded union listeners that "it becomes a solemn obligation of all members of our union to report for picket duty at 5:30 A.M. . . . I urge you to take this obligation and its responsibilities seriously and I am sure that you will conduct yourselves in such a manner as to bring credit and dignity to yourself and your organization."[64]

The next day, when the mill "opened" under the injunction, hundreds of Local 689 members turned out on the picket line. Although Pedigo denied knowledge of the injunction on the first day, it was unlikely that he did not know about it. Since the Anchor strike, local TWUA officials had made it their business to become informed about matters in the court. The Anchor strike had also taught TWUA officials lessons about southern justice. During the strike at Anchor, union pickets had observed the specifications of the court injunction and "the union dribbled away," in the words of a Local 689 officer. Celanese workers "figured they might as well go down hard as get eaten away." So they fought the injunction by ignoring it. On the day the mill opened, deputies "chased around, wrote down names and hauled 140 members into court," but the union soon overwhelmed the local court system with mass arrests. Where Anchor strikers had maintained a picket of the rail line with only 4 people, Local 689 placed 150 people on the railroad tracks. When the company obtained warrants for the arrest of pickets blocking the rail switch, Pedigo remarked only: "It is a matter of common knowledge that we are picketing the tracks leading into the plant but I don't see how we could forcibly stop a train." Day after day, hundreds of workers turned out on the picket line around plant entrances. Every day dozens were arrested on the charge of contempt of court. Before the strike ended, the superior court would issue over 392 contempt of court charges against Celanese strikers. Judge Nichols began to hear the cases in "batches" of ten to twenty at a time. Although the strike persisted for several more weeks, the union had a reserve of over 1,200 members to place on the picket line, and "no more than 100 people went in [to work]," according to one shop chairman.[65]

[64] Speech delivered by Joe Pedigo, WRGA, Oct. 24, 1948, as printed in appendix 14, *Labor-Management Relations*.

[65] Memo recording conversation between Barry Wright and Pedigo, July 15, 1948, "Correspondence Barry Wright, 1945–49" folder, box 2, acc. 85-10, Joint Board Papers; *Rome*

Fortunately, Celanese managers did not adopt the strong-arm tactics employed by Anchor Rome managers or encourage physical violence. In comparison to the Anchor strike, the Celanese protest remained relatively less dangerous, though scattered reports of vandalism surfaced. Two strikers arrested for speeding and reckless driving were discovered to be carrying three pistols. The most serious incident occurred in November when someone shot a striker's son while firing into the backyard of his mill village home. Police arrested a strikebreaker, but Celanese management did not appear to be involved. As a precaution, Judge Nichols asked the county ordinary to refuse gun permits to any person who "is working or has worked at Celanese."[66]

The sheer length of the strike, however, took its toll. Even though rayon workers were better-paid, as the strike moved into three, then four months without paychecks, workers and their families suffered. However, when Celanese attempted to recruit replacement workers rather than reopen negotiations with union members, strikers' commitment increased. Many began to think that the strike originally called over wages had become a struggle for the union itself. Local 689 member Lester Patty believed that the strike lasted so long because "management was trying to get rid of the union. I think that was their intentions—to make it so tough, to make it so that people that worked there wouldn't hold out for it." Continuing to support the strike into the final weeks required enormous sacrifices, but most workers proved willing to make them. Celanese striker Oscar Allen undoubtedly spoke for many when he explained, "I wanted to work, I needed to work, but I'd of dug a ditch from here to [the town of] Armuchee ten feet deep before I'd cross that picket line."[67]

As Celanese plant managers increasingly resorted to legal maneuvers and arrests and the stakes grew higher, Local 689's tactics and public statements became even bolder. In early November, as the number of contempt of court summons issued to strikers approached two hundred, the union purchased a full page of advertising in the *Rome News-Tribune* announcing that the "Textile Workers Union of America stands for law and order" and calling "on the arrogant Celanese Corporation of America to do likewise." Celanese, the union's statement charged, was the "first corporation in the United States" to reject a call from the director of the Federal Mediation and Conciliation Service. Since then, the union charged, company officials had also refused to meet with NLRB officials. Echoing the demands of none other than Dr. W. H. Lewis, Local 689

News-Tribune, Nov. 3, 4, 22, 23, 26, 28, 29, 18, 1948; quote from ibid., Nov. 8, 1948; *Textile Labor*, June 1959.

[66] *Rome News-Tribune*, Nov. 23, Dec. 5, 1948.

[67] Lester Patty, interview with author, Sept. 11, 1994; Oscar Allen interview.

leaders wrapped themselves in the flag and demanded respect for the American government. Holding community leaders to assertions of principle made in the spring of 1948, the statement concluded: "The TWUA believes in law and order and recognition of the United States Government. The strike will continue until the corporation comes to a similar state of mind."[68]

The power of argument undoubtedly aided Local 689, but the union also exerted significant power through the strength of its organization. On the days that Judge Nichols heard contempt cases, for example, hundreds of union workers packed the galleries of the courthouse. Solidarity also allowed the local to put real economic pressure on Celanese. At a time when other rayon producers were collecting hefty postwar profits, Celanese could produce nothing. Constant pickets, and the community's perception that unionists meant to keep scabs out, succeeded. Although many had been willing to cross the Anchor Rome picket line, Local 689 member Walter Brooks remembered, "They didn't dare come out here. A few of them came out, but they got in trouble—they would have got in trouble. We just wouldn't permit it. You know it's the only way you can do it." When supervisors came in through the front gate, pickets were never further than a few inches away. One day when they were picketing the front gate, Brooks recalled, "The plant manager . . . touched—I'll never forget—old Alexander, with the fender of his car, [the strikers] turned it over. They turned the car over. They told him to get out, and then they turned it over. We didn't take stuff like that." Not only did union members roll the supervisor's car, they also issued a warrant for the arrest of the supervisor on charges of assault and attempt to murder with a vehicle.[69] Local 689 members also held a grudge. One Celanese union official remembered that the union office maintained a list of scabs from the 1948 strike until well into the 1970s. Almost fifty years later, workers still remembered who on their street, in their department, or in their church had crossed the picket line. One former shop steward even refused to rent his trailer to the grandson of someone who worked during the strike.[70]

In the final weeks of the strike, Celanese claimed that the mill was running. Full-page ads ran in the *Rome News-Tribune* informing workers that the mill was operating and supplying registration forms for work. But union members knew that it was not. "They said they were running so much of this and so much of that, but they weren't," Brooks remem-

[68] *Rome News-Tribune*, Nov. 4, 1948.

[69] Brooks interview; Local 689 TWUA-CIO, *Comment*, Nov. 6, 13, 1948, box 1614, folder 70, Joint Board Papers.

[70] Brooks interview; Frank and Pat Baker interview.

bered. "This was a complicated process. Oh no, there was no way. But they just kept the lights on, kept the power house going, but they didn't run on." Poking fun at the managers during the first week of the company's back-to-work movement, the union's strike paper featured a cartoon of a Local 689 member holding his nose and looking down on a skunk bearing plant superintendent W. Y. Brown's initials. The caption read, "There sure *is* a funny odor—I wonder if somebody has stuck one of the newspaper advertisements around this spot? I mean the one about the plant is operating!"[71]

Within four weeks of the failed back-to-work movement, Celanese managers, undoubtedly motivated by the profitable contemporary market for rayon, capitulated. When George Baldanzi and Local 689 officials met the plant superintendent at the bargaining table on December 9, the union won its fifteen-cent wage increase and wage equity with northern Celanese workers. More than two thousand people jammed the city auditorium for the vote on the company's offer that evening. When Baldanzi finished speaking, thousands of union workers, family members, and children formed a spontaneous parade and marched down Rome's Broad Street. On the same evening, according to the *Rome News-Tribune*, announcement of the strike settlement to members of the Rome Retail Merchants Association as they held their annual supper meeting likewise brought "an immediate demonstration of cheering and applause."[72]

The stunning success of Local 689's seventeen-week strike at Celanese and the failure of the Anchor Rome Local 787 even to maintain its union local in the face of a hostile management revealed much about the postwar fortunes of the TWUA in Floyd County. In particular, the strikes suggested southern workers' continuing vulnerability to regional underemployment, hostile local officials, and the failure of federal labor policy to overcome these local obstacles. The vicissitudes of the hypercompetitive cotton textile industry undermined workers' collective power in 1948 just as it had in 1934. When workers needed jobs and hours, it was difficult for the union to persuade them that union representation was worth bucking the safety of company paternalism and a steady job. Even in a labor market artificially circumscribed by race, the 1948 strike proved that employers had access to plenty of white strikebreakers. Moreover, cotton textile industrialists' willingness to close down factories elsewhere undermined community support for labor actions that seemed to put local industry and industrial recruitment at risk. Organized workers simply could not command economic or community leverage against companies willing to move or liquidate assets to avoid signing contracts. Even in the

[71] Brooks interview; *Comment*, Nov. 6, 1948.

[72] *Rome News-Tribune*, Dec. 10, 1948.

Celanese conflict, where Local 689's tactics and solidarity had been crucial to the strike victory, the healthy demand for rayon, the capital-intensive nature of production, and the fact that the local could put real economic pressure on the corporation were equally critical advantages in the union's favor.

The strikes also suggested the continuing power of community opinion to make or break workers' struggles to improve their conditions in the South. As Rome boosters sought further outside industrial investment in northwest Georgia, many feared that strikes and unionism would inhibit further development. Thus, even when Anchor Rome managers violated the traditional understanding of corporate paternalism by assaulting white women, city and county leaders proved reluctant to speak out against Anchor management's misbehavior. Although many disapproved of Redmond's actions, the community's silence ultimately lent validity to the claims of Anchor management that they, rather than the TWUA, were truly concerned about workers. In turn, a lack of support for the strike also had the effect of inhibiting community pressure that might have kept strikebreakers from crossing the picket line.

In the realm of community opinion, however, Local 689 leaders gained a critical advantage by articulating their goals in accordance with prevailing cultural beliefs, particularly in terms of the cooperative relationship between white consumers and merchants and by demonstrating the wide support among Celanese workers for their goals. Workers did not mention whiteness, but they did not have to. Booster rhetoric, embellished by allusions to carpetbaggers and regional identity, permitted Celanese workers to make effective cross-class, intraracial appeals to other white Romans. When whites spoke of "the South," they invariably spoke of, and were understood as referring to, the white South. Local 689's willingness to extend their organization to pocketbook matters within their community made the union a more powerful adversary for anti-union editors and businessmen. And although many businessmen would have undoubtedly been reluctant to admit it, Local 689's insistence on wage parity with other Celanese workers actually did help the community at large. In the mid-1950s, even the Rome city manager recognized that "the union has made a real contribution to the welfare of local workers in wages and working conditions."[73]

For members of the Celanese union, the strike also served as a major formative experience for the families and workers in Local 689's community. The "big strike," as it subsequently became known, and the role that all community members had played in it became central elements of the local's institutional memory, a story passed down and repeated by succes-

[73] *Textile Labor*, June 1959.

sive generations of Celanese workers. Decades later, Celanese workers would still talk about the strike in terms of the sacrifice the first generation of Local 689 members had made for them.

However, Local 689's success in the strike did not represent any sort of final victory for the union. Winning the strike and a grudging recognition from city elites did little to redress the many forces arrayed against organized labor in the postwar South. Judges and other elected officials with the power to limit and punish union activism still posed a major obstacle to the future of organized labor in the South. All Georgia unions still had to contend with "right to work" laws, hostile public officials, and boosterism's suspicion of unions in a region where federal protections of organized labor's rights provided meager protection. Though Local 689 had won its fight with the corporation in 1948, union members were still fighting the decisions of Floyd County courts over a year and a half later. Celanese dropped most of the charges against those who violated the injunction, but in the course of TWUA appeals during the following months, the Georgia Supreme Court changed the eight remaining civil contempt cases to "criminal" contempt charges. In 1950, despite Local 689's many legal appeals, including a final appeal to the U.S. Supreme Court to hear the case, eight Rome unionists arrested for violating the injunction against mass picketing faced stiff fines and jail sentences. Such encounters with local "justice" in Georgia reflected larger and more persistent problems facing organized labor in the postwar era.

Fallout from the Anchor Rome strike and Operation Dixie also continued to undermine the image of the International in Floyd County. In May 1948, for example, the union had been pilloried in the Georgia press for a widely publicized CIO convention statement made by TWUA vice president George Baldanzi. Dr. Lewis, the *Rome News-Tribune*, the *Atlanta Journal*, and many other southern papers seized upon Baldanzi's prediction: "I am telling you that before we get through the Southern Drive, based on what we are now facing, there is going to be bloodshed. There will be people killed in the South." Of course, Baldanzi referred to the CIO organizers who would probably be injured or perhaps killed during Operation Dixie. The *News-Tribune*, however, seized upon the statement as an example of the "utter lack of responsibility so often found among labor leaders" and warned that the statement would "only result in more tense feeling, bitter hatred and could easily provoke violence." Instead of "fanning the flames of hatred," the *News-Tribune* had moralized in a veiled reference to the Anchor strike, Baldanzi "should be exercising his influence to prevent intimidation, threats, beatings, and shootings of persons going about their own business." Baldanzi's statement and the general southern resentment of Operation Dixie would frequently come back to haunt the union in the early 1950s.[74]

After the "big strike," Local 689 and the Joint Board made gaining the influence and cultural legitimacy necessary to stop such anti-union attacks a major postwar goal. Politics, of the traditional electoral sort represented by PAC, as well as a community politics of patronage, became the union's defining focus. However, as the issue of African American civil rights increasingly dominated politics, white textile workers' activism became increasingly problematic. In 1948, the union's struggle had been a relatively straightforward one between classes of whites over what the terms of the bargain between boosters, industrialists, and white employees would be. In the 1950s, the civil rights movement complicated white workers' identification with the labor movement and reinvigorated the logic of their identification with southern elites. Union politics became enormously complicated, as conflicts that had always been shaped by whiteness emerged as issues more explicitly about race relations. As textile workers labored to extend union influence in the 1950s, they also faced the unanticipated challenge of reconciling the politics of whiteness with the politics of the CIO PAC.

[74] *Rome News-Tribune*, May 9, 1948; *Atlanta Journal*, Apr. 30, 1948; W. M. Thompson to Kenneth Douty, May 3, and Henderson Lanham to Kenneth Douty, May 5, 1948, both in Baldanzi convention speech folder, box 4, series 10A, MSS 129A, TWUA Records.

Six

Making Friends and Enemies: Political Action in Postwar Georgia

SPEAKING TO A CROWD of over two thousand cheering members and sympathizers of the TWUA in the Rome city auditorium on January 30, 1950, Georgia TWUA director H. D. Lisk promised that a "good PAC job" could "change the thinking of those in public office—including judges." Political action would ensure that "we will never again see such treatment as we are now protesting." The rally, called to honor four unionists released after a ten-day sentence in the county jail, was one of the largest in Rome history. The principal speaker, TWUA executive vice president George Baldanzi, assailed Floyd County Superior Court judge H. E. Nichols for his use of an anti-union injunction and his harsh sentencing of eight TWUA members "whose only offense—committed a year and a half ago—was to picket in violation of a court order." The perception of unfair treatment, more than the jail terms, infuriated TWUA members. While pickets for Local 689 were imprisoned, Baldanzi reminded the audience, a strikebreaker who shot a striker's ten-year-old son went unpunished. Real justice, TWUA leaders promised the crowd, could and would be delivered at the polls in 1950. Baldanzi delivered the final plea for Nichols's defeat: "Even though I'm not a citizen of Rome I hope to God, I pray to the Lord, that come November you vote so many votes against that Judge he'll never even be elected janitor in any place, never mind a judge."[1]

The "take it to the polls" advice Baldanzi offered to Rome unionists reflected the thinking of many postwar American labor leaders, who envisioned labor's future, particularly in the South, as inseparable from politics. In spite of the problems PAC encountered in 1946, Rome's white textile unionists took that advice to heart. In the late 1940s and early 1950s, TWUA members continued to support PAC programs, embarking on an ambitious campaign not only to oust Judge Nichols, but to repeal Taft-Hartley, expose southern anti-unionism, and extend organized labor's political influence in the state and the Seventh Congressional District. The structural complexities of county unit politics, the ideological obstacles posed by boosterism, the generally anti-labor and anti-PAC lean-

[1] *Rome News-Tribune*, Jan. 31, 1950; *Textile Labor*, Feb. 4, 1950.

ings of Georgia Democrats, and the intensifying struggle within labor and Democratic Party circles over civil rights made this a daunting task, to say the least, but Rome unionists achieved a remarkable degree of success. Though PAC activism remained risky, given that traditional Democratic candidates' ability to demonize the CIO could easily make labor's endorsements or activism counterproductive, Local 689's leaders became remarkably adept at working within the southern political system. And contrary to conventional wisdom, the Georgia Democratic Party proved flexible enough on numerous occasions to serve as a vehicle for white working-class interests. To that end, TWUA activists courted both traditional enemies and friends of organized labor, developing a distinctively southern PAC strategy that took advantage of the collective power that unionists commanded as white voters and consumers.

By the mid-1950s, however, as the Democratic Party and the labor movement divided along regional lines over civil rights, southern PAC groups were forced to negotiate a more complicated set of loyalties—to union, region, party, race, and class. Despite national union leaders' contention that segregationists were inherently anti-labor, many Rome unionists were not persuaded that segregation was inconsistent with unionism as they knew it. Such a position represented in many ways a logical, if tragic, extension of the South's segmented labor market and white southern unionists' experiences with working-class activism, Jim Crow, and whiteness. Although Baldanzi, for example, probably meant no harm by his final statement about how he hoped Nichols could not "even be elected janitor," his comment inadvertently appealed to the South's culture of race, and he must have known that it would have had a distinct meaning for this white audience. In effect, Baldanzi equated the position most commonly held by black industrial workers, including members of Local 689, with the lowest status his working-class audience might imagine for the offending judge. Baldanzi's chance comment also reflected the extent to which race served as an immediate reference point even when blackness or whiteness was not explicitly mentioned. This was often the case in the 1940s. Local 689's own race-based allegiances did emerge more explicitly in the mid-1950s, drawing strong criticism from TWUA International leaders. However, the unique history of union and class activism in postwar Georgia rewarded white Rome unionists in the twin pursuit of race and class interests.

In the 1930s and early 1940s, structural segregation within southern industry had often served to insulate Rome union activism from facing any contradictions between race and class interests. In fact, southern textile union membership, composed almost exclusively of whites, often seemed deceptively divorced from race altogether. Even in the 1950s, other Floyd

County workers who joined the local union fold, including a large International Union of Electrical Workers local established at the new General Electric plant in 1955, did little to change the racial profile of the Floyd County labor movement. Given the local dominance of the textile mills, which continued to employ about half of the entire wage-earning population in Floyd County, the practical result was a largely white labor movement.[2] Though the support of the International TWUA and CIO for civil rights at the national level sometimes served as a convenient target for anti-unionists, southern union members successfully avoided conflicts over race for many years by treating it as a specious distraction from the real issues concerning the region's working class.

Union politics, at least in the 1940s, also at times seemed similarly uncomplicated by race, even though few issues in the segregated South were truly unaffected by racial politics. Many leaders of the International TWUA and CIO, for example, had long hoped that union activism in the South might someday result in a political alliance between working-class blacks and whites and a dramatic transformation of the southern Democratic Party. This remained an important, if less visible, aspect of International CIO leadership strategy throughout the 1940s. In the South, however, the difficulty of recruiting white workers and deflecting regional anti-unionism forced union staff to be more circumspect. Day-to-day operations and publicity focused on the more immediate problems of countering anti-unionists and building sympathy for organized labor. For example, even though many CIO leaders envisioned the organization of southern workers as a vehicle to pursue long-term political and civil rights goals for the South, Operation Dixie staff were advised to emphasize the economic benefits of union membership and avoid controversial subjects such as the FEPC.

In a similar fashion, southern PAC leaders described and pursued a narrower vision of union politics than that espoused by the International CIO. As southern leaders implemented PAC programs, the implications of union activism for racial politics were seldom defended or described in such explicit terms. Rather, PAC directives in the late 1940s generally pressed political organization along the lines of simple union partisanship—getting union members registered and voting on candidates' labor records. But because many TWUA and CIO staff believed that the defenders of segregation and the opponents of labor were one and the same, union partisanship was merely one of the means to pursue many ends.

[2] Textile mills still represented the four largest industrial concerns. Of the six largest concerns, employing a total of 7,797 people, the textile mills employed 7,332. On Rome employment, see *Advantages of Rome, Georgia, as a Location for New Industry* (n.d., ca. 1950), copy in Sara Hightower Library.

However, a similar slippage between agreed-upon means and intended ends occurred in the other direction as well. In Rome, organization around union partisanship also happened to correspond to political organization along the color line.[3] In the 1950s and 1960s the differences between International and white rank-and-file views would become a serious point of contention, but in the 1940s at least it did not seem to pose an obstacle to southern unionists allying with CIO PAC.

Political activity quickly became an important facet of union culture in Floyd County. In spite of PAC's difficulties in 1946, leaders of the TWUA's Northwest Georgia Joint Board had continued to place a heavy emphasis on political activism, urging members to register, get out the vote, and make their views known to Georgia politicians. During the 1948 strike, for example, Celanese workers supplemented picket duty with doorbell ringing, leaflet distribution, and arrangements to get TWUA members to the polls to help reelect President Harry Truman. Union leaders self-consciously fused the fate of the Truman Democrats to their own struggle. When Truman won, Local 689's newspaper headline proclaimed, "Well Whad'ya Know! President Truman Elected, Democratic Congress Named. Big Business Takes a Licking. Newspapers are Laughed At and *Celanese Workers Are Winning Strike*."[4] Local 689's record of activism at the polls and within the Georgia legislature indicated that members had internalized the wisdom of their state leaders that "it is not sufficient to pay our union dues . . . if we, or the members of our families neglect to do our duty on the political field."[5] Although Georgia politics rarely offered an opportunity to vote for someone who was openly pro-labor, the enthusiasm demonstrated by Local 689 in the late 1940s and early 1950s belied the assessment of Georgia politics as inherently off-limits to organized labor.

In 1949, Rome's TWUA members even joined the CIO in PAC's major postwar political standoff—the fight to repeal the Taft-Hartley Act. Though the southern Democrat–Republican alliance in Congress, which included several of Georgia's representatives, still served as a potent coun-

[3] On CIO and AFL-CIO aspirations for a political realignment in the South, see Robert Korstad and Nelson Lichtenstein, "Opportunities Found and Lost: Labor Radicals and the Early Civil Rights Movement," *Journal of American History* 75 (Winter 1988): 786–811; Michael Honey, *Southern Labor and Black Civil Rights: Organizing Memphis Workers* (Urbana: University of Illinois Press, 1994), 19, 39, 48–62; and Alan Draper, *Conflict of Interests: Organized Labor and the Civil Rights Movement in the South, 1954–1968* (Ithaca: ILR Press, 1994), 86–106. On the CIO leadership's general approach to the South after World War II, see Zieger, *The CIO*, 230–34.

[4] *Rome News-Tribune*, May 27, July 19, 1946; *Textile Labor*, Feb. 22, 1947; *Comment*, Oct. 30, Nov. 6, 1948, folder 70, box 1614, Joint Board Papers.

[5] H. D. Lisk, *Report for Annual Meeting of Georgia Local Unions, TWUA, 1950*, 1950 H. D. Lisk folder, box 6, series 2A, MSS 129A, TWUA Records.

terweight to organized labor's politicking, political conditions in 1949 presented a real opportunity to force at least a compromise between pro- and anti-labor Democrats, if not repeal. The 1948 election had returned Truman and a Democratic Congress, with organized labor receiving much of the credit. In Georgia, Congressman Henderson Lanham's reelection—and the Georgia electorate's failure to punish him for the negative 1947 vote on Taft-Hartley—suggested that a pro-labor stance was not necessarily tantamount to defeat at the Seventh District polls. Local 689 members, counting on Lanham's support, hoped they might sway other Georgia congressmen as well.

When the 1949 congressional term opened, labor's Democratic allies submitted the Thomas-Lesinski bill, named for the respective chairmen of the Senate and House Labor Committees and based on recommendations made by President Truman in his State of the Union address. Basically, the bill proposed to reenact the Wagner Act with amendments that prohibited certain kinds of jurisdictional strikes and secondary boycotts, and it permitted federal intervention to prevent work stoppages in "vital industries." The GOP forecast a southern Democrat–Republican margin of twenty to thirty votes against repeal, and political analysts predicted that only grassroots pressure could create a majority for the Democrats' bill. CIO leaders accepted the challenge. In March, CIO president Phillip Murray sent all affiliated unions, councils, and regional directors a "Taft-Hartley Repeal field program," directing unionists to write their congressmen, send delegations to Washington, issue public resolutions, organize community meetings, and meet with their representatives personally during the Easter congressional recess.[6]

Although Rome's TWUA members were undoubtedly aware of the difficulty of waging such a campaign in Georgia, their efforts in the spring of 1949 demonstrated the significance that union members attached to political action and labor law reform. In March and April 1949, Floyd County textile unionists issued hundreds of letters and several petitions to inform their legislators that they were an active, organized constituency

[6] Republicans and southern Democrats hoped to substitute the Wood Bill, named for Georgia House member John Wood, which was essentially Taft-Hartley under a new name. "The Labor Story in Congress—Past, Present, and Future," *Congressional Digest*, Apr. 28, 1949, 105–10; "The Labor Bill Rebellion," *Newsweek*, May 9, 1949, 22; "Congress Debates: Labor Bills," *Forum*, June 1949, 12–15; "GOP vs. Lesinski," *Newsweek*, Apr. 25, 1949, 24; *Proceedings of the Eleventh Constitutional Convention of the Congress of Industrial Organizations*, October–November 1949, 99–100. See also Gilbert Gall, *The Politics of Right to Work: The Labor Federations as Special Interests, 1943–1979* (Westport, Conn.: Greenwood Press, 1988), 46; Benjamin Aaron, "Amending the Taft-Hartley Act: A Decade of Frustration," *Industrial and Labor Relations Review* 11 (April 1958): 330–40; Gerald Pomper, "Labor and Congress: The Repeal of the Taft-Hartley Act," *Labor History* 2 (Fall 1961): 323–43.

and wanted their views known. The letters, personalized and written in the words of individual union members, indicated an increasingly sophisticated understanding of southern politics. Many members of Local 689 blamed the Taft-Hartley Act for the injunction against Celanese strikers, the jail terms, and increasing anti-unionism among employers. Lola Truett, for example, a Celanese worker since 1943, claimed that managers "were pretty nice to us before the Taft-Hartley law went into effect, but since then they have treated us quite differently." She believed the 1948 strike would never have lasted seventeen weeks had Taft-Hartley not provided an anti-union impetus to management.[7]

Even Senator Richard Russell, a staunch conservative, received a flood of union correspondence. TWUA letters showed an awareness of Russell's general disdain for unions, but many also demonstrated creative attempts to formulate demands in respect to shared values. C. L. Ross, a mechanic at Celanese and president of Local 689, wrote to Russell, "I realize, Mr. Russell, that you do not represent unions. I would not ask that you be concerned over their welfare as an organization. I do hope that you are concerned with my welfare as a citizen of Georgia and with the welfare of the tens of thousands of other Georgia citizens who work in the textile plants of this state." Similarly, Local 689 member Annie Holtzclaw asserted, "We think we have the right to ask our senators to be our friend and assist us in abolishing the Taft Hartley law." An even more persuasive strategy, perhaps, was that of Clayton Minshew. "[I am] not writing you as a union member, in fact I am disable[d] . . . but am pleading to you as a voting tax payer to do what you can to help pass the Thomas bill . . . as I have just gone through a period of seeing the workers in my home town being beat over the head with the Taft-hartley bill and the courts of my county." Minshew strategically neglected to mention, however, that his wife, Tressa Minshew, belonged to Local 689.[8]

[7] Lola Truett to Richard Russell, Mar. 2, and C. S. Shores to Richard Russell, Mar. 3, 1949, both in folder 4, box 298, Legislative series, subseries M, Russell Papers.

[8] H. H. Gammon to A. E. Barkan, Apr. 17, 1949, 1949 Hugh Gammon folder, box 477, MSS 396, TWUA Records; C. L. Ross to Richard Russell, Mar. 3, and Clayton Minshew to Richard Russell, Mar. 5, 1949, both in folder 1, box 299, Legislative series, subseries M, Russell Papers; *Rome City Directory, 1950* (Richmond: R. L. Polk, 1950), 287; H. H. Gammon to Al Barkan, Aug. 23, 1948, 1948 Hugh Gammon folder, box 479, MSS 396, TWUA Records. See also petitions from Rome and Aragon, folder 4, box 298, Legislative series, subseries M, Russell Papers. Seventh District congressman Henderson Lanham received a similar volume of letter and petitions. See, for example, Kate Johnson to Henderson Lanham and accompanying petition, Mar. 31, 1949, Taft-Hartley 1 folder, and letters in Taft-Hartley 1, 2, and 3 folders, box 34, General series, Henderson Lanham Papers, Richard B. Russell Memorial Library, Athens, Georgia; Pedigo to "Senator," Apr. 16, 1949, Anchor Duck Mills folder, box 2, series 10A, MSS 129A, TWUA Records; Pedigo to Harry Truman and Pedigo to Alben Barkley, both Apr. 16, 1949, 1949 Hugh Gammon folder, box 477, MSS 396, TWUA Records.

Although rates of voter registration and turnout for elections had risen since 1946, only about one-third of Georgia's potential electorate actually participated in postwar elections. As a result, organized labor, as a significant percentage of the county's voters, remained a potentially powerful force in Seventh District politics. In 1948, Local 689 members alone represented 1,244 of the registered voters in Floyd County, a number roughly equal to 10 percent of the votes cast in the 1948 gubernatorial primary.[9] Union petitions and letters thus might have persuaded congressmen that the TWUA represented the most vocal, concerned, and active constituency in the Seventh District had it not been for an equally concerted campaign by their opponents.

Employers, no less than workers, had been politicized by the growing influence of organized labor and the subject of labor law reform. Northwest Georgia factory managers wrote persuasive letters demanding protection of the Taft-Hartley Act. Some even claimed that they wrote on behalf of their employees. Charles S. Heyman, president of Fox Manufacturing in Rome, told Senator Russell, "I do not believe the top union chiefs are the true spokesmen for all laboring people, and many of our employees have so expressed themselves to me."[10] In letters to "pro-labor" Henderson Lanham, some mill managers adopted the conciliatory tone TWUA members had used with Senator Russell. Writing to Lanham, the superintendent of the Celanese mill conceded, "I appreciate that you voted against the law [Taft-Hartley] twice in the 80th congress, but I feel that the past year's experience with Labor Management Relations Act has proved its worth; and I hope you can see fit to change your mind and support the Act rather than its repeal." Others, such as the president of Dellinger Spread Company, warned Lanham, "I dare say that less than 2% of your constituency who are free and uninstructed voters are interested in the Repeal of the Taft-Hartley Act."[11]

[9] Key, *Southern Politics*, 501. In 1948 a total of 12,502 votes were cast in the gubernatorial primary. See *Rome News-Tribune*, Sept. 10, 1948; H. H. Gammon to A. E. Barkan, Aug. 15, 1949, 1949 Gammon folder, box 477, and J. P. Mooney to Al Barkan, Mar. 10, 1948, Georgia 1948 folder, box 479, both in MSS 396, TWUA Records.

[10] Charles S. Heyman to Richard Russell, Mar. 29, 1949, folder 1, box 298, Legislative series, subseries M, Russell Papers.

[11] Wayland Brown to Henderson Lanham, Jan. 31, and W. E. Dellinger to Henderson Lanham, Feb. 5, 1949, both in Taft-Hartley 2 folder, box 23, General series, Lanham Papers. See also E. P. Grant, Standard Stove and Range Co., to Richard Russell, July 21, and E. P. Grant to Henderson Lanham, July 18, 1949, both in Floyd County folder, box 36, series 7; Wayland Brown to Richard Russell, Jan. 31, 1949, folder 3, box 299; A. B. Hammond, General Manager, Berryton Mills, to Richard Russell, Jan. 21, 1949, folder 4, box 299; E. A. Powell, superintendent Good Year Clearwater Mills, to Richard Russell, Mar. 31, and J. Rollins Jolly, General Superintendent American Thread Co., to Richard Russell, Mar. 29, 1949, folder 1, box 298; all in Legislative series, subseries M, Russell Papers.

The issue of federal labor law, perhaps more than any other, stretched the southern Democratic Party coalition to the breaking point, particularly for those candidates who hoped to capture a not insignificant labor vote. Georgia Democrats rarely claimed to represent any citizens other than whites in the years prior to the 1960s, but they did purport to represent *all* white interests, including labor and business, organized and unorganized workers. Taft-Hartley reform required more from Georgia representatives than a balancing act—it called for a vote one way or another. Addressing the prospective bills on the floor of the U.S. House of Representatives in April 1949, Lanham's position reflected the influence and the activism of both organized labor and business, as well as the ideological contortions sometimes elicited by a single party system. First, Lanham recounted a recent visit in his Rome office with a local TWUA member, who informed the congressman that since Taft-Hartley had passed, workers sensed a definite change in management attitude. More than half had dropped out of the union. Then Lanham carefully qualified his position in respect to management, claiming that "there are many factories and mills in my district where . . . there is such an enlightened attitude on the part of management and such cordial relationships between management and labor that union organization is not necessary."

But as Lanham and other southern politicians well understood, appealing to race was by far the safest route to unifying business and labor interests, since virtually all industrial workers and industrialists in the Seventh District were white. Thus Lanham also added "in passing," as a tribute to all his white constituents, organized and unorganized: "We have in the South . . . the finest group of labor in America, because it is homogeneous, because it is Anglo-Saxon." If warring factions in the Democratic Party could not agree on the proper form of labor law, they would theoretically agree on the supremacy of white labor. Only then, with concessions of fairness and goodwill for all, did Lanham finally announce his position. While he opposed the Republicans' alternative bill, he would not support the Truman administration's bill unless it was amended. To do otherwise, he said, "would be recreant to my trust," for "as eager as I am to remove the restrictions that bind and hinder union organization," Lanham declared, "I am more concerned about what may happen to the American public unless we do give the President the right in some way to control Nation-wide strikes."[12]

It was unlikely that Lanham's constituency as a whole supported Taft-Hartley repeal in 1949. In fact, the persistence of an unprecedented number of nationwide strikes since the war and the South's general disaffec-

[12] Henderson Lanham speech in the House of Representatives, Apr. 29, 1949, Taft-Hartley 3 folder, box 34, General series, Lanham Papers.

tion with Truman's administration had probably hardened the lines of opposition to Democratic liberalism.[13] Truman's addition of a civil rights plank to the 1948 presidential platform, which had included a proposal for a permanent FEPC and federal anti–poll tax and anti-lynching statutes, had already alienated many southern Democrats, including party leaders in Floyd County. Although Georgia's political leaders refused to follow the Dixiecrats, who bolted the party and ran their own independent candidates for president in 1948, most Georgia Democrats harbored a lingering resentment against the administration, suspecting, with good reason, that Truman took southern support of the party for granted. Moreover, some political observers believed that Truman had alienated potential allies by threatening to disburse patronage according to votes on Taft-Hartley reform. Southerners read this as an insult to their region's representatives and their role in the party. At the same time, Floyd County unionists agitating for reform still had to contend with local irritation with postwar CIO strikes in national industries like mining and steel and auto manufacturing, as well as the bitter memory of the Anchor strike. Persistent strikes in the coal industry in late 1949 and early 1950 elicited regular *News-Tribune* editorial attacks on John L. Lewis as a "radical" who arrogantly and selfishly "strangled the entire nation to gain, not the welfare of his miners, but power."[14]

In Rome, public resentment of Lewis and the coal strikes in particular played a significant role in strengthening Lanham's commitment to limits on labor, and therefore a limited reform. The threat of coal shortages intensified local frustration with unions in general as both the strike and the debate over Taft-Hartley continued into the winter. In May the *Rome News-Tribune* editorialized on the front page that the coal strikes constituted "the most vicious type of monopoly." By the fall of 1949, the paper claimed that Romans and Floyd County industries were suffering from a strike-induced shortage of coal to fuel furnaces. Notwithstanding the temperate autumn clime of northwest Georgia, the editor shrieked on November 1, 1949, "Hundreds of persons in the Rome area will suffer in freezing temperatures tonight because of John L. Lewis." A Rome "housewife-poet-novelist" asked in an open letter to President Truman, "Is It Cold in Blair House Tonight?" With self-righteous rhetorical flourish, she informed the Trumans that "down here" in Rome, "baby fingers

[13] James T. Patterson, *Grand Expectations: The United States, 1945–1974* (New York: Oxford University Press, 1996), 148–49. On the Dixiecrats, see Key, *Southern Politics*, 329–46; and Kari Frederickson, *Revolt of the Black Belt: The Dixiecrat Party and the End of the Solid South, 1932–1968* (Chapel Hill: University of North Carolina Press, 2001).

[14] On postwar strikes, see Brody, *Workers in Industrial America*, 173–211; Zieger, *American Workers*, 100–108; and Dubofsky, *State and Labor*, 193–94.

and little lips [were] turn[ing] blue with cold." Schools and mills were also experiencing a shortage of coal, the paper reported. Even "pro-labor" Lanham was moved by such complaints to wire President Truman requesting presidential intervention in the coal strike, much to the approval of the *News-Tribune* and other indignant Floyd County residents.[15]

Though the telegram undoubtedly aided Lanham's 1950 prospects for reelection, TWUA members were infuriated by his coddling of Seventh District alarmists. Union member Truman Henderson suggested to Lanham that he had been "misinformed," for in the unionist's travels through the district he had "not found a school or cotton mill closed or on short time because of a shortage of coal." Pepperell and Celanese had large stockpiles, and in reference to recently imprisoned TWUA members, Henderson added, "Even the Floyd County jail is operating full time." Lanham's cordial reply begged to differ with Henderson that there was "a very real and very acute shortage" of coal in Rome, adding that his actions merely reflected a concern for the public. And it was true, the larger public in Rome did appear to be more concerned about a steady supply of coal than the mine workers' struggle.[16]

Lanham's response to the uproar about the coal strike and his stand on Taft-Hartley repeal revealed the limits of what the TWUA could expect from its only Georgia "pro-labor" representative. As a politician who, in Lanham's own words, "appreciate[d] the confidence and support of the laboring people both organized and unorganized," the congressman "desire[d] to legislate for the benefit of the people as a whole and not for a few special interests." Although Lanham valued CIO votes and regularly accepted invitations to speak to organized labor, he refused to acknowledge that Taft-Hartley was all bad and declined to champion the liberal reform that labor sought in Congress. Given the torrent of opinion emanating from other interests in the Seventh District and the nation, Lanham's position was perhaps inevitable. For in the contest to become the Seventh District's squeakiest wheel, those who demanded restrictions on unions had equaled, if not surpassed, organized labor's efforts. If Lanham had spearheaded CIO-led initiatives, he might not have been reelected. A career politician, Lanham owed his success not only to TWUA votes but

[15] The Trumans were living in Blair House in 1949 because of repairs to the White House. *Rome News-Tribune*, May 2, Oct. 27, Nov. 1, 3, 1949. On the coal strike, see Melvyn Dubofsky and Warren Van Tine, *John L. Lewis: A Biography* (Urbana: University of Illinois Press, 1977), 484–90.

[16] Henderson Lanham to Truman Henderson, Feb. 2, and Truman Henderson to Henderson Lanham, Feb. 4, 1950, both in Taft-Hartley 3 folder, box 34, General series, Lanham Papers.

to his own skill in seemingly representing the widely divergent concerns of a broad white constituency.[17]

Other TWUA efforts in 1949 and 1950 may have inadvertently cemented Lanham's commitment to such a lackluster advocacy of organized labor. Looking to labor's political allies outside Georgia, national TWUA officials arranged a Senate investigation of labor relations at two Rome mills. At the urging of TWUA president Emil Rieve and vice president George Baldanzi, Montana's Democratic senator James Murray announced a 1950 Senate subcommittee inquiry into labor-management relations in the southern textile industry. TWUA leaders had long charged that a southwide conspiracy against textile unions existed, and the subcommittee investigation promised an opportunity to draw national attention to the southern anti-unionism and the need for further federal labor law reform to combat it. As one of the few strongholds of textile unionism in Georgia, Local 689 had impressed the TWUA's executive board with its successful seventeen-week strike, and International TWUA officials had long promised an inquiry into the injustices inflicted by the courts and by management on northwest Georgia unionists. As a result, the Celanese plant, the Anchor Rome Mills, and their Haralson County neighbor, the American Thread Mill, became the main focus of the ill-fated Senate investigation. Murray's announcement quickly elicited stinging denunciations of the CIO and the subcommittee from southern congressmen, Senate conservatives, textile industrialists, and Rome business leaders.[18]

When a preliminary and highly partisan report from the subcommittee was leaked to the press in February 1950, southern business and political leaders responded with outrage. Textile industry leaders charged that the subcommittee had already tried and convicted the industry without investigation. The trade paper *Textile Bulletin* claimed that the subcommittee staff was "largely C.I.O. hand-picked, drawn from among union organizers," and warned that subcommittee members were "cooking up a smear of Southern industry such as has never been plastered on before." One southern congressman designated the investigation a "second invasion of carpetbaggers in my state." Senator Russell, at the goading of several Rome businessmen, personally assisted in postponing the investigation. Even Lanham protested to Rome TWUA leaders, "I cannot for the life of me see how it can possibly do the CIO Union any good to stir up more animosity and trouble in Rome and the 7th. District." Writing from Wash-

[17] Lanham served five consecutive terms until his sudden death on November 10, 1957, when his car was hit by a train. Henderson Lanham to Truman Henderson, Feb. 2, 1950, ibid.; *Rome News-Tribune*, Dec. 4, Nov. 11, 1949.

[18] *Textile Labor*, Dec. 4, 1948, Feb. 4, 1950; *Rome News-Tribune*, Nov. 10, 1949.

ington, Lanham continued, "I know pressure is put on by your union heads here, but frankly, I think they are wrong."[19]

When the controversial hearings finally began in August 1950, the outpouring of indignation in the Seventh District surpassed Lanham's predictions. In July and August, the Rome Chamber of Commerce, several mill managers, business owners, and the *Rome News-Tribune* pilloried the investigation as a "ruthless, useless hearing." A *News-Tribune* editorial declared that all "right-thinking persons will instantly deplore the committee's action as unfair," for the " 'inquiry' can only be interpreted as another example of bureaucratic meddling, backed by dictatorial organized labor."[20] Forwarding the same editorial to Richard Russell, the chairman of the Rome Chamber of Commerce's Labor Relations Committee concurred that "hearings such as this one can do nothing but stir up animosities." Rome businessman Parker Arnold pleaded with Russell and Georgia's senior senator Walter George "and other Southern Senators" to "take immediate action in the Senate to have this obnoxious, vicious, trouble-making, South-baiting, C.I.O.P.A.C. sponsored subcommittee of Murray's discharged." Undoubtedly, public perception of the hearing was not helped by the timing of its announcement. The Rome Chamber of Commerce had just introduced a major industrial development campaign. As perennial hawkers of Rome's "Good Native-Born Labor Supply" and the "splendid spirit of cooperation exist[ing] between employer and employee" who relished the influx of new mill payrolls into the local economy, Rome's boosters were collectively infuriated about the hearing's potential for negative publicity.[21]

[19] *Textile Bulletin*, February 1950, 20–22; ibid., May 1950, 34; *Rome News-Tribune*, Apr. 4, July 21, 30, 1950; Alfred Barron to Richard Russell, Aug. 3, 1950, folder 2, box 297, Legislative series, subseries M, Russell Papers; Henderson Lanham to C. N. King, Aug. 8, 1950, C. N. King folder, box 2, acc. 85-10, Joint Board Papers.

[20] Alfred Barron to Richard Russell, Aug. 3, and A. L. Barron to Richard Russell, July 25, 1950, both in folder 2, box 297, Legislative series, subseries M, Russell Papers; *Rome News-Tribune*, Aug. 3, 1950.

[21] Barron to Richard Russell, July 25, and Parker Arnold to Richard Russell, July 22, 1950, both in folder 2, box 297, Legislative series, subseries M, Russell Papers; *Rome News-Tribune*, Apr. 5, 7, 23, 1950; Rome Chamber of Commerce, "Rome," in *Rome City Directory, 1950*, xvi, and "All Roads Lead to Rome," Chamber of Commerce pamphlet, ca. 1955, Rome Chamber of Commerce folder, Special Collections vertical file, Sara Hightower Library. On postwar southern boosterism, see James Cobb, *The Selling of the South: The Southern Crusade for Industrial Development 1936–1980* (Baton Rouge: Louisiana State University Press, 1982), 35–63, 97–121. The fury of Rome's leaders in 1950 had lasting repercussions. Virtually every bit of local evidence that might have documented the Senate hearings and related disputes had mysteriously disappeared. The *Rome News-Tribune* microfilm omitted many issues with stories on labor violence from 1948 to 1951 and skipped the year 1950, a period especially marked by local labor-related disputes. Fortunately, bound issues of the 1950 paper were available in the county courthouse basement.

TWUA Joint Board president C. N. King claimed that despite the protests of Rome's "money boys," the "great majority" of labor people were "looking forward to the investigation." King and Local 689 president C. L. Ross assured Lanham that Rome's unionists had not been pressured by CIO officials. "It should be plain," Ross told Lanham, "that when Celanese workers in Rome, Georgia are mistreated it does not require 'pressure' from union heads in Washington or elsewhere to seek action." Both objected to Lanham's insinuation that the *union* was the party stirring up trouble. "Bias and prejudice" against the CIO, Ross argued, were only "encouraged by the silence of its victims." To remain on the safe side and pull out of the controversial hearings, he told Lanham, would be to strengthen the forces of "injustice against the citizens of the Seventh District." Furthermore, Ross concluded, the Senate hearings were essential to the current Congress for "consideration in making any change necessary in the present laws," because they demonstrated "the actual results of the application of labor or anti-labor laws."[22]

Vindicating TWUA charges about injustice below the Mason-Dixon Line, the Senate subcommittee's final 1952 report rivaled TWUA propaganda in condemning Taft-Hartley, corporate lawyers, southern managers, Judge Nichols, and "the almost inevitably evil effects of the use of injunctions in labor disputes." Revelations about the use of violence and intimidation by Anchor Rome's L. H. "Two-Guns" Rice and his counterparts riddled the final document, laying bare the hypocrisy of southern claims about loyal employees and "enlightened management." The subcommittee's examination of the clearly anti-labor leanings of the courts also lent corroboration to the TWUA's claims of conspiracy. Investigators agreed, for example, with TWUA officials that the state of Georgia had denied Celanese workers their right to collective action under federal laws, and recommended "searching reevaluation of existing labor legislation." National observers, such as the editors of the *New York Times*, predicted that the document would "prove a highly controversial one," but it ultimately turned into a hollow victory for the TWUA. By the early 1950s the political momentum behind Taft-Hartley reform had largely subsided in Congress, and southern officials, as always, were unmoved by charges of anti-unionism.[23]

[22] C. N. King, Jr., to Henderson Lanham, Aug. 11, Henderson Lanham to C. N. King, Aug. 8, and C. L. Ross to Henderson Lanham, Aug. 11, 1950, all in C. N. King folder, box 2, acc. 85-10, Joint Board Papers.

[23] Ross Groshong, interview with author, Mar. 20, 1994; Marshall, *Labor in the South*, 261; U.S. Congress, Senate Subcommittee on Labor and Labor-Management Relations, *Labor-Management Relations in the Southern Textile Industry, Report of the Subcommittee on Labor and Labor-Management Relations*, 82nd Cong., 2nd sess. (Washington, D.C.: Government Printing Office, 1952), 28–45, 52–69, quotes from pp. 38, 69; *New York*

In Georgia, no one seemed to be paying attention to the subcommittee's disclosures. Although the *Rome News-Tribune* had covered the issue of subpoenas to local mill officials and unionists, the details of what transpired at the hearing received little press. While the paper had devoted several column inches to Anchor Rome manager L. H. Rice's April speech before the Rome Kiwanis Club on his employees' "spirit of cooperation and loyalty," the editors chose not to publicize the Senate hearing revelation in August that Rice had provided pistols to scabs during the 1948 strike. When the subcommittee finally published its report, based largely on the events in Rome, editors of the *News-Tribune* did not even treat it as local news. Instead, they carried a wire story placing considerable emphasis on a scathing minority report issued by Senator Robert Taft and newly elected Republican senator Richard Nixon. In agreement with southern industrialists, Taft and Nixon charged that the subcommittee's denunciation of the South's "primitive" policies "constitut[ed] an amazing and unjustified slur upon a great section of our country." Given the resentment of the hearing among the South's traditional business and civic leaders and the general alienation from Truman and the Democratic Party, it was perhaps inevitable that southern opinion makers gave little weight to the pronouncements of men such as Montana's James Murray. In fact, the close association of the TWUA with Yankee senators probably confirmed what had always been a gut-level suspicion of many Floyd County residents—that the unions placed southerners in cahoots with "outsiders." Criticism of the South by northeastern and midwestern Democrats on racial matters such as lynching and poll taxes, for example, had rarely resulted in southern leaders' critical examination of regional policy. The investigation of management-labor relations in southern textiles likewise had little effect on the region's conscience. Until the TWUA commanded more respect in Georgia, even powerful friends outside the South could not compel changes in southern attitudes.[24]

If the voice of labor was "to be heard and heeded" in Floyd County, northwest Georgia TWUA leaders had to prove once and for all that it was worthwhile and necessary for politicians to listen to their labor constituents. While leading letter-writing campaigns and coordinating political publicity from 1948 to 1950, TWUA PAC leaders also continued to organize the organized. Because the TWUA represented a minority interest group in the Seventh District, a good grassroots organization of union voters had to include more than 100 percent of TWUA members. The TWUA PAC needed, and hoped to influence, several votes from each

---

Times, May 10, 1952; Zieger, *American Workers*, 119; *Rome News-Tribune*, Apr. 11, Aug. 17, 1950.

[24] *Rome News-Tribune*, Apr. 11, Aug. 17, 1950.

union household. By 1948, Local 689 had already made greater progress than other Georgia TWUA locals. Registration had increased from less than one-quarter of the workforce in 1944 to over two-thirds in 1948. In contrast, Local 689's Seventh District neighbors at the Crown Mill and the American Thread locals in Dalton had only 389 of 633 members and 310 of 700 members registered, respectively.[25]

Securing the rank and file's cooperation on registration should have been the most simple of PAC's formidable political tasks, but postwar opposition to civil rights in Georgia indirectly complicated even this modest union proposal. In February 1949, Georgia Democrats, under the direction of newly elected Governor Herman Talmadge, who had pledged to carry out his father's plans to curb the black vote in Georgia, passed a voter qualification control law requiring an entirely new voter registration list. A reaction to the increase in African American votes cast in 1946, the reregistration law intended to limit the black vote by requiring that prospective voters be able to read and write and to "understand and explain" the Constitution. As a result of the reregistration law, PAC faced having to start their own registration job from scratch. But accustomed to the difficulty of union politics in Georgia, the director of Seventh District PAC, Hugh Gammon, faced the challenge with characteristic enthusiasm. Gammon, a member of Local 689, tackled reregistration for the 1950 primaries with a "four point PAC Program." The program entailed first setting up a meeting with union officers, selling them on the job of registration, then holding a mass meeting of local union members to sell the rank and file, and finally, forming a committee that secured commitments for the time and the people to do the work. A good judge of human character, Gammon also added his own fifth point: "Get up a good issue of some political nature . . . find out who most of the union workers don't like and who is no good to them in office. Also find a good man who is holding office that we want to see re-elected." By doing this, Gammon found that he "could kill two birds with one stone." People would "register, also give their $1.00 [PAC donation,] and work hard to carry this program out."[26]

Gammon's confidence in 1950 belied the complexities of Georgia politics. If Georgia's system of factions did produce an acceptable candidate

[25] H. D. Lisk, "Annual Report of Georgia Local Unions 1950," 1950 H. D. Lisk folder, box 6, series 2A, MSS 129A; H. H. Gammon to A. E. Barkan, Aug. 15, 1949, 1949 Gammon folder, box 477, MSS 396; J. P. Mooney to Al Barkan, Mar. 10, 1948, Georgia 1948 folder, box 479, MSS 396; all in TWUA Records.

[26] Emory Via to HCF, July 16, 1958, box 1, acc. 89-34, Emory Via Papers, Southern Labor Archives, Atlanta; "Voters' Registration Act," 1949, voter qualification folder, box 17, Gubernatorial series, subseries B, Herman E. Talmadge Papers, Richard B. Russell Me-

or a clear "enemy" of labor, the county unit system, with its rural bias, necessitated further calculations. Votes cast for a PAC candidate did not contribute to an overall state total for the chosen candidate, but counted only at the county level. Given the CIO's minority presence in Georgia and the state system's bias toward rural voters, union officials were forced to make more deliberating calculations of overall costs and benefits. Support for a less popular "liberal" candidate could easily throw a county election, and therefore the entire county's vote, to the most conservative candidate. In 1948, for example, the Seventh District PAC chose not to support the Atlanta PAC's choice of Joe Rabun for governor. Instead, Seventh District PAC leaders encouraged their members to support M. E. Thompson, a less desirable candidate than Rabun, because they feared that support for Rabun would have divided the more "liberal" voters in the Seventh District and resulted in a victory for their least favorite candidate at the time, Herman Talmadge.[27]

The defeat of Judge H. E. Nichols in 1950, however, was an ideal PAC program because it was local, was not subject to the county unit system, and was a simple union issue uncomplicated by divisions within the Democratic Party. Well before Baldanzi's speech, Gammon had already begun to use Nichols as a motivating device "to let our people know they must register" and vote "full strength." Nichols had "never been very popular with the average voters," according to Gammon, who believed that the judge's defeat "should be easy." Seventh District PAC proceeded confidently with reregistration. Local 689 publicity reassured union members: "There is nothing to be afraid of in the new voter qualification law. Only three have been turned down in Floyd County." For those union members who still failed to register, the state miraculously granted a final reprieve. In January 1950, a last-minute decision by the Georgia legislature permitted the old voter registration to stand for the upcoming elections. Local 689 PAC now made arrangements for cars to get out the voters.[28]

---

morial Library, Athens, Georgia; *Statesman*, Mar. 3, 1949; Hugh Gammon to A. E. Barkan, Aug. 15, 1949, 1949 Hugh Gammon folder, box 477, MSS 396, TWUA Records.

[27] For example, in the 1948 gubernatorial election, a solid union vote for PAC-endorsed candidate Joe Rabun in the counties where the CIO was strong probably would have resulted in those county unit votes going to Herman Talmadge. Polk County's 1948 elections illustrate the PAC dilemma. Because Polk County's TWUA members had ignored the PAC endorsement and voted for M. E. Thompson, Talmadge had been defeated by twelve votes. Had Polk's unionists voted for Rabun, Talmadge would have won Polk County's unit votes. Ken Douty to A. E. Barkan, Sept. 10, 1948, Georgia 1948 folder, box 479, MSS 396, TWUA Records; on the county unit system, see Bartley, *From Thurmond to Wallace*, 14–15.

[28] Hugh Gammon to A. E. Barkan, July 15, Aug. 15, Dec. 14, 1949, and final quote from "We Agree That We Must Register," Local 689 PAC leaflet, Aug. 9, 1949, all in 1949 Hugh Gammon folder, box 477, MSS 396, TWUA Records. On factions in Georgia Democratic

What Local 689 leaders had not calculated, however, was Nichols's ability to turn recent anti-CIO sentiment to his advantage. A singularly vicious campaign ensued. Overshadowing all other electoral contests in Floyd County, the superior court race became the center of a virulent public debate about organized labor. In his opening radio speech, Nichols informed Floyd County residents that "there [is] only one issue in this campaign for superior-court judge and that issue . . . is the radical element of the CIO versus law and order." While conceding the legal right to join a union, he denounced Local 689's members as duped by "the dribble and tommyrot of a bunch of foreigners whose names I can't even pronounce." Nichols also attacked his opponent, Horace Clary, as an eleventh-hour candidate persuaded to enter the race only by the "golden voiced oratory of Baldanzi and Joe Pedigo" and tens of thousands of CIO dollars. The choice between himself and Clary, Nichols warned, was a decision of "whether our courts shall remain free." In response, Clary, a good friend and legal partner of Henderson Lanham's, issued a "flat and emphatic denial" of any connection with the CIO PAC. Following suit, Lanham quickly issued a statement denying any connection to Clary's candidacy, the CIO, or any aspect of the superior court race.[29]

In short time, the *Rome News-Tribune*, the Rome Bar Association, and County Commissioner W. H. Lewis also entered the fray on the side of Judge Nichols. Suddenly all the bitterness elicited by the 1948 Anchor Rome and Celanese strikes, the national coal strike, and PAC flowed into the superior court race. A series of outlandish charges followed. Lewis recounted how the "C.I.O. under foreign leadership invaded Floyd County" and prophesied that Nichols's defeat would lead to an erosion of "freedom" and an end to "constitutional government." This was not "just another election," Lewis warned. Rather, county voters would be deciding nothing less than the question of whether "constitutional government, equality before the law and freedom of every citizen to work or not to work has the approval of citizens of Floyd County."[30]

The *News-Tribune*, which had immediately endorsed Nichols and editorialized that the honorable judge should run unopposed and therefore

politics, see Bartley, *From Thurmond to Wallace*, 22–30, 48–50, 59, 71–72; and Joseph Bernd, *Grass Roots Politics in Georgia: The County Unit System and the Importance of the Individual Voting Community in Bi-Factional Elections, 1942–1954* (Atlanta: Georgia Institute of Technology, 1960), 6–35. According to Talmadge and the legislature, reregistration was postponed to give small counties time to deal with the expense and trouble of registration. But it was also true that African Americans, Atlantans, and other voters deemed undesirable by the Talmadge faction were the main constituency that had reregistered. *Rome News-Tribune*, Jan. 11, 12, 14, 16, 25, Feb. 4, 14, 1949.

[29] *Rome News-Tribune*, May 10, 1950, May 14, 1949, May 15, June 7, 1950.

[30] Ibid., June 23, 1950.

be "spared the time and expense of a campaign," must have profited immensely. In the week before the primary, the paper was flanked by an unprecedented amount of political advertising—five full pages in four days. It was unclear who had the largest campaign treasury. Clary matched Nichols's radio and newspaper appeals, but Nichols's campaign was certainly aided by the free endorsements by Lewis, the *News-Tribune*, and the Rome bar. Clary charged that the fact that Nichols "had consistently taken the side of the vested interests and politicians in this county" was aiding the incumbent judge's campaign. "If money could buy the race," Clary told a radio audience, "Nichols would win."[31]

Although it avoided the hyperbole of Lewis and Nichols, the Rome Bar Association's endorsement played upon a concern dear to Romans—boosterism. If Nichols lost, the bar warned, "the newspapers in the entire nation will carry the same as a victory for the CIO. And if this happens, we have a very slim chance of getting any more industries and any more jobs." In a second radio address, Rome lawyer Dean Owens reminded Floyd County voters that the George Baldanzi calling for Nichols's defeat was "one of the radical leaders of the CIO," who had warned in 1948 that the CIO's Operation Dixie might result in "blood" running "in the streets of the South." But Nichols's supporters also went to great lengths to show that support for Nichols's anti-CIO platform was not confined to the business class. According to Clary, Nichols campaigned hard among the unorganized workers at the Pepperell and Anchor Rome mills. A group of Anchor Rome workers who had not struck in 1948 appeared in the *News-Tribune* endorsing Nichols as a candidate for "law and order." A photograph of six anti-union employees presenting Judge Nichols with a $757.58 campaign contribution appeared in a full-page political advertisement allegedly paid for "by hourly-paid Anchor Rome supporters of Judge E. Nichols." Clary countered with the claim that local mill managers were soliciting campaign contributions for Nichols on the job and also charged that Floyd County business and mill managers were trying to "intimidate, coerce and force" their employees to support Nichols. At the same time, however, Clary tried desperately to dissociate himself from PAC, emphatically declaring that he had not received "one thin dime from the CIO." Although Baldanzi and Local 689 had cast the original context for the election, by June 1950 it had spun completely out of TWUA control.[32]

In an election that turned into a countywide referendum on the CIO, the union lost. In fact, the prominence of the CIO PAC may have contributed to Nichols's victory by stimulating many opposition voters who oth-

[31] Ibid., Mar. 19, June 25, 1950.

[32] Ibid., Mar. 19, June 22, 25, 27, 1950.

erwise would not have cast ballots in the 1950 primary. The total number of votes cast in the primary was almost 11 percent higher than the turnout for the previous primary in 1948.[33] The election "clearly demonstrated," according to Joint Board president King, "what the money boys can do with keeping the people here against the CIO." Returns from various Floyd County precincts followed predictable patterns. Nichols lost in the Celanese mill village district, of course, but won by a margin of nearly two to one in Rome. The unorganized mill village of Lindale seconded town support for Nichols with a vote of 979 to 454. But in other respects the election represented a victory for PAC in northwest Georgia. The county total—8,365 for Nichols and 5,482 for Clary—indicated that Local 689 had generated thousands of votes for Clary beyond its immediate membership, even if the final tally suggested that labor issues would still fall short of a majority. Local 689 had proven exceptionally effective at mobilizing grassroots action and demonstrating the collective discipline of the union. Voter registration among union members had expanded well beyond normal yearly increases, and the actual turnout of Celanese union members soared in 1950. In the mill village district alone, the number of registered workers had increased more than 20 percent since 1945. The most impressive gain, however, was in the number of these voters who actually turned out to vote in the primary. In successive gubernatorial and congressional primaries, the participation of workers in the Celanese district rose from only 19 percent of registered voters in 1942 (before the union organized), to 51 percent in 1946 (less than a year after Celanese workers joined the TWUA-CIO), to 55 percent in 1948, and finally to well over 70 percent in 1950.[34]

[33] In 1950 the number of votes cast in the primary totaled 13,847. In 1948, in a special gubernatorial primary called by the Georgia Supreme Court in the wake of the "two governors" controversy, the total vote was 12,502. However, an even higher turnout in 1952 local elections of 14,094 voters suggests that it would be a mistake to read too much into the higher vote. In 1954, the next statewide primary, the total number of votes cast dropped to 10,709. *Rome News-Tribune*, Sept. 8, 1948, June 28, 1950, May 12, 1952, Sept. 10, 1954.

[34] C. N. King to Henderson Lanham, Aug. 11, 1950, C. N. King folder, box 2, acc. 85-10, Joint Board Papers. In the Celanese mill village district Nichols was defeated 553 to 339. The mill district represents only a sample of Local 689's voters, since not all millhands lived in the village. Many of the votes for Nichols from the mill district probably came from the approximately 237 managers and office workers—ineligible for union membership—who were registered to vote in that district. Voter registration figures and voter turnout are based on an analysis of voter registration books for the Riverside district (the Celanese mill village) in Floyd County and a subsequent comparison with voting returns published in the *Rome News-Tribune*. The turnout figures for 1950 are based on the "old" books (before reregistration), which would indicate turnout was 75.5 percent. This estimate may be a little high. Books from 1950 were not available. Floyd County Voter Registration Books, ca. 1933–1949, Floyd County Records Retention Center; *Rome New-Tribune*, June 28, 1950.

However, the 1950 primary also revealed early signs of what was to become a much more serious problem for PAC in the South. Historians usually associate the regional divide over white supremacy with the *Brown v. Board of Education* era, but united white southern opposition to federal civil rights initiatives had been building since creation of the FEPC. Especially in the years after Truman's civil rights proposals, state and federal elections in the South were increasingly dominated by race issues. And as Georgia's politicians become ever more preoccupied with issues of race and region, so did many of Georgia's white unionists. Thus, although the late 1940s and early 1950s witnessed the maturity of TWUA plans for PAC in Floyd County, it also marked the appearance of an explicit division between the political sentiments of International TWUA officials and the white southern rank and file. The 1950 election demonstrated that southern unionists, once mobilized by PAC, would not necessarily follow every principle of CIO politics. The solid rebuke delivered to Judge Nichols, for example, was paralleled by a strong vote of approval for Governor Herman Talmadge. This did not necessarily represent a explicit rejection of a PAC endorsement, since PAC officials had often allowed Georgia locals to select their own gubernatorial candidate in order to avoid "divisiveness." However, organized labor generally had voluntarily refused to support either Talmadge since 1934. Until 1950, Local 689's voters had also voted consistently against the Talmadge faction.

There were many reasons why Celanese workers might have chosen not to support M. E. Thompson, including Thompson's indecisiveness during the Anchor Rome strike. Floyd County's traditional business and courthouse leaders had also shifted their support to Talmadge for the first time since 1934, though it is doubtful that Celanese workers would have respected the opinions of, in the words of TWUA leaders, Floyd County's "money boys." Talmadge had made a brief speech courting organized labor in May 1950, and his platform included "vigilant protection of labor's rights to organize and bargain collectively" and the creation of "more job opportunities." But the issues in 1950 also offer other compelling explanations. The most striking difference between Talmadge and Thompson in 1950 was Talmadge's fiery defense of the county unit system and segregation. In fact, the majority of Talmadge's energies in the campaign of 1950 were directed not toward labor, but against civil rights measures proposed by the national Democratic Party.[35]

Campaigning in Rome and other northwest Georgia towns, Talmadge repeatedly stressed in his speeches the "dangers from an FEPC and antisegregation."[36] Since 1948, Talmadge had been stumping on the potential

[35] *Statesman*, June 1, 1950; *Rome News-Tribune*, May 28, 1950.

[36] J. P. Mooney to Al Barkan, Mar. 10, and Kenneth Douty to Al Barkan, June 23, 1948, both in 1948 Georgia folder, box 479, MSS 396, TWUA Records; *Rome News-Tribune*, Jan. 11, 1949, May 28, June 9, 14, 1950, Dec. 7, 1951.

disaster FEPC represented for white southerners, often with specific reference to the textile mills of Georgia. "If an FEPC law [were] forced on the cotton mills of our State," he argued, it would create "strife," "chaos," and an "intolerable situation." Mills would be forced to fill 40 percent of their jobs with black workers. "In New York," Talmadge warned, "where a State FEPC law [was] in force, white women [were] already taking orders from negro foremen." To anyone who might claim that the FEPC, as a federal issue, was irrelevant to the *state* primary, Talmadge supporters recalled their candidate's role in mobilizing southern Democratic opposition at the National Democratic Convention. Thompson, they warned, might not be up to the muster in 1952.[37]

The 1950 electoral returns thus provided a foreshadowing of how civil rights would upend PAC plans for creating a distinct organized labor vote in the South. Except for their vote against Nichols, Celanese workers had voted in striking conformity with Lindale's unorganized workers. The number of Celanese district votes cast for Talmadge in 1950 had more than doubled since 1948. Moreover, 1950 marked the beginning of a pattern of support for the Talmadge faction of the Georgia Democratic Party in the Celanese mill village district. Although rates of voter turnout for the primaries dropped in successive elections, the district remained solidly for Talmadge and thus solidly behind the southern Democratic opposition to the civil rights revolution that was unfolding in the courts and in Congress throughout the 1950s. In the 1954 gubernatorial primary race between six candidates, Celanese mill village voters would deliver a solid plurality of their votes to a Talmadge-chosen successor for the governorship, Marvin Griffin. In 1956, when Talmadge ran for the U.S. Senate, the Celanese mill village district delivered him 87 percent of their votes. In terms of their votes, Celanese union members became virtually indistinguishable from their unorganized counterparts.[38]

The 1950 election also represented a temporary end of sorts for PAC in Floyd County. Organized labor would not make another public endorsement of a candidate until the 1960s. However, Floyd County TWUA leaders did not cease their efforts to increase the union's influence. Rather, electoral failures in the union's early years focused the union's collective energies on more profitable strategies. Many of Local 689's PAC experiences during the first six years of the union's tenure—the failure of Taft-Hartley repeal, Lanham's duplicity, the Senate hearing fiasco, and the Nichols election—had starkly illustrated the limits and the costs of CIO PAC–style political action in Georgia. But Local 689 employed other community experiences, especially their familiarity with southern-style poli-

[37] *Statesman*, June 1, 1950, Apr. 1, 1948, June 15, Mar. 9, 1950.

[38] *Rome News-Tribune*, Sept. 10, 1954, Sept. 13, 1956.

tics and local power, to enhance CIO PAC strategy. As southerners and seasoned residents of northwest Georgia, members of Local 689 had long understood two important aspects of the political economy of Floyd County. First, community leaders did not necessarily care about union efforts to increase the wages of individual workers or to eliminate North-South wage differentials, but they did share a consuming interest in mill payrolls. As boosters frequently reminded local businessmen and workers, textile mill wages were vital components of the community that not only supported the local economy but also lined the pockets of local retail and service proprietors. Second, TWUA members learned that their letters, petitions, and endorsements did not necessarily command the attention and deference of Georgia politicians. But Georgia's elected officials did show a grudging respect for an organized bloc of white votes. Local 689 members, as wage earners and white citizens, collectively controlled a significant share of both these valuable commodities.

Drawing a lesson from the industrial development boosters' preoccupation with the distribution of mill wages and their experiences in the 1948 strike, Local 689 turned boosterism upside down and recast it in a way that served the union. Where community leaders had often made special concessions to lure industrial capital, union members now organized as consumers demanded a similar sort of concession to draw the union's collective capital. Retail consumption thus became the basis for an ambitious countywide campaign to reward friends and punish enemies of labor.

In part, Floyd County TWUA members were acting in accordance with the principles of the national labor movement's "union label" drive. In a campaign befitting the postwar ascension of industrial workers into middle class consumption, the newly merged AFL-CIO attempted to use union buying power to bolster union manufacturers and strengthen the labor movement. The TWUA established its own union label department in 1958 and created a structure of local, city, state, and national union label committees to coordinate textile workers' spending. Local 689, for example, had its own union label chairman who informed members of recommended union providers for an enormous range of consumer goods, from shoes, hats, shirts, and overalls to cigarettes, lawn furniture, plumbing fixtures, and even vending machine coffee.[39] Local officers distributed lists of manufacturers under TWUA contract and shared catalogs for union-made goods available through mail order. Local 689's union label chairman also wrote to every Rome merchant with a request for

[39] William Pollock to All Locals, Joint Boards and Staff, June 9, 1958, and Resolution No. 21, Union label, n.d., both in "Union Label 1958" folder, box 111, MSS 396, TWUA Records.

information on which union products he or she carried. Rome's ostensibly anti-union businessmen were surprisingly cooperative. Cordial replies expressing gratitude for "the business that [union members] have always given them" simultaneously attested to the power that union dollars held in the community. Moreover, Local 689's officers took the whole project very seriously. When one local department store ignored labor's request for buyers to acquire union-made goods, members of Local 689 circulated a petition of protest and presented it to the management.[40]

Floyd County unionists also moved well beyond observance of the federation's program. Consumption became an organizing tool. In 1958, an officer of the TWUA noticed that the barber in the Celanese village did not display a union card. After he made inquiries with the barbers' union and discovered that the local man had never applied to join, Local 689's president directed the union label committee to visit him and every other barbershop in the city. Local 689 subsequently became an informal partner of the barbers' union in a citywide organizing campaign. In the early 1960s, union minutes regularly included updates on which barbers had joined, which shops were being picketed, and which shops to patronize. Although a few of Local 689's sixteen hundred members apparently broke the boycott, union sanction was strong enough to force them to sneak in the back door.[41] Union members also extended their concerns beyond tradesmen and manufactured goods to retail service employees. In 1961 the union boycotted a local grocery when its managers, in order to subvert an organizing campaign, assigned workers new titles to make them ineligible to vote in an upcoming NLRB election.[42]

While contributing to the overall goal of supporting union labor everywhere, Local 689's selective spending also clearly influenced local opinion. By the late 1950s, Local 689 members were treated with courtesy and a heavy dose of respect by local merchants, who—no matter what their personal feelings about organized labor might have been—courted union spending. In 1959, when Local 689 opened its new union hall, dozens of local merchants and service providers donated door prizes for the opening-day celebration, including a radio, one hundred baby chicks, a coffeemaker, material for three dresses, three oil changes, a twenty-five-

[40] Local 689 minutes, July 24, 1958, and Mar. 26, 1959, folder 1; Mar. 17, 1960; (quote from Hilburn Shoe Co. as recorded Mar. 17, 1960), folder 2; Jan. 10, 1963, folder 7; all in box 1, MSS 78-071, TWUA Records.

[41] Local 689 minutes, July 10, 1958, folder 1; Apr. 21, 1960, folder 3; Sept. 15, 1960, and Apr. 5, 1962, folder 4; May 30, 1962 folder 5; July 19 and Sept. 20, 1962, folder 6; all in ibid.

[42] Local 689 minutes, Feb. 16, 1961, folder 4, ibid.

dollar food order, a set of stainless steel kitchen implements, and a permanent wave.[43]

Local 689 did not call another major plantwide strike for almost twenty years, but the treatment accorded the union during that strike reflected the effects of the union's selective spending, and as a result, the union's new position in the community. Union member Frank Baker remembered, "Everything we had was donated to us . . . I'd call bread companies and they'd be in competition to bring us bread over there, to give it, just stack it up. Milk companies—they had coolers out there of milk. We had eggs—goddern egg companies, just wanted me to stack them eggs 'til it was ridiculous. Cigarette companies, everybody, back then, this was in the sixties now, they would come out." The union also called in favors. Reckoning that the union had spent about $500 a month on flowers for sick or deceased union members, Baker called the local florist and asked for some support. "I called him up on Saturday. I said, 'Mr. Whitehead,'—he always got on me about cussing—and I said, 'I want to know how many damn orchids you got up there.' He said, 'Why?' I said, 'Look, we're going to have about 25 or 30 women walking picket line out there at Celanese and I'd like to see an orchid on every one of them.' 'You got to be kidding,' " Whitehead said, but Baker got a "refrigerator full of damn orchids for a week."[44]

In the more formal arena of city and county government, TWUA leaders also drew lessons from the ways in which the "money boys" had historically bent the region's judicial and political system to support the South's peculiar brand of injustice for unions and workers. Without challenging these basic tenets of Georgia political culture—in fact, by exploiting them when possible—TWUA members made aggressive and creative use of their resources as white citizens. In the long run, making these concessions to the southern political system, rather than issuing challenges, proved to be their most effective tactic. Though all of the strategies employed on this level could not be defined as "politics" in the conventional sense, they were in fact the essence of the money- and power-driven partisanship that governed twentieth-century southern communities like Rome.

Taking a cue from traditional southern justice, for example, the union finally redressed its grievances with Floyd County courts through the time-honored southern method of jury packing. Since juries were selected from applications by white citizens, rather than a random selection process, the system potentially allowed the jury to be controlled by the court-

[43] Local 689 minutes, Mar. 26, 1959, folder 1, ibid.

[44] Frank and Pat Baker interview.

house crowd or anyone who took an interest in court affairs. In 1948, as both unions found themselves at the mercy of Georgia courts, TWUA Joint Board manager Joe Pedigo decided "to see if some working people can't get on the damn jury for a change." At the same time that PAC chairman Hugh Gammon registered voters, he and Pedigo coordinated jurist applications. On the day in 1948 when Judge Nichols was holding contempt of court hearings for Celanese strikers, he also drew a jury for the next session of Floyd County criminal court. It "was quite funny," according to Gammon, when, before an audience of Celanese workers, Nichols drew the names of four Local 689 members, including the local's president, J. S. Whithurst. In all, Gammon was able to get seventy-five members of Local 689 on jury duty in 1949. Of course this was too late to reverse the 1948 criminal charges against union, but the union's new friends in the courthouse served Local 689 well in the future.

Local 689 and the Joint Board also cultivated friends among the county's law enforcers. The next time the company obtained an injunction without a public hearing, a superior court judge warned union officials to "scatter them pickets out" in order to avoid arrests. Although the police remained duty-bound to uphold Georgia's antilabor laws, company officials claimed that local law enforcers were prejudiced in favor of union members. The treatment accorded TWUA members sometimes suggested they were right. When TWUA members were sentenced to serve time in 1950, sheriff's deputies fixed up the jail and replaced all the mattresses.[45]

Local 689's cultivation of friends for the union also aided working-class efforts in the more formal arena of electoral politics. Although Local 689 still had to figure out "the best of two evils" in most elections, union members found productive ways to use their eighteen hundred votes. Though white Georgia Democrats such as Talmadge considered a bloc of black votes "one of the most dictatorial practices carried on in our nation today," few could ignore an organized bloc of white union votes, PAC or no PAC.[46] Local 689's experience suggested that Georgia officials fully understood the value of union votes even if they did not want to identify themselves as labor candidates. In the 1940s, as one union member explained, "these little old companies they owned the politicians, see. Then in the 60s . . . we didn't *own* them, but we . . . *supported* them." Local 689 officials found that state officials "would do you a little favor, but they didn't want the public to know about it, you know. They'd sneak

[45] Memo recording conversation between Barry Wright and Joe Pedigo, July 15, 1948, Barry Wright folder, box 2, acc. 85-10, Joint Board Papers; Hugh Gammon to Al Barkan, Oct. 31, 1948, 1948 Gammon folder, box 479, MSS 396, TWUA Records; Pat and Frank Baker interview; *Textile Labor*, Feb. 4, 1950; McCarthy, "Rome Memo," ca. March 1948, Celanese strike folder, box 6, series 10A, MSS 129A, TWUA Records.

[46] Herman Talmadge, *You and Segregation* (Birmingham: Vulcan Press, 1955), 22–26.

around that way." In 1948, union officials had discovered that Governor Thompson would not help strikers until union members "put the dough on the line." After 1948, TWUA officials used their "dough" to greater effect. Even Governor Herman Talmadge was not above making concessions to organized labor. Throughout his tenure as governor and senator, Talmadge regularly corresponded with union leaders about minimum wage bills, workers' compensation, industrial development, and other issues of interest to labor. In 1952 Talmadge promised Georgia unionists that he would support a bill proposing to make union shop agreements legal again. He met with Rome TWUA members in Washington and even hosted a 1960 meeting with Floyd County union leaders in his home. In the 1960s, when Local 689 officers explained to Senator Talmadge that strikers were too embarrassed to apply for food stamps in a welfare office, he arranged to have food stamp applications delivered and filled out at the mill. Although Local 689 never transformed Talmadge into a pro-labor candidate by CIO standards, the union often benefited from its association with him.[47]

Rome's TWUA leaders also realized that politicians could be swayed if the favors requested could be carried out with minimal political cost. Lanham, for example, who had been unwilling to crusade for Taft-Hartley reform in 1949, was more than glad to phone and write letters to the NLRB on behalf of Floyd County unions. When the Joint Board manager complained in 1956 of unnecessary delays in the Anchor Rome Mills case, Congressman Lanham "made it his business to get after the NLRB in Washington." Talmadge, Russell, and Lanham's successor, John C. Davis, worked tirelessly to curb textile imports and bolster southern industry, an issue as dear to Rome labor as to businessmen in the 1950s and 1960s.[48]

Although these informal networks and political connections rarely surfaced in the papers or the documents recording Local 689 history, they were the events associated with political action that left permanent impressions on Celanese union members. They also had the most lasting impact on the community. It was a paradox of southern politics, perhaps, that unionists frequently complained that Rome was an anti-union town

[47] Waddell interview; Pat and Frank Baker interview; Mac to Larry, ca. April 1948; "Recommendations," ca. April 1948; "Anchor Rome-Political Background" ca. April 1948; all in Celanese strike folder, box 6, series 10A, MSS 129A, TWUA Records; H. D. Lisk, "Annual Report of Georgia Local Unions 1952," 1952 Lisk folder, box 6, series 2A, ibid.; James O'Shea to Boyd Payton, Nov. 1, 1956, folder 8, box 1609, Joint Board Papers; see also frequent references to communications with Talmadge in Local 689 minutes, 1958–68, box 1, MSS 78-071, TWUA Records.

[48] Henderson Lanham letters to NLRB, Aug. 9, 1951, Nov. 1, 16, 1949, Jan. 16, 18, 1951, all in NLRB folder, box 19, General series, Lanham Papers; see also Local 689 minutes, 1958–1968, box 1, MSS 78-071, TWUA Records.

and Georgia an anti-union state, but also claimed that "we had real power in Rome." By the late 1950s, Local 689 members had achieved real power in their community. Local politicians and judges made a point to learn the names of union officials. Harold Waddell, a union officer in the 1960s, for example, recalled his surprise when a local judge he had never met addressed him by name. The judge had memorized every officer's name and face from a photograph hanging in the union hall. Throughout the 1950s and 1960s, a steady parade of candidates for city, county, and Seventh District office—even some of the most anti-union candidates—requested the privilege of addressing a union meeting. Officers of Local 689 began to receive invitations to Democratic Party functions such as the traditional southern Jefferson-Jackson Day dinner. Judges and state representatives frequently dropped by the union hall or had drinks with union officers. In 1956 the TWUA Joint Board manager was invited to serve on Talmadge's campaign staff. Rome never became a true "union town," but the union taught many Georgians and Democrats to respect Local 689.[49]

Surprisingly, Local 689's successes in building alliances with Georgia Democrats such as Talmadge did not immediately upset their relationship with the International. In the 1940s and early 1950s, CIO PAC support for civil rights policies and Georgia Democrats' opposition to those policies managed to coexist in an uneasy equilibrium within the Seventh District PAC. Although national CIO leaders were among the strongest supporters of civil rights, the literature, speeches, and programs designated for southern consumption generally avoided issues that might undermine the labor movement's tenuous presence in the region.[50] Occasionally, national TWUA or CIO leadership would take Floyd County TWUA leadership to task for their politics, but in the 1950s it was relatively rare. In 1952, for example, Hugh Gammon received an angry letter from the Georgia State CIO executive secretary Dave Burgess, informing him that Floyd County's delegates to the Georgia assembly "voted *wrong*" on a Talmadge-sponsored bill connected to civil rights. "This is a disgrace," Burgess wrote. "Here are representatives from a six unit county, from a county with a great number of CIO members, voting against the interest of organized labor and against the National Democratic Party in favor of the Dixiecrats."[51]

[49] Pat and Frank Baker interview; Waddell interview; James O'Shea to William Pollock, June 4, 1956, "NW GA Joint Board" folder, box 23, MSS 129A, series 2A, TWUA Records.

[50] Korstad and Lichtenstein, "Opportunities Found and Lost"; Michael Goldfield, "Race and the CIO: The Possibilities for Racial Egalitarianism during the 1930s and the 1940s," *International Labor and Working Class History* 44 (Fall 1993): 1–27; Honey, *Southern Labor*, esp. chapters 8 and 9.

[51] Dave Burgess to H. H. Gammon, Feb. 7, 1952, folder 15, box 1609, Joint Board Papers.

International TWUA staff, however, were well aware of organized labor's support of Herman Talmadge. The Joint Board manager informed TWUA staff that labor was supporting Talmadge for the U.S. Senate in 1956 long before the primary vote was cast. Perhaps International staff reconciled themselves to labor's alliance with the author of the 1955 anti–civil rights tirade *You and Segregation* because the alliance was a pragmatic one. In the 1940s and early 1950s, the International generally seemed to have accepted that Georgians would choose their local candidates in accordance with local custom. National staff had historically also turned a blind eye to practices such as segregated union meetings.[52]

In the mid-1950s, however, more serious tensions began to surface between southern unions and the national leadership of the labor movement. The prominence of debate over the Supreme Court's 1954 *Brown v. Board of Education* decision mandating the desegregation of public schools, as well as the emerging grassroots movement for civil rights, made it much more difficult for the CIO and the AFL to contain the contrary views of their members. In 1956, as southern governors, congressmen, state legislatures, and white citizens' councils prepared for massive resistance to school integration, the newly merged AFL-CIO Executive Council issued a strongly worded support for the Supreme Court's decision. AFL-CIO leaders also denounced the white citizens' councils, a "new Ku Klux Klan without hoods," as essentially "anti-union and anti-democratic." In 1957, when President Eisenhower called out federal troops to protect black students entering a Little Rock high school from an angry mob of white segregationists, the AFL-CIO publicly announced its approval for the principle of desegregation and Eisenhower's actions. Southern workers responded to both incidents with angry letters and mass disaffiliations from AFL-CIO state councils. One such letter, issued in 1956 from Local 654 of the Papermakers Union in Rome, reflected southern workers' relatively new culture of organized protest as well as southern labor's cultural roots in the region. In a language that echoed the anti-"outsider" regionalism of traditional southern conservatives, the letter contended that it was not the Klan or the citizens' councils, but the NAACP that was "truly subversive" and deserving of the labor movement's contempt.[53]

[52] James O'Shea to William Pollock, July 9, 1956, "NW GA Joint Board" folder, box 23, MSS 129A, series 2A, TWUA Records.

[53] Draper, *Conflict of Interests*, 17–40, quote from 21. Two TWUA locals in Dalton, Georgia, Local 689, and the Northwest Georgia Joint Board disaffiliated from the Georgia State AFL-CIO council in 1955 because, the manager of the Joint Board explained, it was "felt the dues of eight cents per member per month is excessive for the benefits derived" and "the locals in this area have been by-passed on policy discussions which were made in Atlanta by a few without consulting this area." Whether these "policy decisions" concerned

Rome TWUA members did not write letters of protest, spearhead private school initiatives like their counterparts in Front Royal, Virginia, or otherwise distinguish themselves as outspoken defenders of segregation in the 1950s. However, political action and survey responses from the late 1950s suggest that northwest Georgia textile workers disapproved of *Brown* and the AFL-CIO's position on civil rights, even if they avoided more drastic means of expressing their objections. Surveys of white union opinion, conducted in 1957 under the auspices of the AFL-CIO Civil Rights Department, also revealed a decidedly working-class slant to anti-integration sentiment among white workers. Of 110 union locals surveyed, two TWUA affiliates of the Joint Board—Local 943 at Cedartown and Local 789 in Aragon—were among the respondents.[54] According to the Local 789 officers who answered the survey, "few" of the local's 450 members had "antagonistic feelings toward Negroes," were "in favor of the White Citizens Councils," or were "opposed to Negroes voting." But "most" (the strongest answer available) were "opposed to Negroes having the same economic opportunities on the job as white workers have," and "most" were in favor of segregation in general. "Most" favored the plan in Georgia, and many other southern states, of putting public schools under private control in order to circumvent the Supreme Court's order. The majority also disapproved of the AFL-CIO's support for the civil rights movement. Answers provided for the thirty members of Local 943 were identical. Overall, union leaders confirmed what election results had suggested since 1950—that white union members were most concerned about job competition with black workers, opposed to integration of public schools, and angry about the pro–civil rights position taken by the AFL-CIO.[55]

Survey responses in 1957 undoubtedly reflected the upheaval of emotions aroused by Little Rock, but as late as 1960, when many of Georgia's white citizens had adopted a more moderate position on school desegregation, northwest Georgia unionists remained stalwart defenders of segregated schools. In 1959, when a court order desegregating Atlanta schools

civil rights is unclear, although both the AFL and CIO state councils had opposed Georgia's "private school" amendment in 1954. James O'Shea to John Chupka, Nov. 28, 1955, folder 3, box 1609, Joint Board Papers.

[54] Union locals were chosen to participate in the survey according to two categories. Priority was given first to locals "where the race issue was known to have arisen," and second to "typical" locals of the area. Because Locals 789 and 943 did not report any specific problems, they were presumably in the "typical" category. Records and subsequent reports on the survey provide no other explanations of how or why particular locals were chosen to participate. Emory Via, "Interim Report on Survey of Southern Trade Unions and the Race Problem," May 10, 1957, box 1, acc. 89-34, Via Papers.

[55] "Local Union Questionnaires" for Locals 789 and 943, n.d., ca. 1957, both in folder 11, box 1277, Via Papers.

appeared imminent, Governor Ernest Vandiver orchestrated statewide hearings to canvass opinion on how to proceed. The hearings, held in each congressional district, asked respondents whether they preferred to close public schools in the event of court orders to integrate, or whether they preferred a local option or "freedom of choice" plan, which accepted the inevitability of some integration and maintained the public school system. In Rome, among the many individuals and groups that responded, including the board of education, the League of Women Voters, the chamber of commerce, and the Rome Christian Council, the great majority voiced their support for maintaining the public school system. The Rome Central Labor Union, a coalition of area AFL-CIO leaders, however, returned a unanimous vote to the state commission in favor of avoiding integration at all costs, even if it meant abolishing the public school system. The unions and a post of the American Legion stood alone among local organizations favoring such a strong position. As the "better sort" moved toward a tentative acceptance of, or at least a resignation to, integration of schools, organized labor was becoming one of the most conservative constituencies in Georgia.[56]

International TWUA staff also discerned an emerging class dynamic in the conflict over school desegregation. In a memorandum on the South penned just weeks after the Little Rock standoff, research director Solomon Barkan advised International staff that "southern society has come to a turn in the road with the Little Rock incident." Although race had historically tied southern whites of all economic groups together, the region's "low-income whites," in his words, were newly "resentful" as a result of traditional elites' attempts to restore order. Ironically, Barkan saw in the post–Little Rock southern fury the "first evidence of a class structure and cleavage within the South" and the "first time we can truly [see] economic class conflict." Unfortunately, the labor movement, given its own commitment to desegregation, was not well placed "to take advantage of the increasing division between the dominant groups and the workers." Moreover, civil rights–related conflict also required labor leaders to figure out a way to "avoid becoming the scapegoat on whom the lower-income white groups direct their hatred for the desegregation."[57]

The national labor movement's general strategy for addressing segregationist sympathies among its southern members was to argue simply that citizens' councils and anti-integration southern officials were anti-labor.

[56] Jeff Roche, *Restructured Resistance: The Sibley Commission and the Politics of Desegregation in Georgia* (Athens: University of Georgia Press, 1998), 117–19; *Rome News-Tribune*, Mar. 9, 10, 11, 1960.

[57] "Memorandum on the South," Solomon Barkan to William Pollock et al., Oct. 21, 1957, "Southern Organization" folder, box 109, MSS 396, TWUA Records.

From the perspective of AFL-CIO leadership, of course, opponents of civil rights had always been inherently anti-labor in the larger scheme of liberalism, though labor leaders had not always championed this position. But confronted with massive resistance, national union leaders drew much stricter lines and attempted to persuade the southern rank and file to join them. Southern governors who had once received endorsements from the AFL-CIO but became outspoken defenders of segregation, such as Arkansas governor Orval Faubus and Alabama governor George Wallace, were reevaluated by the federation as enemies of labor in the late 1950s. Research produced by the newly created AFL-CIO Civil Rights Department, for example, argued that the leaders of citizens' councils were frequently anti-labor businessmen who had historically opposed union organizations. However, some southern political leaders clearly defied these conventions. Even Lanham, a man with considerable credit within labor circles, resolutely condemned the Supreme Court's decision and vowed to protect segregation. Under such circumstances, many members of the white southern rank and file proved reluctant to abandon relationships established prior to *Brown* and Little Rock. Leaders of the Georgia State AFL-CIO, for example, remained allied with the Talmadge wing of the party throughout the 1960s.[58]

In spite of Barkan's prescient analysis of white working-class resentments, AFL-CIO staff generally tended to interpret anti–civil rights feeling among the southern rank and file as simply a misguided emotionalism mobilized by cynical southern conservatives who sought to undermine organized labor as well as civil rights. However, northwest Georgia textile workers' history suggests that the choice to side with southern conservatives constituted something more substantial, and unfortunately more powerful, than mistaken loyalties or "false consciousness." As historian Alan Draper has observed, AFL-CIO locals below the Mason-Dixon Line "were not just unions that simply happened to be located in the South, they were *southern* unions."[59] As such, they were shaped by the broader culture of segregation that surrounded them. But more important than their regional character was their racial character. Given the strict segregation of industrial jobs, southern unions were overwhelmingly *white* unions in the South. Although conventional wisdom has suggested that black southerners were more amenable to unionism than whites, 1957 union surveys actually reveal that the great majority of southern unionists were white.[60] Moreover, the structure of southern industry also meant

[58] Draper, *Conflict of Interests*, 41–62, 107–22, 104.

[59] Ibid., 15–16, 39.

[60] Although historians have given a disproportionate amount of attention to integrated unions, these unions were also exceptional in the general pattern of union membership in

that white southern workers had much to gain from maintaining the privileges of whiteness.

The segregation of industrial work, as well as the choices made during the early years of the union's tenure not to confront segregation or press the rank and file to internalize important aspects of CIO liberalism, made it difficult, if not impossible, to challenge southern conservatism by the 1950s. Especially given white Georgia workers' ability to accommodate union goals to the political status quo, by the 1950s it would have been nearly impossible to persuade textile workers that support for candidates such as Talmadge and Lanham was bad for the union movement or that broad social changes in the South such as integration served the interests of white workers. As newly enfranchised and empowered members of the southern community who had always benefited from segregation, textile union members had a stake in conducting business as usual. Local 689's community-based successes also meant that they had a lot to lose in bucking the general segregationist sway of southern politics. Floyd County unionists insisted on "running [their union] like we thought it ought to be run," in the words of one former union member, in part because they had derived concrete benefits from doing so. Local accomplishments were particularly meaningful given the failure of national efforts by the CIO to make the South more accommodating to organized labor. Although CIO efforts to repeal Taft-Hartley and investigate southern employers' hostility to unions had done little to aid northwest Georgia's labor movement, local political action had "changed the thinking" of friends as well as enemies in Floyd County.[61]

The structure of southern industry and politics undoubtedly encouraged white unionists' alliances with traditional southern Democratic defenders of segregation. The racial homogeneity of the textile workers and their unions permitted unionists to support defenders of segregation with little internal debate or awareness of potential contradictions between race and class interests. Indeed, it is remarkable in the late 1940s and early 1950s how seldom race emerged as an explicit issue in local textile union records. All prominent Georgia Democrats supported segregation, which allowed political activism to seem as though it revolved exclusively around labor issues and alliances for many years. Since Rome unionists were never offered an opportunity to vote for candidates who supported both contemporary labor issues such as repeal of Taft-Hartley *and* civil

---

the South. For a 1957 racial breakdown of southern union membership, see Emory Via, "Interim Report on Survey of Southern Trade Unions and the Race Problem," May 10, 1957, box 1, acc. 89-34, Via Papers.

[61] Pat and Frank Baker interview.

rights in the 1950s, it is impossible to know whether they would have made different choices. However, the more exacting test of race and class allegiances emerged in the mid-1960s. After 1964, southern workers' structural isolation from civil rights issues began to give way as the whole edifice of southern segregation, including the segmented market for southern labor, began to collapse under the weight of federal legislation.

Seven

The "So-Called 'Civil Rights' Bill" and the Republicanization of Rome

In 1964, ten years after *Brown v. Board of Education*, the Civil Rights Act declared finally and unambiguously that all racial discrimination was illegal. The secretary of the Rome NAACP chapter hailed the law as "one of the greatest steps forward in this century." But unfortunately, this decisive action by the U.S. Congress did not settle the issue for many white southerners. A *Rome News-Tribune* poll taken the day after the act passed the Senate revealed sharp divisions along racial lines in Rome. One respondent, Georgia Power employee Bill Blaylock, declared that it was "time for the people of this nation to stand up and fight for what's right and for the principals [*sic*] for which our forefathers died." He referred, however, to the rights of whites to continue practicing segregation. Without recognizing the incongruity of the metaphor, he claimed that "with the passage of this bill, you are no longer a free citizen—you are now a slave of the federal government." A Rome minister, Rev. Thomas Wheelis, echoed the sentiment: "I regret the passage of the civil rights bill,"he told the *Tribune*. "The public accommodations feature is an open invitation to complete government dictatorship . . . every person in America has less freedom because the bill was passed." A doctor, a restaurant operator, a motel operator, a member of the Rome City Commission, and the president of the Rome Citizens' Council joined him in lamenting the passage of what the paper had lately taken to calling the "so-called 'civil rights' bill." The editorial page went even further to claim that the bill's alleged violation of private property, business practices, and the employer's discretion in matters of employment "may well mark the most serious blow to constitutional government in American history."[1]

Locally, passage of the bill had particular resonance, as it finally settled an intensifying struggle between African American residents and the white city leadership over segregation in Rome. Like their counterparts in Greensboro, Birmingham, and other southern cities, black high school students had begun to challenge Rome's Jim Crow practices in the early 1960s with a series of sit-ins at downtown lunch counters. In one of the largest sit-in protests, in March 1963, a rolling strike of several groups of

[1] *Rome News-Tribune*, June 21, 1964.

students had forced the Rome city police to create a three-car shuttle from town to jail to accommodate the sheer volume of students arrested. The courts convicted the teenagers of violating city ordinances and sentenced fifty-seven of them to time, served on weekends, in the city jail. But suddenly, in spite of local white opposition, less than a month after passage of the Civil Rights Act, black residents of Rome were attending movies, eating out in cafés, and frequenting drive-in restaurants that had once been strictly segregated. Just days after the bill became law, the Rome NAACP chapter filed a petition to integrate the city's schools. The customs of segregation so zealously guarded by so many white southerners had begun to crumble.[2]

At least as revolutionary as the integration of public venues were the Civil Rights Act's implications for employment. Title VII of the act explicitly forbade the sort of race- and gender-based discrimination that had historically governed the market for southern labor. Although many local employers, such as motel operator William M. Slaughter, protested that they already believed in "free employment" and hired "according to the qualifications of the job and the applicant's education . . . regardless of race, creed or color," civil rights legislation and its enforcement arm, the Equal Employment Opportunity Commission (EEOC), placed a much greater burden on employers, as well as unions, to practice nondiscrimination in good faith. Indeed, the Civil Rights Act compelled more radical actions than even a determined labor movement could enforce among its membership—actions that undermined the very basis of the racial segmentation of the working class.[3]

Interestingly, local textile unions were initially at the forefront of changes in race relations as local union leaders voluntarily, if somewhat grudgingly, began to comply with some of the International TWUA's civil rights policies long before the passage of the Civil Rights Act. Under increasing pressure from their black membership, national leadership, employers, and the federal government, the predominantly white textile unions adapted to the demands of civil rights throughout the decade. However, the culture and practices of observing whiteness and blackness proved difficult, if not impossible, to dislodge. Many Rome labor leaders

[2] On sit-ins, see ibid., Feb. 14, 29, Mar. 31, Apr. 1, 3, 1963, Feb. 27, Mar. 1, 1964; *Atlanta Journal-Constitution*, Apr. 3, 1963; on the NAACP petition, see *Rome News-Tribune*, June 24, 1964; on the integration of Rome restaurants and theaters, see ibid., July 6, 1964.

[3] Quote from *Rome News-Tribune*, June 21, 1964; on the significance of the Civil Rights Act of 1964 and EEOC litigation in textile mills, see Timothy J. Minchin, *Hiring the Black Worker: The Racial Integration of the Southern Textile Industry, 1960–1980* (Chapel Hill: University of North Carolina Press, 1999), 4, 36–40, 42–62, 112, 219–25, 231.

simply did not accept civil rights as part of a working-class or union program. In spite of a younger cadre of whites and blacks committed to change, there was a considerable lag between compliance with the law on the one hand and genuine acceptance of its principles on the other. Ironically, the integration of jobs actually nudged working-class whites closer to traditional southern political conservatism. As the social value of whiteness came under attack, new rhetorical justifications of the racial status quo—articulated in the language of classical conservatism—emerged to disguise, and ultimately preserve, the politics of whiteness. A break in the racial segmentation of the southern workforce put the invention of a race-blind working class in the realm of possibility, but alone it could not ensure its creation.

Although the late 1950s and early 1960s are generally regarded as the height of the movement for integration, segregation in workplaces, labor markets, and most aspects of working-class life remained deeply entrenched in Rome. Unless they were among the many spectators who thronged in front of store windows to observe sit-ins along Broad Street, or had children attending a county school affected by the token integration imposed by the "freedom of choice" plan, white textile workers remained fairly isolated from direct contact with the civil rights movement. Segregation persisted in the mills, the villages, and the plant facilities. White workers were still most likely to encounter black workers in positions of service to whites: tending the village and grounds in Lindale, unpacking cotton bales, manning the Pepperell laundry, or filling the cafeteria and custodial staff at the Celanese mill.[4]

Union operations also permitted a generous amount of space for southern locals to accommodate local customs of segregation. A postwar TWUA manual on problems of discrimination and prejudice, for example, provided dozens of constructive suggestions for dealing with prejudice among managers and the rank and file, but it also encouraged caution. If segregated meetings were "a matter of the accepted pattern of the community," the handbook advised, "the issue should not be argued." Instead, union officers were encouraged to try to build black-white solidarity through common actions and activities. Even in the late 1960s, TWUA leaders decided not to "spearhead the civil rights fight," favoring instead "simply continu[ing] to take a positive position." Given the reaction to *Brown* and Little Rock, many TWUA leaders feared that a strong position leading civil rights in the South would jeopardize the stability of

[4] On the small number of black workers who labored in nontraditional textile jobs in other southern locales prior to the 1960s, see Minchin, *Hiring the Black Worker*, 23–28.

its small southern membership. In Floyd County, International leaders did not intervene until black workers issued their demands directly to the TWUA regional director.[5]

As a result, the relationship between whites and blacks in the union continued within established patterns of paternalism. White officers recognized black members as part of the local, but whites clearly held most of the power. The nature of the union relationship encouraged blacks and whites to cooperate in some union activities, such as volunteer organizing efforts, and Local 689 officers avoided the extremes of segregationists, voting in 1959, for example, to rent their new union hall to other local unions but not to the Ku Klux Klan.[6] However, the local union's practice of holding segregated meetings and the de facto segregation of leadership clearly begged the question of union solidarity. White members met weekly; black members met monthly. In fact, some black members complained that their meetings were "merely a scheme designed to justify the white[s] in taking our money" because the black membership meeting had "no importance in . . . business functions of the union."[7] Paternalism in the union, like paternalism in the village, meant that black workers were dependent upon the goodwill of whites. In contract negotiations, for example, black members had no one to represent their departments. "We just had to take what they said was there for us," explained Lewis Shelton, a black employee who worked in village maintenance. The union re-created its racial character in more subtle ways as well. When issues of interest to black workers came up in union meetings, they were not presented by black workers, or as issues of concern to workers, but by white members as a concern of "our colored brothers."[8]

However, the efforts of black union members and the International leadership led to the integration of union meetings long before that of other institutions and groups in Floyd County. In 1961, a committee of two janitors, R. A. Scott and Elbert Bray, representing black workers at Celanese authored a "Statement of Position" and took their case to the regional director of the TWUA. The white rank and file, they claimed, was holding elected officers hostage to the white members' desire to maintain segregated meetings, and exclusion from whites' meetings had thus denied

[5] Draper, *Conflict of Interests*, 17–40; "Handbook on Shop Problems in the Field of Discrimination and Prejudice," n.d., ca. 1950s, "Discrimination and Prejudice" folder, box 5, series 8A-1, MSS 129A, TWUA Records; TWUA policy quoted in Minchin, *Hiring the Black Worker*, 234.

[6] Local 689 minutes, Dec. 12, 1960, folder 4, box 1, MSS 78-071, TWUA Records.

[7] "Statement of Position," Nov. 2, 1961, "689, Rome, GA" folder, box 437, MSS 396, TWUA Records; Shelton interview.

[8] See, for example, Local 689 minutes, Apr. 7, Oct. 13, 1960, both in folder 4, box 1, MSS 78-071, TWUA Records; Shelton interview.

black workers "the right of collective bargaining." Evidently, white officers had initially approached black representatives about the possibility of establishing integrated meetings, and the black membership responded enthusiastically. But, Scott and Bray charged, once white officials sensed the rank and file's disapproval and saw the "white reaction" to the possibility of "the colored voting" in union meetings, they refused to follow through. Although they believed officers had come to them in "good faith," the same officers had become "engulfed by political fears," Scott and Bray informed the International, and "refused to use the moral and legal persuasion of their office to secure our rights."[9]

The regional and international offices of the TWUA responded promptly and firmly. TWUA International president William Pollock sent Local 689 members a telegram informing them that the matter had been referred to the union's civil rights committee and a hearing had been scheduled. TWUA staffers Ralph Cline and Michael Botelho attended the following weekly meeting and reminded white Local 689 members of the International constitution's guarantee that all members had the right to attend and participate in meetings. Unfortunately, minutes from the meeting provide few details of the reaction or the discussion that followed, noting only that "a number of questions were asked by the members and answered by Bros. Cline and Botelho." Botelho, the regional director in Georgia, Alabama, and Florida, appealed to the white rank and file to settle the matter "in a manner becoming local 689, which in his opinion was one of the best locals anywhere." He also appealed to their sense of independence, reassuring them that the local "could take care of this problem without interference from any one and keep [the] local in good standing." Two of Local 689's officers spoke up and said that they felt it "was the duty of the Local to take care of this matter within the local."[10]

The following week, white members voted to integrate their meetings, and apparently with very little fanfare—at least at the union hall. Several members spoke in favor of accepting the recommendation, and if there were any arguments against, union minutes did not preserve them. At least some union regulars opposed. The vote was twenty-five for, five against. Unfortunately, the small number of votes provides few clues about how the white rank and file felt about integrated meetings, but white union officers generally claimed that Local 689 members were moderate on race relations. Walter Brooks, a business agent in the mid-1960s and local president in the 1970s, recalled most workers at Celanese accepting change in union race relations without protest. Certainly in the

[9] "Statement of Position," Nov. 2, 1961, "689, Rome, GA" folder, box 437, MSS 396, TWUA Records: see also Local 689 minutes, folder 5, box 1, MSS 78-071, TWUA Records.

[10] Local 689 minutes, Mar. 8, 1962, folder 5, box 1, MSS 78-071, TWUA Records.

local's official record, business continued as usual without any discussions of integration, or even any note of black attendance recorded in the minutes. However, in contrast to Brooks's recollection, Shelton recalled that when union leaders first suggested integrated meetings, "it was awful. Some guys even went down there [to the mill village] and threw rocks at the president's house and broke his windows out." Shelton also remembered that even when the meetings were integrated, black and white workers sat separately, in effect re-creating segregation within an integrated meeting.[11]

Although inclusion in meetings certainly represented a victory for black workers, many of the other side effects of segregation persisted. Given the proportions of black and white, black workers did not have the power to change company or union practices. "Back in those days," Shelton explained, "you had to just take whatever they offered . . . you couldn't strike because you were outnumbered. So I guess you had to just go with the flow, just vote whatever they voted for whether you liked it or not." Even the right to vote in union meetings did little to redress problems, he explained, "because the biggest majority was white anyway." Given the strict segregation of jobs and departments that had always existed in the plant, whites still outnumbered blacks by about twenty-seven to one in the early 1960s.[12]

The allocation of jobs by race and sex persisted at the Rome plant for much of the decade, in spite of federal fair employment initiatives in the early 1960s designed to enlarge opportunities for black workers. President Kennedy's 1961 Executive Order 10925, which strengthened nondiscrimination standards for companies holding government contracts, seems to have scarcely affected Floyd County employers. Although Celanese officials approached officers of Local 689 about implementing civil rights laws as early as 1962, company officials were evidently reluctant to change employment practices.[13] The Civil Rights Act of 1964, however, held the potential to change the balance of power in southern industries and, consequently, in the labor movement, by opening up more jobs for black workers everywhere. Although southern textile firms soon acquired a reputation for dragging their feet on Title VII requirements, a few months after its passage, Celanese officials initiated a meeting with the officers of Local 689 to discuss "ways and means of insuring compliance

[11] Local 689 minutes, Mar. 15, 1962, ibid.; Brooks interview; Shelton interview.

[12] Shelton interview.

[13] Many southern mills, including Celanese, balked at hiring black workers in traditionally white jobs, even under pressure of losing contracts, because they considered the risk of causing unrest among white workers to be too great. See also Minchin's discussion of management fears related to equal employment opportunity in *Hiring the Black Worker*, 67–97.

with our existing employment policies regarding equal employment opportunity."[14] However, adoption of equal employment opportunity policy did not immediately result in substantial changes in the workforce. Past discrimination had lingering effects, including many that were seemingly outside union and company control. Even with union cooperation, several structural obstacles stood in the way.

First, company and union policy meant that the company did not make many new hires. Celanese continually adjusted to fluctuations in demand with layoffs, and as jobs opened up the contract required managers to call workers back according to departmental seniority. Workers retained a right to reinstatement for two years. Thus even when Celanese managers added workers, a majority were hired from an existing pool of former employees, and former employees in historically white departments were, of course, white employees. Since Celanese continued to be regarded as one of the better places to work in Floyd County, most workers accepted layoffs as a part of the job and waited to be called back.[15] This had important implications for equal employment opportunity, since Celanese actually presided over very few new job "opportunities."

The plant's system of seniority presented a further structural barrier. Under the contract, Celanese workers accrued department seniority and plant seniority. Plant seniority entitled them to bid on jobs in other departments, should a new opportunity arise, if they were qualified for the position. The maintenance department, for example, which employed the most highly skilled and best-paid workers in the plant, almost always hired from other departments. However, departmental seniority determined the order for layoffs, thus discouraging interdepartmental transfers. The last hired in a department was the first laid off. Moreover, even if the personal satisfaction derived from pioneering in a historically white job was great, the economic compensation did not necessarily merit the risk of layoff. In 1964, for example, an operator in the twisting department, a position with about average compensation for white workers, earned a base rate of $1.568. Among historically black positions, a helper or second-class cook in the cafeteria earned $1.690, a janitor earned $1.674, and a general laborer earned $1.740. Although the policy did not directly discriminate against black workers—white workers were forced to make the same calculations when they considered transfer—it placed a substantial burden on workers seeking to take advantage of equal employment opportunity policy.[16]

[14] B. B. Lucas to Melvin Thacker, Nov. 25, 1964, "689, Rome, GA" folder, box 437, MSS 396, TWUA Records.

[15] Patty interview; Oscar Allen interview; Brooks interview.

[16] For example, one white worker I interviewed, Herman Anderson, waited nearly twenty years for an opportunity to bid on a job in maintenance, but when a job came open he

Celanese did control plant facilities, however, and in response to federal legislation the company made tentative steps toward integration in the early 1960s. In 1961, plant officials removed all "white" and "colored" signs from the cafeteria, locker rooms, rest rooms, and drinking fountains. Company and union reports indicate that self-segregation persisted for years after the signs came down. Union officer Harold Waddell recalled that on the day Celanese integrated the cafeteria, managers, expecting trouble, "called the president and the business agent and myself and we three went to the cafeteria and just seated ourselves and it was about 10:00 in the morning." When black employees came into the white dining room, "they seated themselves in different areas." Although Waddell recalled that "it didn't cause any problems, whatsoever," it did suggest the tenacity of segregation and racial consciousness among blacks and whites. According to company reports, "true integration" did not happen until 1964, presumably in response to the Civil Rights Act. The delay between the company's initial action and actual integration also suggested the important role that practices in the broader community played in governing behavior inside the mill gates.[17]

White union leaders, such as Melvin Thacker, who was president of Local 689 in the late 1960s, were generally under the impression that "the integration problem here had been handled nicely" and frequently expressed their desire in union meetings that "all of our people get along good." However, some white workers did not readily accept integration. Another former union president, Max Proctor, who had become a supervisor by the time Celanese integrated, recalled that some whites balked at using integrated facilities. When "they integrated the cafeteria," Proctor recalled, "this guy quit eating out there. He wouldn't go eat with no 'niggers.' "[18] Integration of locker rooms and showers, Proctor recalled, also elicited white resistance. The company had just spent millions to completely renovate the plant's extensive locker rooms—"They were big, nice ones. Everybody had 2 lockers, [in] big rooms with ceramic tiles." In fact, company records indicated that plant managers upgraded the facilities in order to ease the transition to integration. Proctor recalled the day the

---

decided it was not worth risking the seniority he had accrued in the textile department. On company layoff policy, see Ralph Cline to William Pollock, Nov. 18, 1964, "689, Rome, GA" folder; and on wage rates, see Local 689 contract, Feb. 12, 1962 (wage rates effective until May 1964), unmarked folder; both in box 437, MSS 396, TWUA Records.

[17] Waddell interview; "Rome Affirmative Action, Celanese Fibers Company Plans 1969–70," folder 67, box 46, Wharton School's Industrial Research Unit Papers, University Archives and Records Center, University of Pennsylvania, Philadelphia (hereafter cited as Wharton Papers).

[18] Melvin Thacker quoted in union minutes, June 2, 1965, folder 9, box 1, MSS 78-071, TWUA Records; Max Proctor, interview with author, July 15, 1994.

policy went into effect. The superintendent called a meeting and told everyone "the blacks and the whites are all going to be in the same locker room. Everybody's going to have to lock together." The company's authority to introduce changes, however, did not compel acceptance by workers. Proctor recalled, "This guy [at the meeting] jumped up and he said, 'I'll tell you one thing, I'm not going to take no bath with no nigger.' And he got up and walked out. And he got away with that, [it] upset that superintendent. He didn't know what to say and he just dismissed everybody." Some white workers who felt put out by integration made black workers suffer. Lewis Shelton remembered, for example, that someone broke into a black man's locker and put acid on his clothes.[19]

Integration of jobs, perhaps a more radical departure in the racial culture of the plant, proceeded slowly, since, unlike plant facilities, it could not be accomplished by a centralized decree. Union minutes and company reports indicate that at least some jobs were integrated as early as 1966, but the number of black operatives remained far below what could reasonably be termed the goals of the Civil Rights Act. In 1966 only twelve black workers, less than 1 percent of the total workforce, held jobs in predominantly white departments.[20] Legal observance of the Civil Rights Act, however, only required Celanese not to discriminate; it did not compel the company to find and hire black and female workers for nontraditional jobs or to change seniority rules. Thus, despite Title VII, changes in Celanese hiring policy had a limited impact on the community at large. In the short term, however, seniority and bidding rules may have helped ease the transition. Herman Anderson, a white worker who had worked at Celanese since 1941, remembered that there was little trouble when they integrated because "most of the black folks they put into the plant had worked somewhere or other in the plant, so you knew them. It wasn't like they'd go off on the street [and get just anybody]." Lewis Shelton also recalled that he "never did have any trouble, as far as integrating goes, because I worked out there, cut their grass, stuff like that." Shelton had also had experience working with many whites, since his crew supplied helpers to the skilled workmen in maintenance.[21]

[19] "Rome Affirmative Action," folder 67, box 46, Wharton Papers; Proctor interview; Shelton interview; Brooks interview.

[20] When I interviewed workers, most people recalled integration happening in the 1970s. Workers' memories may correspond to their own experiences of when their department or shift integrated. Since company records confirm that integration proceeded very slowly, it is entirely possible that many workers had no direct experience with integration until then. On black workers at the Rome plant, see the 1966 and 1968 reports on Rome, Georgia, folder 66, and "Rome Affirmative Action," folder 67, all in box 46, Wharton Papers.

[21] Anderson interview; Shelton interview. Minchin notes that some black workers felt that being a "pioneer" put an unfair burden on them, as black textile workers were expected to be "super negroes," not just good workers. See *Hiring the Black Worker*, 116–25.

How this translated into changes in the culture of Local 689, however, was more complicated. The racial views of the employees at the Rome Celanese plant spanned the entire spectrum of opinion. Some white workers clearly resented integration of historically white jobs. Brooks recalled that the first black man to get a job in the spinning department was harassed so much that he quit after about three weeks. Some of the white workers in the spinning room threw his locker out the window. Some whites in the plant, through a decidedly racialized sense of "fairness," felt put out when their departments were integrated and others were not. Celanese supervisor Max Proctor, for example, once refused to interview a group of prospective black employees. "I've got all the blacks I want," he protested to a personnel officer. "I've got more than anybody in this plant." Personnel staff pressed the issue, but ultimately Proctor was allowed to refuse the applicants. White disapproval of black advancement at the plant made it particularly difficult to get African American workers into the more highly skilled and desirable positions in operations, maintenance, and engineering.[22]

However, some white workers were clearly supportive of black workers' rights. Lester Patty, a white instructor in acetate spinning, recalled that integration elicited "a little trouble. There was some of them that was really bad opposed to it. . . . Some of them didn't want to have nothing to do with them." But Patty's job included training new workers, so, he said, "I had to treat them just like they were white. I couldn't do no otherwise." Besides, he added, "I thought it was right to do that. I didn't worry about what other people thought."[23] Brooks, who sponsored several black workers' bids to take jobs in all-white departments, proudly recalled getting sixteen black workers hired for formerly white jobs. Most of them were people who already worked in the cafeteria and on the janitorial staff, and in Brooks's estimation they deserved better treatment because they earned it. "They were awful good people. . . . They came to every union meeting regular," he remembered, "and that's what I stand for. I mean if you're not going to represent them, don't take their dues."[24]

The white workforce's collective action is also difficult to categorize. A strike in 1966 over the issue of integration, for example, provides a fascinating perspective on how civil rights shifted, but did not immediately transform the culture of Local 689. The local held a weeklong wildcat strike in the acetate spinning room over integration, but the circumstances were much more complicated than simply whites' refusal to work with blacks. Although company officials, when interviewed some years

[22] Brooks interview; Proctor interview.

[23] Patty interview.

[24] Brooks interview.

later for a study of black workers in the textile industry, claimed that the strike was a protest against integration, the workers had not demanded that Celanese reverse integration.[25] Rather, the business agent told the company that "the union felt that if the plant is to be integrated, it should be integrated in every department in the plant and not place a few colored people in a group in just a few departments." And contrary to the claims of Celanese management, this was not simply a position adopted by recalcitrant whites—it was supported by white *and* black members of Local 689. Even if the strike originated as a rebellion among difficult whites, it became something much larger. In an unusual display of interracial solidarity, black and white members of the department held meetings with the business agent and came to a joint agreement on the principle behind the strike. Moreover, reporting on the strike at a union meeting, the business agent concluded with the radical assertion to the members that "a man has right to work where he wants to." He noted that two black employees were scheduled to start jobs in another department the following week, and asserted that "this is making some progress."[26]

However, even a joint job action—even one seemingly focused on equal employment opportunity—could not entirely change the racial culture of the union. An account of the strike in the union minutes betrays the persistence of a racial perspective in the union: the minutes note "the colored people felt as we do . . . and said they will stick with us." At least some union members apparently still thought in terms of a white "we" and a black "them" instead of a race-blind "us." The wording of the account in the minutes also leaves open the possibility that the local's position on absolute integration might have been offered to blacks only after whites adopted it first.[27] But given that white and black rights had historically been mutually exclusive positions, the fact that local officers were able to use this issue as a tool to demand further black employment and full integration throughout the plant was truly quite remarkable. Unfortunately, on this point the union lost. Celanese managers refused to negotiate during the wildcat, and when the issue went to a mediator, the mediator ruled that although the employees were "right in principle," they were contractually "wrong in [calling] a wildcat strike."[28]

[25] Minchin's *Hiring the Black Worker* (20) cites this strike as an example of unions resisting integration, but this is only partially true. When Richard Rowan, a researcher associated with the Wharton School's studies of black workers in various industries, visited the Rome Celanese plant, managers told him that the union called a wildcat strike "when the company tried to integrate certain departments."

[26] Local 689 minutes, Apr. 7, 14, 1966, folder 10, box 1, MSS 78-071, TWUA Records.

[27] Local 689 minutes, Apr. 7, 1966, ibid.

[28] Local 689 minutes, Apr. 7, 14, 1966, ibid.

In general, after the dispute in 1962 about integrated meetings, the officers and the local union, at least in its official capacity, consented to further integration without resistance. In fact, given all the prior indicators of white working-class opinion on civil rights issues, particularly the responses to the 1957 surveys and the Rome Central Labor Union's strong stand on segregated schools in 1960, Local 689 was surprisingly compliant. Indeed, Local 689's officers seem to have taken their own positive steps to become informed about the Civil Rights Act of 1964. A month before the act officially took effect, union officers and several downtown business owners met with a local judge for a briefing on the "fair labor law." After a report was delivered to the membership meeting, Local 689 president Melvin Thacker encouraged everyone to "get along" and reminded those in attendance that he had taken "an oath that he would try to defend everyone and that our bylaws and contract would be enforced."[29]

Local 689's positive actions on civil rights in the plant are even more striking when compared with all the negative comment on equal employment opportunity in the white community at large. The Civil Rights Act and the political controversies that followed its passage elicited more letters to the editor and more public outcry among whites than any other major event in the mid-twentieth century, including the "two governors" controversy and *Brown v. Board of Education.* Of course, letters printed in the paper did not necessarily represent the views of all Romans, but they did lend authority to the position and project the appearance of a consensus around opposition. Resistance to the Civil Rights Act by whites in official positions of community and city leadership played a similar role. A Rome city commissioner went so far as to claim that the legislation was un-American because "the American tradition is that we earn our situations in life and that we shouldn't have to force these things by law." The president of the Rome Citizens' Council warned of businessmen being arrested and predicted a massive voter protest in the next election. In one of the most strident letters to the paper, Floyd County resident Howard Keeler claimed that the day the Senate passed the Civil Rights Act would "surely . . . go down in history as the blackest of all Black Fridays." In reference to city leaders meeting with members of the black community about implementation of the Civil Rights Act, Keeler said, "I am afraid to say that right here in Floyd County that there is a (blank) in the woodpile. So I will say that there is a colored gentleman in the fuel supply here."[30]

[29] Local 689 minutes, June 2, 1965, folder 9, ibid.

[30] *Rome News-Tribune*, June 21, and letters to editor, June 24, 1964.

Although the core objections to Title VII represented essentially the same emotions and impulses driving opposition to the FEPC, white Rome's reactions to the Civil Rights Act also represented an essential turning point in the history of southern whiteness. In the 1940s Romans had expressed opposition to "fair employment" by ridiculing African Americans, waving the banner of white supremacy, and warning of the "evils of both races in the same spinning department." Although appeals to racism clearly played an important role in the 1940s, appeals to preserve *segregation*, which commanded extraordinary power as an cultural norm among southern whites, frequently served as the final justification for protecting traditional employment practices. In 1955, Governor Herman Talmadge had gone so far as to oppose the FEPC and *Brown* on the grounds that "God advocate[d] segregation."[31] But by the 1960s it was beginning to dawn on most white southerners, even Talmadge, that the principle of segregation no longer carried the same moral authority in the world of politics and ideas. Nor did open defenses of white privilege. What had once been frank arguments for the right to discriminate and maintain white supremacy in the workplace were transformed in the 1960s into a more subtle and insidious rhetoric about "qualification." Although Title VII did not compel affirmative action and merely demanded that employers not discriminate, many whites jumped to the conclusion that the act would require employers to hire black and—they assumed and asserted at the same time—necessarily "less qualified" applicants.

Writing to the editor of the *Rome News-Tribune* in 1964, for example, Rome residents Gary Allen and Bobby Wright explained that they were "not saying that the Negroes are inferior, just that it isn't right for them to take jobs they are not qualified for." Quoting Arizona senator Barry Goldwater, they argued that "any man has the right to employ the people qualified for the job." Their paraphrase of Goldwater, often repeated in the late 1960s, captured a critical moment in the shift from segregationist to conservative rhetoric defending whiteness. The new argument, articulated in the seemingly principled language of Goldwater, nevertheless rested on essentially racist premises. References to "qualification" implied that current labor markets were the products of objective judgments of workers' skills. Had black workers been capable and competent to perform other jobs, Allen, Wright, and others implied, they would already have opportunities. In the 1960s, "qualified" served the same purpose that "experienced" had served in the 1940s—as a code word for whiteness. Both were seemingly race-neutral terms, but they also functioned as uniquely relative terms in the context of the post–Jim Crow South. As

[31] Talmadge, *You and Segregation*, 44.

the arguments in favor of simple white supremacy went underground, "qualified" therefore incorporated much of the ideological and emotional baggage that had once resided in whiteness.[32]

Although the editor of the paper, city and county leaders, and Seventh District congressman John Davis appealed to white Romans to obey the laws peacefully, a considerable amount of resistance to civil rights remained. Even some local government facilities remained segregated. County officials integrated the public library, but the city and county boards of education assigned faculty to schools by race until nearly the end of the decade. In July 1964, just a month after the act became law, when three black city residents tried to buy tickets to the Rome city swimming pool "set aside for whites," they were denied admission. The city manager announced that "our policy is at present and has been that we will not integrate our pools." The commission simply closed white and black facilities. The Celanese pool was segregated by de facto custom as late as 1969. One white Roman who owned a privately run swimming pool filled it with concrete. Nor was resistance confined to older Romans. Some of the faculty at local Berry and Shorter Colleges were involved in the local civil rights movement, but a 1964 poll of students at Berry College revealed that should the school be integrated, five out of six students planned to leave.[33]

If Local 689's moderation on equal employment opportunity issues in the union set them apart from many in the white community, it was also essentially the limit of their commitment to civil rights. In spite of Local 689's involvement in a broad range of community and service projects in the 1960s, they did not join sit-ins or sign NAACP petitions. Nor, apparently, did they approve of their International's support for civil rights issues and organizations. Historically, "moderate" white southern locals such as Local 689 and the international leadership of the TWUA had managed to sustain working relationships despite their differences of opinion on race. But by the summer of 1963, the intensifying southern struggle over segregation made it difficult for any political activism to remain distinct from the issue of civil rights. Television and newspapers riveted public attention on the southern civil rights struggle as Birmingham police turned nightsticks, police dogs, and high-pressure fire hoses on the nonviolent activists led by Dr. Martin Luther King, Jr. Even President John F. Kennedy, who had tried to remain publicly distant from the civil rights movement for fear of alienating southern Democrats, was

[32] *Rome News-Tribune*, June 21, 24, 1964. Employers also used "qualifications" as an excuse for their failure to hire black workers. See Minchin, *Hiring the Black Worker*, 67–98.

[33] *Rome News-Tribune*, July 7, June 24, 1964; Shelton interview.

moved to make a major public address in favor of federal civil rights legislation in June 1963.[34]

Revealing the strain that civil rights had placed on the relationship between New York City and Rome, a dispute arose within Local 689 in July 1963 over TWUA political funds that nearly resulted in Local 689's abandoning its allegiance to AFL-CIO political action. Some members suspected that contributions to the Committee on Political Education (COPE), which had replaced PAC in the years after the AFL-CIO merger, were being diverted to civil rights organizations. Under pressure from the rank and file, John Williams, the Local 689 COPE chairman, wrote the International TWUA's general secretary-treasurer, informing him of the "controversy" over COPE donations and asking whether their donations were used "to finance controversial issues such as Civil Rights." Within a few days, before Local 689 even received a written reply, Regional Director Michael Botelho appeared at the regular membership meeting to explain how funds were used, assuring members that "COPE has never made a contribution to the N.A.A.C.P."[35]

Botelho's appearance, however, did not quell local suspicions. The following week, a major argument about COPE erupted at the Local 689 membership meeting. After a motion passed in favor of supporting COPE, Melvin Thacker, a member of the COPE committee, made a second motion to rescind the local's support and discontinue the COPE fund for three years. Unfortunately, union minutes did not record the details of the discussion, but workers must have been concerned about something other than contributions to the NAACP. Perhaps Rome workers were troubled by the TWUA leadership's alliances with President Kennedy, Vice President Lyndon Johnson, and other liberals whose views more closely corresponded to TWUA's politics than those of the average working-class white voter in Floyd County. Local 689 officers protested that COPE had "done well" and that the "union has to stay in politics if we are to exist." The COPE chairman retorted that if Thacker felt that way he should resign from the committee. But when the motion came to a vote, twenty-nine of fifty people present at the meeting favored discontinuing COPE contributions. Those who supported COPE won the motion, if not the full moral victory, because it fell short of the two-thirds majority required to pass. Discontinuing local support of COPE must have been a fairly

[34] On Birmingham, Kennedy, and civil rights, see Patterson, *Grand Expectations*, 480–81; and Glenn T. Eskew, *But for Birmingham: The Local and National Movements in the Civil Rights Struggle* (Chapel Hill: University of North Carolina Press, 1997).

[35] Local 689 minutes, Aug. 1, 1963, folder 8, box 1, MSS 78-071; John Chupka to John Williams, Aug. 2, 1963, "Southeast, General Correspondence, 1963" folder, box 626, MSS 396; both in TWUA Records.

popular stance, however, because the following year Thacker was elected president of Local 689.[36]

The vote of no confidence in the TWUA-COPE provides an interesting counterpoint to the union's acceptance of civil rights practices within the union. Although members of Local 689 complied with integration of union meetings and equal employment opportunity, as the union constitution required, union political actions, which were completely voluntary, permitted them to set boundaries of what the membership would support. As the COPE dispute made clear, many union regulars were firmly opposed to any extra-union activity or even an indirect contribution to a larger civil rights agenda. It was one of very few times in the union's history that an official union meeting formally entertained opposition to the International TWUA's policy. In taking such an position, Local 689 signaled that the union local would not become a venue for the promotion of civil rights abstracted from their own workplace. For the majority-white workforce at Celanese, and for their political allies in Georgia, civil rights and union business were separate issues.

The COPE fund dispute also foreshadowed a greater political divide between the white members of Local 689 and the national labor movement in 1964. In the past, TWUA COPE and Local 689 had differences over individual candidates and issues, but they had always shared a basic Democratic partisanship. The Civil Rights Act of 1964, however, dramatically altered the South's relationship to the Democratic Party. Although the Seventh District COPE received credit for aiding the Kennedy victory in 1960, and Local 689's officers hailed the election of Kennedy as a great triumph over the forces of prejudice, the federal elections of 1964 proved much more divisive. As the 1964 election neared, Democratic Party leadership in Georgia predicted that they faced "real trouble in keeping Georgia Democratic as always." According to the chairman of the state's Democratic Committee, as early as July they were already receiving "daily reports . . . of increasing support for [Republican presidential candidate Barry] Goldwater," and "nearly all of it stems from his vote against the civil rights bill."

Goldwater's opposition to virtually all social welfare policy did have a strong appeal in the South. A member of the NAACP, Goldwater was a sophisticated conservative who did not champion segregation but was strongly opposed to the Civil Rights Act as just one of many illegitimate federal intrusions into domestic social issues. As one of eight senators to vote against the Civil Rights Act, Goldwater appealed to the same impulses and emotions exploited by segregationists in the 1950s. Anti-government conservatism, in particular, must have resonated with alienated

[36] Local 689 minutes, Aug. 15, 1963, folder 8, box 1, MSS 78-071, TWUA Records.

white southerners in 1964. In fact, it was striking how local condemnations of civil rights so seamlessly turned to endorsements of Goldwater's anti-government rhetoric. In February the *Rome News-Tribune* editorial page condemned the civil rights bill as a move toward "all-powerful, centralized government." In June when the bill passed, a Rome physician compared the law to the "tyranny and oppression of a strong central power" that drove the original American settlers to flee England and form a new government. On the very same day, a letter to the editor asked, "What is so terrifying about this Goldwater? He just believes in the individual." In a muddled reference to the civil rights bill, the letter added that Goldwater "advocates that [if] people, like milk, [were] left alone, cream will rise to the top." In November the *News-Tribune*'s editorial page endorsed Goldwater as an "exponent of the belief that the best government is that which governs least."[37]

That the boosters and business conservatives behind the *Rome News-Tribune* would break with the Democrats over Lyndon Johnson is perhaps not surprising. However, weeks before the newspaper's endorsement, the newly elected president of Local 689, Melvin Thacker, announced his endorsement of Goldwater and the Seventh District Republican candidate for Congress, Ed Chapin. The announcement, an advertisement paid for "by the voluntary contributions of President Thacker and other members of Local #689, TWUA," and issued as a statement from Thacker, claimed that "75% of the Local membership feel the same way." The language of the endorsement was virtually identical to other white Romans' condemnation of civil rights and endorsements of Goldwater. Thacker argued that the election of Goldwater and Chapin was necessary "to preserve American freedom and to stem the tide of socialism and overpowering centralized government." Thacker charged that the incumbent, John Davis, "claims to be a conservative but continues to vote more liberal than any other Georgia congressman." Of Goldwater, Thacker claimed that his "strong stand for states rights, for integrity, morality, and fiscal sanity in government more truly represents the views of the voters of Floyd County."[38]

Although other Georgia unionists endorsed Goldwater, he was clearly no friend of the labor movement, as the International TWUA and Georgia AFL-CIO leadership took pains to point out. In fact, TWUA International president William Pollock labeled him a "menace." Goldwater opposed

[37] *Rome News-Tribune*, July 14, June 21, pp. 1 and 4, Nov. 1, 1964. Bryant Simon also found a pattern of anti–civil rights conservatism taking the form of anti-statism in the postwar period. See Simon, *Fabric of Defeat*, 219–39.

[38] Clipping from *Rome News-Tribune*, Oct. 23, 1964, in "South, General, 1964" folder, box 627, MSS 396, TWUA Records.

the union shop, wanted to return governance of labor relations to the states, spoke out against an increase in the minimum wage, voted against nationwide standards for unemployment compensation, and, ironically, opposed labor's right "to engage in any kind of political activity." He vilified Walter Reuther as "more dangerous to America" than the Soviet Union, and claimed in his 1960 book *Conscience of a Conservative* that "labor unions seriously compromise American freedom." Collective bargaining, Goldwater claimed, resulted in a "weakening of the individual personality and self-reliance." Given the depth, consistency, and seeming sincerity of Goldwater's views on organized labor, it is hard to imagine that workers believed that his election could benefit labor. How "can any good Union Member vote for Goldwater," the *Georgia State AFL-CIO News* exclaimed in July 1964, "after reading what Goldwater thinks of Union people and their Unions?????"[39]

It was a good question. Given that endorsements of Goldwater were typically paired with attacks on Johnson, they seemed to register as much protest against Johnson and COPE as approval of Goldwater. A spokesman for United Automobile Workers Local 34 in Atlanta, for example, said the local "just made up our minds to support Goldwater instead of Johnson to show Walter Reuther he couldn't play the part of dictator to us." Thacker's endorsement similarly carried a heavy condemnation of Johnson and Democratic liberals. Linking Johnson and Humphrey to the liberal pressure group Americans for Democratic Action (ADA), Thacker claimed that Goldwater would "help to restore constitutional government, and halt the spread of ADA liberalism and dictatorial federal power as represented by Lyndon B. Johnson and Hubert Humphrey."[40]

In spite of Thacker's claim to represent the opinions of the rank and file, three days later, four officers of Local 689, including the COPE chairman, paid to publish their own advertisement disavowing the endorsement. Thacker, they claimed, had not contacted the union officers and "did not speak for the membership of Local 689." The announcement avoided any political discussion, except to note that the Rome Central Labor Union had already endorsed Chapin's opponent, incumbent John Davis. In conclusion, the four officers encouraged Local 689 members to disregard the endorsement and charged that "Mr. Thacker [was] using his position in the union to confuse the members of Local 689 and also

[39] William Pollock to TWUA Local Unions, Joint Boards and Staff, Sept. 21, 1964, untitled folder, box 8, ACTWU Tennessee Joint Board Papers, acc. 82-84, Southern Labor Archives, Atlanta. Goldwater quotations and final AFL-CIO quote from *Georgia State AFL-CIO News*, July 1964, Georgia Periodicals, Southern Labor Archives (multiple question marks in the original).

[40] Clippings from *Atlanta Constitution*, Oct. 19, and *Rome News-Tribune*, Oct. 23, 1964, in "South, General, 1964" folder, box 627, MSS 396, TWUA Records.

to deceive the public into believing that the big local union at Celanese is endorsing Goldwater."[41]

Thacker and his supporters did not give up. On the same day, on the back of the very same page, Goldwater supporters struck back. An ad paid for by the Floyd County Goldwater for President Committee announced, "We salute a courageous patriotic American, Melvin Thacker, who has strongly endorsed Barry Goldwater for President and Ed Chapin for Congress." It took courage, the ad contended, because Thacker was "under great political pressure from top national leaders of his Union to support the radical Johnson-Humphrey ADA ticket." Rather than allowing Thacker's repudiation by his own fellow officers to become an embarrassment, the ad tried to make Thacker into a hero and an example of principled independent politics. "When you enter the election booth," the ad encouraged voters, "remember that you, like Mr. Thacker, are a free American." It concluded with a variation of the standard Goldwater pitch: "In your heart, you know that Goldwater and Chapin stand for the same things you stand for."

On election day, Goldwater fell short of Thacker's estimation of support. Nevertheless, he polled the largest number of votes ever cast for a Republican presidential candidate in Rome's mill village districts, revealing the early signs of the Republicanization of Floyd County's blue-collar classes. Although a number of Floyd County voters had split tickets to vote for Eisenhower in 1956, this was also the first time a Republican presidential candidate had ever won in Floyd County. In the Celanese village, still dominated by a majority of union textile workers, Johnson outpolled Goldwater 346 to 265, which was a large turnout for the small precinct and a significant gain for the Republicans over 1960. In Lindale, nonunion workers, presumably not influenced by COPE or Thacker, gave Goldwater a majority of 839 to 814. Except for a couple of rural districts that delivered decisive majorities to Goldwater, however, it was a very close election across the board. Rome City, the largest precinct in the county, chose Johnson 4,239 to 4,092, but Goldwater carried the county 9,849 to 8,750. Although Johnson won a sweeping victory nationwide and incumbent Democratic congressional candidate John Davis won by a substantial margin in the Seventh District, the 1964 election also registered a decisive break in the solid South. In 1960 the Republicans had mustered only enough support to carry 11 of Georgia's 143 counties, but just four years later Goldwater became the first Republican presidential candidate to win Georgia's electoral college votes. Nor was it simply a short-lived backlash. Just two years later, Georgia voters would give a

[41] Clipping from *Rome News-Tribune*, Oct. 26, 1964, in "689, Rome GA" folder, ibid.

plurality of their collective votes to Republican gubernatorial candidate Bo Callaway.[42]

Despite local labor's presidential Republicanism, Local 689 officers still retained a high level of activism and party loyalty in state and local Democratic politics. Although Thacker acknowledged that "labor had been criticized by some of the Democrats" for supporting Republicans, by the 1960s labor's influence in Seventh District politics was such that Local 689 did not always have to seek out friends. At the start of the 1966 primary campaign season, when the Seventh District COPE held its first annual rally at Local 689's labor temple, state legislator George Bagby, former governor and current gubernatorial candidate Ellis Arnall, the speaker of the Georgia House, and Republican candidate Ed Chapin addressed the membership. In the 1960s, virtually every candidate for every office requested an opportunity to address the Local 689 membership meeting. In June 1966, gubernatorial candidate Jimmy Carter made a special visit to the Celanese mill to shake hands and chat with members of Local 689 during shift change. In August 1968 a record number of twenty-nine candidates for city, county, and state offices spoke to the weekly membership meeting. Local 689's activism also continued to earn unionists leadership positions within the Democratic Party establishment. In 1966, longtime Local 689 recording secretary and TWUA staff organizer Mildred McElrath earned a place on the Democratic Party's executive committee. The following year, Thacker was appointed to Governor Lester Maddox's staff, and in 1968 he was elected the first vice president of the Floyd County Democratic Association and was one of two people representing the county at the annual Jefferson-Jackson Day fund-raising dinner in Atlanta.[43]

A crisis at the Rome Celanese plant in 1966–67 also dramatically revealed how important Local 689's members had become to the city, state, and federal political scene. In October 1966 Celanese officials announced plans to close an entire section of the plant the following spring. Changing markets and increasingly stringent federal standards on pollution, man-

[42] Official election returns for 1964 in *Rome News-Tribune*, Nov. 8, 1964; on Goldwater in Georgia, see also Bartley, *Creation of Modern Georgia*, 229; on Goldwater's appeal to southern conservatives, see Jonathan Rieder, "The Rise of the 'Silent Majority,' " in *The Rise and Fall of the New Deal Order: 1930–1980*, ed. Steven Fraser and Gary Gerstle (Princeton: Princeton University Press, 1989), 248–49; Numan Bartley, *The New South* (Baton Rouge: Louisiana State University Press, 1995), 383–87; Earl Black and Merle Black, *The Vital South: How Presidents Are Elected* (Cambridge: Harvard University Press, 1992), 127; Bernard Cosman, *Five States for Goldwater: Continuity and Change in Southern Presidential Voting Patterns* (Tuscaloosa: University of Alabama Press, 1966).

[43] On Carter, see Local 689 minutes, June 23, 1966, folder 12; on McElrath, see Oct. 6, 1966, folder 11; on Thacker, see Sept. 29, 1966, folder 11, and Jan. 25, 1968, folder 13; all in box 1, MSS 78-071, TWUA Records.

agement claimed, made the viscose plant too expensive to continue to operate. As millhands reeled over the closing and the displacement of eleven hundred workers, McElrath suggested that "it would be best if we try to contact our congressmen and Senators and get them to help us out." Within weeks, local judges, state assemblymen, Congressman Davis, Senators Russell and Talmadge, and the candidates for office in November had offered their services to the local. Just two days after the announcement, in fact, Congressman Davis attended at the local membership meeting and had already begun to make inquiries with the Department of Labor about establishing federal retraining programs for Rome Celanese workers. The following week Thacker and Northwest Georgia Joint Board manager James O'Shea met with two local judges. Over the weekend they met with Senator Russell at his home in Winder, Georgia. At the next membership meeting, Chapin, the Republican candidate for Congress in 1966, while admitting his opposition to labor's position on right-to-work, Medicare, minimum wages, and Taft-Hartley, told the membership that "as soon as he heard about the viscose plant closing, he sent to the *Rome News-Tribune* guidelines for getting more jobs and wages for people" and promised that "if elected he would do all in his power to get new industries into Georgia."[44]

However, over the next two years it was Davis's work as a liaison between former Celanese workers and the U.S. Department of Labor, the Office of Economic Opportunity, and the Georgia Department of Labor that offered perhaps the best measure of Local 689's stature by the late 1960s—especially since Local 689's leaders had supported first Davis's Democratic primary opponent, and then the Republican rather than Davis in 1966.[45] Davis's efforts, which resulted in over $85,000 in job training grants for displaced Celanese workers, also indicated that candidates could no longer write off the labor vote, even if they were unwilling to be a close friend of labor.

If Local 689's strength and influence in the Seventh District and the state of Georgia validated a greater independence from the International in the 1960s, local events in the late 1960s probably encouraged them to stray further from labor-liberal Democrats. In the spring of 1968 the U.S. Department of Health, Education, and Welfare (HEW) investigated

[44] Local 689 minutes, Oct. 13, 20, Nov. 3, 1966, all in folder 11, ibid.

[45] Local 689 minutes, May 19, 1966, folder 10, ibid. Davis to W. Willard Wirtz (U.S. Secretary of Labor), Sept. 27, 1967; Davis to James O'Shea, Oct. 2, 1967; Wirtz to Davis, Oct. 5, 1967; a letter from twenty-five former employees of Celanese to Davis, Mar. 5, 1968; Davis to Sam Caldwell (Georgia Commissioner of Labor), Mar. 11, 1968; Davis telegram to Eugene Foley (Assistant Secretary of Commerce for Economic Development), Mar. 15, 1967; all in Floyd County Folder, box 74, subseries C, series VI, John Davis Papers, Richard B. Russell Memorial Library, Athens, Georgia.

Rome's city schools and served notice that Rome would have to make significant changes to comply with the requirements for desegregation under the Civil Rights Act. Although Rome had adopted a "freedom of choice" plan that permitted students to choose their own school, the investigation revealed that only about 25 percent of black students in Rome had transferred to formerly white schools and that staff vacancies were still filled on a racial basis. The Celanese school in Riverside Village, for example, had no black students and only one black teacher. In HEW's opinion, schools were still "racially identifiable" as black or white. The agency ordered the city and county school systems to submit a new plan for the 1968–69 school year and warned that if they did not meet Title VI standards, federal funds would be withdrawn. In short, HEW's standards for eliminating "racially identifiable schools" would require white students to attend black schools.[46]

Although local school officials had known about the stricter standards for at least two years, many Romans reacted with stunned outrage. In the eyes of white Romans, sending white students to black schools was a proposition very different from allowing black students to attend white schools. The *Rome News-Tribune*, which printed the full text of every letter exchanged between HEW and the superintendent of Rome schools, declared that "the systematic rape of Rome public schools" by HEW's "self-anointed arbiters of social planning" had begun. The chairman of the Rome Board of Education, William B. Primm, blasted HEW as "an outfit that calls all the shots and makes all the rules. And their favorite sport is to change the rule in the middle of the game." He even suggested at one point that Rome might forfeit its $800,000 in federal funds rather than follow federal guidelines. Rome school superintendent M. S. McDonald complained that parts of the report were "biased and educationally unfair" because investigators had not physically inspected every single school in the system. As everyone seemed to conveniently forget that the "freedom of choice" plan had originally been concocted by state leaders to *limit* the impact of school integration, Rome officials claimed that the system had "performed its legal function in good faith and . . . the fact that 28% of the Negro children in the City of Rome attended formerly all-white schools during the 1967–68 school term . . . indicates a fair and honest effort." McDonald retorted to HEW that "any insistence to the contrary is counter discrimination."[47]

[46] *Rome News-Tribune*, May 16, 21, 1968.

[47] Ibid., May 21, June 19, 1968; McDonald to Eldridge McMillan and Eldridge McMillan to McDonald, ibid., May 28, June 10, 1968. McDonald quote from M. S. McDonald to Eldridge McMillan, June 6, 1968, as printed in ibid., June 10, 1968.

It was true that HEW had adopted a stricter measure of compliance by the mid-1960s. The "freedom of choice" plan, consistent with the Supreme Court's ruling in *Brown*, only required that the city not confine black students to black schools. In effect, the original plan placed the burden of desegregation on the students and parents, who could then "choose" their school and decide whether the transfer would be worthwhile. As Rome officials complained on behalf of whites in 1968, schools drew students from the communities immediately surrounding them, which were segregated. If students attended a school with a different racial identification, it meant leaving their neighborhood school and traveling, sometimes across town, to another. Of course, this is what "freedom of choice" demanded black students do when choosing a white school. The new standard required that the burden of desegregation be placed equally upon all students, black and white, demanding that some white students also make a change. Rome finally met HEW's requirements by transferring a large number of black and white students around the school system, expanding white schools to accommodate new black students, reassigning faculty, and, significantly, by phasing out the formerly all-black elementary and high schools.

Many white Romans, however, saw a shared effort on behalf of integration as a violation of their rights. Requiring any adjustment by white students to promote desegregation, complained parents, the school superintendent, and the editors of the paper, was "discrimination" against whites. In a letter to HEW officer Elridge McMillen, Rome resident James C. Gardner, Jr., charged that "in your zeal to enforce your present policy you have greatly infringed upon my civil rights as well as those of my fellow citizens in this community." Fifteen parents appealed to Senator Talmadge to use his "influence to see that our children do not become the victims." The letter explained that although the signers were not typical protesters—"draft-card burners, racial activists, rioters, or 'hippies' "—they might take more drastic measures "if it becomes necessary to insure an atmosphere in which our children can receive the kind of education to which they are entitled even though they may be the children of non-poor, non-black parents." A employee at the Rome GE plant similarly complained to Senator Talmadge that HEW's demands were unfair to white people. Full integration, he wrote, "may be well and good for negro students, but I vaguely recall something about freedom of choice. This must apply only to the negro race, since none of the white students here have expressed desire enough to enter a negro school."[48] Another GE

[48] James C. Gardner, Jr., to Eldridge W. McMillan (copies sent to Herman Talmadge, the editor of the *Rome News-Tribune*, Congressman Davis, Senator Russell, and Superinten-

employee protested to Talmadge that our "forefathers would turn over in their graves if they could see the conditions we have let our country get into by letting every department of the Federal Government *dictate* the wishes of a few to the majority."[49]

Floyd County whites' perverse acceptance of some desegregation but resentment at being required to make any further efforts for integration mirrored not only Local 689's position on union civil rights but the general view of most white Georgians in the late 1960s. Polls of Georgia voters in April 1968, for example, indicated that when voters were questioned about "granting negroes equality in Georgia," only one in every ten voters responded that "Negroes have too many rights now." Apparently, massive resistance had become a minority opinion. Only 14 percent of white voters polled believed that blacks in Georgia should have less equality. But in spite of the many obvious inequities that persisted, in schools, employment, health, and wealth, the majority, 56 percent, endorsed the status quo, responding that race matters "should stay same as now." Pollsters summed up the 1968 "moderate" view among whites with a series of rhetorical questions: "[Are whites] concerned and worried? Yes. Blindly hostile to Negroes? No. Prepared to do more for the Negro? Not really."[50]

This "moderate" position, which neatly paralleled the white reaction to the 1968 Rome schools dispute, illustrated some of the general boundaries of the emerging white southern conservatism. Though the dispute clearly revolved around a defense of privileges associated with whiteness, many aspects of this conflict divided it from the massive resistance effort of the 1950s. First and most strikingly, no one, in a public utterance, advocated segregation or the right of whites to discriminate anymore. In fact, by 1968 many Romans opposed to reorganizing the school system appealed to *Brown* to buttress their defense of the "freedom of choice" plan. The main object of their hostility by the late 1960s was not the NAACP or the Supreme Court, but the federal government and its demand that whites do more than peacefully accept change. Interestingly, many of their past political champions of segregation also ceased to encourage them. To all the angry letters, Herman Talmadge responded that he had protested to the president, the vice president, the attorney general,

---

dent McDonald), June 24, 1968; Harry Christian to Herman Talmadge (petition signed by fifteen Rome residents), June 6, 1968; and Jeff T. Freeman to Herman Talmadge, May 29, 1968; all in folder 3, box 84, subseries A-1968, series V, Talmadge Papers.

[49] Carlton J. Littlejohn to Herman Talmadge, June 3, 1968, folder 2, ibid.

[50] "A Survey of the Political Climate in Georgia, April, 1968," p. 39, in folder with same title, box 134, subseries B, series VI, Talmadge Papers.

and the secretary of HEW "without avail," but he made no further promises that he could "correct" the situation.[51]

Indeed, open defenses of white supremacy, segregation, and white privilege seemed to have gone underground. However, just as the explicit rhetoric of white supremacy disappeared, a new discourse, or at least a newly refurbished one, emerged to reunite white southerners across class lines and divide them from black southerners. By 1968 former segregationists had reclaimed the language of freedom, choice, and civil rights to defend their own desire to maintain the remnants of the old system. For white Romans, there was a distinction between letting black residents do as they liked—whether it was applying for a job or entrance into a white school—and making whites do anything to actively participate in or make a contribution to integration. This was considered a violation of their "freedom." Resembling Goldwater's anti-statism, this new conservative southern white position took the form of a bitter hostility to government action in all social—but not explicitly identified as racial—matters. It would be expressed in an overwhelming rebuke to the Johnson administration and the Democratic Party in the elections of 1968.

Local 689's emergent conservatism, highlighted by the number of unionists willing to bolt the party and defy COPE to support Goldwater, foreshadowed the development of a similar 1968 revolt among working-class whites. Although Local 689 and other Floyd County unions did not play a visible role in the controversy over city schools, white workers' mass defection from the labor-Democratic coalition in 1968 made them central partners in the triumph of the new southern conservatism. On the day Thacker announced to the union membership his election to the Floyd County Democratic Association, for example, he also announced to the rank and file that he "could not support [President] Johnson, but if [George] Wallace announced he would run for President, he would back him."

If Goldwater's anti-government conservatism spoke to a white working class increasingly alienated from the federal government, George C. Wallace was a candidate with an even more potent appeal to the politics of white southern workers. A former governor of Alabama who had made a brief run as an Independent candidate for president in 1964, Wallace was in many ways the personification of racially conscious working-class politics in the post–World War II period. He became deeply conservative on racial and general social issues, but he had built his career on close ties to organized labor and the kind of working-class populism that held many

[51] See, for example, Herman Talmadge to Carlton J. Littlejohn, June 13, 1968, folder 2, box 84, subseries A-1968, series V, Talmadge Papers.

southern Democratic coalitions together. In the 1950s, as an Alabama state legislator, he championed the cause of the common white man, fighting against right-to-work laws, supporting liberal unemployment compensation laws, opposing regressive taxation, and earning, in the process, a favorable rating from Alabama COPE.[52] However, Wallace also learned the power of race from his first, failed 1958 bid for the governor's office, and in 1962 he made race a central and successful issue. Inaugurated in 1963, Wallace was immediately catapulted into the spotlight by his vehement defense of white supremacy—declaring himself and the state of Alabama for "Segregation now! Segregation tomorrow! Segregation forever!"[53]

Simply defending segregation did not distinguish Wallace from other southern governors, but he became perhaps the most visible opponent of the civil rights movement in the early 1960s. As the civil rights struggle in Birmingham raged and Kennedy spoke out in favor of a national civil rights act, Wallace became a folk hero of whiteness with his defiant "stand in the schoolhouse door" to block the admission of black students to the University of Alabama. That he lost this battle in the larger war to defend white supremacy did not matter to his largely working-class followers. In 1965, Wallace did nothing as civil rights demonstrators marching from Selma to Montgomery were attacked by mounted troopers with clubs and tear gas on the edge of the state capital. His prominent opposition to civil rights, particularly at a time when the civil rights movement was gaining increasing attention and sympathy from the press, the federal government, and Democratic Party leadership, did change him in the eyes of the national AFL-CIO leadership. The AFL-CIO officially cut ties to Wallace as early as 1963. But even as the federation and TWUA International staffs ended all official contact between the governor and the labor movement, rank-and-file workers remained extremely loyal to Wallace, not just in Alabama but elsewhere in the South.[54]

Race was, of course, central to Wallace's appeal, but it was more than his popular opposition to civil rights that made him such a powerful and

[52] COPE did not officially endorse Wallace in 1962 when he ran in the gubernatorial primary, but he was one of three candidates who received a favorable rating from COPE. He did receive the highest number of votes from the COPE committee, but he was just short of the two-thirds majority required for the endorsement. See Draper, *Conflict of Interests*, 107–8. On Wallace, see Stephen Lesher, *George Wallace: American Populist* (Reading, Mass.: Addison-Wesley, 1994); and Dan Carter, *The Politics of Rage: George C. Wallace, the Origins of the New Conservatism, and the Transformation of American Politics* (New York: Simon and Schuster, 1995).

[53] Lesher, *George Wallace*, 174.

[54] On Wallace's relationship to the Alabama AFL-CIO staff, see Draper, *Conflict of Interests*, 107–21; on his appeal to southern workers, see Bartley, *The New South*, 394–95.

dangerous foe for AFL-CIO COPE in the 1960s. A fiery, powerful public speaker, Wallace, like Tom Watson, Eugene Talmadge, and other southern Populists who preceded him, had the ability to tap the emotions, fears, and grievances of poor and working-class whites. On the 1960s equivalent of the stump, Wallace replicated the Talmadge appeal of "us versus them"—the hardworking people with traditional values versus the over-privileged elite who look down on everyone else. His scathing attacks on "pointy-headed" intellectuals, distant federal bureaucrats, and youthful student protesters resonated with white working-class folk nationwide who felt increasingly alienated from the government and the emerging sensibilities of the modern world. For white southerners, long the object of the nation's condescending gaze, Wallace's message validated their resentment, their anger, and their old expectations of the world at a time when the rest of the nation looked upon them with shame. In 1968, when Wallace reemerged as the presidential candidate of the American Independent Party, his appeal was a perfect melding of economic populism, anti-government reaction, and old-fashioned southern defensiveness. Addressing the issues of the day in language coded to the white backlash, Wallace denounced rioters and welfare mothers, anti–Vietnam War protesters, and the "liberals, intellectuals, and long-hairs" who were turning the country upside down. His message, however, differed from the simple anti-government philosophy of Goldwater in significant ways. While Goldwater's negative program for organized labor provided a straightforward target for COPE, Wallace supported federal job training programs, a higher minimum wage, and better protection for workers who lost their jobs. He did not cross picket lines, and he defended union seniority against government mandates that new hires meet equal employment opportunity mandates.[55] Indeed, Wallace's platform differed very little from the traditional southern Democrat's, save his positive embrace of working-class and labor issues.

Given textile workers' involvement in state and national politics, they were undoubtedly aware of Wallace's record in Alabama and his break with the AFL-CIO COPE. Local 689 leaders also anticipated the TWUA's efforts to build support for Johnson, and later for Vice President Hubert Humphrey when Johnson decided not to seek the Democratic nomination. But in 1968, union leaders and members were also willing to ignore COPE. In a declaration that echoed countless southern Democrats' declaration of independence from the traditional political parties, President Thacker announced to the union that neither the "Democratic association, International union, nor [anyone] else could tell him how to vote."

[55] Patterson, *Grand Expectations*, 698–99; Rieder, "Rise of the Silent Majority," 243–68.

In April, when Wallace supporters held an opening rally to launch a Floyd County campaign, Thacker was one of three nominated to chair the county committee and won election as treasurer of the association. His wife became the corresponding secretary.

In August and September, as candidates for city, state, and county office gave their final pitches at Local 689's weekly meetings, union officers stepped up the local's own political activities, including a straw poll of the membership on the 1968 presidential campaign. Although Local 689 usually did not endorse specific candidates, officers did participate in the Georgia State AFL-CIO, and Local 689 COPE committee members intended to use poll results to guide the local's representatives at the upcoming Georgia convention. Despite the International's consistent post-1963 opposition to Wallace, the straw poll of Local 689 revealed that 86.4 percent of the rank and file supported the former governor of Alabama. There was a negligible amount support for Humphrey, but Humphrey could not even outpoll Republican Richard Nixon. The regular party candidates split the remaining 13.6 percent evenly—6.8 percent each.[56]

TWUA International staff realized that union support for Wallace posed a major obstacle to Humphrey's election. In September, a TWUA staff member informed President Pollock that there was "no chance that Humphrey can carry Georgia against either Nixon or Wallace." Lamenting the Georgia State AFL-CIO's recent endorsement of Herman Talmadge over the former NLRB attorney and liberal African American Maynard Jackson in the 1968 Democratic primary for U.S. Senate, he declared, "I do not understand such a decision; I really think the world is mad." Perhaps, he speculated, they had endorsed Talmadge "in order to protect what little the Democrats have left in Georgia against the inroads of Wallace supporters among the Union ranks." However, TWUA staff probably also underestimated the popularity of traditional Democrats, and of Talmadge in particular. In Floyd County, for example, Talmadge won 82 percent of the primary vote.[57]

In addition to his customary election-year letter to joint boards and locals, Pollock issued a letter to all TWUA members in October 1968 on the subject of Wallace. The letter to locals, read at the weekly Local 689 meeting, began with the traditional pitch about the importance of political action, then declared that "one phase of this campaign deserves special

[56] On AFL-CIO state councils' role in union politics activity, see Draper, *Conflict of Interests*, 8; Local 689 minutes, Oct. 10, 1968, folder 13, box 1, MSS 78-071, TWUA Records. Unfortunately, union minutes do not contain any details on the poll other than the breakdown of votes cast.

[57] Daniel Jordan to William Pollock, Sept. 4, 1968, "South, General, 1968" folder, box 630, MSS 396, TWUA Records.

attention . . . the candidacy of George C. Wallace." The "overwhelming majority of TWUA members," Pollock asserted, "knows that Wallace's appeal for votes is a fraud. . . . But there undoubtedly are some who are still being taken in by Wallace's propaganda." Though Wallace was "posing as a 'friend' of the workingman and as a champion of 'law and order,' " Pollock claimed, "he is neither, and his record proves it beyond a doubt." Citing Wallace's weaknesses on labor, Pollock noted that Alabama workers' average income lagged far behind the national average, that the state tax structure favored the wealthy, and that Wallace had failed to improve unemployment and workers' compensation or to gain a state minimum wage. Moreover, Pollock charged that Wallace had used the State Highway Patrol against strikers (though he did not identify a specific incident), defended Alabama's right-to-work law, and received financial support from union busters. As for Wallace's stand for "law and order," Pollock ignored the obvious reference to recent rioting, student protests, and civil rights demonstrations and noted that Alabama had one of the highest murder rates in the nation. In the letter to the rank and file, Pollock did not go into as much detail about Wallace's labor record, claiming simply that "George Wallace offers textile workers nothing," and added that Wallace had allowed "Alabama's crime rate to soar far above the national average" while "workers in his state remained glued to the bottom of the national wage ladder."[58]

What is most striking about the International's letters is that neither made an effort to *persuade*. No concessions were made concerning why Wallace might be appealing to anyone. Nor was there any attempt to persuade workers that Wallace's conservatism on government activism might be damaging to labor. Even a point-by-point comparison of Humphrey versus Wallace, both of whom claimed to be labor's friend, would have clearly been to Humphrey's advantage. However, Pollock wrote a highly partisan letter to his audience as though they shared exactly the same set of values as International staff at a time when rank-and-file partisanship and regional consensus could hardly be taken for granted. Nor is there any evidence that Pollock or International staff wrote a specific letter addressed to the perspective of southern members, who remained in many ways still marginal members of the International TWUA. Southern COPE activists such as the officers of Local 689, who lobbied, canvassed voters, and worked on political education themselves on a regular basis in less-than-ideal circumstances, were sophisticated voters and political activists.

[58] Pollock to "Fellow Members" n.d., ca. October 1968; Pollock to all local unions and joint boards, Sept. 9, 1968; both in "Political Letters, 1968 Pres. Election" folder, box 651, ibid.

So was Wallace, and his supporters were unlikely to be swayed by such a simplistic appeal.

Pollock, of course, was correct in identifying Alabama's faults, but the letters did not make workers come to their liberal Democratic senses. It was more like throwing gasoline on a smoldering fire. Although Alabama did have much lower wages, regressive taxes, and less-than-ideal statutes governing workers' compensation, these statistics did little to distinguish it from any other state in the Southeast, and particularly states like Georgia that were dominated by labor-intensive industries such as textiles. Nor did allegations about the murder rate in Alabama persuade southerners that Humphrey, whose own nominating convention was the scene of a violent confrontation between demonstrators and the Chicago police, was a more competent defender of "law and order." Instead, Pollock's letter elicited many angry replies. A letter from 150 members of TWUA Local 1465 in LeMoyne, Alabama, for example, protested to Pollock, "We are capable and qualified to judge for ourselves; and we would like to vote for whom we desire in the upcoming election." In a direct rebuttal to Pollock's letter, it continued, "Wallace may offer the textile workers nothing," but "after having Mr. Humphrey as Vice President for four years, we feel we could not tolerate another four years with him as President." Moreover, the letter concluded with a suggestion that Pollock "check the FBI records on crime rate and you will find that Minnesota (Mr. Humphrey's home state) far exceeds Alabama in crime increase." Local 1465's letter was one of the more caustic ones, but Pollock received pro-Wallace letters from union members in South Carolina, Virginia, Alabama, North Carolina, and Georgia, as well as Kansas and Pennsylvania.[59]

No one from Local 689 wrote Pollock, but when President Thacker received the endorsement and the COPE materials supporting Humphrey, he wrote to Montgomery, Alabama, to request Wallace literature. Both were placed in the lobby of the union hall. On the same day that the union membership heard Pollock's letter to local unions, Thacker announced that the Joint Board manager, the 689 COPE chairman, and he would attend the upcoming Georgia AFL-CIO COPE convention and that he "would endorse George Wallace for President."[60]

But a week later in Savannah, neither Local 689 nor any other Wallace sympathizers made an endorsement. Although a telegram from Wallace addressed to the secretary of the Georgia State AFL-CIO and delegates was read to the convention, in which he pledged his support for "your right of collective bargaining and the presentation of grievances, improve-

[59] Members of Local 1465 to Pollock, Oct. 28, 1968, "Political Letters, 1968 Pres. Election" folder, ibid.

[60] Local 689 minutes, Oct. 10, 1968, folder 13, box 1, MSS 78-071, TWUA Records.

ment in the conditions under which you work and live and increase in the benefits rightfully due you for your labors," no positive discussions of Wallace were recorded in the proceedings. Area COPE director Wilbur Hobby discussed the labor records of Humphrey, "Chicken Nixon," and Wallace, conceding that Wallace "made a couple of fairly favorable responses" to a poll on business and labor issues, but he insisted that "if we look at the record in Alabama, the record is not there." Wallace had "a whole lot of our union members buffaloed," Hobby claimed, "because he talks a good game."[61]

Appeals for support of Humphrey at the Georgia convention did differ significantly from Pollock's. Hobby, for example, appealed to Democratic partisanship in a way that directly addressed practical politics. "You people have got legislators that are going every day to capitol hill asking these people to vote on issues that affect the working people. . . . Here is a man [Humphrey] who has voted right 191 times for us and wrong none. And it doesn't look like but about 60 or 65 percent of the union members around this country are going to vote for him." This, Hobby argued, was dangerous because legislators might not bother to listen to labor in the future. In conclusion, he made an indirect reference to the ever-present but unspoken issue—race. He pleaded with attendees to "search your own minds and consciences about being a trade union member and not vote on a racious [*sic*] [racial?] platform but vote what's right for the United States and for the majority of its people."[62]

Reporting to membership after the convention, Thacker complained that no delegates could get recognized to speak on behalf of Wallace. Though one of Hobby's comments—that his proposal "looks like it might be too hot for you"—suggested there was some dissension on the floor, state speakers at the convention managed to keep all endorsements in the party. But back in Rome, when Local 689 COPE chairman Ed McSwain reported to the membership on the meeting, he concluded his remarks with the assertion that in his opinion, there was "only one man to vote for, and that was the man from the South," George Wallace. At this point, one union member, Louise Mays, who had been the shop steward for the plant's traditionally black departments, spoke up and expressed her disapproval of the COPE chairman's remarks. If McSwain wanted to campaign for Wallace, she accused, "he should do it on his own time," since his views did not represent her own. Thacker countered that at the convention there were "always lots of politicians and campaigning," this time all of it for Humphrey and Muskie, and that the "convention hall

[61] Georgia State AFL-CIO Annual Convention Proceedings (October 1968), published December 1968, p. 43, box 51, Georgia Periodicals.

[62] Ibid., p. 32.

was covered with their literature." Thacker did offer Mays an opportunity to speak on behalf of Humphrey, but if she did, union officers did not bother to include her remarks in the minutes. At the close of the meeting, McSwain took the floor and made a final appeal in which he asserted that he "was a union man 100% and asked that [members of the local] back the man for President that is for our union."[63]

Local 689 had deviated from COPE's election line in the past, but the break in 1968 was a much more significant one. The COPE chairman and president not only openly bucked the TWUA and AFL-CIO endorsement, but they also used the union meeting as a venue to proselytize for his opponent. An officer in the Wallace campaign organization, Thacker also put his experience with political education to work. Before the campaign Thacker and another union officer, department chairman Frank Baker, traveled to Tennessee and put Wallace leaflets "in every mailbox in Chattanooga." Simply voting for Wallace would have expressed a backlash against Johnson Democrats; actively campaigning for him represented a backlash of sorts against Pollock and the TWUA.[64]

In openly boosting Wallace, Local 689 officers such as McSwain and Thacker undoubtedly expressed what historians have long identified as a white working-class alienation from, and disdain for, the federal government. Southern workers in particular could not have helped but notice that federal commitment to civil rights waxed as federal support for the labor movement seemed to wane. Though the federal government, in a matter of just a couple of years, had imposed tougher pollution standards on Celanese, forced the integration of facilities at the plant, compelled downtown business owners to open their lunch counters and sales positions to African Americans, and fully integrated Floyd County schools, contemporary federal protections of labor routinely failed. The Taft-Hartley Act and the NLRB, for example, still could not force southern employers to deal straight with unions in the South or deliver such timely results to the TWUA. Floyd County unionists had many years of direct and frustrating experience with the enforcers of federal labor law, first in the decade-long struggle to win back pay and compensation for Anchor Rome strikers, and in the 1960s with their efforts to get a fair union election and a contract in Lindale. As political debate focused on the proper role for the federal government, Floyd County unionists were carrying out their own protracted struggle to get even the minimal promises of federal labor law enforced.

After twenty years of failed efforts, union activists had finally won a union election in Lindale, but because of the intransigence of the company

[63] Local 689 minutes, Oct. 24, 1968, folder 13, box 1, MSS 78-071, TWUA Records.

[64] Pat and Frank Baker interview.

and the NLRB's inability to enforce national labor law, it remained a hollow victory for many years. Slow but significant progress in organizing Lindale had begun in the early 1960s.[65] In 1961 the International had assigned a new full-time organizer, and in 1962 it hired Mildred McElrath to help organize among the plant's eleven hundred women workers. Both were aided by O'Shea and several volunteer organizers from Local 689 and the Central Labor Union, including an African American janitor at Celanese, Joe Lawrence, who volunteered his services to sign up the small number of black workers at the plant. In March 1962 the company announced a wage raise—a typical tactic to defeat organizing. Calling the company's bluff, organizers backed off, and within a few months managers cut hours and effectively took back the wage increase. Sympathy for the TWUA reached an all-time high. By 1963, according to Walt Curtis, a retired member of Local 689 who had spent a lot of time handbilling at the Pepperell plant before and after his retirement, there were "more people [at Lindale] interested in a Union at this time than ever before." In fact, Curtis reported to the regional director, even some of the past opponents of the union were interested in joining.[66]

Eighteen months later the entire organized labor community in Rome, from the barbers to the electrical workers, had joined the effort to organize Pepperell. To the TWUA's standard pitch on wages, holidays, pensions, insurance, and grievance procedures, the Rome Central Labor Union added a new one: "When in Rome, do as the Romans do." Organizers also compared Lindale millhands to workers in other industries to show how Pepperell wages had fallen behind community and national averages.[67] Pepperell managers, however, still attempted to employ the old arguments about "outsiders." "After all these years of rearing our families, enjoying fine schools and churches and our wonderful community," a newspaper advertisement accused, "these outsiders say we need a union. . . . Why did these people, whose names you or I cannot pronounce, become so interested in our community and our welfare all at

[65] Local TWUA volunteer organizers and International staff never completely gave up gave up organizing activities at Lindale after 1946. The TWUA only had "active" campaigns in 1955, 1958, 1959, 1961, 1963, and 1965, but Joint Board and Local 689 records indicate that unionists maintained contacts and occasional activities at other times as well.

[66] Frank Joseph to Michael Botelho, Nov. 27, 1961; Special Notice to Pepperell Workers (copy), Mar. 2, 1962; "It's Your Decision to Make" (TWUA leaflet), Oct. 11, 1962; Walt Curtis to Michael Botelho, July 25, 1963; all in "Pepperell 1962 Campaign" folder, box 2, MSS 81-295, TWUA Records; Local 689 minutes, Mar. 29, 1962, folder 5, box 1, MSS 78-071, TWUA Records; see also Local 689 minutes, May 30, June 21, 1962, folder 5; July 26, Oct. 4, 1962, folder 6; all in ibid.

[67] Clifford Weeks (Rome Central Labor Union) to members, n.d., ca. 1965; TWUA letter to Pepperell Workers July 1962; Robert Freeman to Pepperell workers, July 7, 1966; all in "Pepperell 1962 Campaign" folder, box 2, MSS 81-295, TWUA Records.

once?" Managers did not try to race-bait the union, perhaps because the Civil Rights Act had already settled the issue of fair employment, but they did make the mistake of offering their own assessment of the differences between Pepperell's workforce and others in Floyd County. Pepperell general manager G. H. Smith repeatedly pointed out that union organizers "keep trying to talk about electrical contracts at General Electric and Chemical contracts at Celanese" and implied that the wages and benefits organizers spoke of had no relevance to workers in the Lindale mill. After generations of being told how important and valuable they were, Lindale workers were now warned by management that it was unwise to compare themselves to others. In direct response to a TWUA letter, Smith warned that the union "will be talking about automobile plants, steel plants, synthetic chemical plants. . . . Our company does not run and YOU DO NOT WORK IN, an automobile plant, a steel plant, or a synthetic chemical plant."[68] Smith might as well have told them they were "lintheads."

In the final weeks before the March 1965 election, affiliates of the Central Labor Union ran a campaign blitz of leaflets, letters, newspapers ads, meetings, house calls, and telephone canvassing. When the NLRB conducted an election, 959 workers, the largest number yet, voted for the TWUA. This was not enough to defeat the 1,155 who voted "no union." However, in an NLRB investigation of TWUA charges filed after the election, board investigators concluded that among Pepperell management's many efforts to compare the Lindale mill to other plants—particularly, organized cotton mills such as Anchor Rome that had recently shut down—lay violations of federal labor law. After "sitting on [the] appeal for months," the NLRB ordered another election. The TWUA quickly reactivated its committees and leaflet distributions, and nearly seventeen months after the original election, workers at the Lindale plant, now owned by West Point Pepperell as the result of a 1965 corporate merger, voted for the union 1,139 to 917.[69]

As TWUA members knew well, winning a union election in the post-Taft-Hartley era by no means guaranteed a contract. The very day after the TWUA's victory, West Point Pepperell management, represented by the prominent anti-labor Atlanta law firm of Lovic, Brooks, and Constangy, filed what TWUA staff deemed "lengthy and frivolous objections

[68] The company statement about outsiders was allegedly written by one of the West Point Pepperell employees, whose name was not printed. See *Rome News-Tribune*, Mar. 3, 1965; G. H. Smith to Fellow Employee, July 16, 1966 (underline and caps in original), "Pepperell Lindale, Ga. 1965–1969" folder, box 2, MSS 81-295, TWUA Records.

[69] "Hearing Officer's Report and Recommendation on Objection," NLRB Case 10-CA-6214, and "General President's Representation Election Questionnaire," both in "Pepperell, Lindale, 1965–69" folder, box 2, MSS 81-295, TWUA Records.

to the election."[70] Though the NLRB certified the TWUA as Lindale workers' bargaining unit five months later, it took *years* for the TWUA and the NLRB to force West Point Pepperell management to even sit down with union representatives for the first bargaining session. West Point Pepperell attorneys challenged every court decision before the NLRB and in the regular courts, adding almost a year to the first appeal alone by repeatedly asking for extensions of time to file materials.[71] The appeals court finally ruled in favor of the union, but this was nearly four years after the original election. Writing to the NLRB, a TWUA attorney charged that the courts' handling of the matter was "a disgrace. . . . The company's only objective in appealing was to obtain delay and its success has been overwhelming."[72] But even after the company lost on appeal, West Point Pepperell managers refused to meet with union representatives. The TWUA was forced to go back to the NLRB and file charges against the company for refusing to bargain, and the whole process of appeals began again. In theory the NLRB protected the rights of workers through this entire process, but in practice, federal law and the courts became tools used by management to avoid collective bargaining. Nor was the West Point Pepperell workers' plight unusual. TWUA leaders described it as a typical example of how the union was forced to wait "for the slow processes of the law to catch up with industrial textile giants."[73]

In August 1968, as Wallace and Nixon crisscrossed the nation talking about what was wrong with the federal government, frustrated members of the new Local 1716 TWUA AFL-CIO wrote to the chairman of the NLRB about the "travesty of justice" that had been permitted in Lindale. "We are proud to be considered good, loyal citizens of this great country of ours," the letter began, "but begin to have doubts when people, whether Management, the National Labor Relations Board or the Courts,

[70] "Hearing Officer's Report and Recommendation on Objection," NLRB Case 10-CA-6214, ibid; quote from Georgia State AFL-CIO Annual Convention Proceedings, p. 28. On the slow pace of the NLRB and anti-union attorneys, see Brattain, "A Town as Small as That." The most infamous case of corporate stalling is the case of J. P. Stevens's battle with its Burlington, North Carolina, workers. See James Hodges, "The Real Norma Rae," in *Southern Labor in Transition, 1940–1995*, ed. Robert Zieger (Knoxville: University of Tennessee Press, 1996), 251–72.

[71] For example, when filing for appeal in the Fifth Circuit, company attorneys were granted four extensions before they even submitted their materials for the case, adding nearly a year before briefs were even filed. Daniel B. Jordan to Marcel Mallet-Prevost, July 18, 1969, "Pepperell, Lindale, 1965–69" folder, box 2, MSS 81-295, TWUA Records.

[72] Daniel B. Jordan to Marcel Mallet-Prevost, July 18, 1969, "Pepperell, Lindale, 1965–69" folder, box 2, MSS 81-295, TWUA Records; "West Point Pepperell Mills, Previous Organizing History," Nov. 26, 1968, "South, General, 1969" folder, box 631, MSS 396, TWUA Records.

[73] 1968 Georgia State AFL-CIO Annual Convention Proceedings, p. 28.

use what ever means they can to defeat the majority." In conclusion, the letter reminded the chairman that they had "a right as citizens of this great country, as well as taxpayers, to equal protection under the law," and requested that he "cut out the stalling" in the courts. However, West Point Pepperell managers did not even meet with workers to begin bargaining until late 1969. Local 1716 would not sign a contract until January 1970.[74]

Traditionally, the TWUA and AFL-CIO had linked problems securing labor's rights to the need for political action. The national PAC's major efforts in the 1940s, for example, had been to repeal Taft-Hartley. In the 1950s and early 1960s Rome unionists had also sought to replace local anti-unionists with friends of labor in order to improve state labor laws. In 1968, as Pepperell's case moved slowly through the courts, southern TWUA staff tried to make a similar link between current organizing problems and the upcoming elections. Reporting on the Lindale situation at the 1968 Georgia State AFL-CIO convention, for example, the southern director of the TWUA, Scott Hoyman, reminded delegates that a "liberal Democratic congress" had given labor the Wagner Act, and a Congress with a "republican majority and . . . the assistance of conservative Southern democratic representatives" had given them Taft-Hartley. He drew a direct connection between the problem in Lindale and the 1968 elections. For unionists to "finish this piece of unfinished business for the labor movement and finish the organization of the south, we need a stronger Labor Act, and we need a more effective National Labor Relations Board." He concluded with the advice that "we need to give a lot of thought, not just based on emotion, but based on where we want to go and where we want our unions to go . . . before we cast that vote on the first Tuesday in November."[75]

Historically, such pitches had coincided with the majority of Floyd County's textile workers trooping out to the polls and voting for the Democrats, but by 1968 many white southern workers had different analyses of what was wrong with the United States and who could fix it. The traditional labor-Democratic project of picking away at federal labor law one clause at a time, an agenda that had sustained the alliance between northern and southern labor Democrats since 1947, was now eclipsed by working-class concern about riots, civil rights, and big government. Moreover, workers' commitment to labor liberalism and federal solutions to labor's problems had been put to the test of decades of frustration. What was wrong with the NLRB, in the Wallace worldview, was less its connection

[74] Local 1716 to Frank W. McCulloch, Aug. 5, 1968, "Pepperell, Lindale, 1965–69" folder, box 2, MSS 81-295, TWUA Records; *Textile Labor*, January 1970.

[75] 1968 Georgia State AFL-CIO Annual Convention Proceedings, p. 28.

to partisan politics than its implication in the hopelessly bureaucratic federal government and its failure to enforce the law.

For white working-class southerners, "thought," "emotion," and many recent experiences with their employers, their schools, and (for some) even with their union undoubtedly pointed to Wallace as an ideal candidate to represent their race and class. Wallace frequently claimed that his movement was not a "white backlash" but a "backlash against big government in this country." His supporters certainly did not recall the overtly racist antics of a Eugene Talmadge. However, racially charged rants about "lawlessness," government pandering to black urban rioters, and excessive intervention in the name of civil rights pressed similar buttons. Wallace claimed, for example, that he supported rights as defined by the Constitution, but he adamantly opposed federal efforts "in the name of civil rights trying to control the property rights of people, the seniority list of labor unions [or] telling [restaurateurs] who they must serve." More concerned about the suppression of riots and demonstrations than the injustices that might have caused them, Wallace supporters expressed the most recent incarnation of whiteness and white resentment—namely, that whites bore no responsibility for black and white inequities. They could not legitimately be forced by the federal government to participate in improving the position of minorities at any inconvenience to themselves. Implicitly, then, the Wallace message about government appealed to racial identity, even when he did not use the words "white" and "black." But if Wallace identified himself with anyone explicitly, it was the working classes. In an interview that effectively launched his 1968 campaign, he argued that this backlash represented "a movement of the people. . . . And I think if the politicians get in the way . . . a lot of them are going to get run over by this average man in the street—this man in the textile mill, this man in the steel mill, this barber, the beautician, the policeman on the beat . . . the little businessman." It was the basic list he repeated throughout the 1968 campaign.[76]

Writing to the *Rome News-Tribune*, for example, a worker at West Point Pepperell asserted his disapproval of what seemed to him to be unnecessary government pandering to disorderly minority groups, and he linked these discontents to support for Wallace."I have always been a Democrat," he explained, "but today our two party system has merged and deteriorated to a point that the American people should look forward to supporting someone who pledges to restore our constitutional government, regardless of party affiliation." Echoing the reactions to the Civil Rights Act, the letter incorporated the new coded rhetoric of "qualifica-

[76] Lesher, *George Wallace*, 390–421, quotes on 413, 421, 390; see also Sugrue, *Origins of the Urban Crisis*, 265–67.

tions" to argue against further government action along Humphrey-Johnson lines to correct social inequities. "As to civil rights," he argued, "we feel that they are greatly exaggerated as all races and creeds have the same opportunities and equal rights to work at any job for which they are qualified." He was particularly upset about Humphrey's and the Johnson administration's "catering to minority groups who call themselves poor people." The "general public," the letter scolded, "knows the marches, demonstrations, rioting and burning are not committed by the poor people, but by hoodlums."[77]

Wallace supporters kicking off the local campaign in Floyd County put it more simply: "The country [was] a mess." Leonard Wilson, a Wallace representative from Alabama, opened the first Floyd County meeting with the cry, "Damn the leftwingers, damn the people who destroy our country, Full speed ahead!" He described the Wallace campaign as more than electoral politics—it was a people's "movement" that originated "at the crossroads of America, not in Washington, but in Alabama." Wallace, he promised, would save the "Republic from lawlessness, looting and rioting and from a no-win policy in Vietnam." Aside from the loaded discussion of riots, Wilson did not mention race—he did not need to. However, following the general anti-intellectual, anti–"party politics as usual," and anti–civil rights bent of 1968 politics, he reserved high praise for segregationist Georgia governor Lester Maddox, a man with "the courage of his convictions—and an axe handle."[78]

White Floyd County residents were generally united in their opposition to Humphrey, but interestingly the backlash against the Johnson-Humphrey Democrats also suggested a general break along class lines. Those who officiated the Wallace campaign in Floyd County included Thacker, his wife, a service station owner, the owner-manager of a trailer park, a secretary at West Rome High School, and the wife of a truck driver—all members of the working class or proprietors of small local businesses. Nixon supporters included the business and professional elite such as the editor of the *Rome News-Tribune* and Dr. John I. Dickinson, the chair-

[77] J. J. Rush, Rte 4 to Roman Forum, *Rome News-Tribune*, Aug. 25, 1968; *Polk's Rome City Directory, 1968* (Richmond: R. L. Polk, 1968), 348.

[78] Maddox was catapulted into politics by his well-publicized stand, armed with an ax handle, in the door of his restaurant to prevent African Americans from being served in spite of the Civil Rights Act. Elected by the largely Democratic Georgia legislature in 1966 after an election too close to call, he was considered something of an embarrassment by many well-heeled Georgians. In spite of the fact that he owed his entire career to the Democrats, Maddox also bolted his party to support Wallace. On Maddox, see Bradley R. Rice, "Lester Maddox and the Politics of Populism," in *Georgia Governors in an Age of Change*, ed. Harold P. Henderson and Gary L. Roberts (Athens: University of Georgia Press, 1988), 193–210; *Rome News-Tribune*, Apr. 17, 1968.

man of the Republican Party in Floyd County.[79] In another type of loaded language, Nixon supporters also gestured toward the class difference between Wallace, Nixon, and their respective supporters. The newspaper described Wallace as a " 'give 'em hell' type" who "says things simply and quickly the way many like to hear it," and portrayed Nixon as a "stable and astute public servant," an "outstanding constitutional spokesman," and a "true" conservative. Wallace, the editorial page argued, could not gain the backing of Congress, unite the country, or command "prestige abroad." Moreover, it warned, a third-party candidate could not win. Just as the AFL-CIO argued that "a vote for Wallace is a vote for Nixon," the *Rome News-Tribune* warned that "a vote for Wallace is one for Humphrey."[80] A letter to the editor in favor of Nixon pointed out the other significant class difference between Nixon and Wallace. "People should take note," the letter began, of a statement Wallace made on national television that "if he went to work for company that had a labor union one of the first things he would do would be to join that union, or to organize a union if the company had no union." Harking back to the old conservatives' charges against PAC, the letter even went so far as to suggest that labor's support might be the key to Wallace's "extraordinarily well-directed, managed, and financed nationwide" third-party campaign.[81]

On November 5, 1968, in the greatest election turnout in Floyd County's history, Democrats swept all state and local offices except the presidency, which Wallace won with a comfortable majority. With over 21,000 of Floyd County's citizens casting ballots, Humphrey mustered a mere 4,029 votes. Nixon made a strong showing with 7,428, but he fell far short of the 1964 Republican vote for Goldwater. Wallace was a clear winner with 9,984.[82]

By 1968, unfortunately, there are no longer any records that provide a neat analysis of votes by class, race, or union affiliation. By then, former Celanese mill houses had been privately owned for over ten years, and the Celanese workforce, and thus Local 689's membership, itself had dropped by nearly half. However, the village remained overwhelmingly working class and white. Of those voters who could be located in the

[79] *Rome News-Tribune*, Apr. 17, Aug. 30, Nov. 7, 1968.

[80] Ibid., Oct. 27, 1968.

[81] This was the only pro-Nixon letter the paper published. From South Carolina, it might have been written by a Floyd County resident—perhaps someone in the service—or may have simply been chosen by the editors for its content. The author, Allston Calhoun, did not appear in the 1968 city directory. *Rome News-Tribune*, Oct. 31, 1968.

[82] Georgia General Election Returns, 1968, all returns, consolidated and district, Fayette–Fulton Counties, microfilm 196-69, Georgia Department of Archives and History, Atlanta; *Polk's Rome City Directory, 1968*, pp. 2–448.

1968 city directory (86 percent), about 38 percent were employed at Celanese or lived in households with someone else who worked at Celanese. Nearly 80 percent of the total held working-class occupations. The greatest majority worked at one of Floyd County's factories or at local retail businesses such as barbershops, department stores, pharmacies, or service stations. These voters overwhelmingly favored Wallace. In the Celanese district, Wallace received twice as many votes as Nixon and almost three times as many as Humphrey.[83] In the Lindale district, which had by far the largest number of textile workers in the county in 1968, the majority for Wallace was even greater, with 1,078 ballots cast for Wallace and only 218 and 623 cast for Humphrey and Nixon, respectively. However, Rome city's precinct, perhaps the best measure of opinion among Rome's business and professional classes, reversed the order, with 1,417 votes for Nixon, 601 for Humphrey, and 934 for Wallace. If the backlash began with Talmadge in 1950 and gained momentum with Goldwater in 1964, it was emphatically expressed in 1968. Humphrey could not even win 20 percent of Floyd County's votes.

According to former Local 689 COPE chairman Oscar Allen, who worked at Celanese from the 1930s through the 1960s, Local 689's COPE never regained the same discipline or shared sense of purpose it once commanded in the 1940s and 1950s. "When I first started," Allen recalled, "I could go to a seminar. . . . I'd come back to the local, I'd talk to people . . . [and say] 'vote for so-and-so' and they'd do it, most of them." In the 1960s, however, "it got to where they'd say, 'Well you can go to hell, I'll vote for anyone I want to.' " Even the newly organized Lindale workers

[83] To determine who voted in 1968, I compared the state's official list of who voted with the 1968 *Rome City Directory*, which provides addresses and occupations. Fourteen percent of the people who appeared on the voter's list were not listed in the city directory. They may have been younger or older voters who lived in someone else's household, and the city directory primarily lists male heads of households and wives who appear under the husband's name. Seven percent appeared in the directory but had no occupation listed, and may have been retired or temporarily unemployed. Fourteen percent were listed as retired, and most likely had worked at Celanese or some other working-class occupation given the character of the community as a whole. It is also likely that the occupations of those people who could not be identified with a job or former job were distributed in roughly the same percentages as those that could be identified. But to gain a more accurate measure, I excluded those who could not be clearly identified and calculated the percentages in the above as the proportion of those workers who were clearly identified with an occupation or household in the city directory. Celanese workers, for example, were 38 percent of the 404 that could be identified. Managers, foremen, and supervisors were 12 percent. For the sake of determining the working-class vote I excluded managers and foremen, two pastors and their wives, five teachers, six students, an optician, two insurance agents, two bookkeepers, a member of the Floyd County Board of Roads and Revenue, and an assistant police chief. Georgia General Election Returns, 1968, Georgia Department of Archives and History; *Polk's Rome City Directory, 1968*, pp. 2–448.

voted overwhelmingly for Wallace, and when the local finally got on its feet in the 1970s, officers did not even establish a COPE committee.[84]

Historians often identify the Wallace phenomenon with the persistence of antagonism toward civil rights and the final dissolution of the New Deal coalition. White trade unionists' support for Wallace has also been well documented, and it might be tempting to end a history of white workers there, and chalk up workers' support for Wallace as simply a measure of racism among the rank and file. Floyd County's history certainly conforms to the well-known racial dynamics of the 1968 elections. But, in the context of workers' other experiences during the 1960s, the Wallace candidacy also revealed a more complicated history of the changing nature of racism, the character of the emerging southern conservatism, and the persistence of working-class identification with whiteness in spite of a superficial acceptance of civil rights.

In the broadest sense, Local 689's Wallace endorsement and workers' votes starkly revealed the long-term effects on the labor movement of not simply racism, but also segregation. The working-class agenda of Rome unionists had always been shaped by race, even though the primary focus on class issues in Democratic and PAC politics had permitted them to pursue class-based politics and maintain a cooperative relationship with the CIO PAC. When the Democratic Party began to change, shifting its emphasis from labor to civil rights, it stripped away the race-blind rhetoric of class that had often served to hide the differences between the South's white working class and the International. At the same time, the prominence of the civil rights movement and the intensification of white southern resistance to it clearly compelled International union officers to make their own civil rights allegiances more explicit. Rome unionists' responses—first, to the integration of union meetings; second, to the Civil Rights Act and Title VII hires; and finally, to the candidacy of Wallace—made it clear just how far they were willing to follow. Although Local 689 members could claim that "the integration problem here had been handled nicely" and maintain their good standing with the TWUA, interracial unionism was clearly not the same as sharing a race-blind working-class agenda. Humphrey and the labor movement clearly stood for this particular kind of activism, which would have required further government involvement and by necessity a greater degree of white activism in, and commitment to, racial matters. The 1968 elections provided white workers an opportunity to reject that avenue. Thus, even as explicit racism was excised from the labor movement in the 1960s, the privileges of whiteness remained. Acceptance of the status quo—the very essence of

[84] Oscar Allen interview; Poole interview.

conservatism—was ideally suited to resist further erosion of those remaining privileges.

The local reaction to the Civil Rights Act, HEW, and the 1968 election also suggested that this conservatism was shared among a broad white constituency. White assessment of what had been accomplished in civil rights by 1968 and apathy about further change revealed that the elimination of open discrimination had been a limited victory at best. In Floyd County there was a difference between accepting the cessation of active, open discrimination on the one hand and making a greater ideological and emotional leap to recognize the role that past discrimination continued to play once segregation was eliminated. Though segregation lost its claim to cultural legitimacy, it was replaced by a new and more insidious position, characterized by a general indifference to the lingering effects of Jim Crow. The defensive reactions to Title VII and HEW standards, for example, expressed in whites' appropriation of "qualification" and "rights" to defend the status quo, highlighted an important turning point in the history of whiteness. Even if social and cultural obstacles remained, structural barriers to racial equality had been removed, and clearly that was all that most Floyd County whites believed they could be held responsible for. Though African Americans continued to be underrepresented in white jobs and schools and marginalized within southern politics and the labor movement, most whites, as expressed in their votes for Wallace, did not see the need for further federal action on behalf of civil rights. In other words, workers and employers, and many other citizens of the white South, could not, or would not, see how whites continued to benefit from whiteness.

Epilogue

In the summer of 1971, racial tensions and black frustration in Rome finally boiled over in what the white editor of the *Rome News-Tribune* declared a "racial outbreak." In late August and early September, vacant homes, construction sites, and businesses fell victim to Molotov cocktails, arson, and even a makeshift bomb. Although arrests included at least one group of five white youths, much of the destruction, aimed at white-owned businesses within or bordering black neighborhoods, was attributed to a more "radical," or at least impatient, element of the black community. White city leaders had just begun to hear and respond to black grievances about the schools, job opportunities, and unequal representation within city government, when in a single night, August 31, five downtown groceries and retail firms were firebombed. A few days later, on September 2, just hours after some eight hundred black city residents met with local officials in a mass meeting at the city auditorium, someone placed a dynamite bomb at the entrance of a local bowling alley. Two weeks after the first firebomb fell, on September 15, two hundred black residents took to the streets and marched across the South Rome bridge into the "cotton block" of downtown Broad Street. Rome police arrested sixteen marchers, the city commission ordered a 9 P.M. to 6 A.M. curfew, and the Rome unit of the Georgia National Guard went on standby alert. On the same day, about three hundred black students "struck" and refused to attend classes. The night before, someone had set a vacant home on fire; when firemen arrived they were pelted with rocks from a group of black bystanders.[1]

The immediate trigger, according to the paper, may have been rumors about the nature of an alleged black-on-white crime and police "mistreatment" of eight black men subsequently arrested. Local black leaders, however, had warned only a few days prior to the beginning of the disorder that unless Rome whites took the black community's needs and demands seriously, riots, vandalism, and destruction of property were likely to come to the city. "You haven't had a demonstration yet. . . . You haven't had any real serious vandalism or rioting," a black leader warned the readers of the *News-Tribune* in August, "but you see it's something that can happen." Younger leaders charged that the older black leadership, traditionally solicitous of white approval and content with promises of gradual change, no longer represented the black community. "It's to

[1] *Rome News-Tribune*, Aug. 31, Sept. 2, 5, 15, 16, 1971.

the point now, especially with the young blacks," said Jimmy Hardy, a twenty-two-year-old leader of Rome's Black Coordinating Committee, a body elected by the black community, "that we don't care, really, how you feel about us. But we want to see some effective action taken on what we want." Hardy and others wanted more than integration of public accommodations, and had been "trying to get the people of the community to do now . . . what has come about after violence has occurred in other cities." Whites just did not know "what happens in the black community," Hardy explained. "They leave their jobs, and get in their cars, and roll up their windows and turn on their air-conditioners and they go back home" to "their side of town."[2]

Even if the precipitating rumors of police misconduct were false, black grievances were many and justified. In spite of many white Romans' perceptions that civil rights had been accomplished in 1964, many residual effects of segregation and discrimination remained in employment, housing, education, and health care. As Hardy and others predicted, disorder prompted a new level of white awareness and attention. The pace and progress of black-white negotiations increased noticeably in the first weeks of September 1971. Local African American leaders met with city police, the city and county commissions, the chamber of commerce, and the school board. They demanded more black police and firemen, black representation on appointed boards and commissions, better pay and working conditions for black city workers, and black cheerleaders, coaches, and band instructors in Rome Main High. And consistently in every venue, they demanded more job opportunities in local business and government. Not only elected officials, but local businesspersons and the chamber of commerce met with black leadership to discuss ways of opening up more jobs to black Romans.

Despite Title VII, job discrimination—the source of economic inequality for so many years in Rome—remained entrenched. Black leaders charged that white businesses in Rome and Floyd County made only superficial efforts toward nondiscrimination in hiring, especially in supervisory, managerial, and administrative positions. While black college graduates might obtain jobs on the production lines of local industries in 1971, they found themselves largely shut out of better-paying, higher-status positions. Hardy complained that when African American leaders asked why no black workers held such jobs, "the white answers that 'if there are qualified blacks here in the Rome area we'll be glad to put 'em in these positions.' " "Qualification," as Hardy understood, located the source of the problem, and the burden of its solution, in the worker, not the em-

[2] Ibid., Aug. 25, 1971. On the long-term economic and structural causes of urban unrest in the 1960s, see Sugrue, *Origins of the Urban Crisis*.

ployer.[3] Too often, claimed Jeffrey Jackson, another young black community representative, "we've been given one clerical job or one job in front of the show window. They [employers] want people to walk by and say 'that place is integrated' but it's not really integrated because when you go upstairs, you do not see any blacks in any responsible positions." Both claimed that a "stereotype still persist[ed] in the white business and industrial world that blacks, regardless of their education[, were] simply not capable of performing well in anything but menial jobs."[4]

By 1971, black Romans were even more dependent upon white employers, since "urban renewal" programs, financed by federal grants, had a disproportionate and negative effect on the black business community and black employers. Begun in 1968, local "slum clearance" and "urban renewal" programs in north Rome had eliminated an entire neighborhood of black-occupied homes, replaced them with thirty-six units of public housing, and subsequently torn down sixteen black businesses that had once occupied a block of buildings in Rome's Five Points district. Though urban renewal provided compensation to homeowners and business proprietors, few businesspeople had recovered their losses by 1971. The homes were removed first, eliminating local customers and foot traffic. Some businesspeople relocated, but the dispersal of black business and north Rome residents upended what had been an economically self-sustaining black community for generations. Callie Martin, for example, once owned a north Rome grocery and employed two workers. In 1971 she struggled to run a café on her own and was "not really making ends meet at that," she said. Hubert Holland, who ran a barbershop dislocated by urban renewal, likewise felt that his business was adversely affected by the program. Largely dependent upon the East First Street neighborhood for his livelihood, Holland was already in dire financial condition before he was forced to move to a more expensive location. "The way I see it," he complained, urban renewal "destroyed the Negro businesses, what little they had." In August 1971 only three of the sixteen local black-owned businesses had reopened.[5]

Other leaders complained that indirect discrimination still prevented black entrepreneurs from starting independent businesses. Bankers, Jackson complained, were more than willing to grant a loan for purchases such as a car, but "if you want it for a business, you're not going to get it if you're black." The bank "might give you some petty excuse such as

[3] When the Rome City Commission made a public announcement of its efforts to involve black citizens in local government, for example, it used the word "qualified" four times in six sentences. *Rome News-Tribune*, Sept. 2, 1971.

[4] Ibid., Aug. 29, 1971.

[5] Ibid., Aug. 3, 4, 1971.

'you're not stable enough,' or 'you're not qualified for a business,' something of that nature," but Jackson felt it was "a ways and means for keeping you down." Meanwhile, white merchants were "getting rich off the black community. They're taking the money out of the black community and into [the white subdivisions of] Garden Lakes or Horseleg Estates or wherever they live."[6]

Jackson's emphasis on independent black business echoed the growing influence of black nationalism as well as wider frustration with integration's failure to correct economic disparities between blacks and whites. Even when managers and businessmen made positive efforts to expand job opportunities for black workers, equal employment proceeded very slowly. Aggregate figures may have indicated compliance, but they also disguised the long-term effects of generations of discrimination. Between 1960 and 1970, for example, black workers in Floyd County had increased their share of manufacturing jobs from 8 percent to 13 percent, a level roughly proportional to their representation in the workforce. However, the ghettoization of black workers in particular jobs and particular industries remained a problem. In spite of an increase in industrial employment and a decrease in agricultural employment, the largest categories of black employment in 1970 still included service industries, domestic work, and general labor among the top four. Thirty-eight percent of black workers labored in furniture mills. Eighteen percent worked in private households.[7] Statistics from individual firms also revealed that occupational segregation within industries remained a problem. As of mid-1969 at the Celanese plant, for example, there were no black plant officials, managers, or professionals, only six technicians, four black office workers, four black craftsmen, and seventeen black operatives. Of the eighty African Americans employed at Celanese in 1969, 50 percent were service workers. Although Celanese managers adopted an affirmative action plan at the end of 1969, their projection for black hires in 1970 called for an additional 19 black workers to augment a workforce of 886 people.[8] Nineteen hires represented progress to be sure, but progress at a very slow rate.

[6] Ibid., Aug. 29, 1971.

[7] Of 3,462 black Floyd County residents employed, 889 were operatives, 488 were service workers in cleaning, food, health, or personal service, 650 were private household workers, 310 were non-farm laborers, and 293 were craftsmen. Figures calculated from U.S. Bureau of the Census, *Census of Population: 1970*, vol. 1, pt. 12 (Washington, D.C.: Government Printing Office, 1973), table 127, p. 555; and U.S. Bureau of the Census, *Census of Population: 1960*, vol. 1, pt. 12 (Washington, D.C.: Government Printing Office, 1962), table 88, p. 347.

[8] "Rome Affirmative Action, Celanese Fibers Company Plans 1969–70," folder 67, box 46, Wharton Papers.

Jackson's and Hardy's comments also revealed that even as elements of structural discrimination theoretically ended, elements of the South's older culture of segregation and white privilege persisted. Policy changes, as segregationists were fond of noting, did not necessarily result in immediate attitude changes. But because attitudes translated into treatment on the job and evaluation of "qualifications," white beliefs did matter. Some of the very same people who spoke out so vociferously against the Civil Rights Act in 1964 and the reorganization of Rome schools in 1968 were undoubtedly still present in local workplaces and still bitter in 1971. Even in union plants with nondiscrimination policies, harassment of black workers by white workers indicated not only that white working-class resentments lingered, but also that blacks and whites did not receive equal treatment at work or within the union. Politics in the late 1960s similarly revealed that even if white southerners could be made to accept the end of formal discrimination, they did not necessarily accept responsibility for correcting other aspects of racial inequality. Southern white attachments to the privileges of whiteness might have shifted or been reconstructed by civil rights laws, but they were not summarily eliminated by structural changes in labor markets. The new and seemingly objective rhetoric of "qualifications," for example, replaced older segregationist arguments and provided a new language to defend the status quo. This was a major innovation in whiteness because it allowed former segregationists to argue that the edge whites held over blacks in jobs and income was simply the product of market forces.

While it is not surprising that inequities remained in 1970, it perhaps is surprising that so many whites could not, or would not, recognize how the modern South and the relative status of black and white workers were the end products of discrimination. For nearly a century, Rome's economy and the South's industrial development had been rationalized according to prevailing racial views and the demands of segregation. From the rhetoric of the cotton mill campaigns at the turn of the century, to the defenses of higher white wages in the early twentieth century, to the protests against fair employment during the 1940s, Rome's major employers had reserved the best jobs, the highest wages, and the perks of welfare capitalism for whites only. Although at times southern leaders did not make the racial content of policies and ideologies explicit, as in the case of boosterism, all southerners understood that "opportunity," at least prior to 1964, applied to whites only. No less than Jim Crow laws, de facto segregation in industry and employment had divided and differentiated the black and white working classes for almost a century. As a result of these long-term structures of discrimination, white workers were in fact more experienced and "qualified." But, given Rome's history, "qualified" was not a race-neutral word. In fact, Rome employers and U.S. Employment

Service managers themselves had once used a variation of "qualified"—the designation "experienced"—as a code word for "white" under the regime of the FEPC. In the 1960s, as in the 1940s, real equality of opportunity demanded truly race-blind terms of evaluation that did not reward unfairly acquired advantages.

Race did not simply serve to exclude blacks; it also had a profound effect on whites. The South's pairing of Jim Crow segregation with industrialization allowed whiteness to become a primary influence in southern class formation and working-class culture. Especially in southern Piedmont and upcountry communities dominated by textiles, the reservation of not only social privilege but also economic opportunity had historically given white workers a reason to believe they shared interests with their employers and the traditional white leaders of the South. In time, the selective provision of employment opportunity intensified perceptions of difference associated with race by reifying racial difference within the categories of occupation. All Romans understood that textile workers and managers were white, maids and janitors were black. For much of the twentieth century, white workers, managers, and political leaders united around the project of policing those boundaries. Such boundaries may have served the immediate economic interests of whites, but they did little to challenge existing inequalities among whites. The pairing of factory wages with whiteness and paternalism often disguised the real poverty of the South's whole economic system by creating an illusion of common white interests served by boosterism. In the context of southern poverty, the provision of jobs, wages, and welfare did benefit white workers, but it also reinforced a generally favorable view of business that constituted a significant obstacle to the formation of independent working-class institutions well into the twentieth century.

Segregation also placed limits on the vision and the activism of southern unionists. Against a background of Jim Crow and extreme white opposition to the FEPC, the TWUA organized southern workers into locals that were profoundly influenced by the effects of occupational segregation. In the mid-1940s, when most of northwest Georgia's textile locals organized, union leaders had not made acceptance of the CIO's racial liberalism a prerequisite for union membership. The union's marginal position in the postwar South made union leaders understandably reluctant to undertake such a difficult project. Occupational segregation also meant that organizers did not have to sell workers on the idea of shared interests between blacks and whites in order to sell them on the union. In fact, since CIO leaders were forced to combat anti-union arguments portraying industrial unionism as race mixing, occupational segregation may have served to facilitate TWUA organizing.

However, the segregated nature of southern unions and the failure to incorporate racial liberalism into white union consciousness ultimately undermined the CIO's long-term plans for an interracial movement capable of transforming the politics of the South. The segmentation of the South's workforce alone would have placed sharp limits on what a union local could accomplish in the way of interracial cooperation. Moreover, the failure to incorporate new ideas about race into workers' consciousness of class permitted southern textile locals to become venues for exclusively *white* working-class interests. Even if only by their unwillingness to challenge the status quo, Floyd County textile union locals re-created segregation in the labor movement. In fact, some union agreements institutionalized racial difference in the language of union contracts. The historic pairing of work with race gave white southern workers a reason to think that their interests were served by segregation and traditional southern Democratic conservatism, and by the 1950s white union members had a substantial stake in the maintenance of the racial and political status quo. When the national labor movement became more visibly allied with the civil rights movement in the 1950s and 1960s, angry letters and disaffiliations made it painfully clear that white southern workers had internalized only trade union–based, and therefore white-based, allegiances. Although southern unions such as Local 689 were capable of adapting to legal aspects of civil rights law, the rank and file as a whole refused to join labor liberals in a coalition for civil rights and labor in the 1960s.

Integration of textile jobs did begin to challenge the relationship between race and work, even if it did not immediately undermine the connection between unions and the politics of whiteness in Rome. In the 1970s a new generation of white workers, such as union president Walter Brooks and recording secretary Mildred McElrath, put an end to white bias in the Local 689 contracts and worked to extend new opportunities to black workers within the plant. Brooks risked his position as president of Local 689 to sponsor a black man's bid to join an all-white department. Lindale's Local 1716, organized in a post–Civil Rights Act workplace, had black representation among its first officers and included a nondiscrimination clause on the first page of its contract. Although a fair amount of racial tension and racism remained in both locals, the TWUA's postwar plan to build solidarity and trust by encouraging black and white union members to work together finally did make some headway after the integration of the mills.[9]

For CIO and other national labor leaders, industrial unionism had always held out the promise of such transformations. When blacks and

[9] Brooks interview; Poole interview; Local 1716 contract, in printed materials, ACTWU, GTA Joint Board Papers, acc. 81–10, Southern Labor Archives.

whites worked together, shared a common adversary, and cooperated on collective goals, the logic of interracial solidarity was powerful. The mines and mills of the South where workers had been able to overcome racial division to mount interracial movements for change had historically served as a inspiring vision of how things could have been different. If the South's largest industry had not operated within a racially constrained labor market, and the unions formed at the end of World War II had represented a broader segment of the southern working class, the TWUA might have contributed to an economic and political transformation of the American South. Unfortunately, the dissociation of industrial work from whiteness came too late.

The industry that played such an important role in the creation of the New South of low-wage industries, a single party, and segregation was not destined to play a significant or lasting role in the transformation of the South to more a industrially diversified and integrated region. By the 1950s the South's textile industry had already entered a steady decline, marked by reduced workforces, plant liquidations, and permanent closures as international textile capital increasingly turned to production facilities in Asia and Latin America, for the same reasons that once attracted them to the American South. Between 1946 and 1960, 202 southern textile mills closed, eliminating 54,290 jobs. In the same period in Floyd County, five organized textile mills closed down. In the 1960s, textile employment in Georgia cotton mills, historically the core of the state's industry, declined another 17 percent.[10] The Northwest Georgia Joint Board, once a symbol of the TWUA's postwar confidence and ambition, dissolved, and the remaining Floyd County unions transferred to a regional board stretching from eastern Tennessee to northeastern Alabama. Permanent layoffs and partial liquidations also took a toll on the textile jobs that remained. In 1977, when the Celanese mill closed down for good, it employed only about five hundred workers. Of all the original mills established at the turn of the century, only the Lindale plant remained in the 1980s, and it employed even fewer workers. Almost as rapidly as the South had risen to dominate the American textile industry, it fell to defeat by other lower-wage regions beyond U.S. borders.[11]

[10] Figures on plant closings are not available for the 1960s.

[11] Flamming, *Creating the Modern South*, 311; handwritten notes of James O'Shea, ca. 1958, folder "Wage Rates, 1952–58," box 1613, Joint Board Papers; John Gaventa and Barbara Ellen Smith, "The Deindustrialization of the Textile South: A Case Study," in *Hanging by a Thread: Social Change in Southern Textiles*, ed. Jeffrey Leiter, Michael D. Schulman, and Rhonda Zingraff (Ithaca: ILR Press, 1991), 183; figures on the 1970s calculated from Textile Mill Liquidations reports compiled by the Textile Workers Union of America Research Department, filed by year, 1970–76, box 7; 1980s figures from "Textile Plant Closings and Partial Liquidations, 1980–1985," box 8; all in MSS 97–196, TWUA Records.

Despite its rapid and brutal demise, the textile industry and its workers contributed to the shape and character of southern politics, society, economy, and history in extraordinary ways. For almost one hundred years, textile mills and textile work had been dominant forces in the economy of the region and the lives of many of its inhabitants. Shaped by boosterism and paternalism and the Jim Crow world in which it arrived, the textile industry served as the race-conscious entry to industrial wage work for many of northwest Georgia's whites. But it was not simply that textile work was shaped by the circumstances of its birth. The association of textile work with race also made further contributions to constructions of segregation and whiteness, creating a particular conception of the industrial working class, the ramifications of which were felt in politics, union organizing, and beyond. Whiteness began to change under the influence of workplace integration, the disappearance of explicit white supremacist political rhetoric, and the end of Jim Crow, but the changes were slow. As the riots of 1971 so tellingly demonstrated, occupational segregation and its effects were deeply embedded in the society of the post–civil rights South. Textile workers and the textile unions had begun to respond to some of the challenges of creating a real interracial workforce and union movement, but the concurrent decline of the industry meant that textiles would not play the same role in any new definition of the southern working class. While there is every reason to think that whiteness still occupies a central role in northwest Georgia, it no longer plays itself out among spinners, doffers, weavers, and fixers.

Bibliography

Manuscripts

Felix Hargrett Rare Book and Manuscript Library, Athens, Georgia
  Georgia Collection
Floyd County Records Retention Center, Rome, Georgia
  Floyd County Voter Registration Books
  Rome City Directories
George Meany Memorial Archives, Silver Spring, Maryland
  AFL-CIO Civil Rights Department Records
Georgia Department of Archives and History, Atlanta
  Employment Security Agency Records
  Georgia Department of Labor Records
  Georgia Supreme Court Case Files
J. Murrey Atkins Library, University of North Carolina, Charlotte
  Payton, Boyd. Papers
National Archives, Southeast Region, East Point, Georgia
  War Manpower Commission Records
National Archives, Washington, D.C.
  Cotton Textile National Industrial Relations Board Records
  National Recovery Administration Records
National Archives II, College Park, Maryland
  National Labor Relations Board Papers
Richard B. Russell Memorial Library, Athens, Georgia
  Davis, John W. Papers
  Lanham, Henderson. Papers
  Russell, Richard B. Papers
  Talmadge, Herman E. Papers
Sara Hightower Library, Special Collections, Rome, Georgia
  Battey, George MacGruder. Papers
  Harris, John L. Papers
  Tubize Yarns
  Vertical Files
Southern Labor Archives, Atlanta, Georgia
  ACTWU, GTA Joint Board Papers
  ACTWU Tennessee Joint Board Papers
  AFL-CIO Southern Area Civil Rights Department Records
  Georgia Periodicals
  Kennedy, Stetson. Papers
  Ramsey, John. Papers
  TWUA Northwest Georgia Joint Board Papers
  Via, Emory. Papers

State Historical Society of Wisconsin, Madison
Textile Workers Union of America Records
University Archives and Records Center, University of Pennsylvania, Philadelphia
Wharton School's Industrial Research Unit Papers
William R. Perkins Library, Durham, North Carolina
Mason, Lucy Randolph. Papers

Newspapers and Periodicals

Atlanta Constitution
Atlanta Journal
Floyd County Herald
Rome News-Tribune
The Statesman
Textile Bulletin
Textile Labor
Textile Labor Banner

Interviews

(All interviews conducted by author in Floyd County, Georgia, in author's possession, unless otherwise specified.)
Oscar Allen, August 28, 1994
Opal and J. C. Allen, September 12, 1994
Herman Anderson, July 20, 1994
Ellis Arnall, interview by James F. Cook, March 25 and April 17, 1986, Georgia Government Documentation Project, Southern Labor Archives, Atlanta, Georgia
Pat and Frank Baker, July 12, 1994
Blondell Bishop, June 28, 1994
Walter Brooks, July 7, 1994
Pat and Ernest Burch, September 12, 1994
Earl Fricks, July 5, 1994
Polly Gammon, May 16, 1994
Ross Groshong, Greensboro, North Carolina, March 20, 1994
Claudie Knowles, June 28, 1994
Ruth Knowles, June 28, 1994
Callie Martin, July 28, 1994
Lester Patty, Centre, Alabama, September 11, 1994
Joseph Pedigo, interview by Bill Finger, April 2, 1975, transcript, Southern Oral History Project, Louis Round Wilson Library, Chapel Hill, North Carolina
Grady Poole, July 5, 1994
Max Proctor, July 15, 1994
Opal Scott, September 10, 1994
Lewis Shelton, August 14, 1994
Forrest Shropshire, May 3, 1994
Fanny Smith, July 20, 1994
Rufus Turner, July 18, 1994

Vicky Vinson, July 13, 1994
Harold Waddell, July 23, 1994
Dean Wood, September 10, 1994
H. O. Yarbrough, July 14, 1994

Books, Articles, and Theses

Aaron, Benjamin. "Amending the Taft-Hartley Act: A Decade of Frustration." *Industrial and Labor Relations Review* 11 (April 1958): 330–40.

Adams, Leonard P. *The Public Employment Service in Transition, 1933–1968: Evolution of a Placement Service into a Manpower Agency.* Ithaca: Cornell University Press, 1969.

Allen, John E. "The Governor and the Strike: Eugene Talmadge and the General Textile Strike, 1934." Master's thesis, Georgia State University, 1977.

Anderson, William. *The Wild Man from Sugar Creek: The Political Career of Eugene Talmadge.* Baton Rouge: Louisiana State University Press, 1975.

Angoff, Charles, and H. L. Mencken. "The Worst American State." *American Mercury* 24 (September, October, November 1931): 1–16; 175–88; 355–71.

Arnall, Ellis. *The Shore Dimly Seen.* Philadelphia: Lippincott, 1946.

Aycock, Roger. *All Roads to Rome.* Roswell, Ga.: W. H. Wolfe Associates, 1981.

Baron, Ava, ed. *Work Engendered: Toward a New History of American Labor.* New York: Cornell University Press, 1991.

Bartley, Numan. *The Creation of Modern Georgia.* 2nd. ed. Athens: University of Georgia Press, 1990.

———. *From Thurmond to Wallace.* Baltimore: Johns Hopkins University Press, 1970.

———. *The New South.* Baton Rouge: Louisiana State University Press, 1995.

———. *The Rise of Massive Resistance: Race and Politics in the South during the 1950s.* Baton Rouge: Louisiana State University Press, 1969.

Bartley, Numan, and Hugh D. Graham. *Southern Politics and the Second Reconstruction.* Baltimore: Johns Hopkins University Press, 1975.

Bass, Jack, and Walter DeVries. *The Transformation of Southern Politics: Social Change and Political Consequence since 1945.* New York: Basic Books, 1976.

Battey, George MacGruder, Jr. *A History of Rome and Floyd County, Georgia.* Atlanta: Webb and Vary, 1922.

Berger, Maurice. *White Lies: Race and the Myths of Whiteness.* New York: Farrar, Strauss, Giroux, 1999.

Bernd, Joseph. *Grass Roots Politics in Georgia: The County Unit System and the Importance of the Individual Voting Community in Bi-Factional Elections, 1942–1954.* Atlanta: Georgia Institute of Technology, 1960.

Bernstein, Irving. *The Lean Years: A History of the American Worker.* Boston: Houghton Mifflin, 1960.

Billings, Dwight B., Jr. *Planters and the Making of a "New South": Class Politics and Development in North Carolina, 1865–1900.* Chapel Hill: University of North Carolina Press, 1979.

Black, Earl, and Merle Black. *Politics and Society in the South.* Cambridge: Harvard University Press, 1987.

Black, Earl, and Merle Black. *The Vital South: How Presidents Are Elected* (Cambridge: Harvard University Press, 1992.

Blicksilver, Jack. *Cotton Manufacturing in the Southeast: An Historical Analysis.* Atlanta: Georgia State University, School of Business Administration, Bureau of Business and Economic Research, 1959.

Boyte, Harry. "The Textile Industry: Keel of Southern Industrialization." *Radical America* 6 (March–April 1972): 4–49.

Brattain, Michelle. "Making Friends and Enemies: Textile Workers and Political Action in Postwar Georgia." *Journal of Southern History* 63 (February 1997): 91–138.

———. "The Pursuits of Post-exceptionalism: Race, Gender, Class, and Politics in the New Southern Labor History." In *Labor in the Modern South*, ed. Glenn T. Eskew. Athens: University of Georgia Press, 2001.

———. " 'A Town as Small as That': Tallapoosa, Georgia, and Operation Dixie." *Georgia Historical Quarterly* 81 (Summer 1997): 395–425.

Brody, David. *Workers in Industrial America: Essays on the Twentieth-Century Struggle.* New York: Oxford University Press, 1986.

Byerly, Victoria. *Hard Times Cotton Mill Girls: Personal Histories of Womanhood and Poverty in the South.* Ithaca: ILR Press, 1986.

Carlton, David. *Mill and Town in South Carolina, 1880–1920.* Baton Rouge: Louisiana State University Press, 1982.

Carter, Dan T. *The Politics of Rage: George Wallace, the Origins of the New Conservatism, and the Transformation of American Politics.* New York: Simon and Schuster, 1995.

Cash, W. J. *The Mind of the South.* New York: Vintage Books, 1941.

Chafe, William. *The American Woman: Her Changing Social, Economic, and Political Roles, 1920–1970.* New York: Oxford University Press, 1972.

———. *The Unfinished Journey.* New York: Oxford University Press, 1986.

Cobb, James. *Industrialization and Southern Society, 1877–1984.* Lexington: University Press of Kentucky, 1984.

———. "Not Gone, but Forgotten: Eugene Talmadge and the 1938 Purge Campaign." *Georgia Historical Quarterly* 59 (Summer 1975): 197–209.

———. *The Selling of the South: The Southern Crusade for Industrial Development 1936–1980.* Baton Rouge: Louisiana State University Press, 1982.

Cohen, Lizabeth. *Making a New Deal: Industrial Workers in Chicago, 1919–1939.* New York: Cambridge University Press, 1990.

Coleman, Kenneth, ed. *A History of Georgia.* Athens: University of Georgia Press, 1977.

Conway, Mimi. *Rise Gonna Rise: A Portrait of Southern Textile Workers.* Garden City, N.Y.: Anchor Press, 1979.

Cook, Sylvia Jenkins. *From Tobacco Road to Route 66: The Southern Poor White in Fiction.* Chapel Hill: University of North Carolina Press, 1976.

Corson, John. *Manpower for Victory: Total Mobilization for Total War.* New York: Farrar and Rinehart, 1943.

Cosman, Bernard. *Five States for Goldwater: Continuity and Change in Southern Presidential Voting Patterns.* Tuscaloosa: University of Alabama Press, 1966.

Daniel, Pete. *Standing at the Crossroads: Southern Life in the Twentieth Century.* New York: Hill and Wang, 1986.

Draper, Alan. *Conflict of Interests: Organized Labor and the Civil Rights Movement in the South, 1954–1968.* Ithaca: ILR Press, 1994.

Dubofsky, Melvin. *The State and Labor in Modern America.* Chapel Hill: University of North Carolina Press, 1995.

Dubofsky, Melvyn, and Warren Van Tine. *John L. Lewis: A Biography.* Urbana: University of Illinois Press, 1977.

DuBois, W.E.B. *Black Reconstruction in America, 1860–1880.* 3rd ed. New York: MacMillan, 1992.

Dyer, Richard. *White.* New York: Routledge, 1997.

Eskew, Glenn T. *But for Birmingham: The Local and National Movements in the Civil Rights Struggle.* Chapel Hill: University of North Carolina Press, 1997.

Faue, Elizabeth. "Anti-Heroes of the Working Class: A Response to Bruce Nelson." *International Labor and Working-Class History* 44 (Fall 1993): 377–88.

Fields, Barbara J. "Ideology and Race in American History." In *Region, Race and Reconstruction: Essays in Honor of C. Vann Woodward,* edited by J. Morgan Kousser and James M. McPherson, 143–77. New York: Oxford University Press, 1982.

Fink, Gary M. *The Fulton Bag and Cotton Mills Strike of 1914–1915: Espionage, Labor Conflict, and New South Industrial Relations.* Ithaca: ILR Press, 1993.

Fink, Gary M., and Merle E. Reed, eds. *Essays in Southern Labor History: Selected Papers, Southern Labor History Conference, 1976.* Westport, Conn.: Greenwood Press, 1974.

———. *Race, Class, and Community in Southern Labor History.* Tuscaloosa: University of Alabama Press, 1994.

Fite, Gilbert C. *Cotton Fields No More: Southern Agriculture, 1865–1980.* Lexington: University Press of Kentucky, 1984.

Flamming, Douglas. *Creating the Modern South: Millhands and Managers in Dalton, Georgia.* Chapel Hill: University of North Carolina Press, 1992.

Flynt, J. Wayne. *Dixie's Forgotten People: The South's Poor Whites.* Bloomington: Indiana University Press, 1979.

Flynt, J. Wayne, and Dorothy S. Flynt. *Southern Poor Whites: A Selected Annotated Bibliography of Published Sources.* New York: Garland, 1981.

Foley, Neil. *The White Scourge: Mexicans, Blacks, and Poor Whites in Texas Cotton Culture.* Berkeley: University of California Press, 1997.

Foster, James Caldwell. *The Union Politic: The CIO Political Action Committee.* Columbia: University of Missouri Press, 1975.

Frankenberg, Ruth. *White Women, Race Matters: The Social Construction of Whiteness.* Minneapolis: University of Minnesota Press, 1993.

———, ed. *Displacing Whiteness: Essays in Social and Cultural Criticism.* Durham: Duke University Press, 1997.

Fraser, Steve and Gary Gerstle, eds. *The Rise and Fall of the New Deal Order, 1930–1980.* Princeton: Princeton University Press, 1989.

Frederickson, Kari. *Revolt of the Black Belt: The Dixiecrat Party and the End of the Solid South, 1932–1968.* Chapel Hill: University of North Carolina Press, 2001.

Frederickson, Kari. " 'The Slowest State' and 'Most Backward Community': Federal Civil Rights Legislation, 1946–1948." *South Carolina Historical Magazine* 98 (April 1997): 177–202.

Gall, Gilbert. *The Politics of Right to Work: The Labor Federations as Special Interests, 1943–1979.* Westport, Conn.: Greenwood Press, 1988.

Gaston, Paul M. *The New South Creed: A Study in Southern Mythmaking.* New York: Knopf, 1970.

Gerstle, Gary. *Working Class Americanism: The Politics of Labor in a Textile City, 1914–1960.* New York: Cambridge University Press, 1989.

———. "Working-Class Racism: Broaden the Focus." *International Labor and Working-Class History* 44 (Fall 1993): 33–40.

Gibbons, Jim. *A History of Lindale: The Research of Polly Gammon.* Rome, Ga.: Art Department of Rome, 1997.

Goldfield, Michael. *The Decline of Organized Labor in the United States.* Chicago: University of Chicago Press, 1987.

———. "Race and the CIO: The Possibilities for Racial Egalitarianism during the 1930s and the 1940s." *International Labor and Working Class History* 44 (Fall 1993): 1–27.

Goodwyn, Lawrence. *Democratic Promise: The Populist Moment in America.* New York: Oxford University Press, 1976.

Gordon, David M., Richard Ewards, and Michael Rich. *Segmented Work, Divided Workers: The Historical Transformation of Labor in the United States.* New York: Cambridge University Press, 1982.

Greene, Julia. "The Strike at the Ballot Box: The American Federation of Labor, Local Trade Union Leadership, and Political Action." Ph.D. diss., Yale University, 1990.

———. " 'The Strike at the Ballot Box': The American Federation of Labor's Entrance into Election Politics, 1906–1909." *Labor History* 32 (Spring 1991): 165–92.

Griffith, Barbara. *The Crisis of American Labor: Operation Dixie and the Defeat of the CIO.* Philadelphia: Temple University Press, 1986.

Gross, James A. *The Making of the National Labor Relations Board: A Study in Economics, Politics, and the Law, 1933–1937.* Albany: State University of New York Press, 1974.

———. *The Reshaping of the National Labor Relations Board: National Labor Relations Policy in Transition, 1937–1947.* Albany: State University of New York Press, 1981.

Hahn, Stephen J. *The Roots of Southern Populism: Yeoman Farmers and the Transformation of the Georgia Upcountry, 1850–1890.* New York: Oxford University Press, 1983.

Hale, Grace Elizabeth. *Making Whiteness: The Culture of Segregation in the South, 1890–1940.* New York: Pantheon, 1998.

Hall, Jacquelyn Dowd, James Leloudis, Robert Korstad, Mary Murphy, Lu Ann Jones, and Christopher B. Daly. *Like a Family: The Making of a Southern Cotton Mill World.* Chapel Hill: University of North Carolina Press, 1987.

Harris, Cheryl I. "Whiteness as Property." *Harvard Law Review* 106 (June 1993): 1709–91.

Harris, Howell. *The Right to Manage: Industrial Relations Policies of American Business in the 1940s.* Madison: University of Wisconsin Press, 1982.

Henderson, Harold Paulk. *The Politics of Change in Georgia: A Political Biography of Ellis Arnall.* Athens: University of Georgia Press, 1991.

Henderson, Harold P., and Gary L. Roberts, ed. *Georgia Governors in an Age of Change.* Athens: University of Georgia Press, 1988.

Herring, Harriet. "Cycles of Cotton Mill Criticism." *South Atlantic Quarterly* 28 (1929): 113–25.

———. *Welfare Work in Mill Villages: The Story of Extra-Mill Activities in North Carolina.* 1929. Reprint, Montclair, N.J.: Patterson and Smith, 1968.

Hill, Herbert. "Myth-Making as Labor History: Herbert Gutman and the United Mine Workers of America." *International Journal of Politics, Culture, and Society* 2 (Winter 1988): 132–200.

Hill, Mike, ed. *Whiteness: A Critical Reader.* New York: New York University Press, 1997.

Hitz, Alex M. "Georgia Militia Districts." *Georgia Bar Journal* 19 (February 1956): 20–23.

Hodges, James. *New Deal Labor Policy and the Southern Cotton Textile Industry, 1933–1941.* Knoxville: University of Tennessee Press, 1986.

Honey, Michael. "Operation Dixie: Labor and Civil Rights in the Postwar South." *Mississippi Historical Quarterly* 45 (Fall 1992): 439–54.

———. *Southern Labor and Black Civil Rights: Organizing Memphis Workers.* Urbana: University of Illinois Press, 1994.

Hunter, Tera. *To 'Joy My Freedom: Southern Black Women's Lives and Labors after the Civil War.* Cambridge: Harvard University Press, 1997.

Irons, Janet. "Testing the New Deal: The General Textile Strike of 1934." Ph.D diss., Duke University, 1988.

Kelley, Robin D. G. *Race Rebels: Culture, Politics, and the Black Working-Class.* New York: Free Press, 1994.

———. " 'We Are Not What We Seem': Rethinking Black Working-Class Opposition in the Jim Crow South." *Journal of American History* 80 (June 1993): 75–112.

Kennedy, Stetson. *Southern Exposure.* New York: Doubleday, 1946.

Kessler-Harris, Alice. *Out to Work: A History of Wage-Earning Women in the United States.* New York: Oxford University Press, 1983.

———. *A Woman's Wage: Historical Meanings and Social Consequences.* Lexington: University Press of Kentucky, 1990.

Key, V. O. *Southern Politics.* New York: Random House, 1949.

Kirby, Jack Temple. *Rural Worlds Lost: The American South, 1920–1960.* Baton Rouge: Louisiana State University Press, 1987.

Knowlton, Evelyn H. *Pepperell's Progress: History of a Cotton Textile Company, 1844–1945.* Cambridge: Harvard University Press, 1948.

Korstad, Robert, and Nelson Lichtenstein. "Opportunities Found and Lost: Labor Radicals and the Early Civil Rights Movement." *Journal of American History* 75 (Winter 1988): 786–811.

Kousser, J. Morgan. *The Shaping of Southern Politics: Suffrage Restriction and the Establishment of the One-party South, 1880–1910.* New Haven: Yale University Press, 1974.

Kousser, J. Morgan, and James M. McPherson, eds. *Region, Race, and Reconstruction: Essays in Honor of C. Vann Woodward.* New York: Oxford University Press, 1982.

Lawson, Steven R. *Black Ballots: Voting Rights in the South, 1944–1969.* New York: Columbia University Press, 1976.

Leiter, Jeffrey, Michael D. Schulman, and Rhoda Zingraff, eds. *Hanging by a Thread: Social Change in Southern Textiles.* Ithaca: ILR Press, 1991.

Lesher, Stephen. *George Wallace: American Populist.* Reading, Mass.: Addison-Wesley, 1994.

Letwin, Daniel. *The Challenge of Interracial Unionism: Alabama Coal Miners, 1878–1921.* Chapel Hill: University of North Carolina Press, 1998.

Lewis, Earl. *In Their Own Interests: Race, Class, and Power in Twentieth-Century Norfolk, Virginia.* Berkeley: University of California Press, 1991.

Lewis, Sinclair. *Cheap and Contented Labor: The Picture of a Southern Mill Town in 1929.* New York: United Textile Workers of America and Women's Trade Union League, 1929.

Lipsitz, George. *The Possessive Investment in Whiteness: How White People Profit from Identity Politics.* Philadelphia: Temple University Press, 1998.

Logue, Calvin McLeod. *Eugene Talmadge: Rhetoric and Response.* New York: Greenwood Press, 1989.

MacDonald, Lois. *Southern Mills Hills: A Study of Social and Economic Forces in Certain Textile Mill Villages.* New York: Alex L. Hillman, 1928.

Marshall, F. Ray. *Labor in the South.* Cambridge: Harvard University Press, 1967.

McGill, Ralph. *The South and the Southerner.* Boston: Little, Brown, 1959.

McKiven, Henry M., Jr. *Iron and Steel: Class, Race, and Community in Birmingham, Alabama, 1875–1920.* Chapel Hill: University of North Carolina Press, 1995.

McLaurin, Melton. *The Knights of Labor in the South.* Westport, Conn.: Greenwood Press, 1978.

———. *Paternalism and Protest: Southern Cotton Mill Workers and Organized Labor, 1875–1905.* Westport, Conn.: Greenwood Press, 1971.

McMath, Robert C. *Populist Vanguard: A History of the Southern Farmers Alliance.* Chapel Hill: University of North Carolina Press, 1975.

Milkman, Ruth. *Gender at Work: The Dynamics of Job Segregation by Sex during World War II.* Urbana: University of Illinois Press, 1987.

Millis, Harry A., and Emily Clark Brown. *From the Wagner Act to Taft-Hartley: A Study of National Labor Policy and Labor Relations.* Chicago: University of Chicago Press, 1950.

Minchin, Timothy J. *Hiring the Black Worker: The Racial Integration of the Southern Textile Industry, 1960–1980.* Chapel Hill: University of North Carolina Press, 1999.

———. *What Do We Need a Union For? The TWUA in the South, 1945–1955.* Chapel Hill: University of North Carolina Press, 1997.

Mitchell, Broadus. "Fleshpots in the South." *Virginia Quarterly Review* 3 (1927): 169–78.

———. *The Rise of the Cotton Mills in the South.* Baltimore: Johns Hopkins University Press, 1921.

Morland, John Kenneth. *The Millways of Kent.* Chapel Hill: University of North Carolina Press, 1958.

Neather, Andrew. " 'Whiteness' and the Politics of Working-Class History." *Radical History Review* 61 (Winter 1995): 190–96.

Nelson, Bruce. "Class, Race, and Democracy in the CIO: The 'New' Labor History Meets the 'Wages of Whiteness.' " *International Review of Social History* 41 (1996): 351–76.

Newby, I. A. *Plain Folk in the New South: Social Change and Cultural Persistence, 1880–1915.* Baton Rouge: Louisiana State University Press, 1989.

Newitz, Annalee, and Matthew Wray. *White Trash: Race and Class in America.* New York: Routledge, 1997.

Newman, Dale. "Work and Community Life in a Southern Textile Town." *Labor History* 19 (Spring 1978): 204–25.

Nichols, Jeannette P. "Does the Mill Village Foster Any Social Types?" *Journal of Social Forces* 2 (March 1924): 350–57.

Nixon, Raymond B. *Henry Grady: Spokesman of the New South.* New York: Knopf, 1943.

Norrell, Robert J. "Labor at the Ballot Box: Alabama Politics from the New Deal to the Dixiecrat Movement." *Journal of Southern History* 57 (Spring 1991): 201–34.

———. "Labor Trouble: George Wallace and Union Politics in Alabama." In *Organized labor in the Twentieth-Century South,* edited by Robert Zieger, 250–72. Knoxville: University of Tennessee Press, 1991.

Odum, Howard W. *Race and Rumors of Race: The American South in the Early Forties.* Baltimore: Johns Hopkins University Press, 1997.

Patterson, James T. *Congressional Conservatism and the New Deal: The Growth of the Conservative Coalition in Congress, 1933–1939.* Lexington: University of Kentucky Press, 1967.

———. *Grand Expectations: The United States, 1945–1974.* New York: Oxford University Press, 1996.

Pomper, Gerald. "Labor and Congress: The Repeal of the Taft-Hartley Act." *Labor History* 2 (Fall 1961): 323–43.

Pope, Liston. *Millhands and Preachers: A Study of Gastonia.* New Haven: Yale University Press, 1942.

Potwin, Marjorie. *Cotton Mill People of the Piedmont: A Study in Social Change.* New York: Columbia University Press, 1927.

Preiss, Art. *Labor's Giant Step: Twenty Years of the CIO.* New York: Pioneer, 1964.

Reed, Merle E. "The Augusta Textile Mills and the Strikes of 1886." *Labor History* 14 (Spring 1973): 228–46.

———. *Seedtime for the Modern Civil Rights Movement: The President's Committee on Fair Employment Practice, 1941–46.* Baton Rouge: Louisiana State University, 1991.

Regensburger, William Edward. "Ground into Our Blood: The Origins of Working-Class Consciousness and Organization in Durable Unionized Southern Industries, 1930–1946." Ph.D. diss., University of California at Los Angeles, 1987.

Reynolds, Hughes. *The Coosa River Valley from DeSoto to Hydroelectric Power.* Cynthiana, Ky.: Hobson Book Press, 1944.

Richards, Paul David. "The History of the Textile Workers of America, CIO, in the South, 1937 to 1945." Ph.D. diss., University of Wisconsin, Madison, 1978.

Roche, Jeff. *Restructured Resistance: The Sibley Commission and the Politics of Desegregation in Georgia.* Athens: University of Georgia Press, 1998.

Roediger, David. *Towards the Abolition of Whiteness: Essays on Race, Politics, and Working Class History.* New York and London: Verso, 1991.

———. *The Wages of Whiteness: Race and the Making of the American Working Class.* New York and London: Verso, 1991.

Rogin, Michael. *Fathers and Children: Andrew Jackson and the Subjugation of the American Indian.* New York: Knopf, 1975.

Salmond, John A. *Gastonia, 1929: The Story of the Loray Mill Strike.* Chapel Hill: University of North Carolina Press, 1995.

———. *Miss Lucy of the CIO: The Life and Times of Lucy Randolph Mason, 1882–1959.* Athens: University of Georgia Press, 1988.

Schulman, Bruce J. *From Cotton Belt to Sunbelt: Federal Policy, Economic Development, and the Transformation of the South, 1938–1980.* New York: Oxford University Press, 1991.

Shannon, Jasper Berry. *Toward a New Politics in the South.* Knoxville: University of Tennessee Press, 1949.

Shaw, Barton C. *The Wool-Hat Boys.* Baton Rouge: Louisiana State University Press, 1984.

Shelton, Willard. "Why Operation Dixie Failed." *Nation* 29 (April 1950): 391–92.

Simon, Bryant. "The Appeal of Cole Blease of South Carolina: Race, Class, and Sex in the New South." *Journal of Southern History* 62 (February 1996): 57–86.

———. *A Fabric of Defeat: The Politics of South Carolina Millhands, 1910–1948.* Chapel Hill: University of North Carolina Press, 1998.

———. "Rethinking Why There Are So Few Unions in the South." *Georgia Historical Quarterly* 81 (Summer 1997): 465–84.

Sosna, Morton. "More Important than the Civil War? The Impact of World War II on the South." In James C. Cobb and Charles R. Wilson, eds., *Perspectives on the American South: An Annual Review of Society, Politics, and Culture* 4 (New York and London, 1987): 145–61.

Sugrue, Thomas J. *The Origins of the Urban Crisis: Race and Inequality in Postwar Detroit.* Princeton: Princeton University Press, 1996.

Talmadge, Herman. *You and Segregation.* Birmingham: Vulcan Press, 1955.

Tannenbaum, Frank. *Darker Phases of the South.* New York: Putnam, 1924.

Tindall, George Brown. *The Emergence of the New South, 1913–1945.* Baton Rouge: Louisiana State University Press, 1975.

Tippett, Tom. *When Southern Labor Stirs.* New York: Jonathan Cape and Harrison Smith, 1931.

Truchil, Barry E. *Capital-Labor Relations in the U.S. Industry.* New York: Praeger, 1988.

Tullos, Allen. *Habits of Industry: White Culture and the Transformation of the Carolina Piedmont.* Chapel Hill: University of North Carolina Press, 1989.

U.S. Bureau of the Census. *Census of Population: 1940.* Vol. 2, *Population*, pt. 2, *Florida–Iowa.* Washington, D.C.: Government Printing Office, 1942.

———. *Census of Population: 1950.* Vol. 2, *Characteristics of the Population*, pt. 2, *Georgia.* Washington, D.C.: Government Printing Office, 1952.

———. *Census of Population: 1960.* Vol. 1, *Characteristics of the Population*, pt. 12, *Georgia.* Washington, D.C.: Government Printing Office, 1962.

———. *Census of Population: 1970.* Vol. 1, *Characteristics of the Population*, pt. 12, *Georgia.* Washington, D.C.: Government Printing Office, 1973.

———. *Fifteenth Census of the United States: 1930.* Vol. 1, *Unemployment.* Vol. 2, pt. 2, *Agriculture.* Vol. 3, *Population*, pt. 1, *Alabama-Missouri.* Washington, D.C.: Government Printing Office, 1932.

U.S. Congress, Senate Subcommittee on Labor and Labor-Management Relations. *Labor-Management Relations in the Southern Textile Industry: Hearings before the Subcommittee on Labor-Management Relations.* 81st Cong., 2nd sess. Washington, D.C.: Government Printing Office, 1950.

———. *Labor-Management Relations in the Southern Textile Industry: Hearings before the Subcommittee on Labor-Management Relations.* 82nd Cong., 2nd sess. Washington, D.C.: Government Printing Office, 1952.

Vorse, Mary Heaton. *Strike!* 1930. Reprint, Urbana: University of Illinois Press, 1991.

Woodward, C. Vann. *Origins of the New South, 1877–1913.* Baton Rouge: Louisiana State University Press, 1951.

———. *Tom Watson, Agrarian Rebel.* Savannah: Beehive Press, 1938.

Wright, Gavin. *Old South, New South: Revolutions in the Southern Economy since the Civil War.* New York: Basic Books, 1986.

Zieger, Robert. *American Workers, American Unions, 1920–1985.* 2nd ed. Baltimore: Johns Hopkins University Press, 1994.

———. *The CIO, 1935–1955.* Chapel Hill: University of North Carolina Press, 1995.

———, ed. *Organized Labor in the Twentieth-Century South.* Knoxville: University of Tennessee Press, 1991.

———. *Southern Labor in Transition, 1940–1995.* Knoxville: University of Tennessee Press, 1997.

Index